Table of Contents

GloomCookie

story
Serena Valentino

art
John Gebbia

edited by
Julia Dvorin

lettering for issues 8,9,10
Chief McFri

president
Dan Vado

publisher
Bob Simpkins

assistant publisher
Jennifer de Guzman Belew

created by Serena Valentino and Ted Naifeh

GloomCookie Volume 2, Third printing, March 2007. Contains material previously published in issues #7 - 12 of GloomCookie. Published by SLG Publishing, P.O. Box 26427, San Jose, CA 95159-6427. Created by Serena Valentino and Ted Naifeh, ™ and © 2002, all rights reserved. All art © 2002 John Gebbia. Foreword © 2002 Darick Robertson. No part of this publications may be reproduced, except for purposes of review, without the written permission of Serena Valentino and SLG Publishing. Printed in Canada.

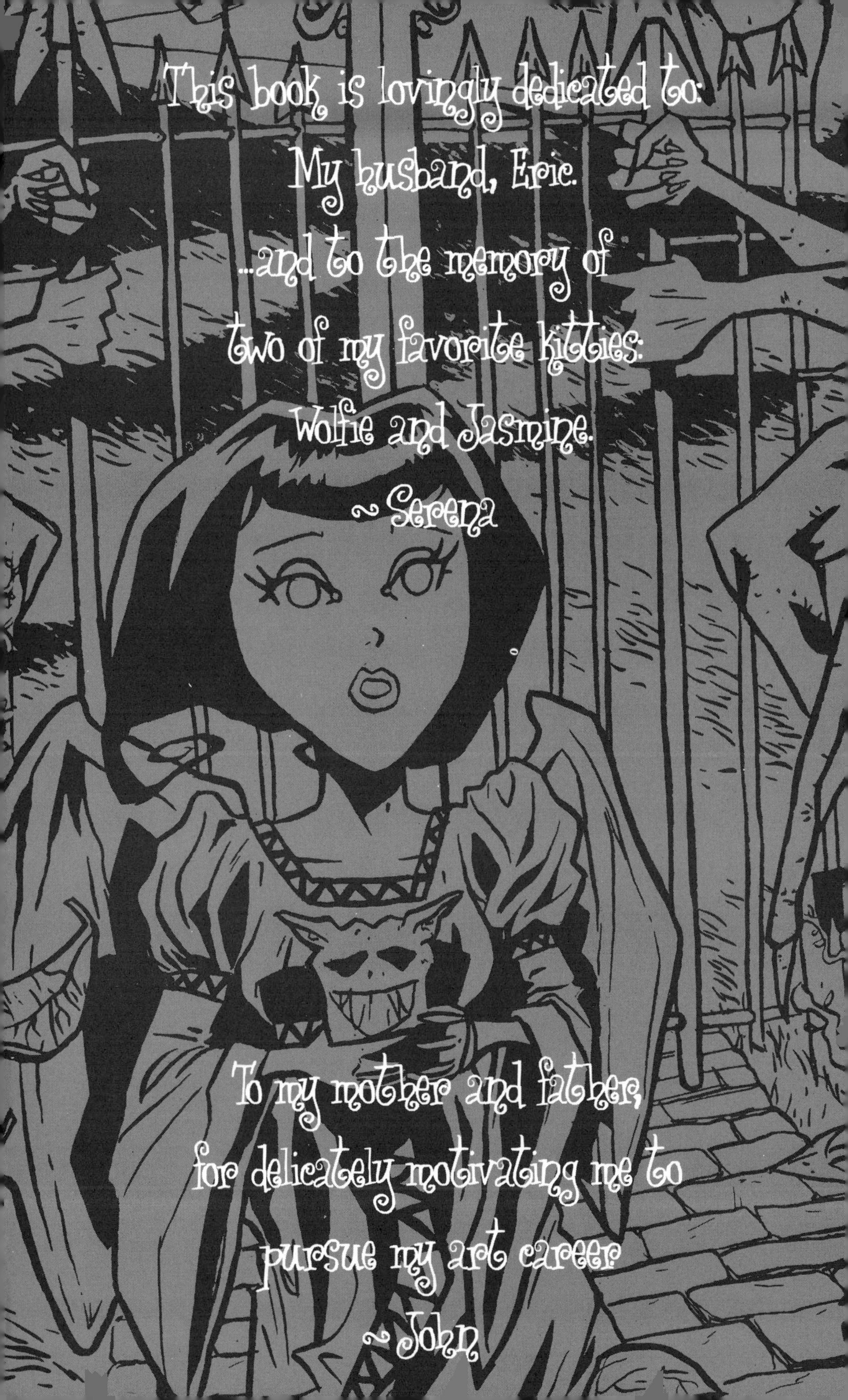

This book is lovingly dedicated to:
My husband, Eric.
...and to the memory of
two of my favorite kitties:
Wolfie and Jasmine.
~ Serena

To my mother and father,
for delicately motivating me to
pursue my art career
~ John

Foreword

By Darick Robertson

I have a confession: Serena broke my heart; on acid. I first met Serena in 1987 when we were still teens and the only one of us dreaming about a career in comics was me. I was publishing my first comic, Space Beaver, and the odds of getting where I am in comics today seemed slim to none. In those days, I was also dressed in my squishiest black outfits and joined in the parade at the dance clubs of San Francisco, though I never achieved the royal level that Serena did. For me, she was that bobbed, raven-haired beauty that Lex is, but in a red velvet dress (and I still see her in Ted's art). Ironically, I was like Lex and she was my Max. (If anyone, I was probably equated to Vermilion, though, as much as I wish I had been like one of the cooler characters, like Max or Sebastian.)

I would draw pictures of Storm (from the x-men, with her black leather and mohawk) and Batman and such for her and she would hang them on her wall (Because she liked the black leather, mohawks and bats). I had a merciless crush on her (you know the kind. It feels like you're drowning in dark chocolate, swirling in a dark cauldron of lust and love and being pulled under the bed by grinning girls with sharp teeth) and we'd talk on the phone for hours. I'd drive to her house after school and we'd make out in that awkward teenage desperate way.

As we were becoming a fledgling couple, Tommy and Jess (who were just then reconciling their on again-off again relationship at the time), invited us to take acid with them. Neither of us had tried it before, so it was exciting. I'd be with her on a beach at night and we'd do this wild thing together. We went with this other couple to a foggy beach in Pacifica and dropped. I was having a fine time, facing my emotional demons, understanding the cosmos, staring at the sea and wondering where Serena had gone. She came back with Tommy, took me aside and told me, as I was peaking, that she was in love. Turns out it was not with me but with Tommy. It wasn't enough that I was getting my heart broken; I had to be hallucinating through the experience. Serena and I had our own on again-off again affairs through the dying years of the eighties that followed and the soundtrack was by Robert Smith and Morrisey. At that time, as I began to look forward, I never imagined Serena would also be involved in the comics industry one day.

It's OK, because over a decade later, maturity has led to a solid friendship that has outlasted teenage infatuation. My point is in all of this is that Serena doesn't write about this world as if she merely observes it and you can tell. She lives it. It's as alive in her imagination as it is in her post modern fairy tales. You think you know where you are, but you don't (and who, or what, is that lurking in the shadows?). You're lost in a world of displaced, heart broken demons and freak shows; Hidden monsters and wicked Queens. You're somewhere between the Brothers Grimm and Tim Burton and Walt Disney on acid.

Fast forward to present day. I'm married and so is she, I'm living in Brooklyn, and she's still living in San Francisco. I talk to her often and share pictures of my baby boy. She tells me of regular trips to New Orleans and does Tarot card readings for me from time to time.

When I first saw Gloom Cookie, it was a little fold over, stapled together Xerox comic that she was handing out at San Diego Comic Con. One look at my old friend Ted Naifeh's (whom I'd known since High School) incredible designs, and I knew Serena really had something. I eagerly presented it to Vertigo editors, but they didn't get it. When I heard Slave Labor did, (good ol' Dan Vado and Slave Labor Graphics) I knew she was in good hands. I offered some initial advice, but I never doubted for second that she was onto something like a vampire onto a vein. I hoped she'd do well.

Well, I'm writing this for a second collection, so apparently my instincts about comics were better than my instincts about raven-haired beauties. It's so funny how life can be, isn't it? One day she's breaking my heart on some far away foggy, LSD enhanced beach in Pacifica and the next, she's a dear friend and I'm wishing her well and singing her praises here in print and laughing about the broken heart that was so devastating when I was 17.

Serena's talented, and she surrounds herself with talent. I would read Gloom Cookie even if there was never a connection between me and the author, because it's really, really good. It rings of truth and sincerity and it makes you laugh. When I see Lex, it takes me away to another time and another place, and I can feel that tugging graying hand from the past pulling me under the bed where it's dark and shiny eyes and teeth await to devour me. It's sweet and dark. It's friendly yet disconcerting. It's Alice in Club-land. It's Gloom Cookie, and there's nothing else like it. It's a sweet trip wherever it takes you.

Darick Robertson
Brooklyn, New York 2002

Chapter 7

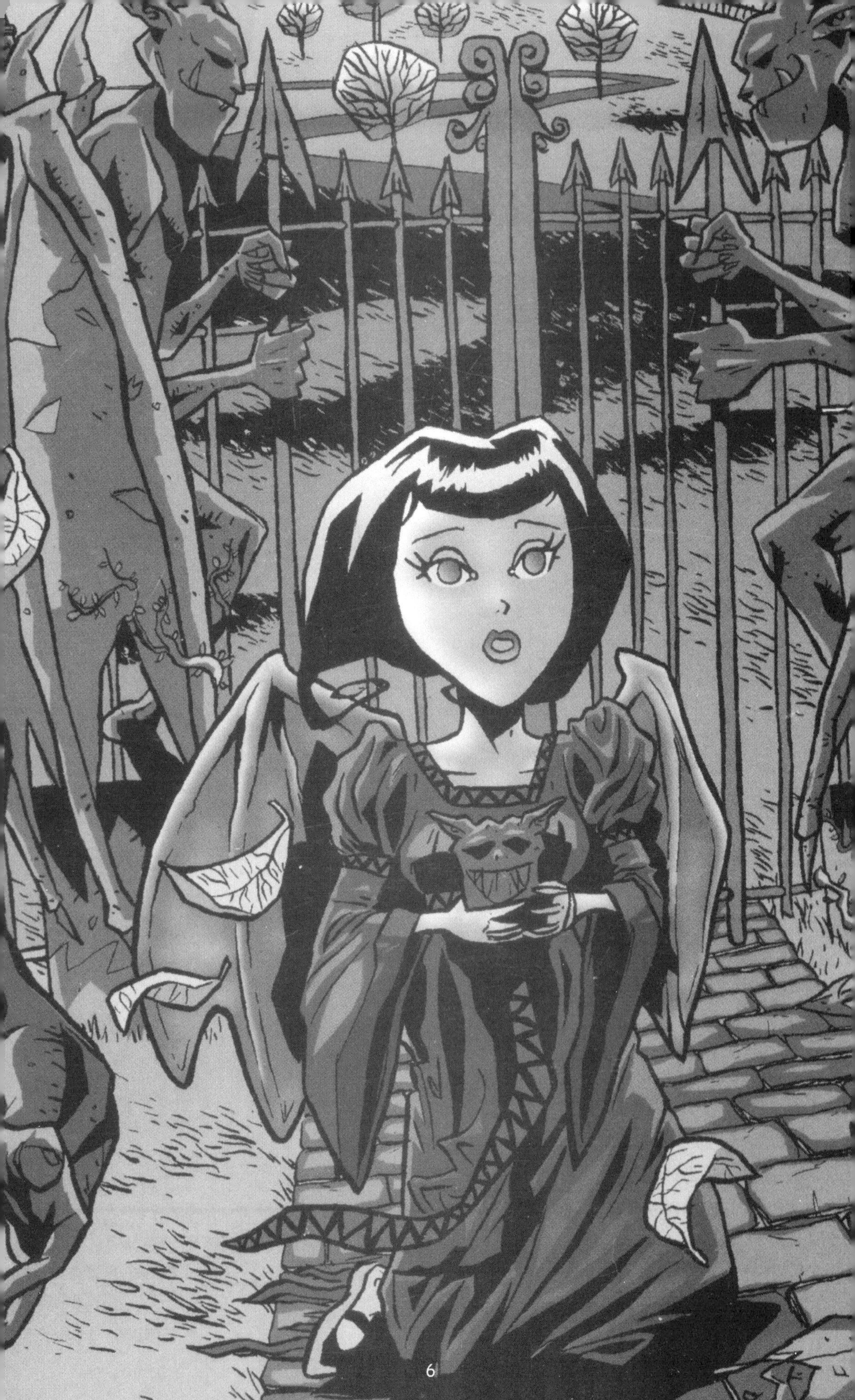

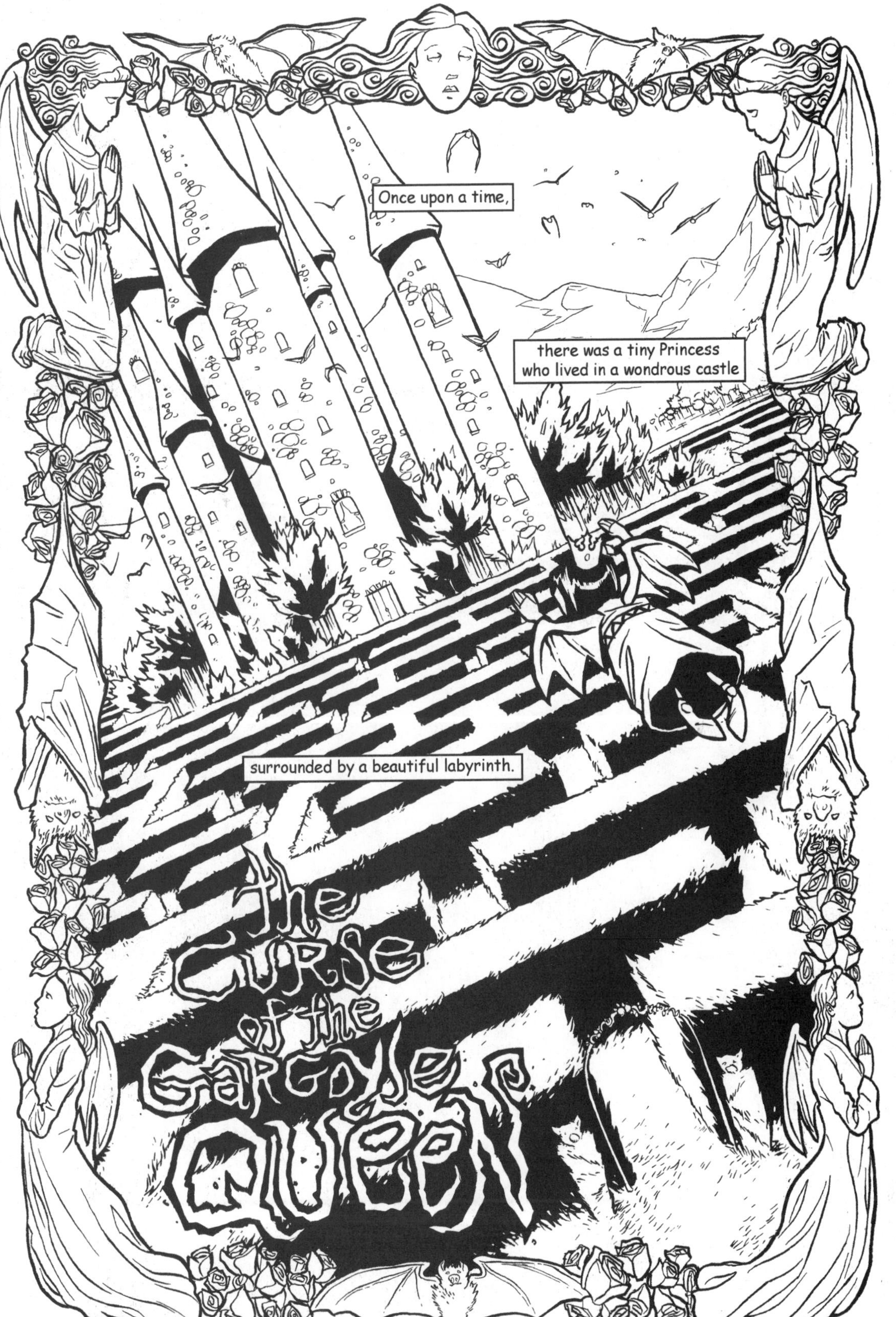
Once upon a time,
there was a tiny Princess who lived in a wondrous castle
surrounded by a beautiful labyrinth.
the Curse of the Gargoyle Queen

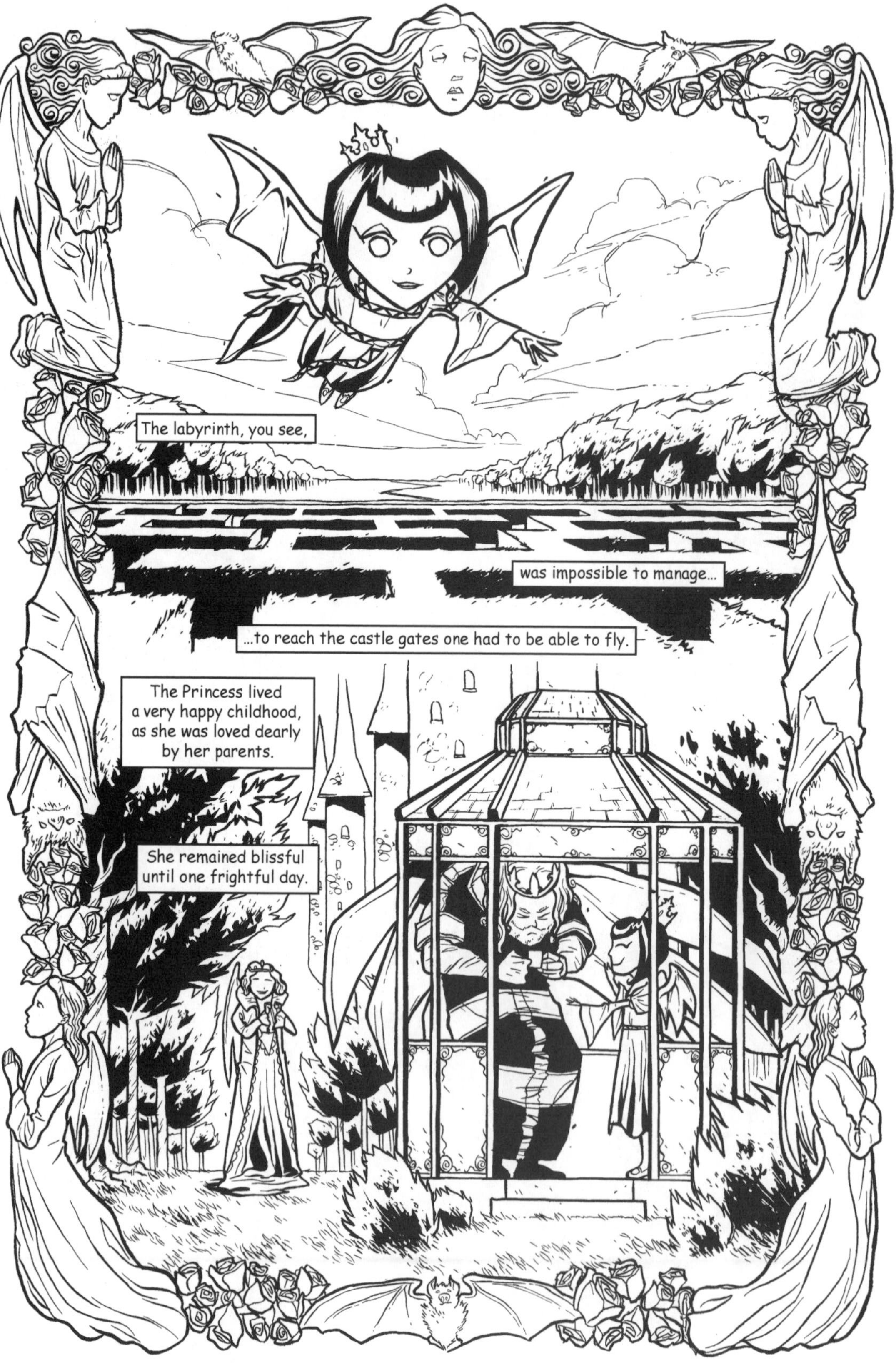
The labyrinth, you see,
was impossible to manage...
...to reach the castle gates one had to be able to fly.
The Princess lived a very happy childhood, as she was loved dearly by her parents.
She remained blissful until one frightful day.

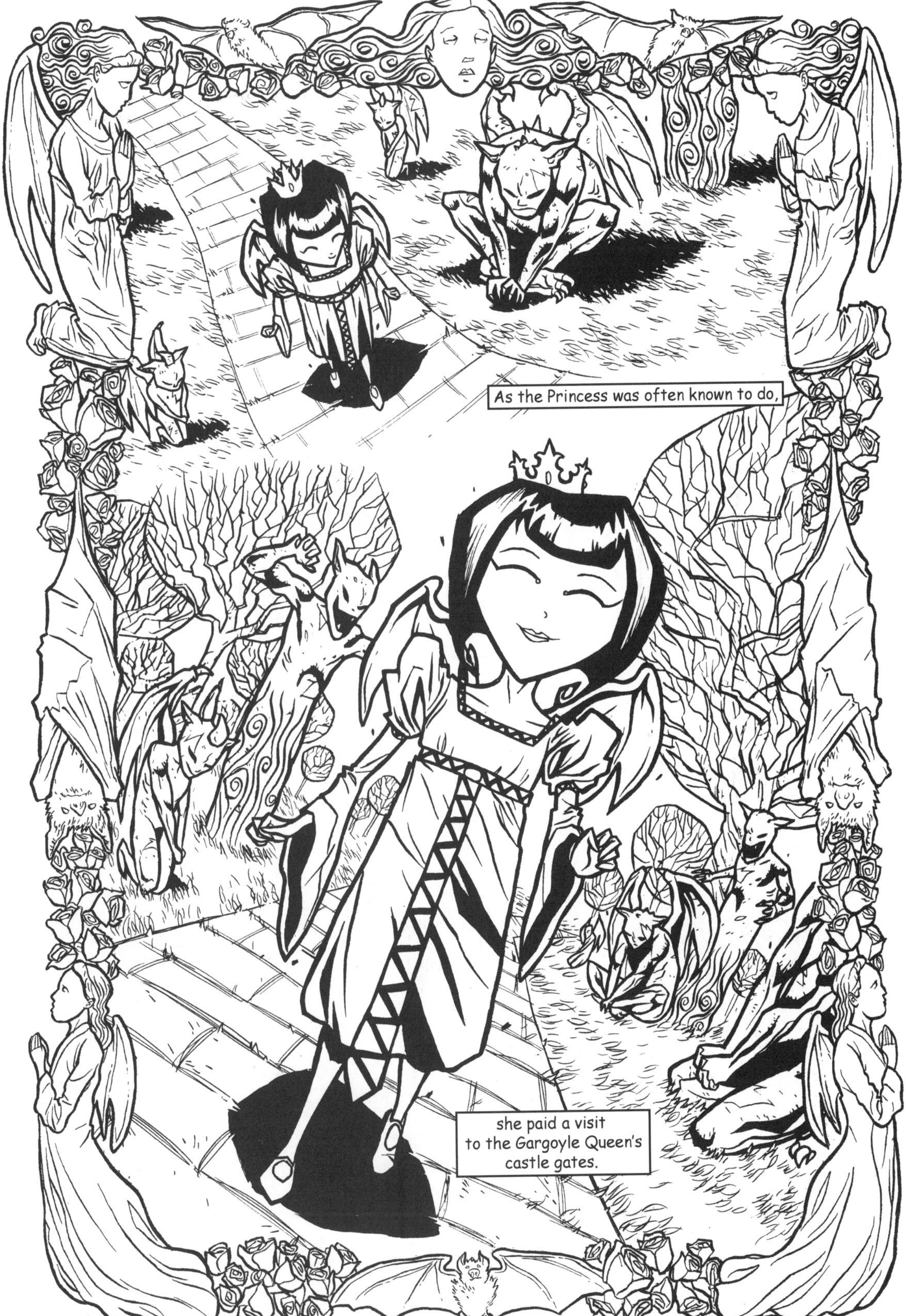
As the Princess was often known to do,
she paid a visit to the Gargoyle Queen's castle gates.

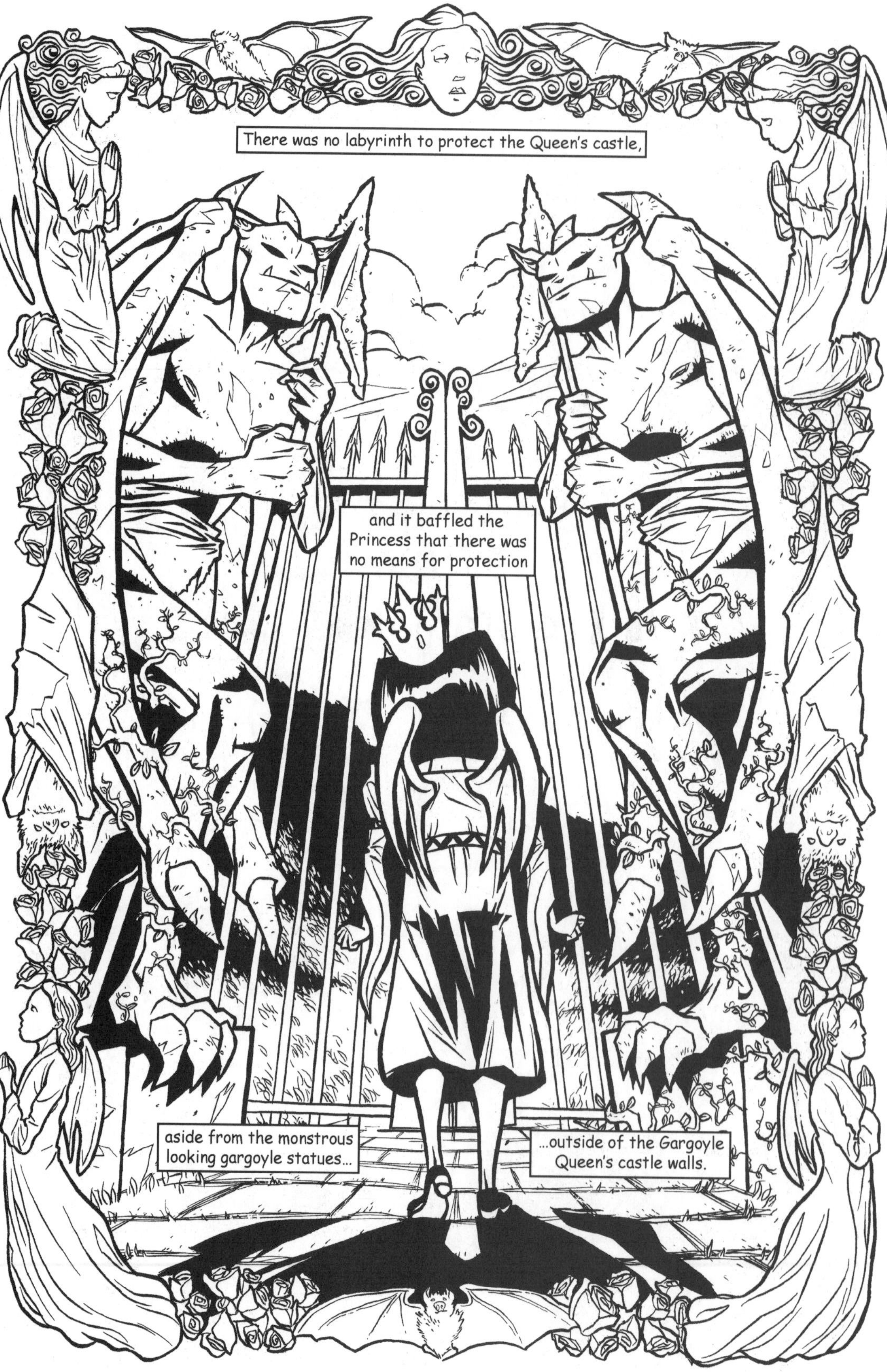
There was no labyrinth to protect the Queen's castle,
and it baffled the Princess that there was no means for protection
aside from the monstrous looking gargoyle statues...
...outside of the Gargoyle Queen's castle walls.

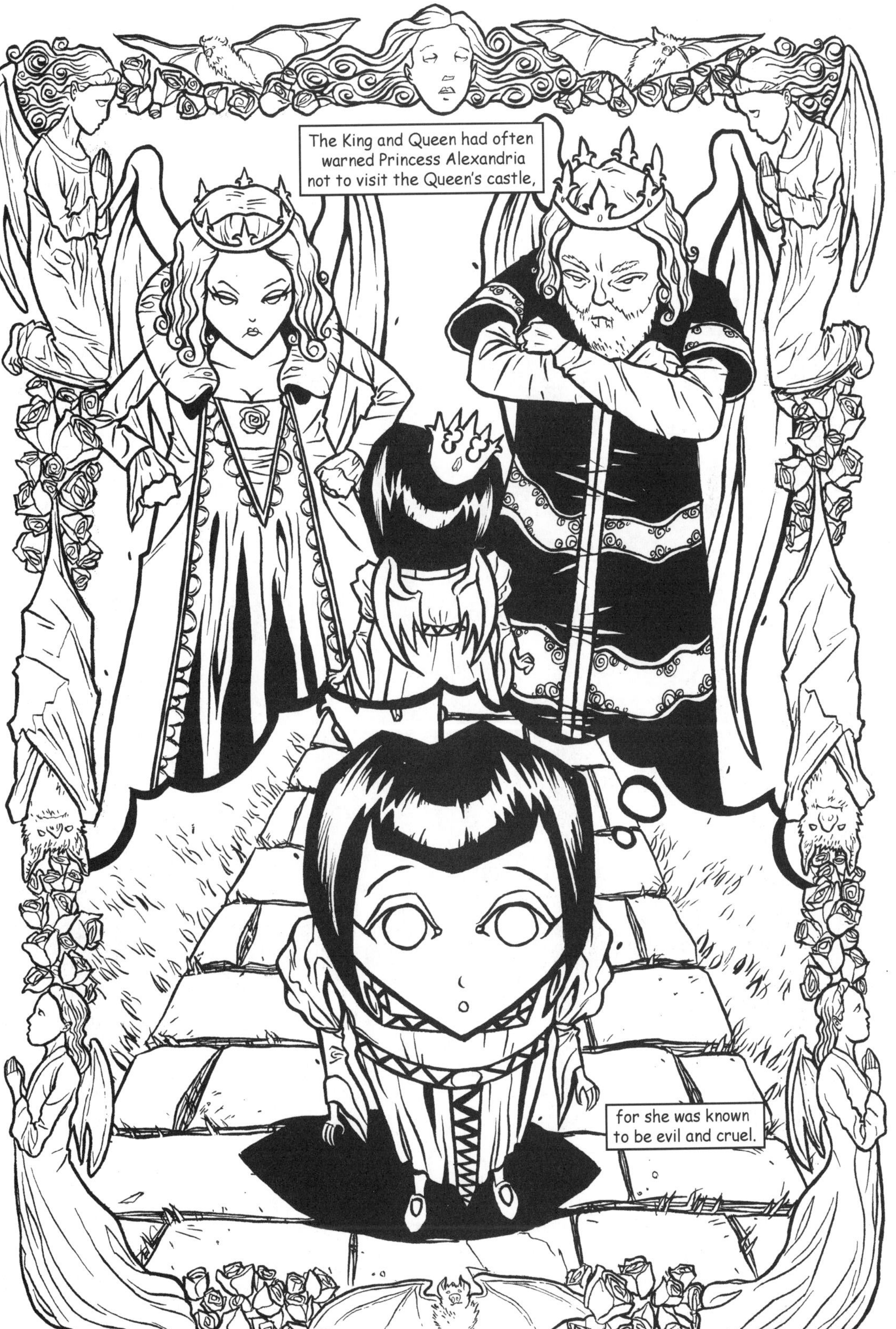
The King and Queen had often warned Princess Alexandria not to visit the Queen's castle,
for she was known to be evil and cruel.

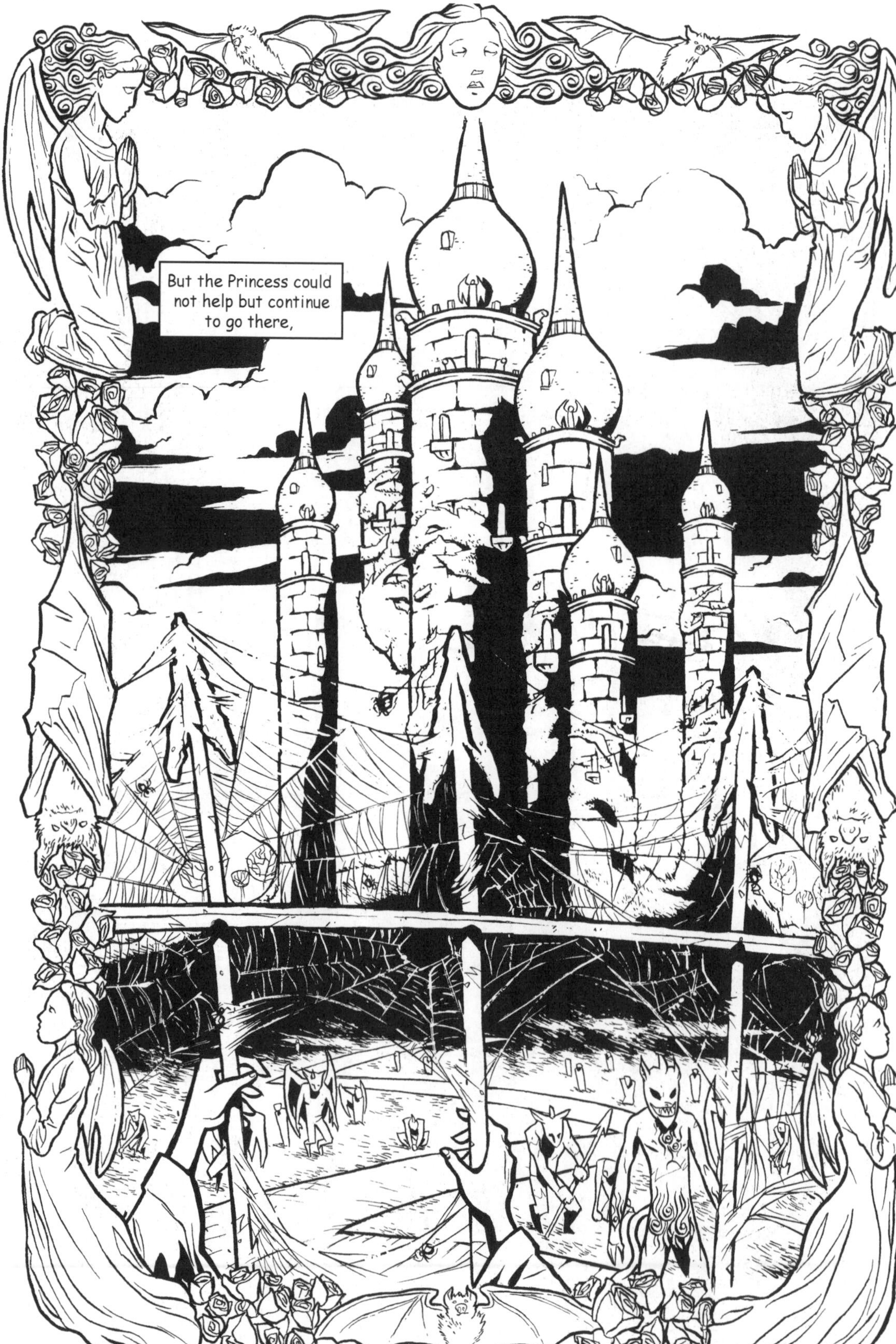
But the Princess could not help but continue to go there,

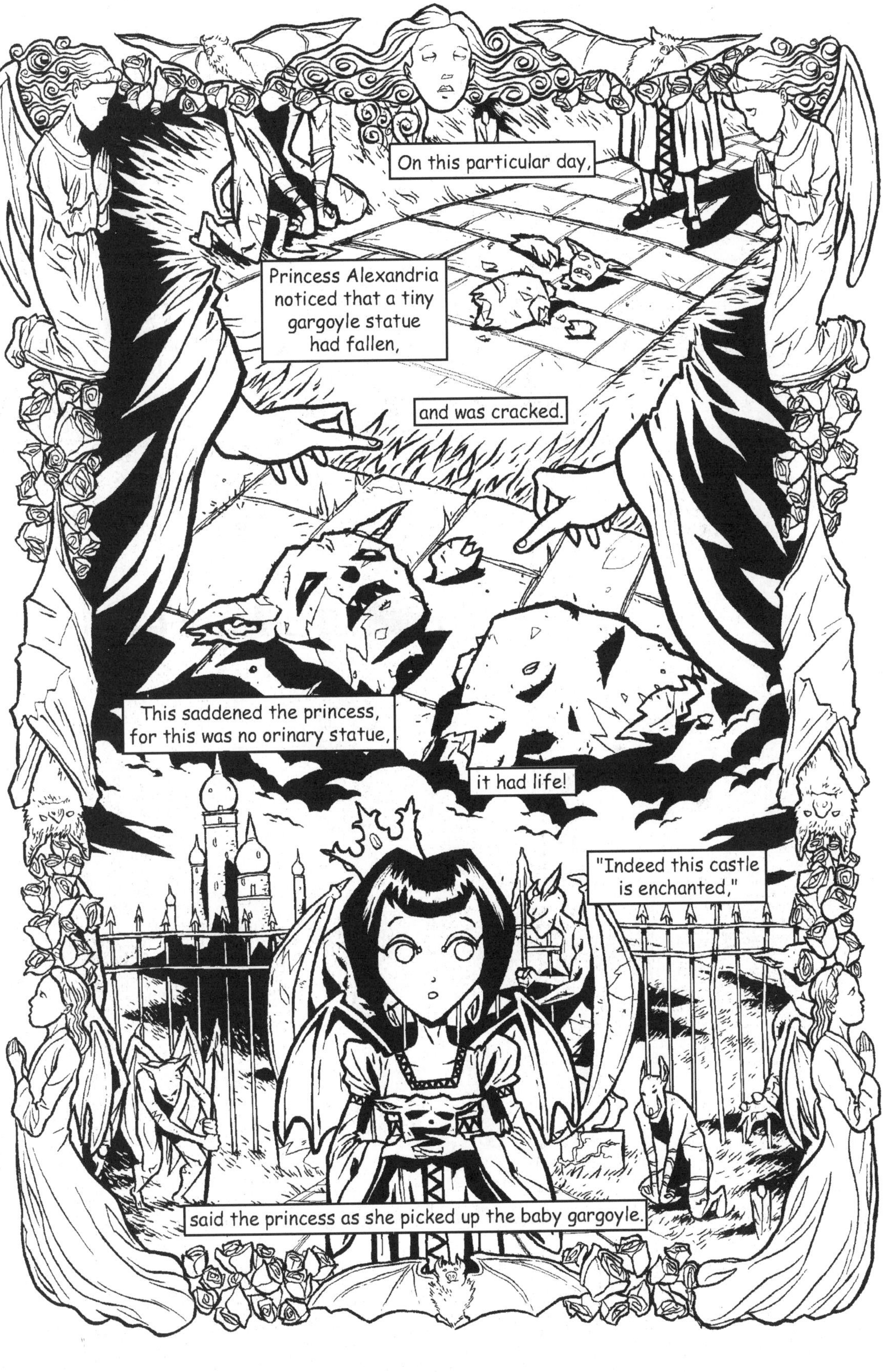
On this particular day,
Princess Alexandria noticed that a tiny gargoyle statue had fallen,
and was cracked.
This saddened the princess, for this was no orinary statue,
it had life!
"Indeed this castle is enchanted,"
said the princess as she picked up the baby gargoyle.

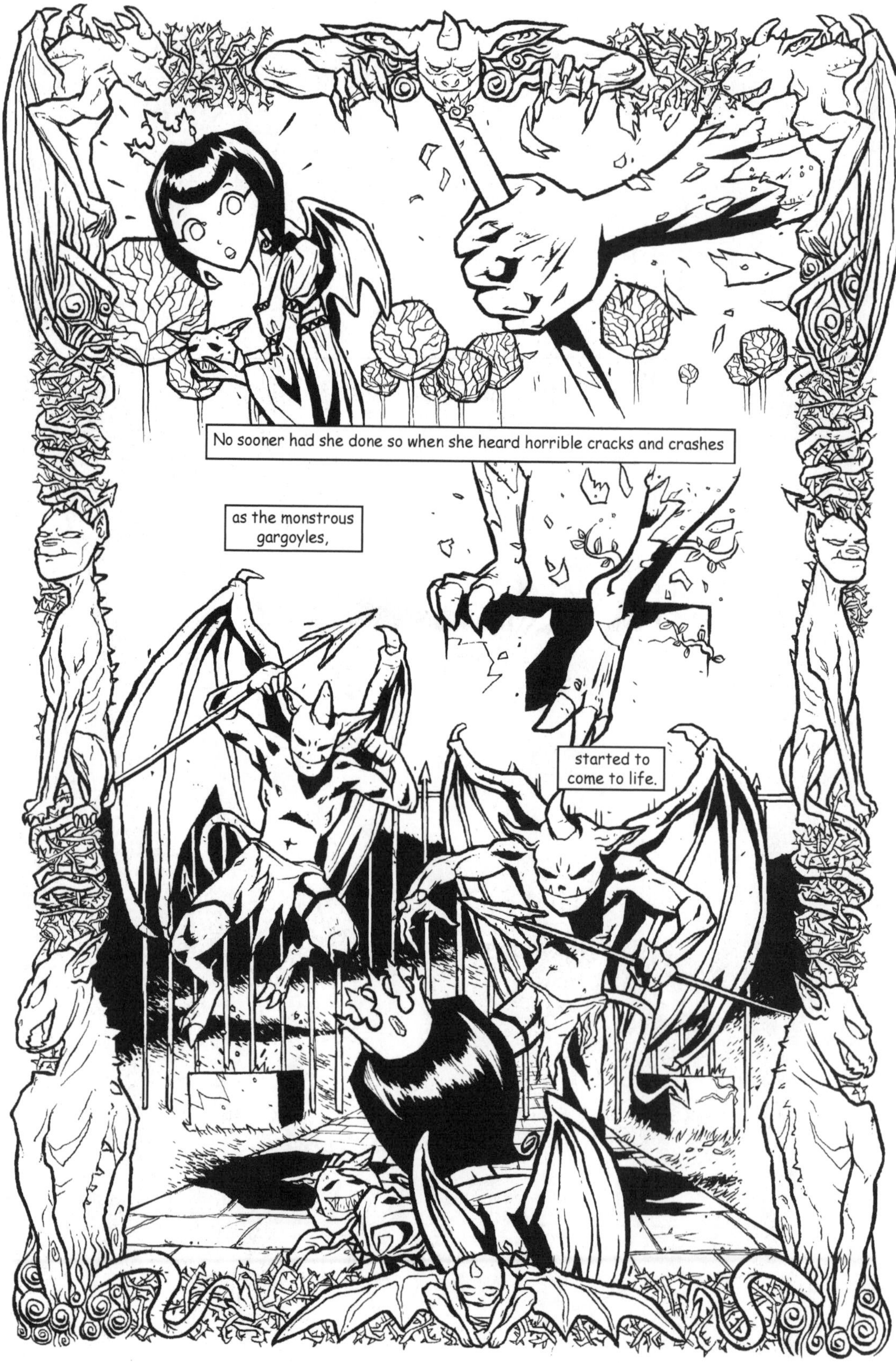
No sooner had she done so when she heard horrible cracks and crashes
as the monstrous gargoyles,
started to come to life.

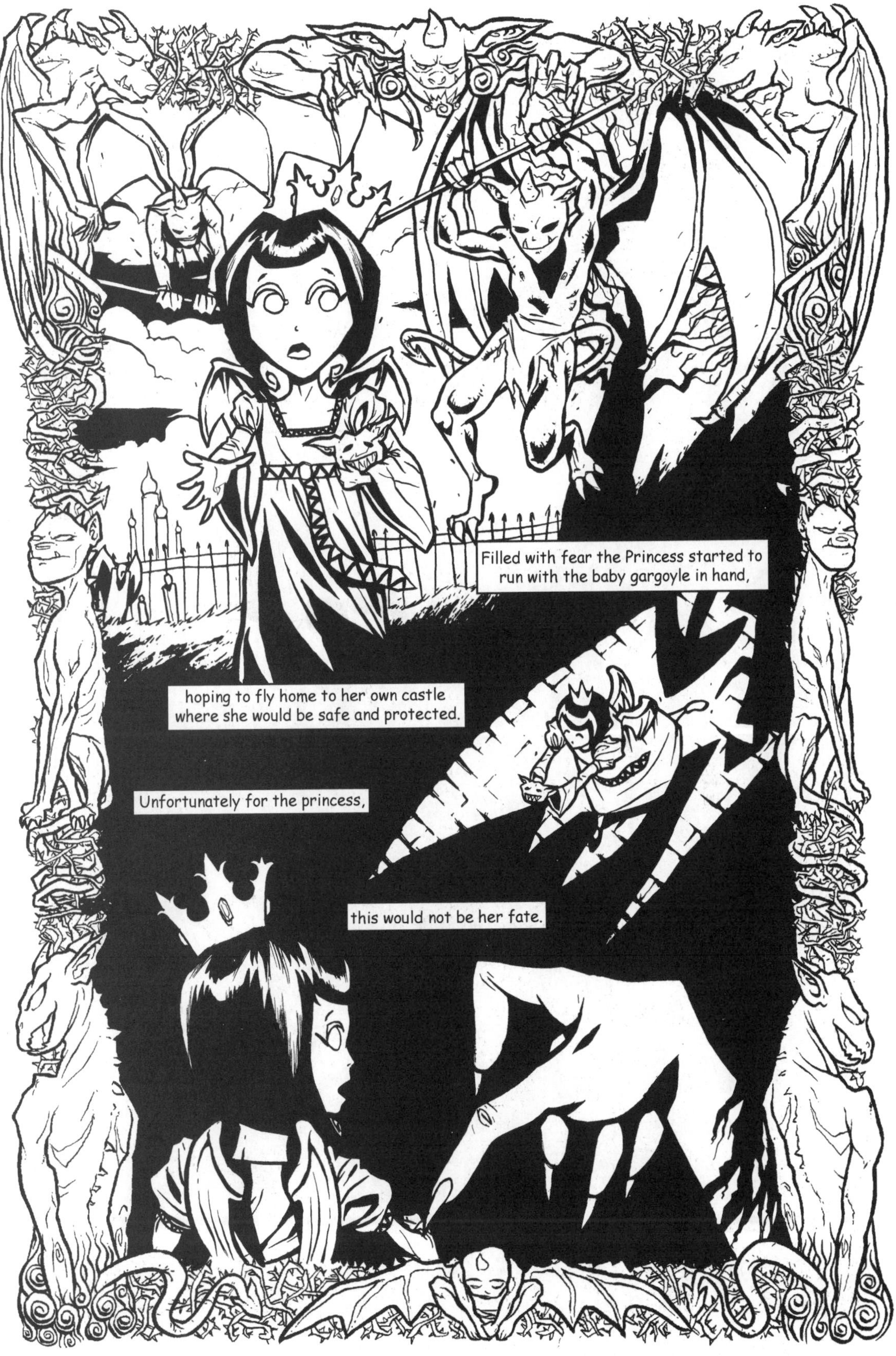
Filled with fear the Princess started to run with the baby gargoyle in hand,
hoping to fly home to her own castle where she would be safe and protected.
Unfortunately for the princess,
this would not be her fate.

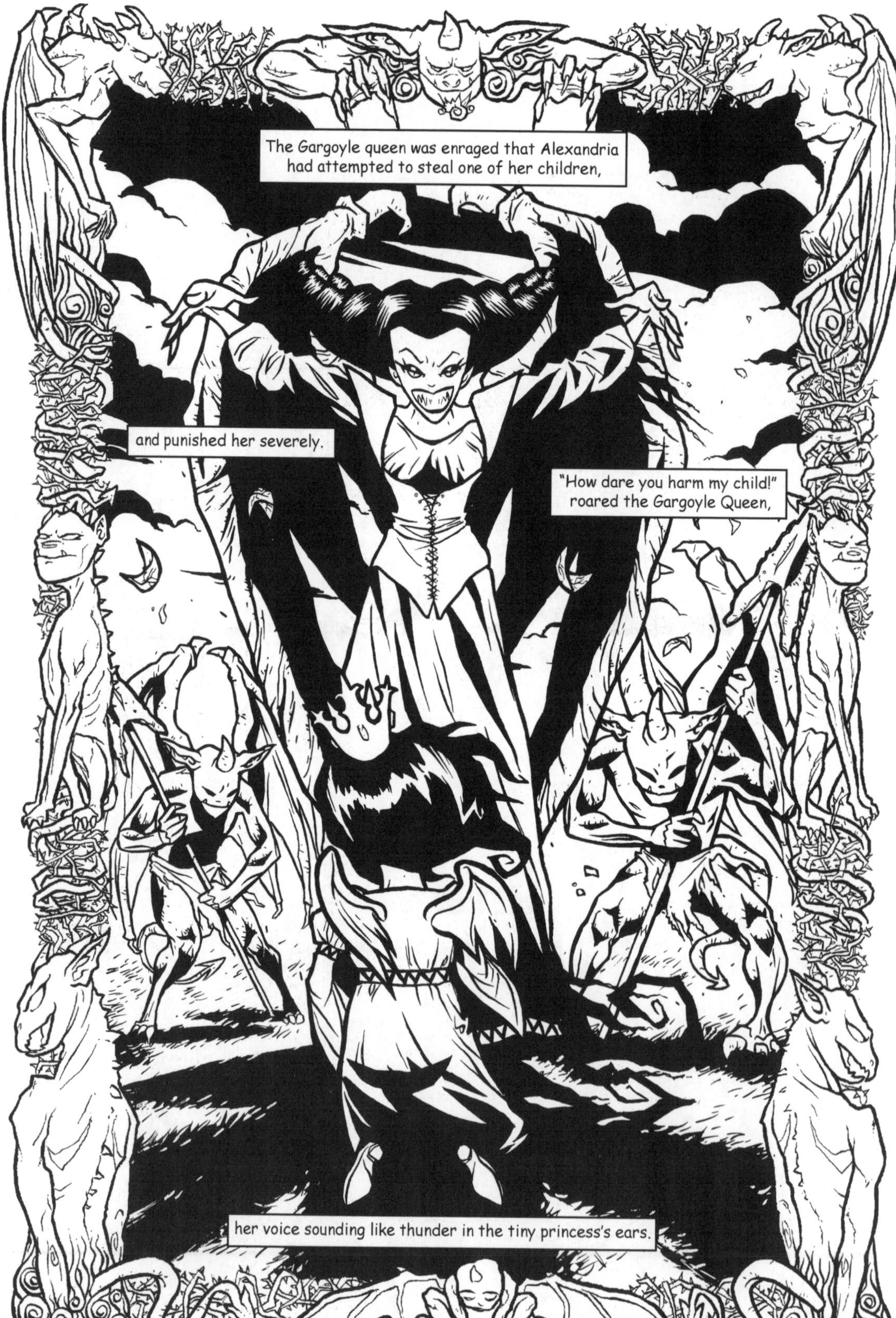
The Gargoyle queen was enraged that Alexandria had attempted to steal one of her children,
and punished her severely.
"How dare you harm my child!" roared the Gargoyle Queen,
her voice sounding like thunder in the tiny princess's ears.

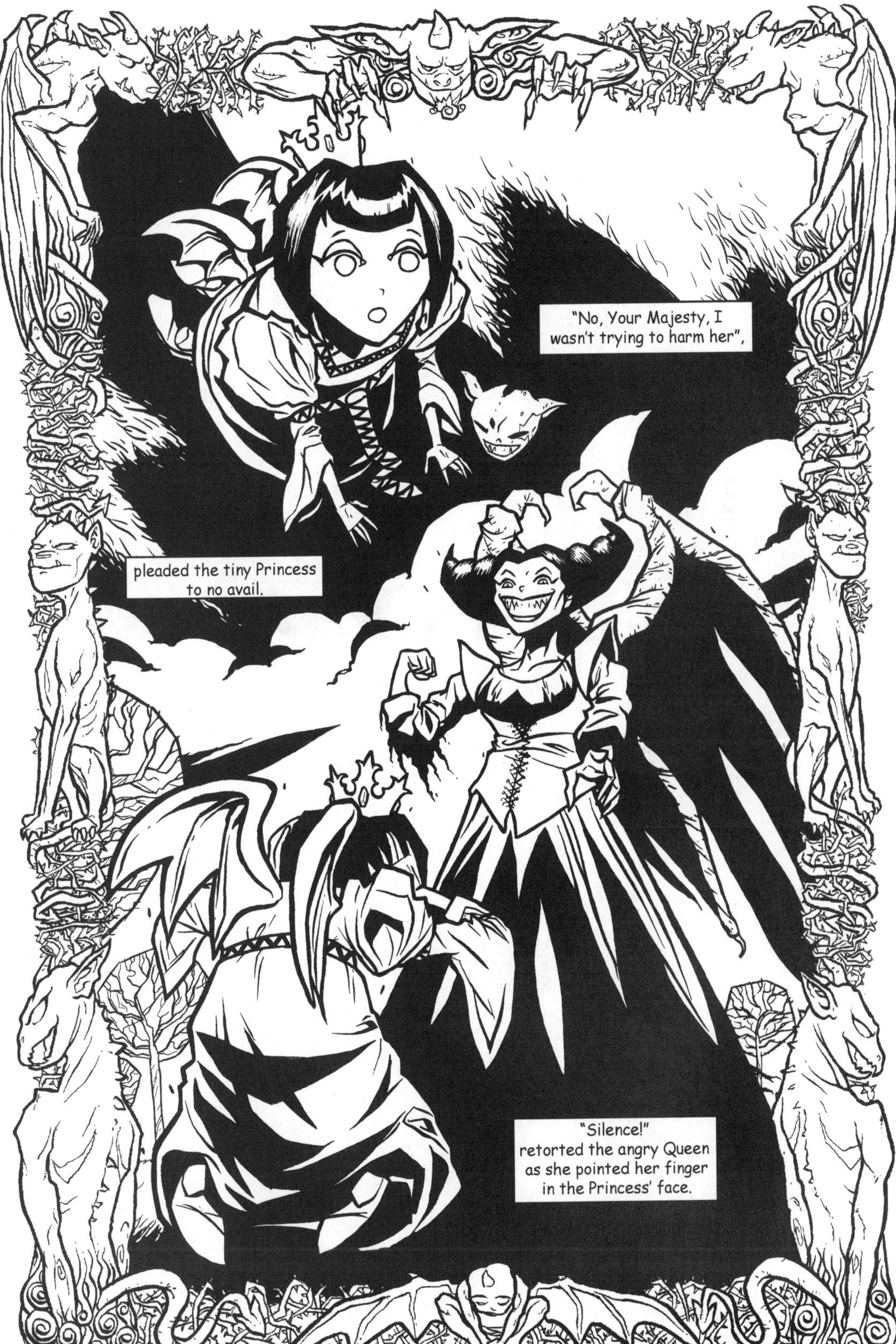
"No, Your Majesty, I wasn't trying to harm her",
pleaded the tiny Princess to no avail.
"Silence!" retorted the angry Queen as she pointed her finger in the Princess' face.

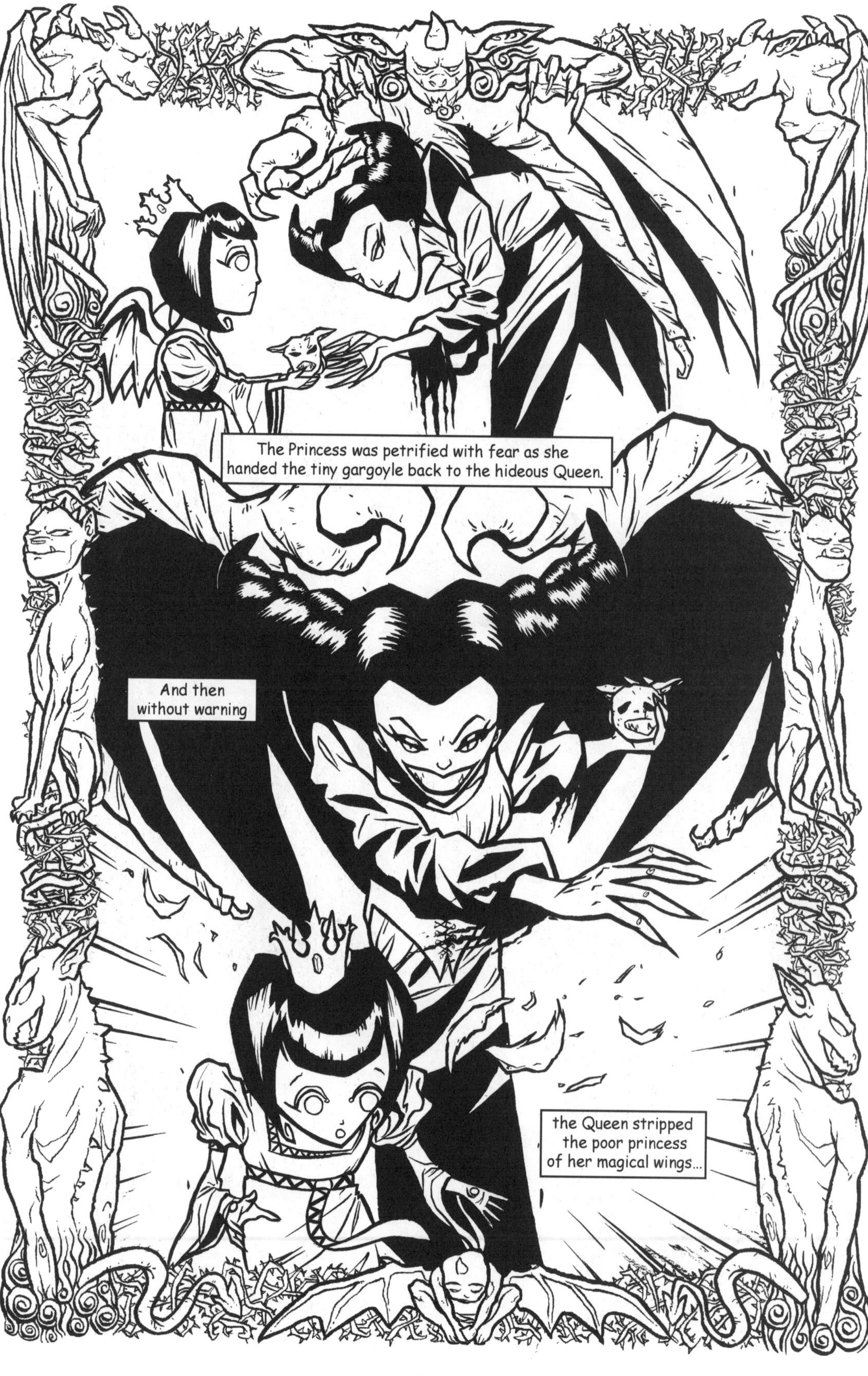
The Princess was petrified with fear as she handed the tiny gargoyle back to the hideous Queen.
And then without warning
the Queen stripped the poor princess of her magical wings...

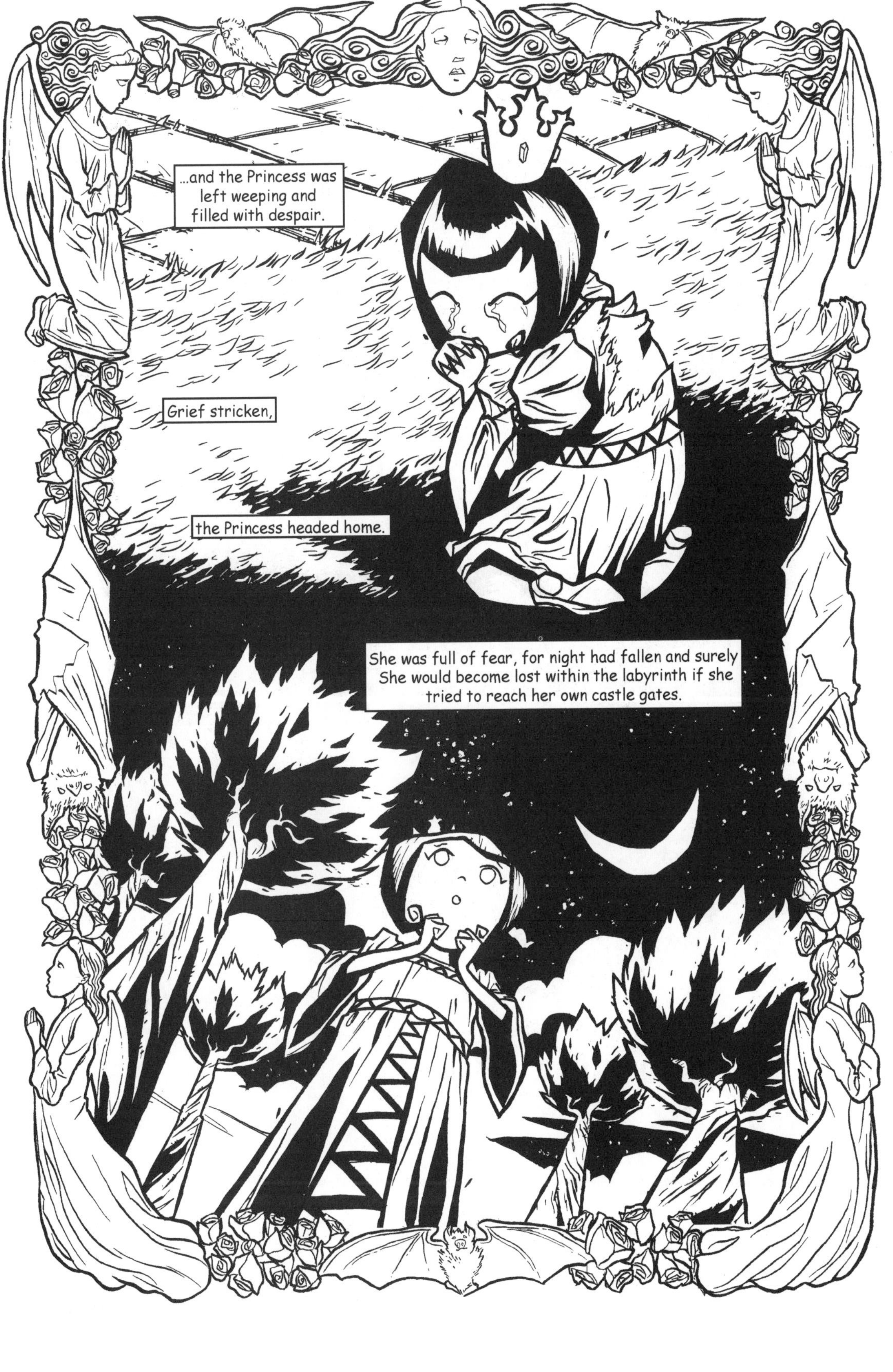
...and the Princess was left weeping and filled with despair.
Grief stricken,
the Princess headed home.
She was full of fear, for night had fallen and surely She would become lost within the labyrinth if she tried to reach her own castle gates.

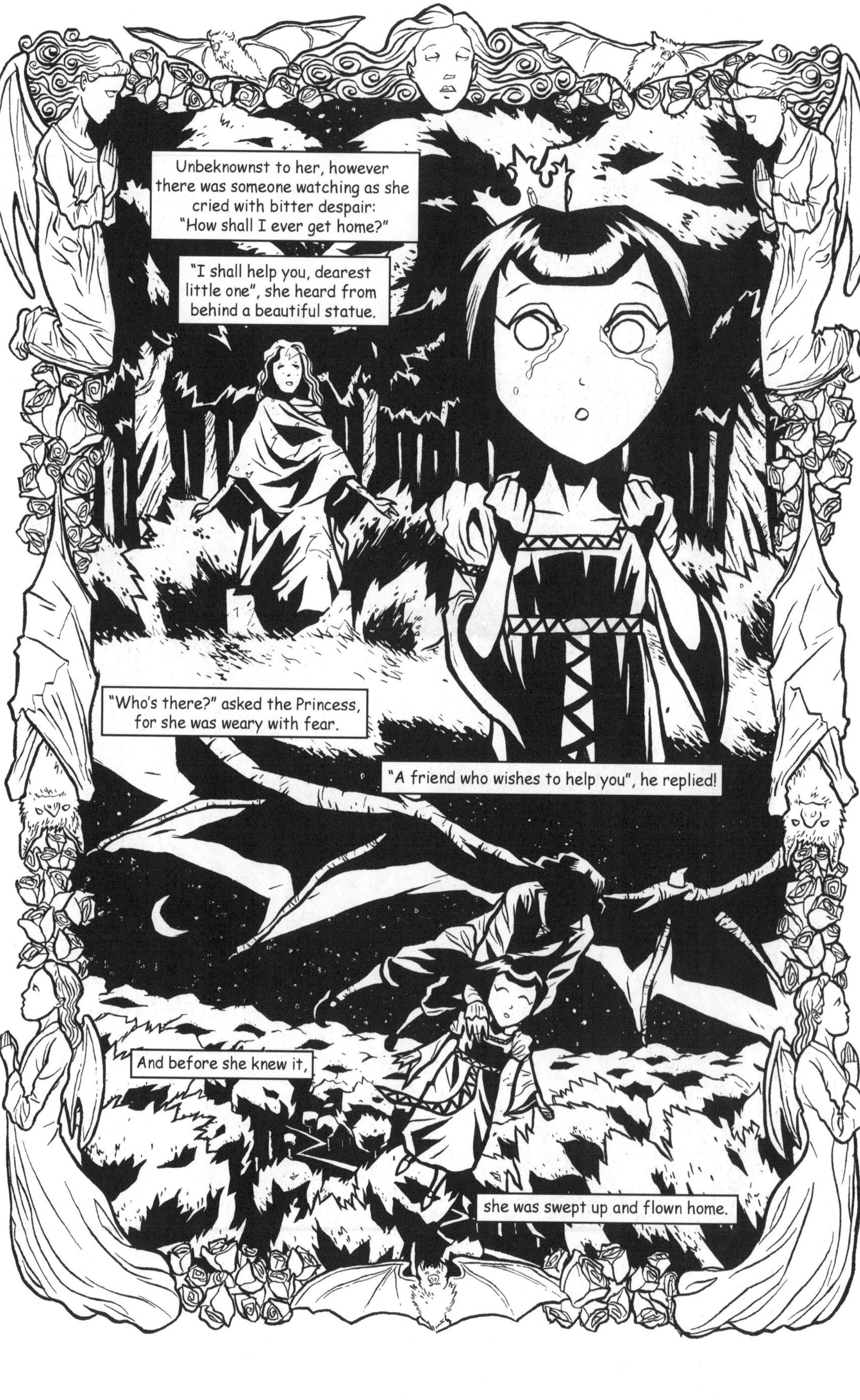

Unbeknownst to her, however there was someone watching as she cried with bitter despair: "How shall I ever get home?"
"I shall help you, dearest little one", she heard from behind a beautiful statue.
"Who's there?" asked the Princess, for she was weary with fear.
"A friend who wishes to help you", he replied!
And before she knew it,
she was swept up and flown home.

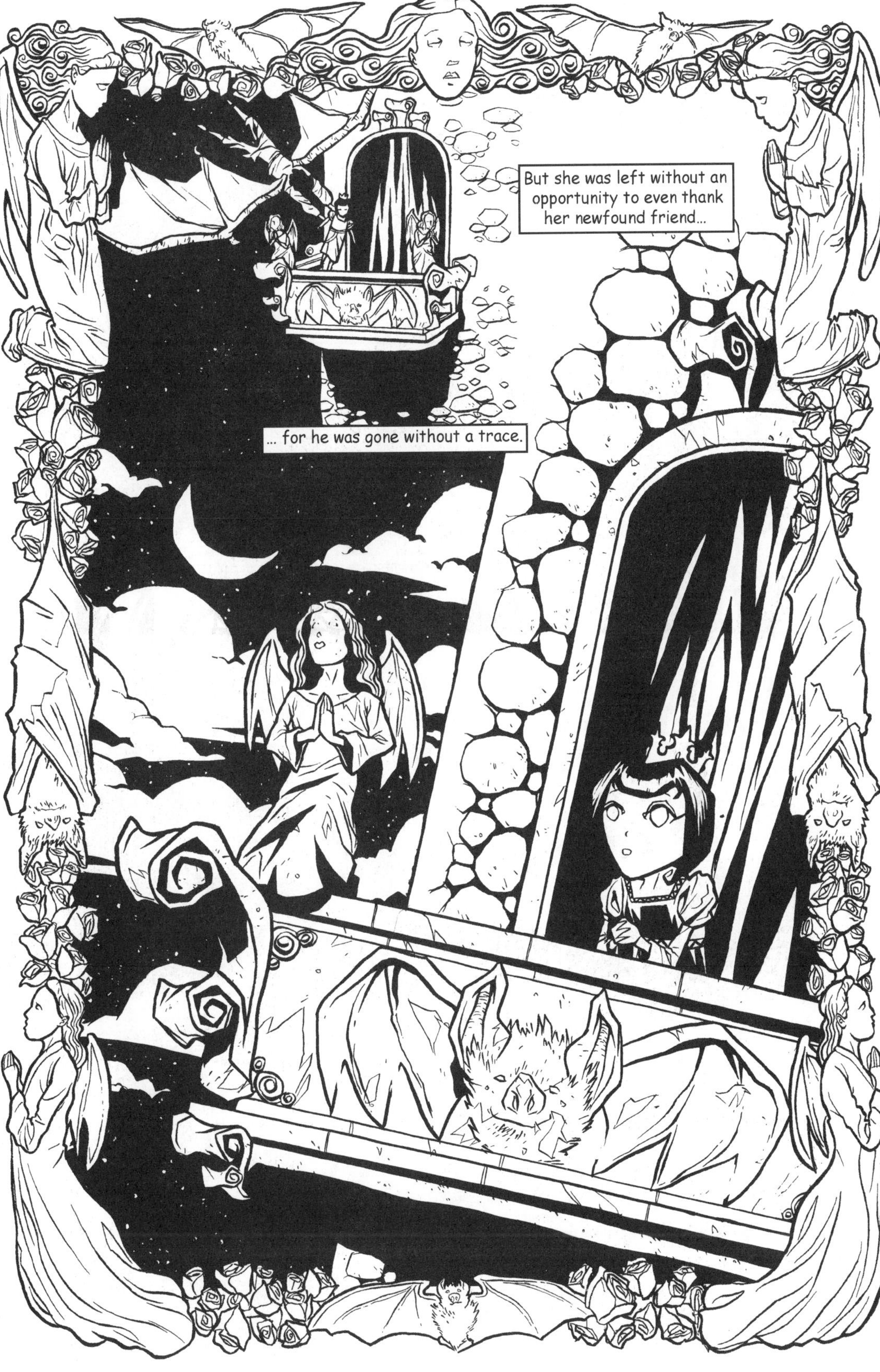

But she was left without an opportunity to even thank her newfound friend...
... for he was gone without a trace.

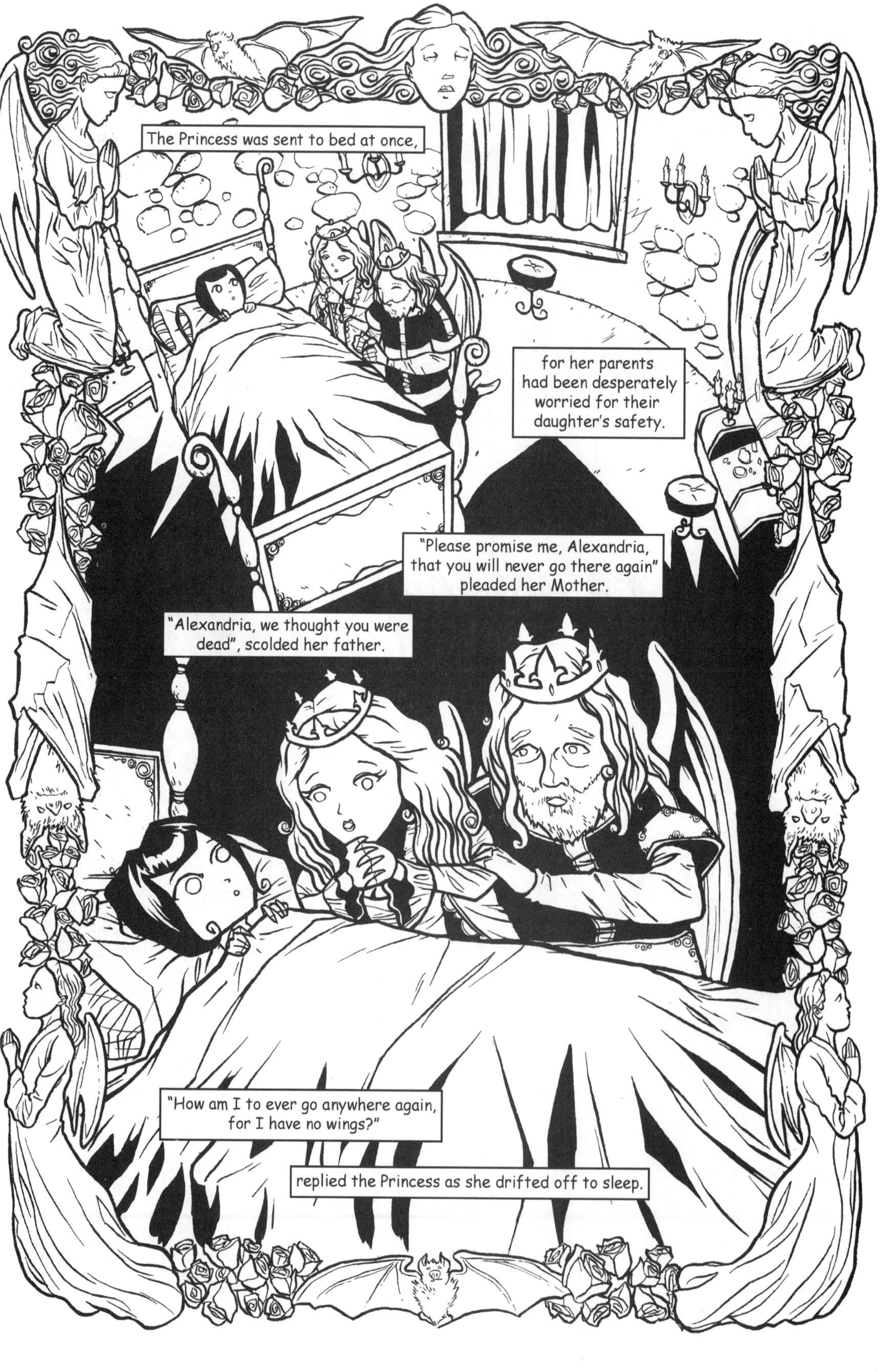
The Princess was sent to bed at once,
for her parents had been desperately worried for their daughter's safety.
"Please promise me, Alexandria, that you will never go there again" pleaded her Mother.
"Alexandria, we thought you were dead", scolded her father.
"How am I to ever go anywhere again, for I have no wings?"
replied the Princess as she drifted off to sleep.

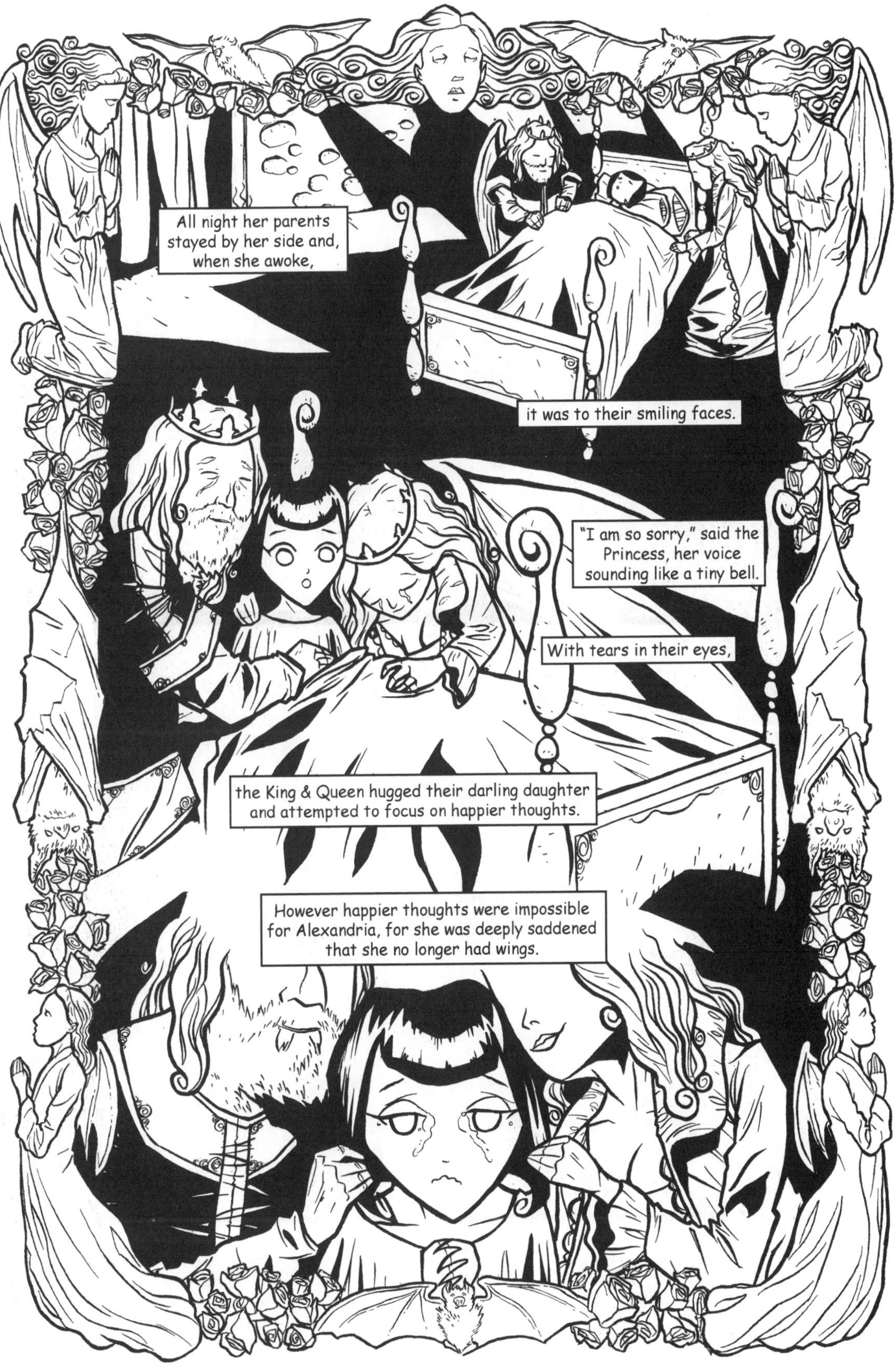
All night her parents stayed by her side and, when she awoke,
it was to their smiling faces.
"I am so sorry," said the Princess, her voice sounding like a tiny bell.
With tears in their eyes,
the King & Queen hugged their darling daughter and attempted to focus on happier thoughts.
However happier thoughts were impossible for Alexandria, for she was deeply saddened that she no longer had wings.

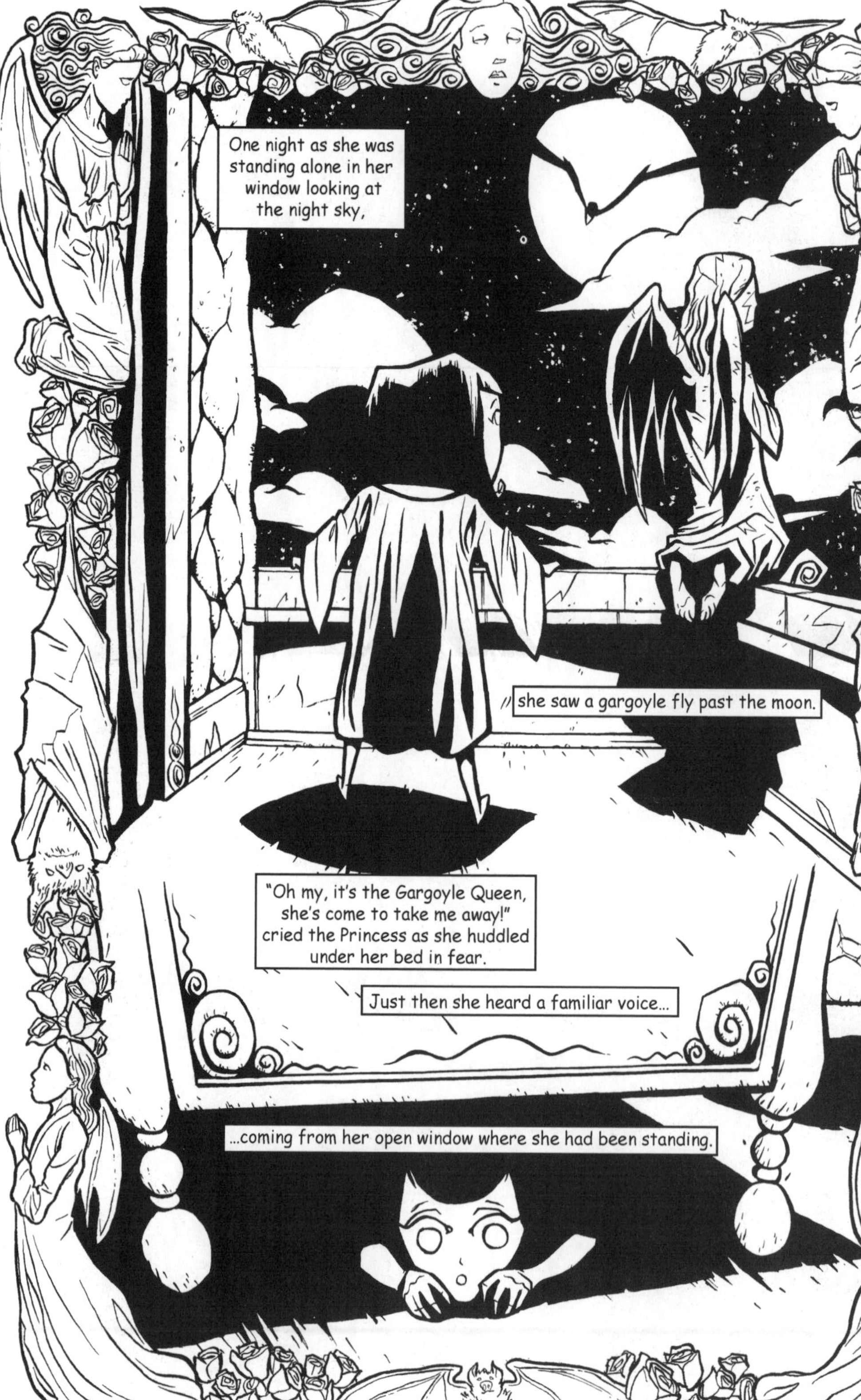
One night as she was standing alone in her window looking at the night sky,
she saw a gargoyle fly past the moon.
"Oh my, it's the Gargoyle Queen, she's come to take me away!" cried the Princess as she huddled under her bed in fear.
Just then she heard a familiar voice...
...coming from her open window where she had been standing.

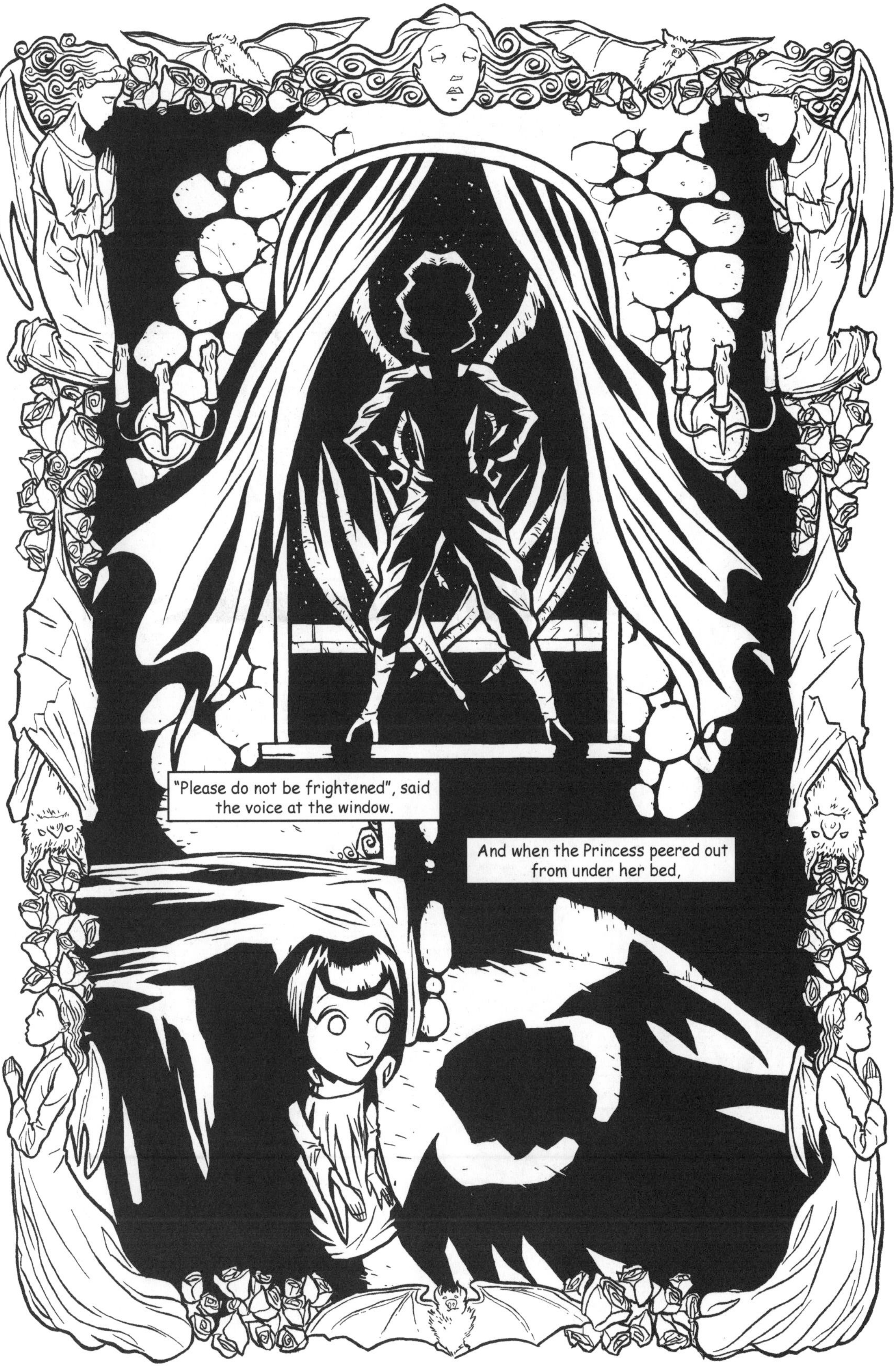
"Please do not be frightened", said the voice at the window.
And when the Princess peered out from under her bed,

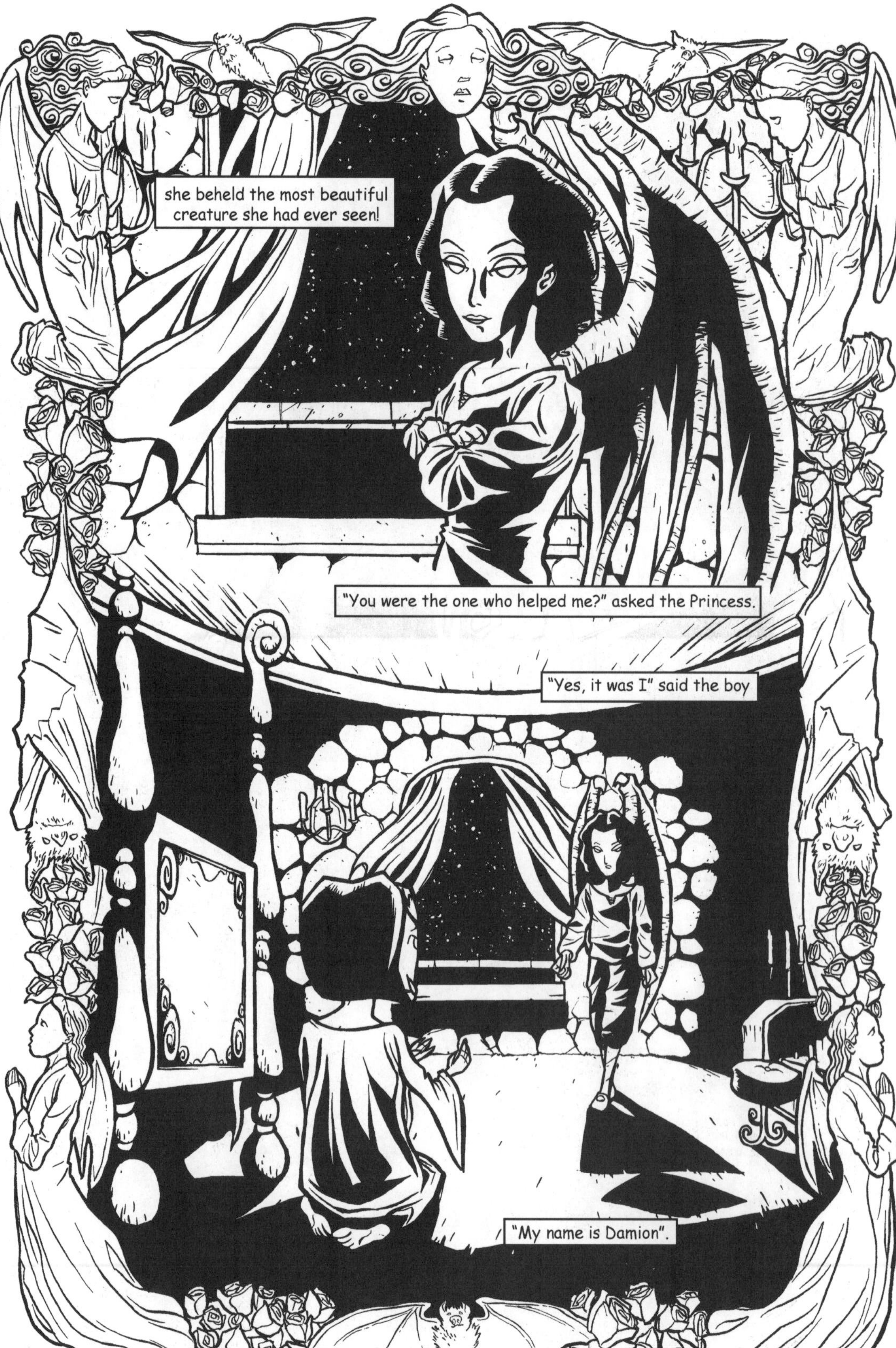
she beheld the most beautiful creature she had ever seen!
"You were the one who helped me?" asked the Princess.
"Yes, it was I" said the boy
"My name is Damion".

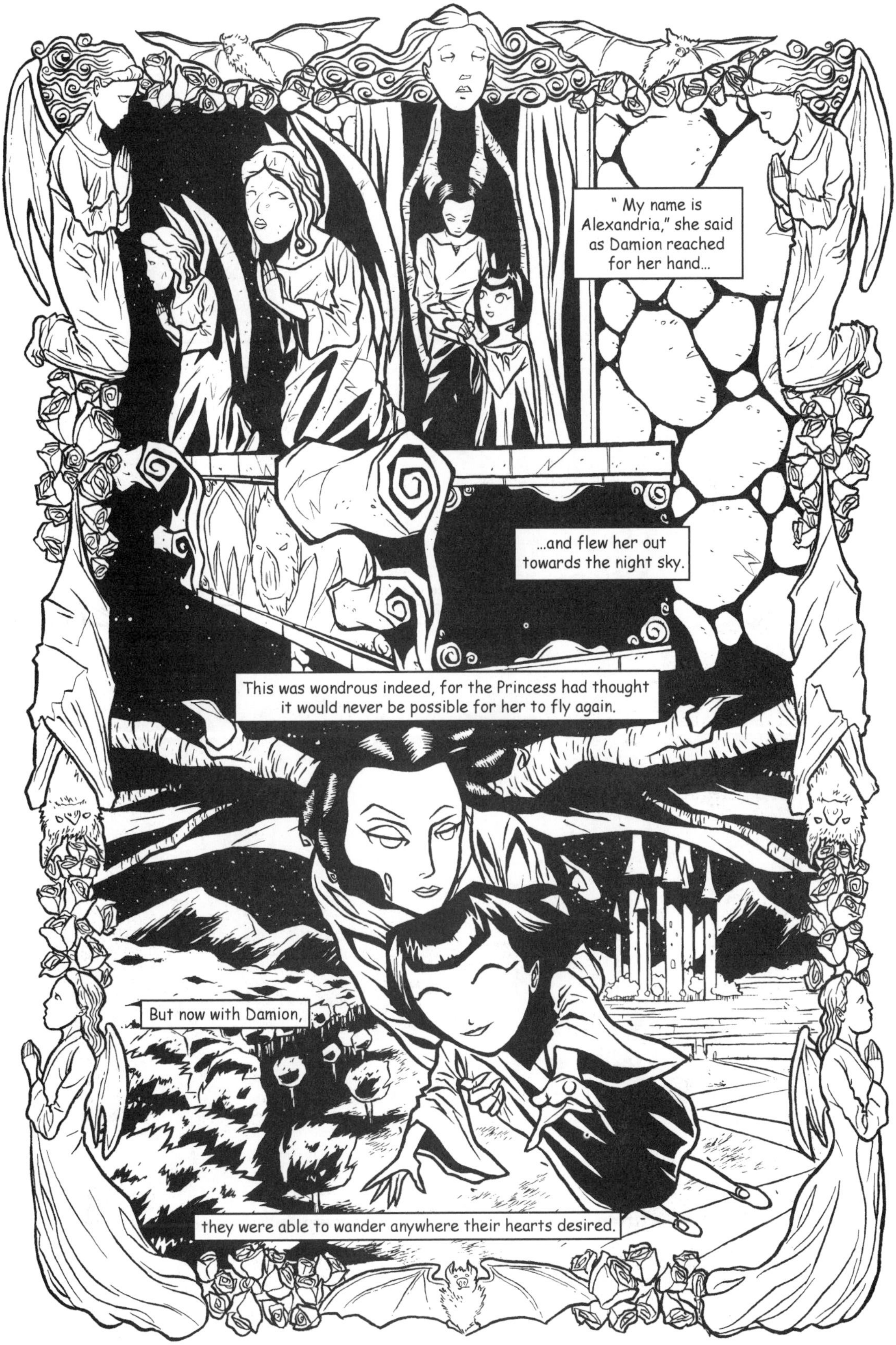

" My name is Alexandria," she said as Damion reached for her hand...
...and flew her out towards the night sky.
This was wondrous indeed, for the Princess had thought it would never be possible for her to fly again.
But now with Damion,
they were able to wander anywhere their hearts desired.

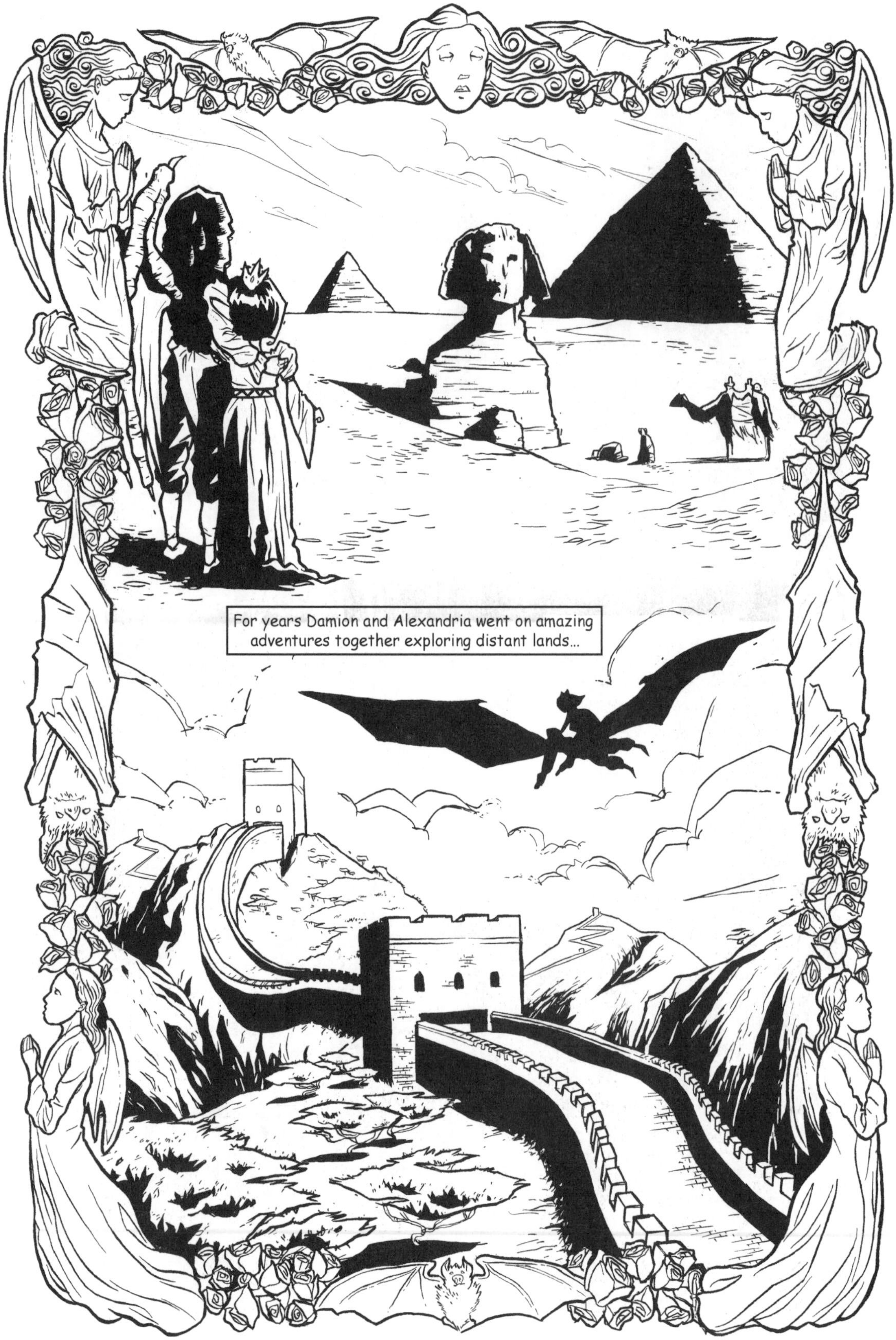
For years Damion and Alexandria went on amazing adventures together exploring distant lands...

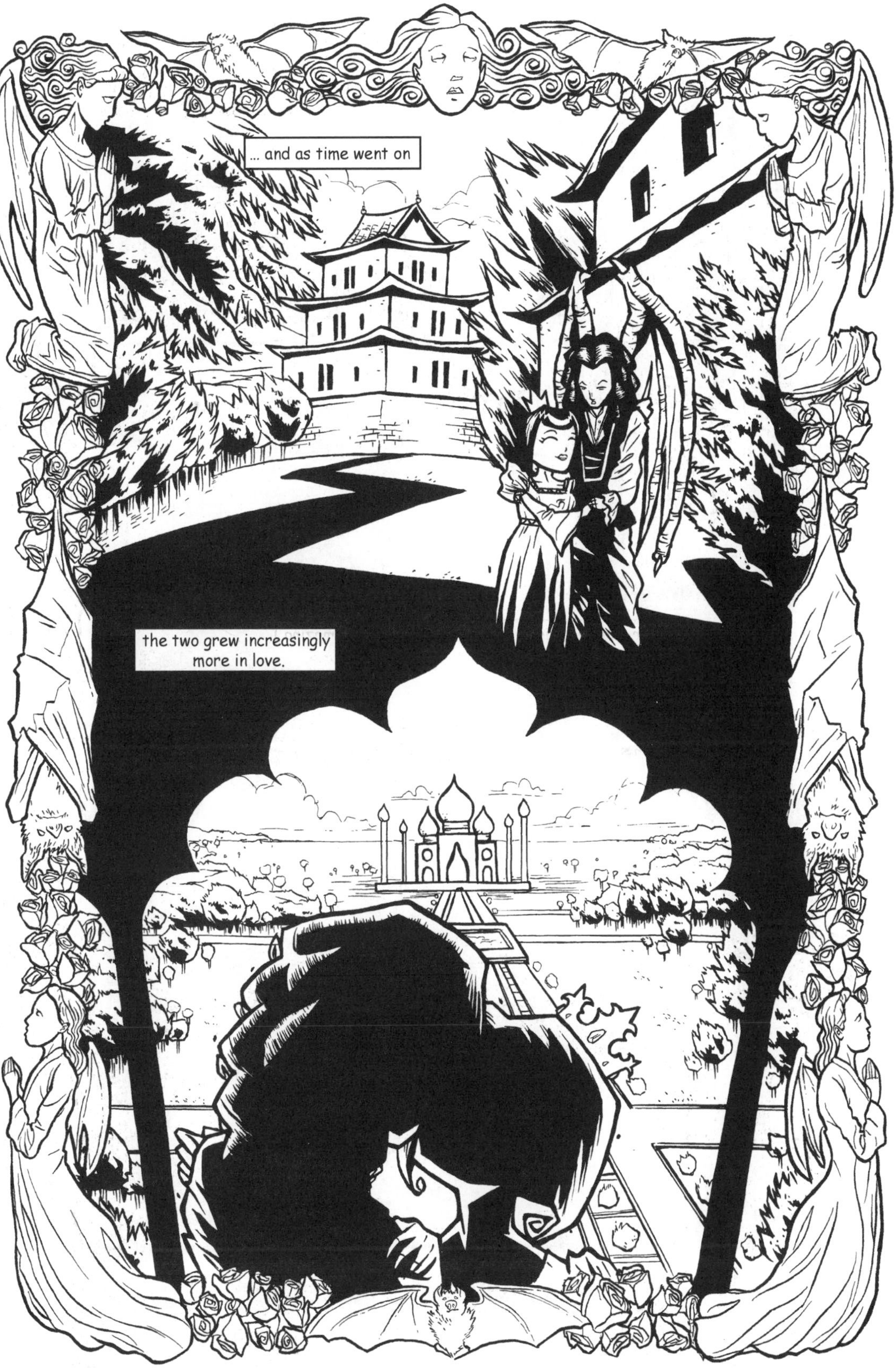
... and as time went on
the two grew increasingly more in love.

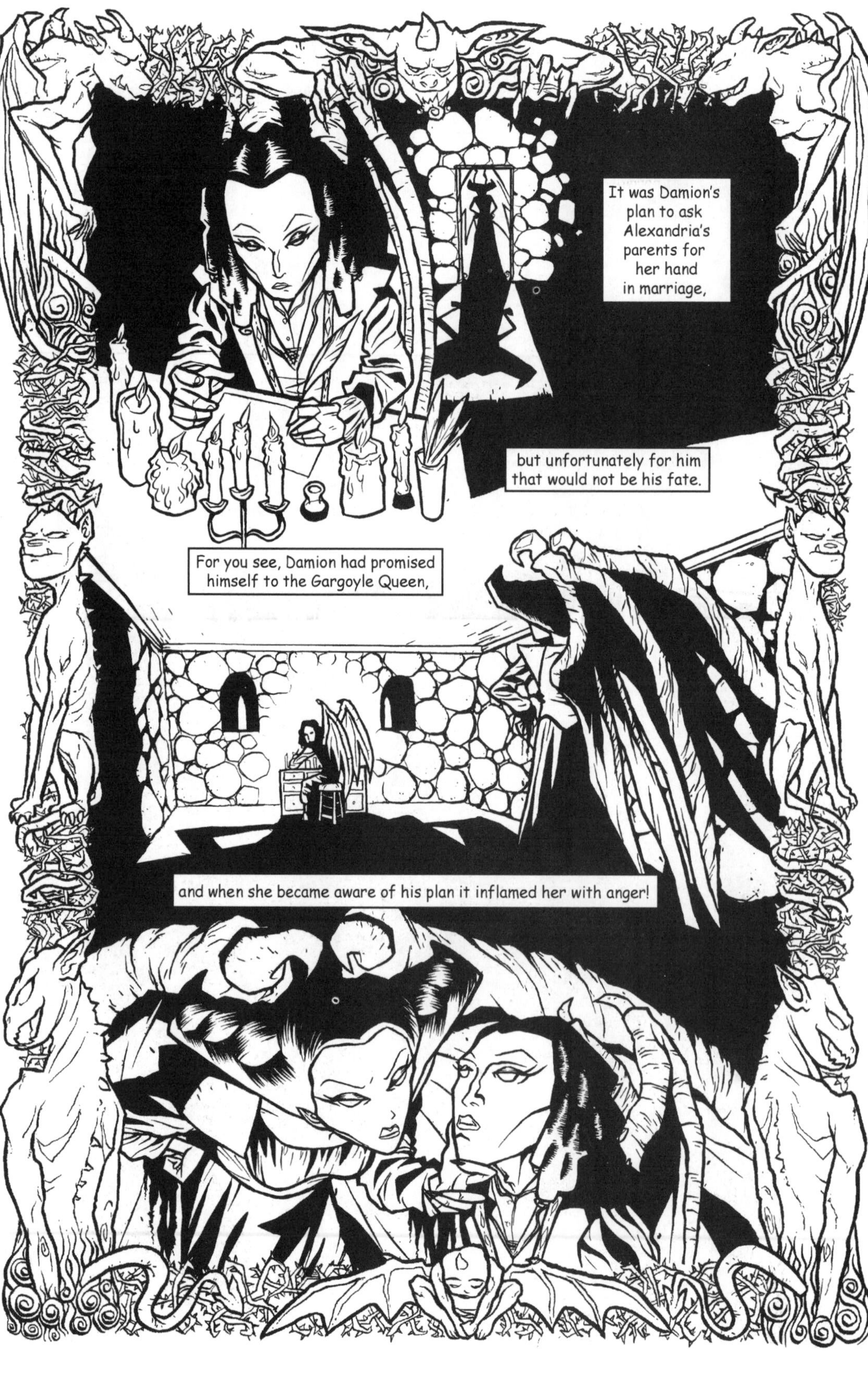
It was Damion's plan to ask Alexandria's parents for her hand in marriage,
but unfortunately for him that would not be his fate.
For you see, Damion had promised himself to the Gargoyle Queen,
and when she became aware of his plan it inflamed her with anger!

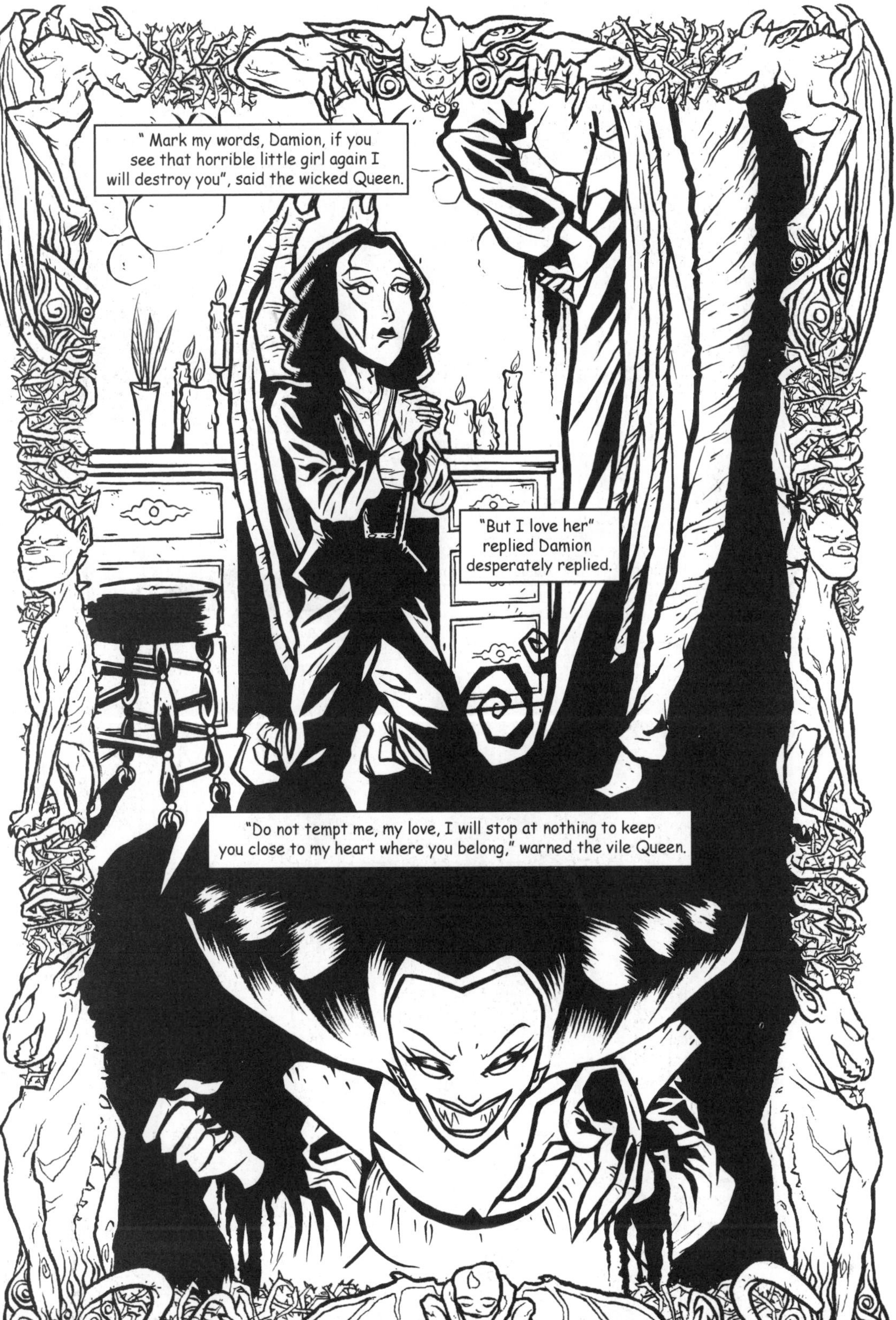
" Mark my words, Damion, if you see that horrible little girl again I will destroy you", said the wicked Queen.
"But I love her" replied Damion desperately replied.
"Do not tempt me, my love, I will stop at nothing to keep you close to my heart where you belong," warned the vile Queen.

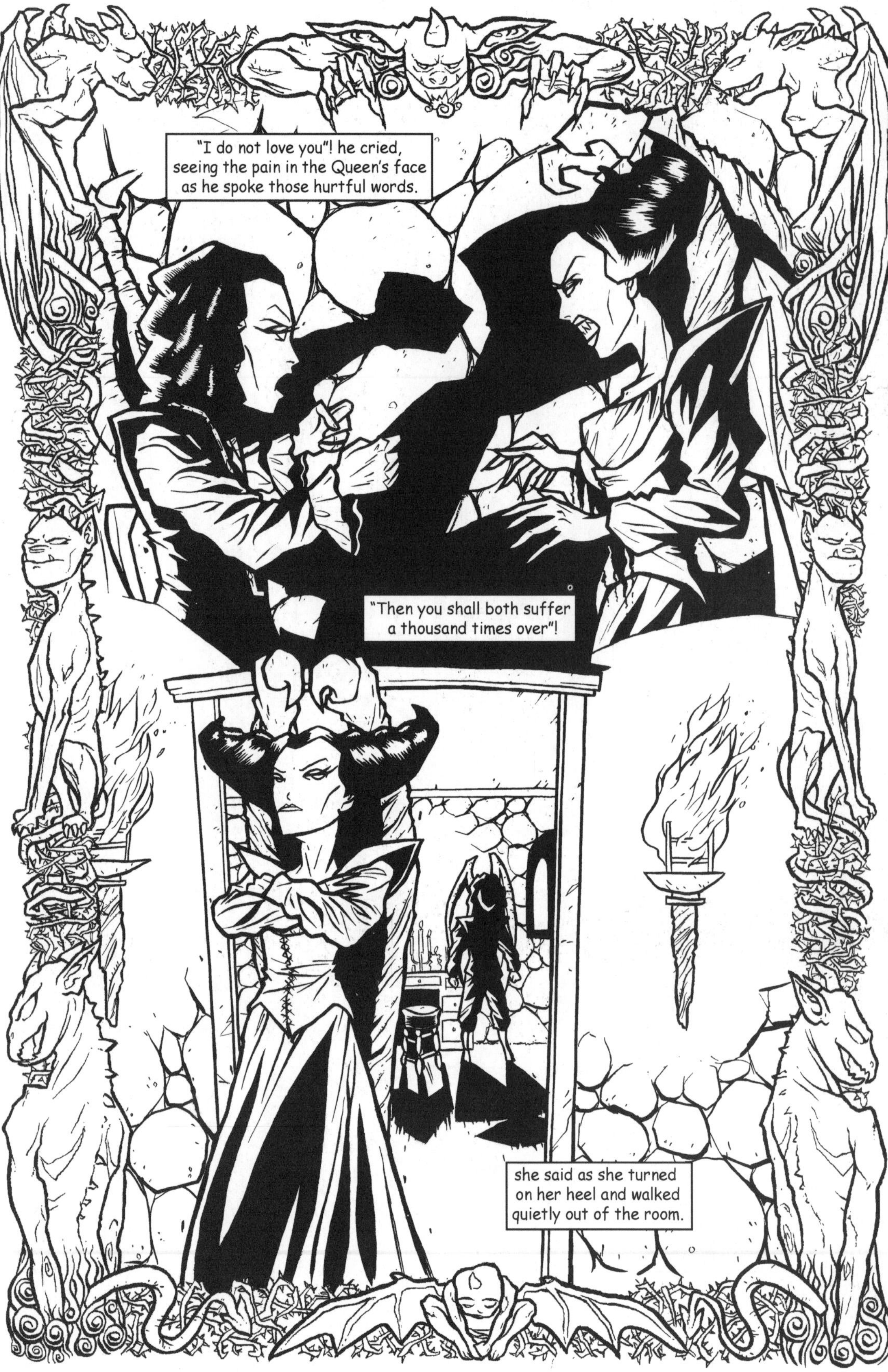
"I do not love you"! he cried, seeing the pain in the Queen's face as he spoke those hurtful words.
"Then you shall both suffer a thousand times over"!
she said as she turned on her heel and walked quietly out of the room.

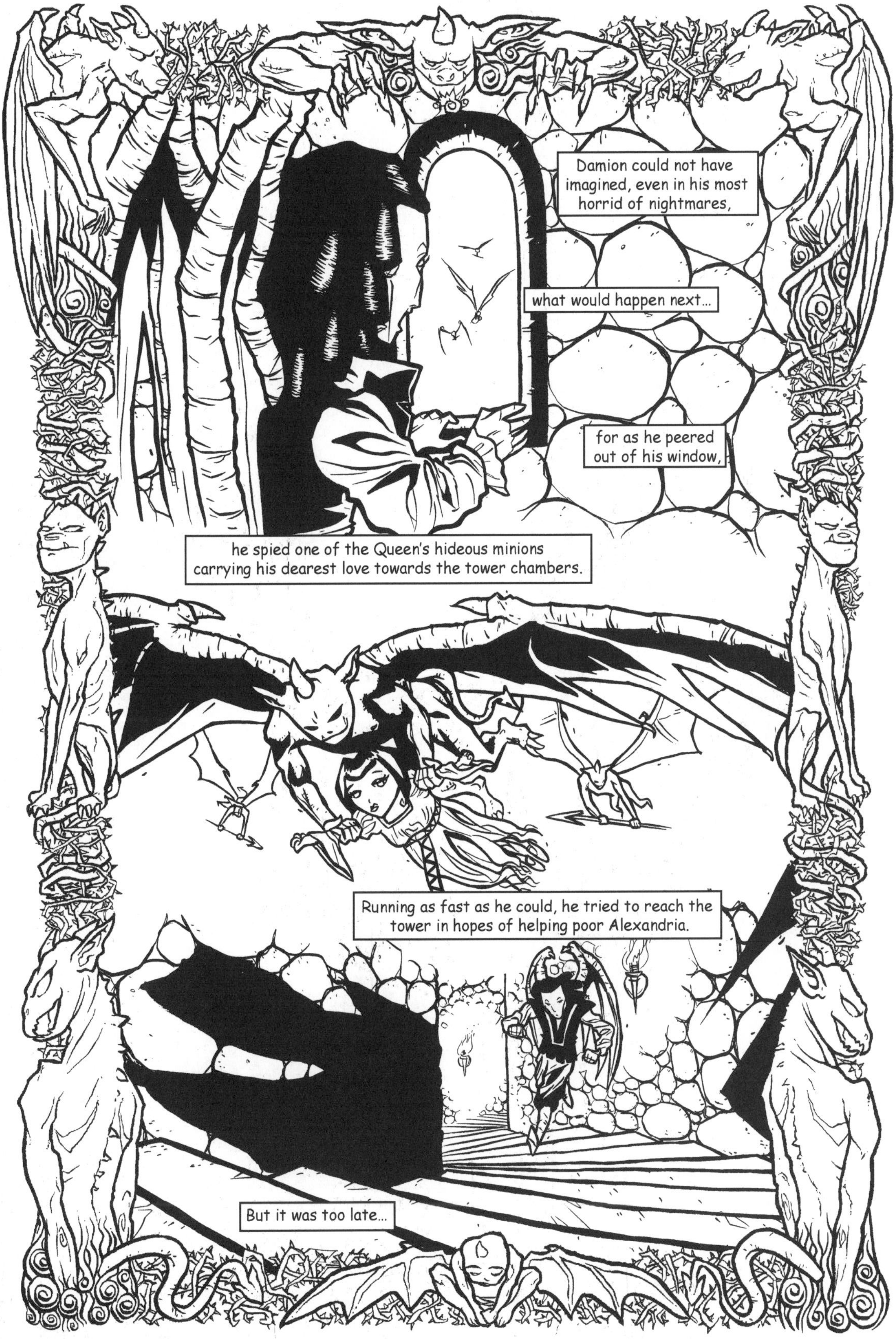
Damion could not have imagined, even in his most horrid of nightmares,
what would happen next...
for as he peered out of his window,
he spied one of the Queen's hideous minions carrying his dearest love towards the tower chambers.
Running as fast as he could, he tried to reach the tower in hopes of helping poor Alexandria.
But it was too late...

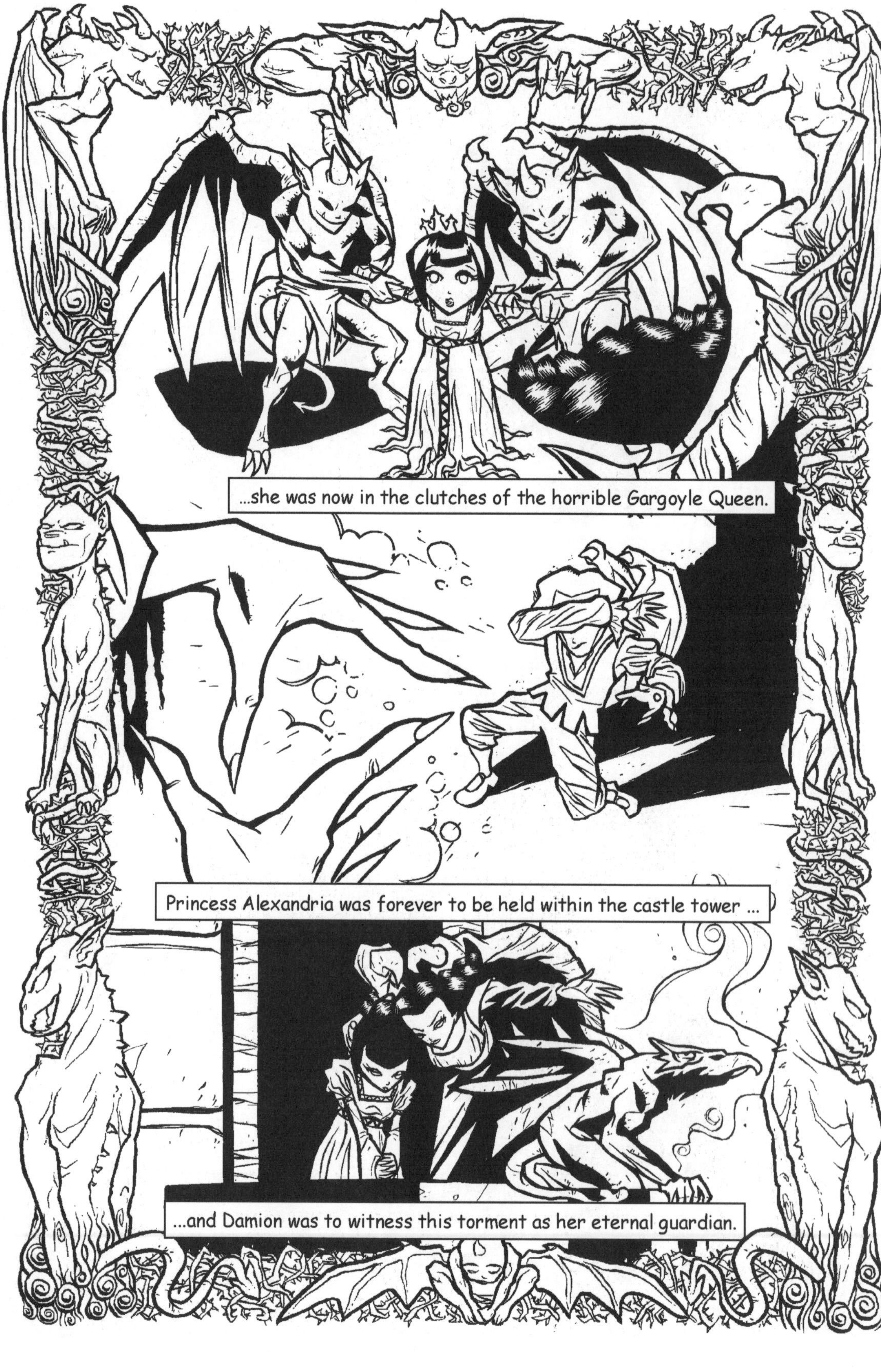
...she was now in the clutches of the horrible Gargoyle Queen.
Princess Alexandria was forever to be held within the castle tower ...
...and Damion was to witness this torment as her eternal guardian.

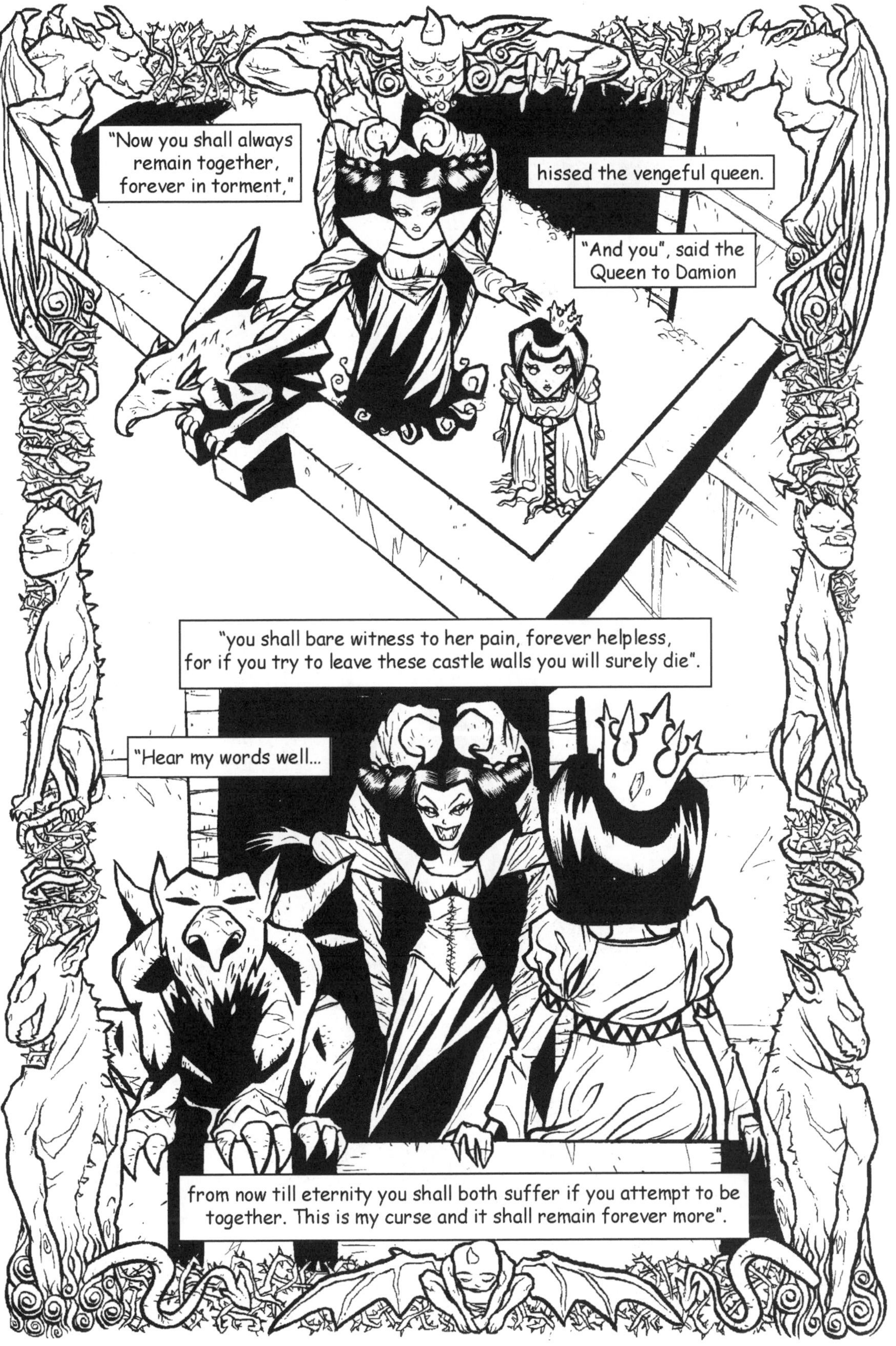
"Now you shall always remain together, forever in torment,"
hissed the vengeful queen.
"And you", said the Queen to Damion
"you shall bare witness to her pain, forever helpless, for if you try to leave these castle walls you will surely die".
"Hear my words well...
from now till eternity you shall both suffer if you attempt to be together. This is my curse and it shall remain forever more".

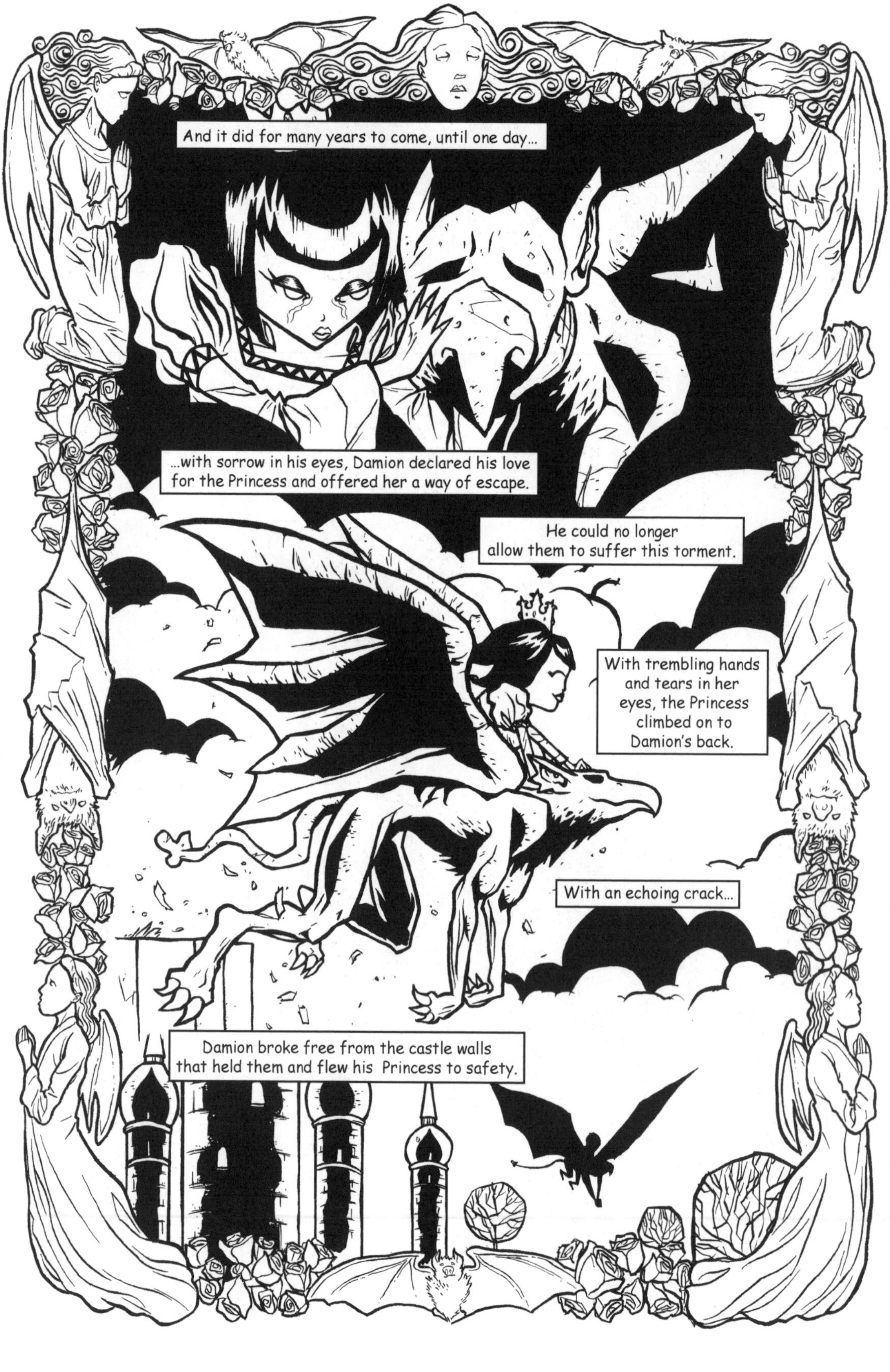

And it did for many years to come, until one day...
...with sorrow in his eyes, Damion declared his love for the Princess and offered her a way of escape.
He could no longer allow them to suffer this torment.
With trembling hands and tears in her eyes, the Princess climbed on to Damion's back.
With an echoing crack...
Damion broke free from the castle walls that held them and flew his Princess to safety.

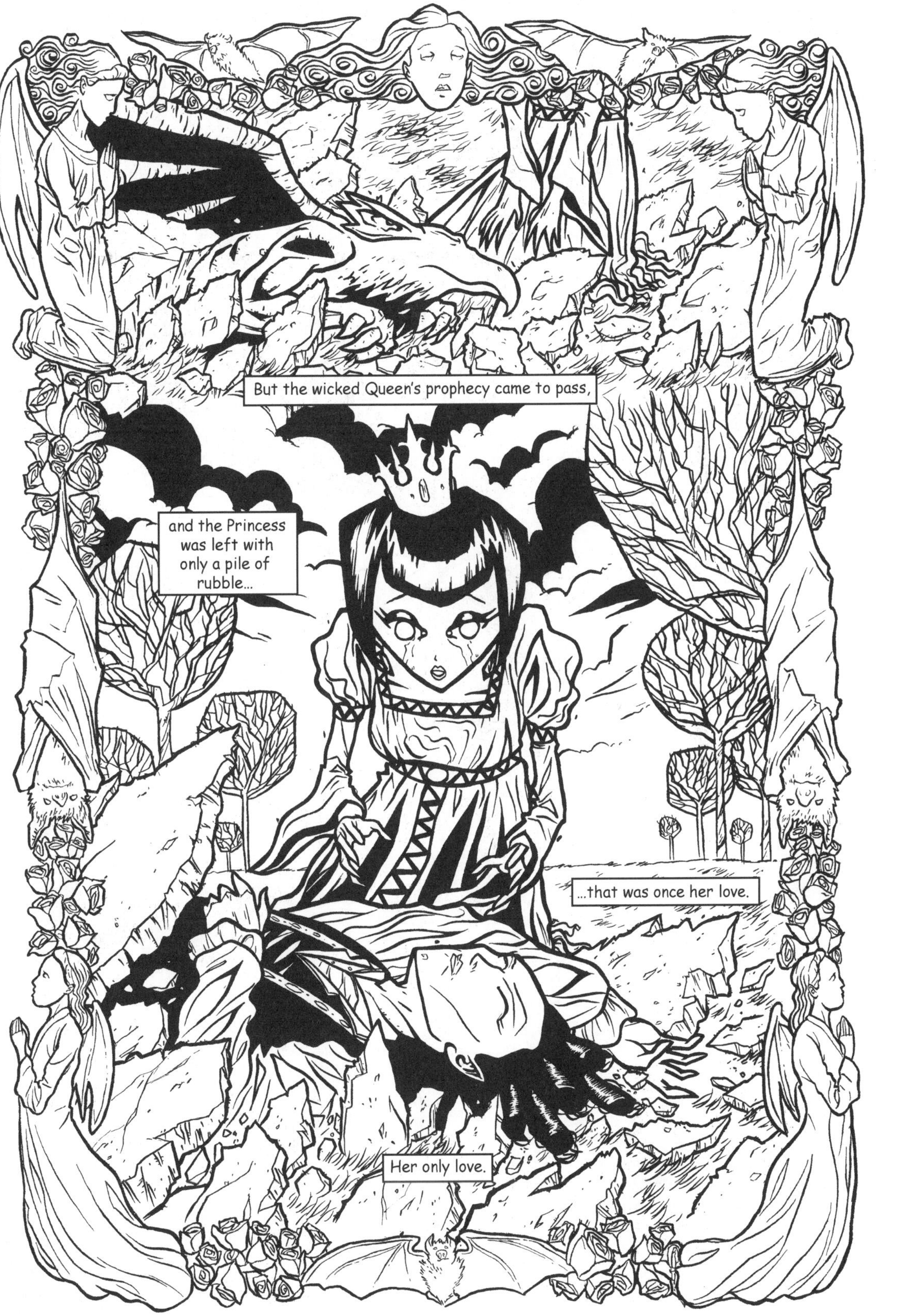
But the wicked Queen's prophecy came to pass,
and the Princess was left with only a pile of rubble...
...that was once her love.
Her only love.

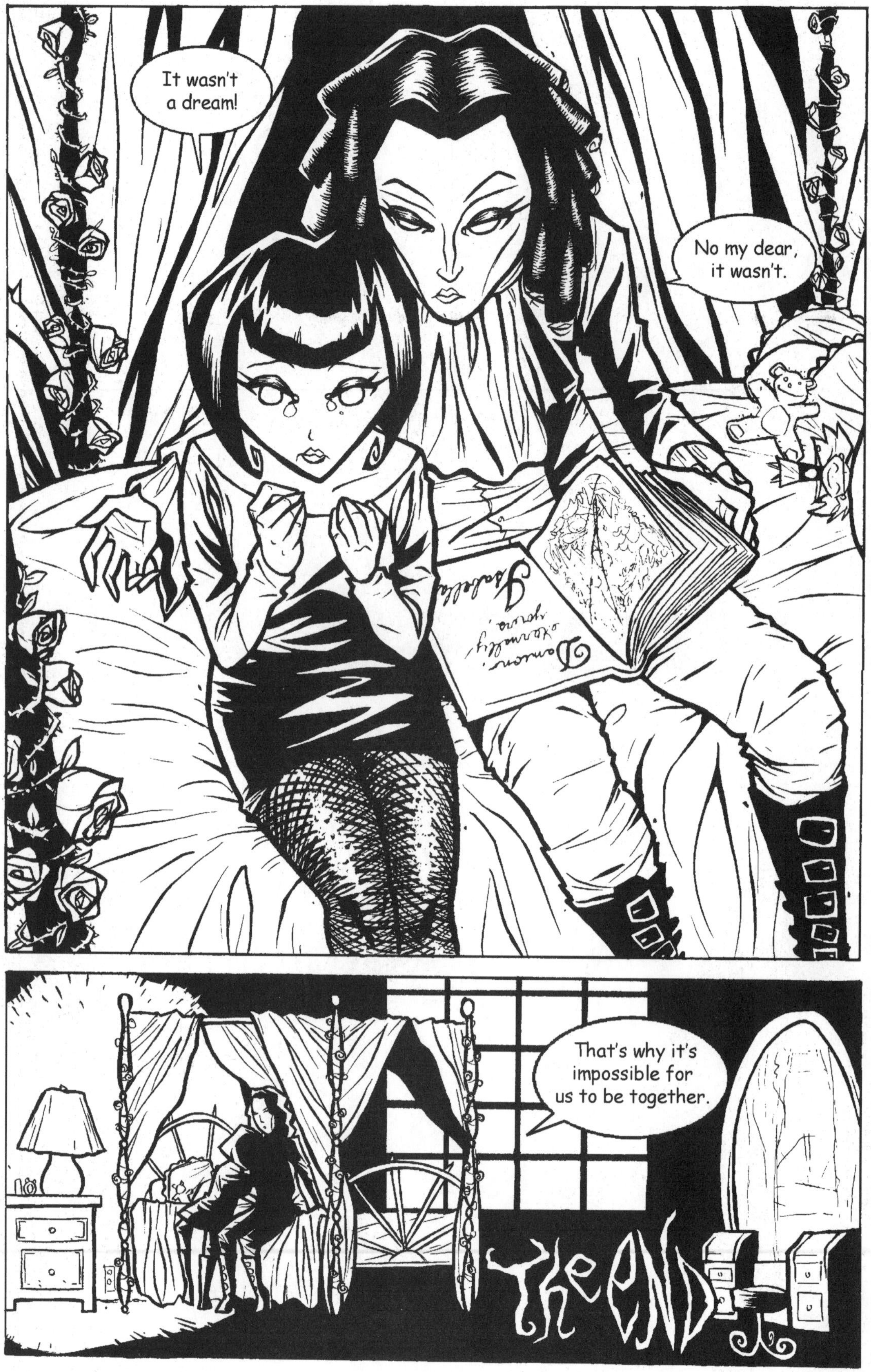
It wasn't a dream!
No my dear, it wasn't.
That's why it's impossible for us to be together.
THE END

Chapter 8

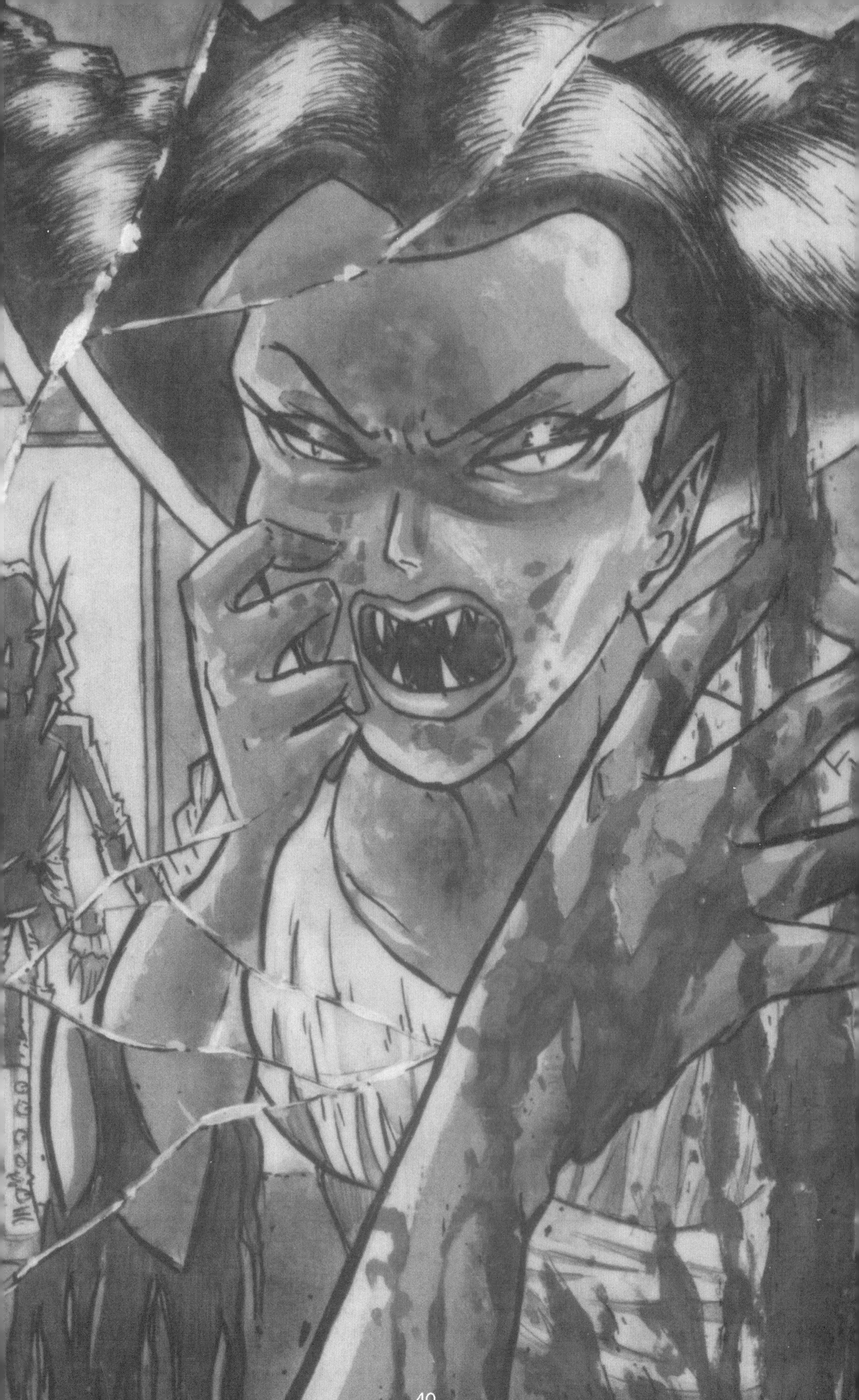

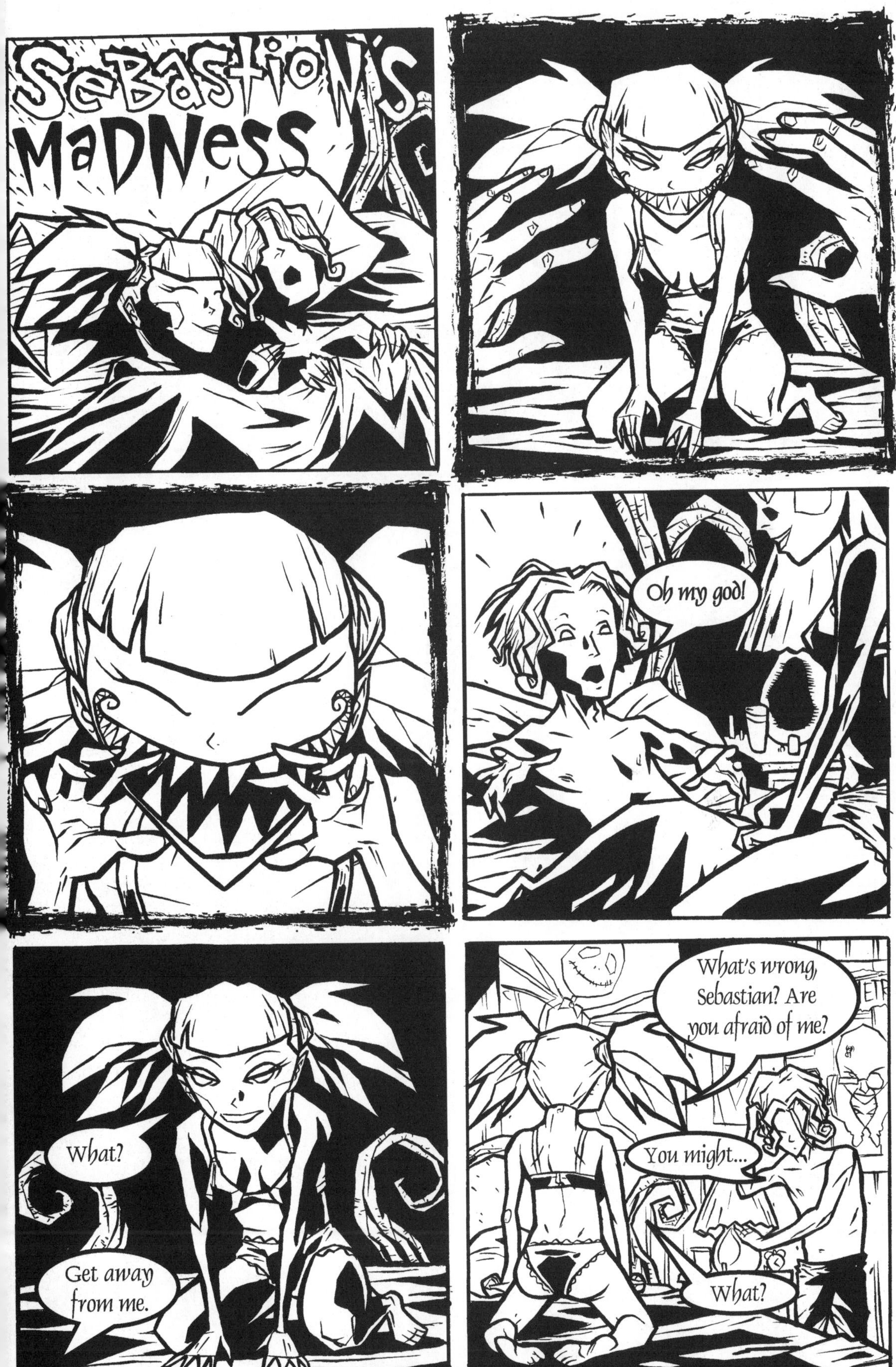
Sebastion's Madness
Oh my god!
What?
Get away from me.
What's wrong, Sebastian? Are you afraid of me?
You might...
What?

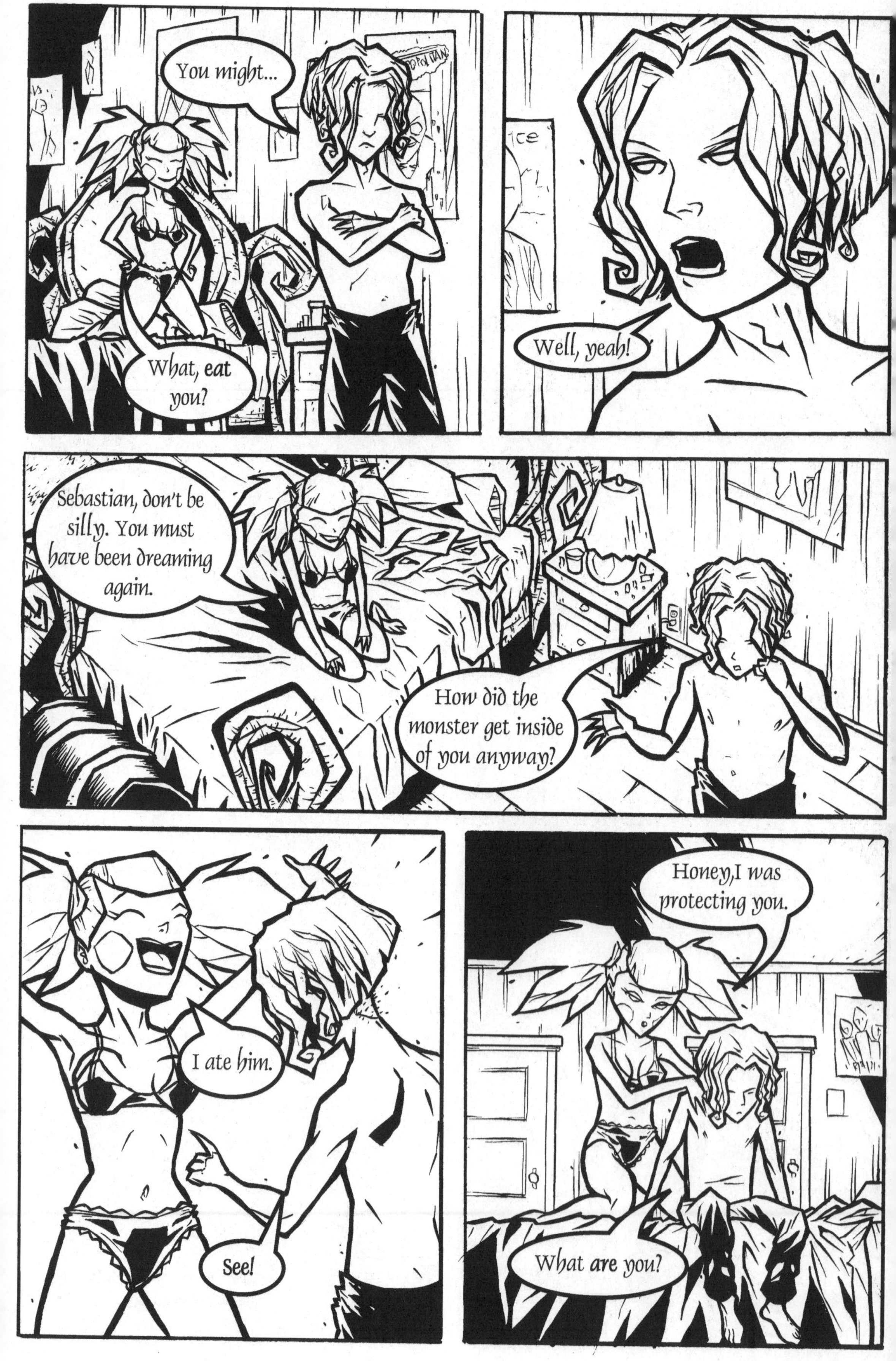
You might...
What, eat you?
Well, yeah!
Sebastian, don't be silly. You must have been dreaming again.
How did the monster get inside of you anyway?
I ate him.
See!
Honey,I was protecting you.
What are you?

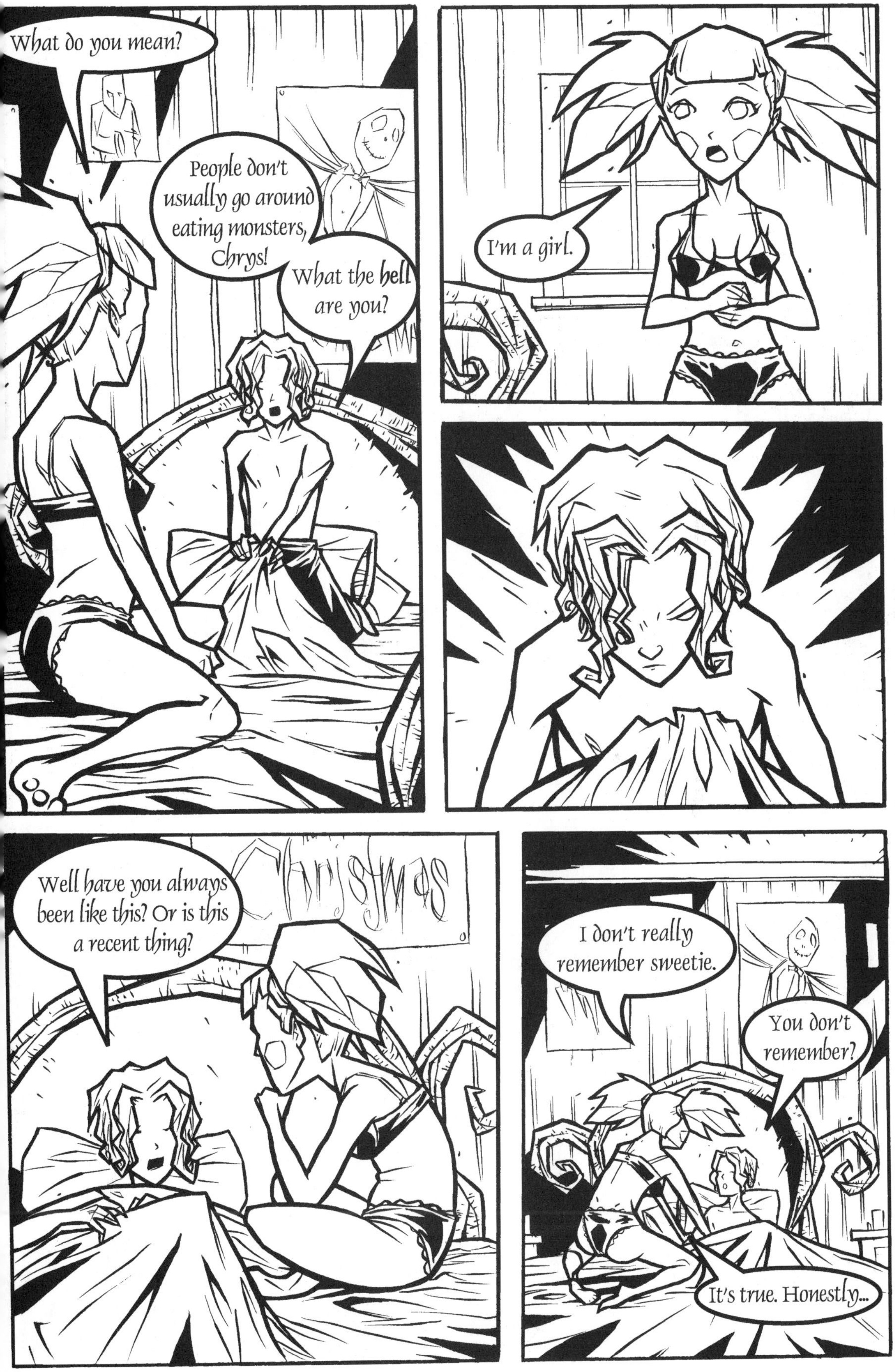
What do you mean?
People don't usually go around eating monsters, Chrys!
What the hell are you?
I'm a girl.
Well have you always been like this? Or is this a recent thing?
Christmas
I don't really remember sweetie.
You don't remember?
It's true. Honestly...

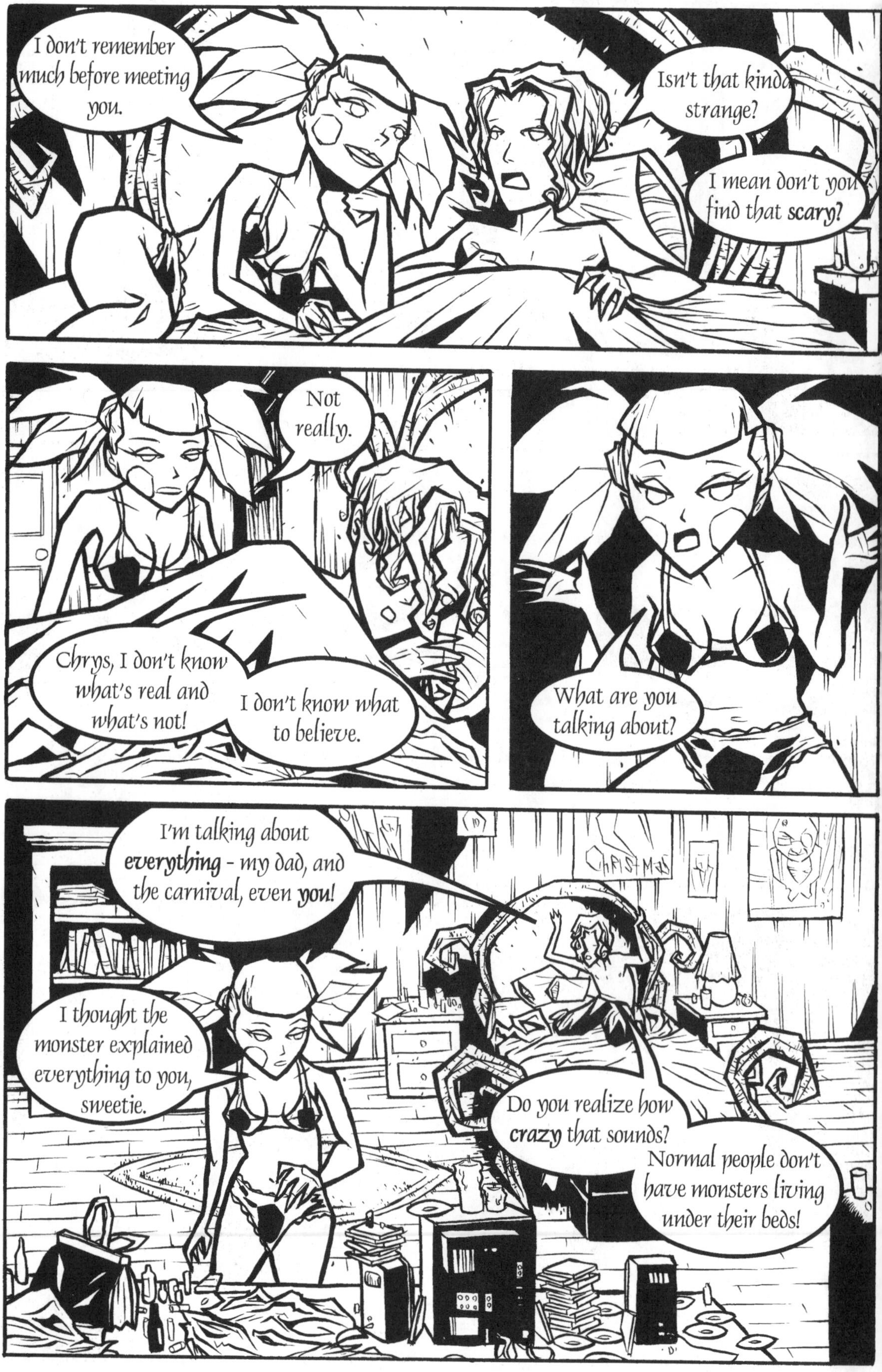
I don't remember much before meeting you.
Isn't that kinda strange?
I mean don't you find that scary?
Not really.
Chrys, I don't know what's real and what's not!
I don't know what to believe.
What are you talking about?
I'm talking about everything - my dad, and the carnival, even you!
I thought the monster explained everything to you, sweetie.
Do you realize how crazy that sounds?
Normal people don't have monsters living under their beds!

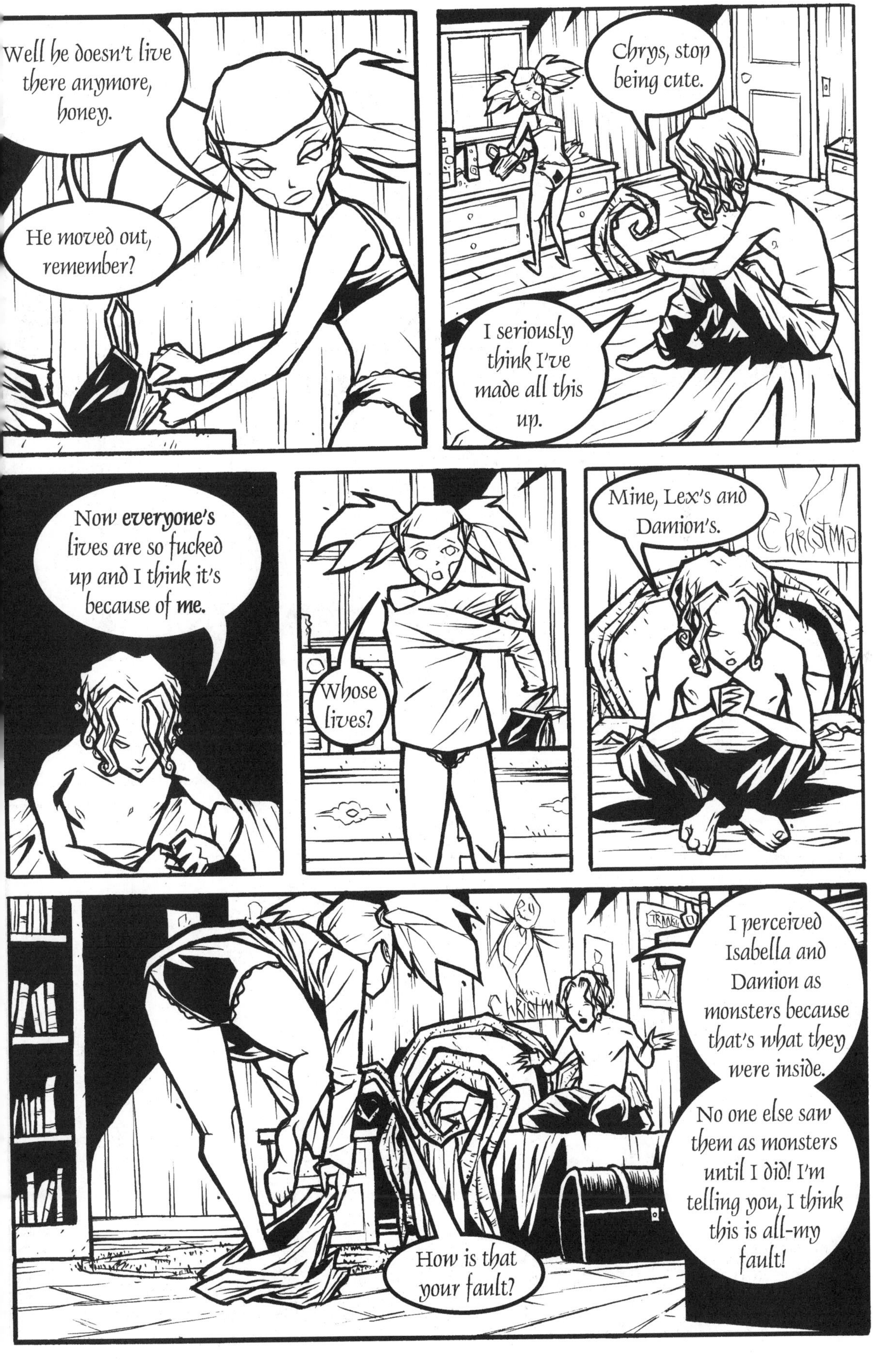
Well he doesn't live there anymore, honey.
He moved out, remember?
Chrys, stop being cute.
I seriously think I've made all this up.
Now **everyone's** lives are so fucked up and I think it's because of **me.**
Whose lives?
Mine, Lex's and Damion's.
CHRISTMAS
I perceived Isabella and Damion as monsters because that's what they were inside.
No one else saw them as monsters until I did! I'm telling you, I think this is all-my fault!
How is that your fault?

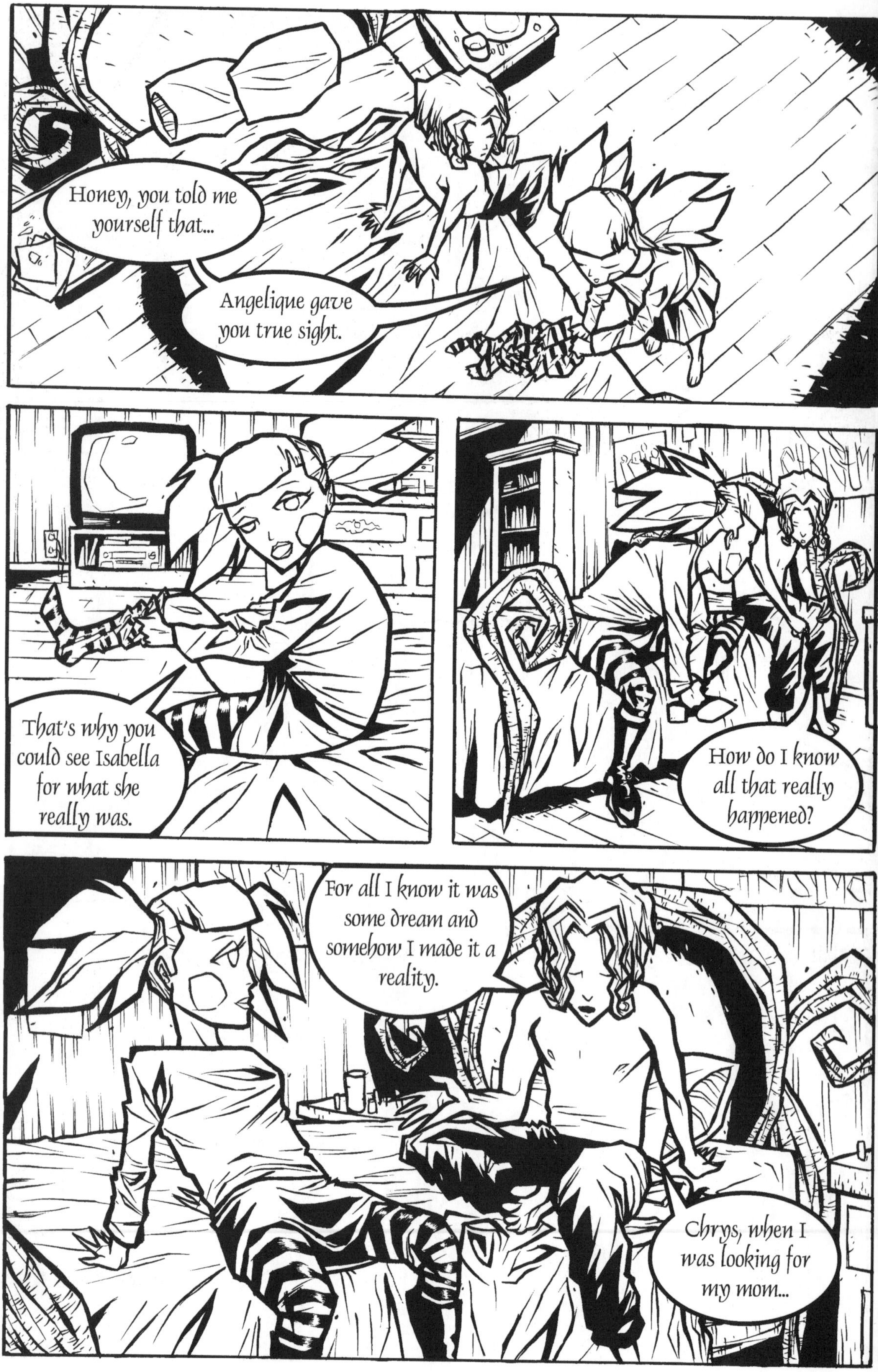
Honey, you told me yourself that...
Angelique gave you true sight.
That's why you could see Isabella for what she really was.
How do I know all that really happened?
For all I know it was some dream and somehow I made it a reality.
Chrys, when I was looking for my mom...

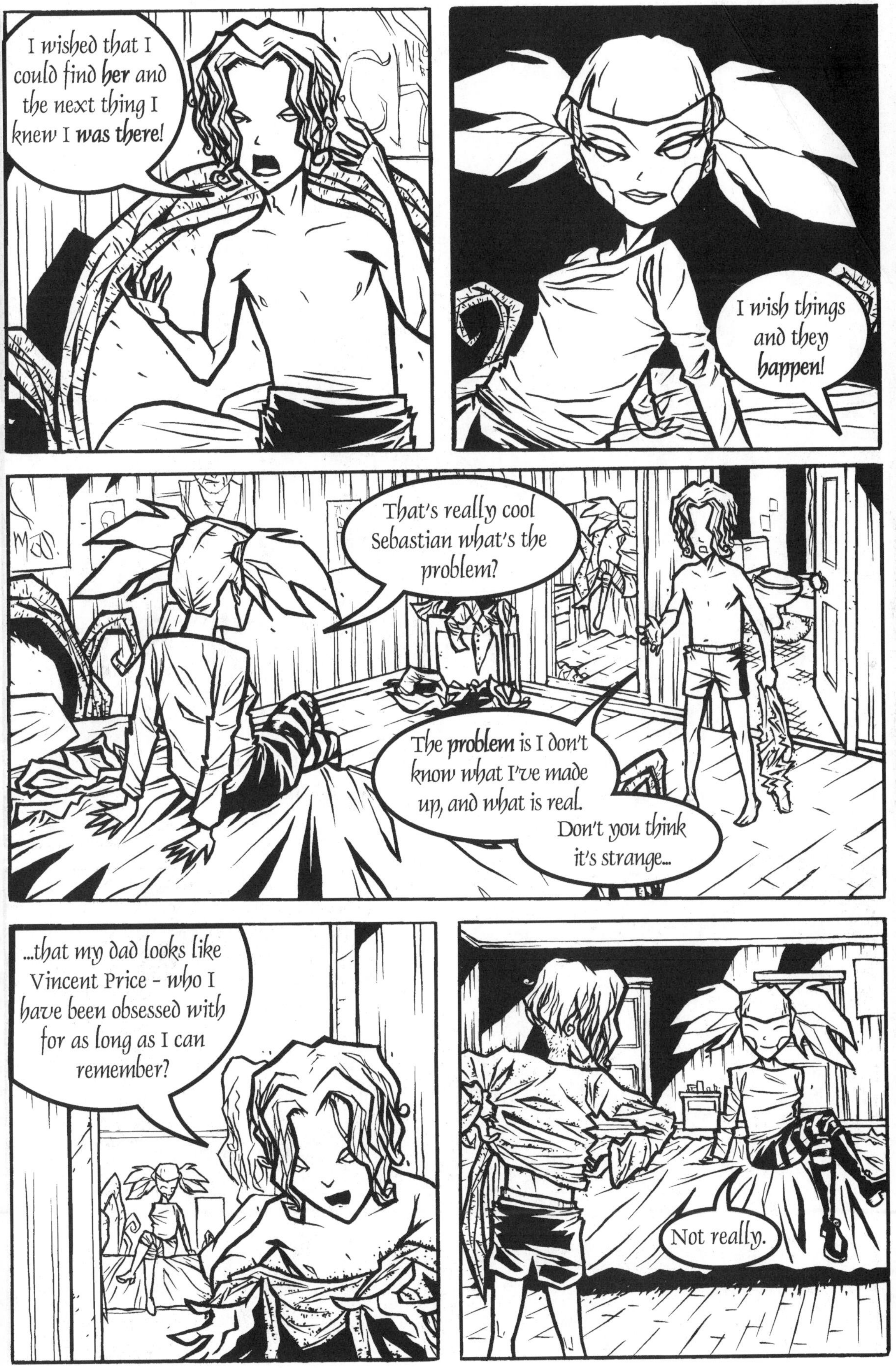
I wished that I could find her and the next thing I knew I was there!
I wish things and they happen!
That's really cool Sebastian what's the problem?
The problem is I don't know what I've made up, and what is real.
Don't you think it's strange...
...that my dad looks like Vincent Price - who I have been obsessed with for as long as I can remember?
Not really.

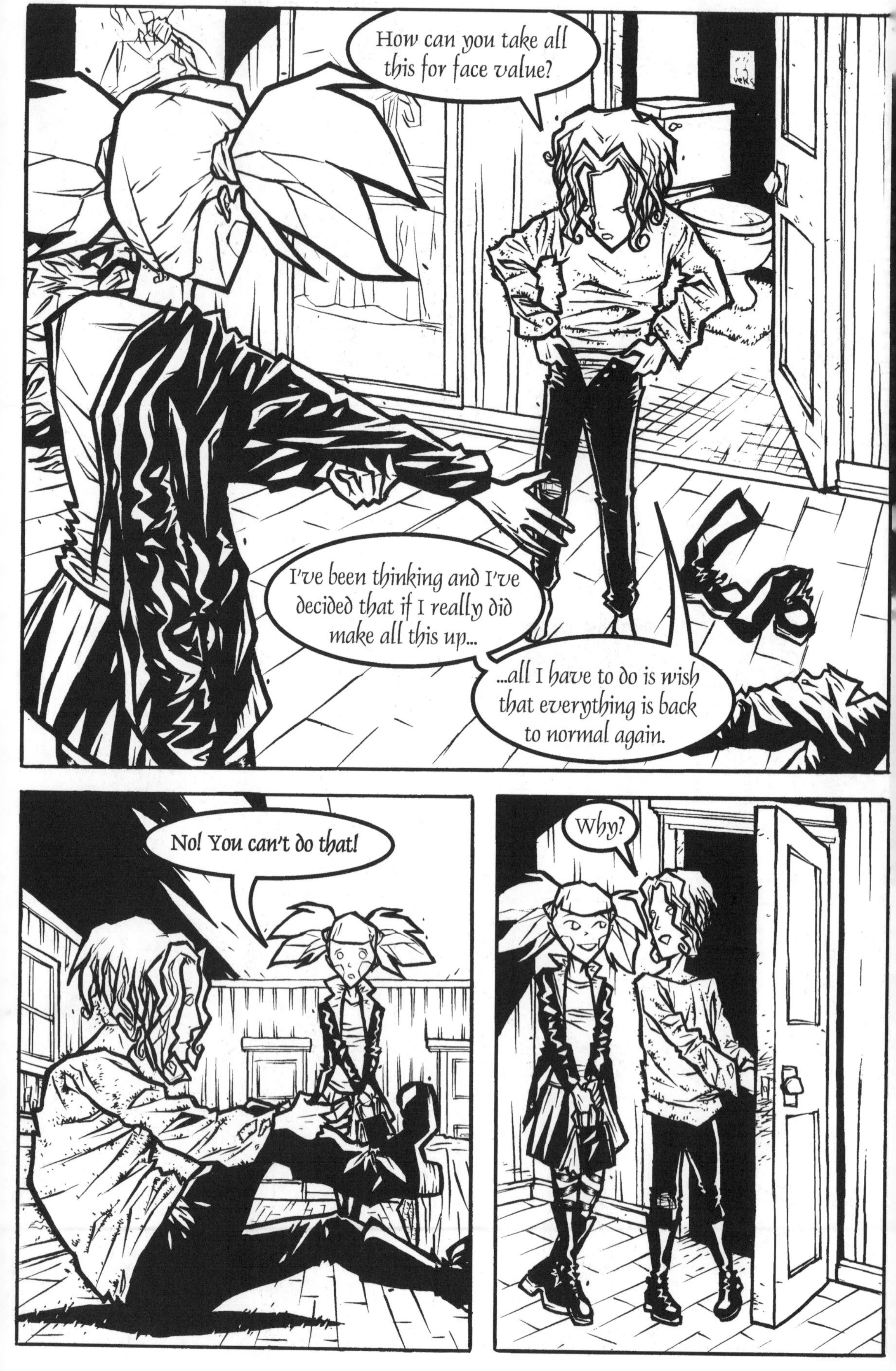
How can you take all this for face value?
I've been thinking and I've decided that if I really did make all this up...
...all I have to do is wish that everything is back to normal again.
No! You can't do that!
Why?

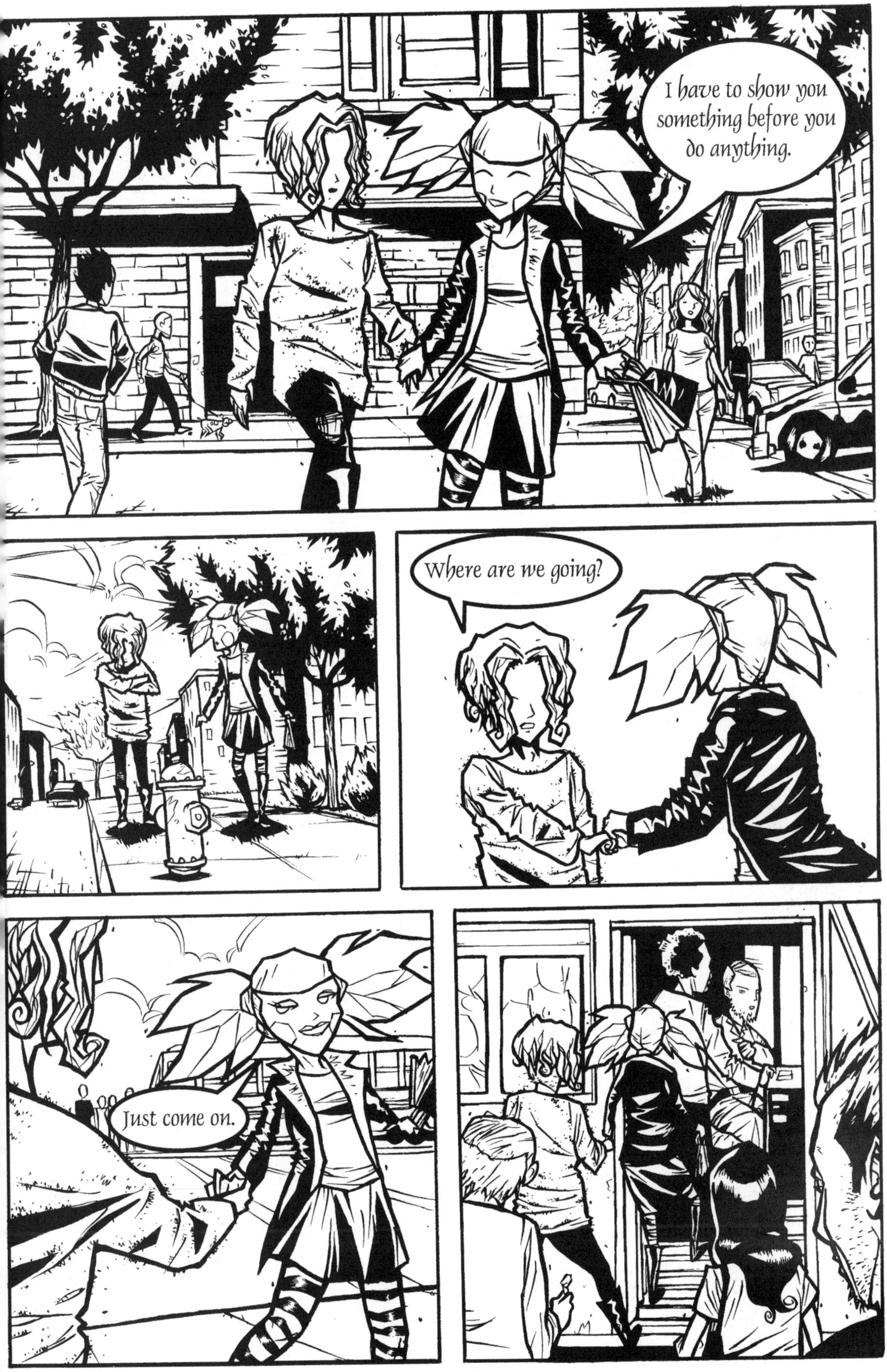
I have to show you something before you do anything.
Where are we going?
Just come on.

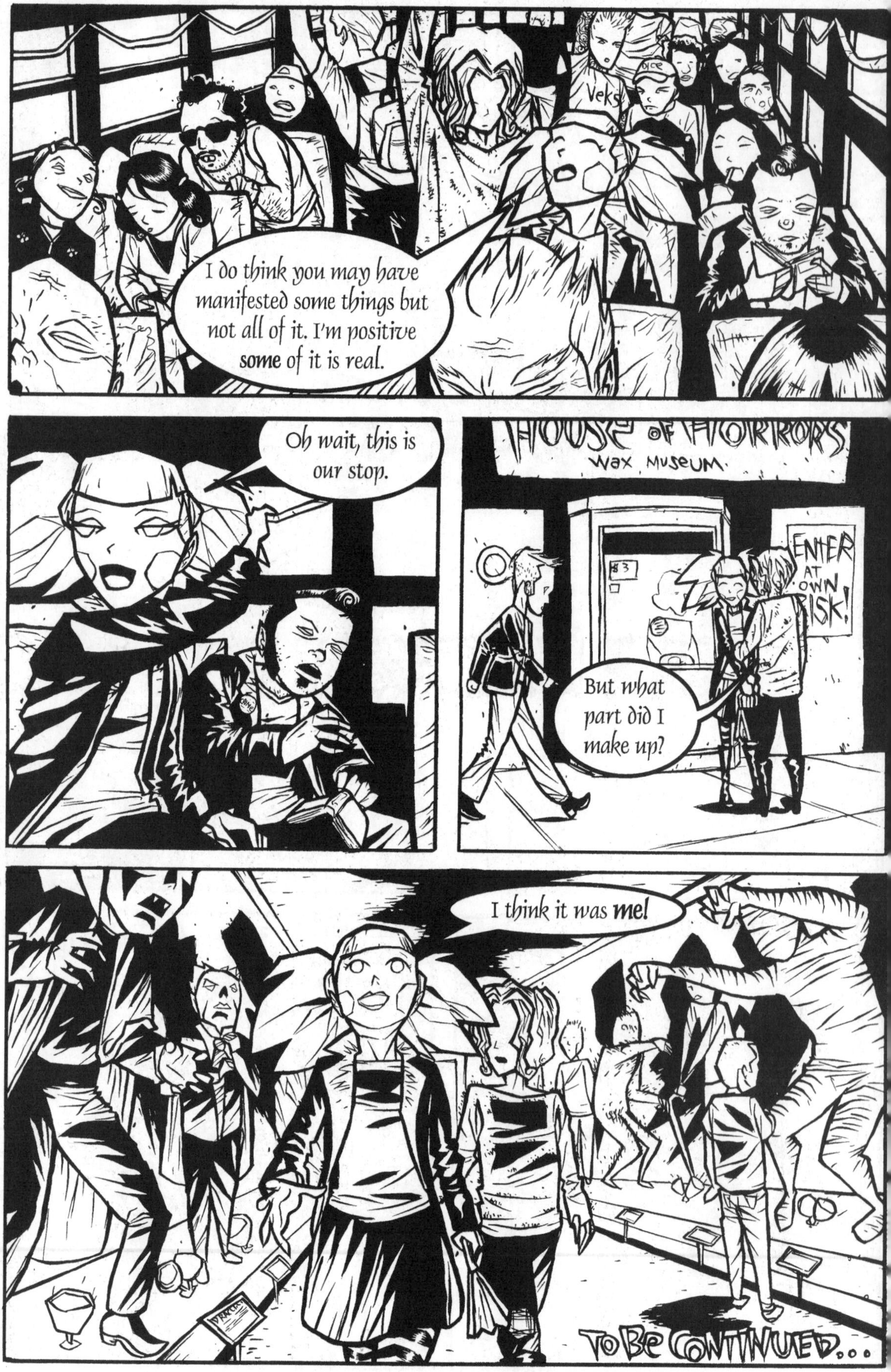
Veks
DICE
I do think you may have manifested some things but not all of it. I'm positive **some** of it is real.
Oh wait, this is our stop.
HOUSE OF HORRORS
WAX MUSEUM
$3
ENTER AT OWN RISK!
But what part did I make up?
I think it was **me!**
DRACULA
TO BE CONTINUED...

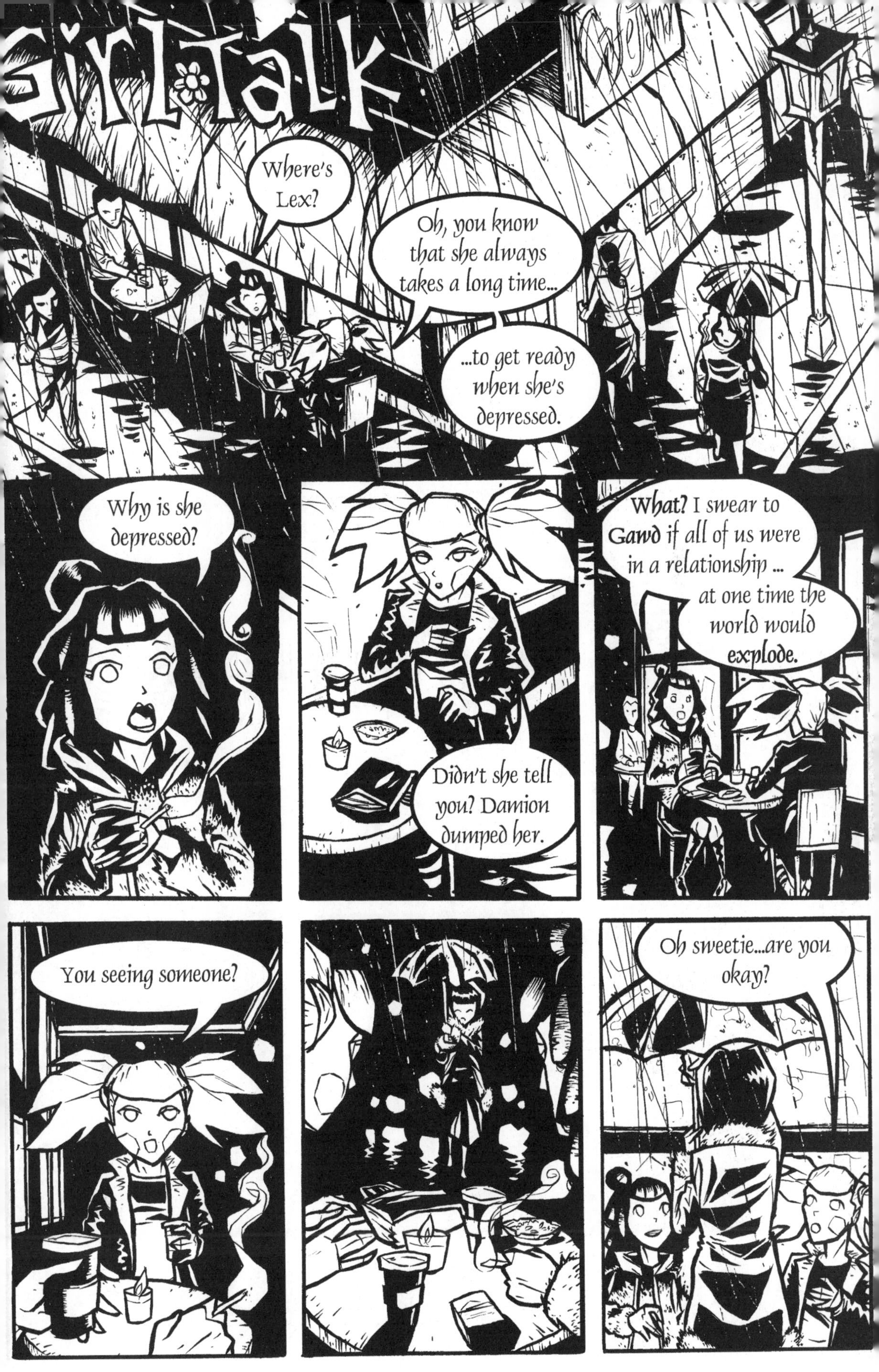
Girl Talk
Cafe Jinny
Where's Lex?
Oh, you know that she always takes a long time...
...to get ready when she's depressed.
Why is she depressed?
Didn't she tell you? Damion dumped her.
What? I swear to Gawd if all of us were in a relationship ...
at one time the world would explode.
You seeing someone?
Oh sweetie...are you okay?

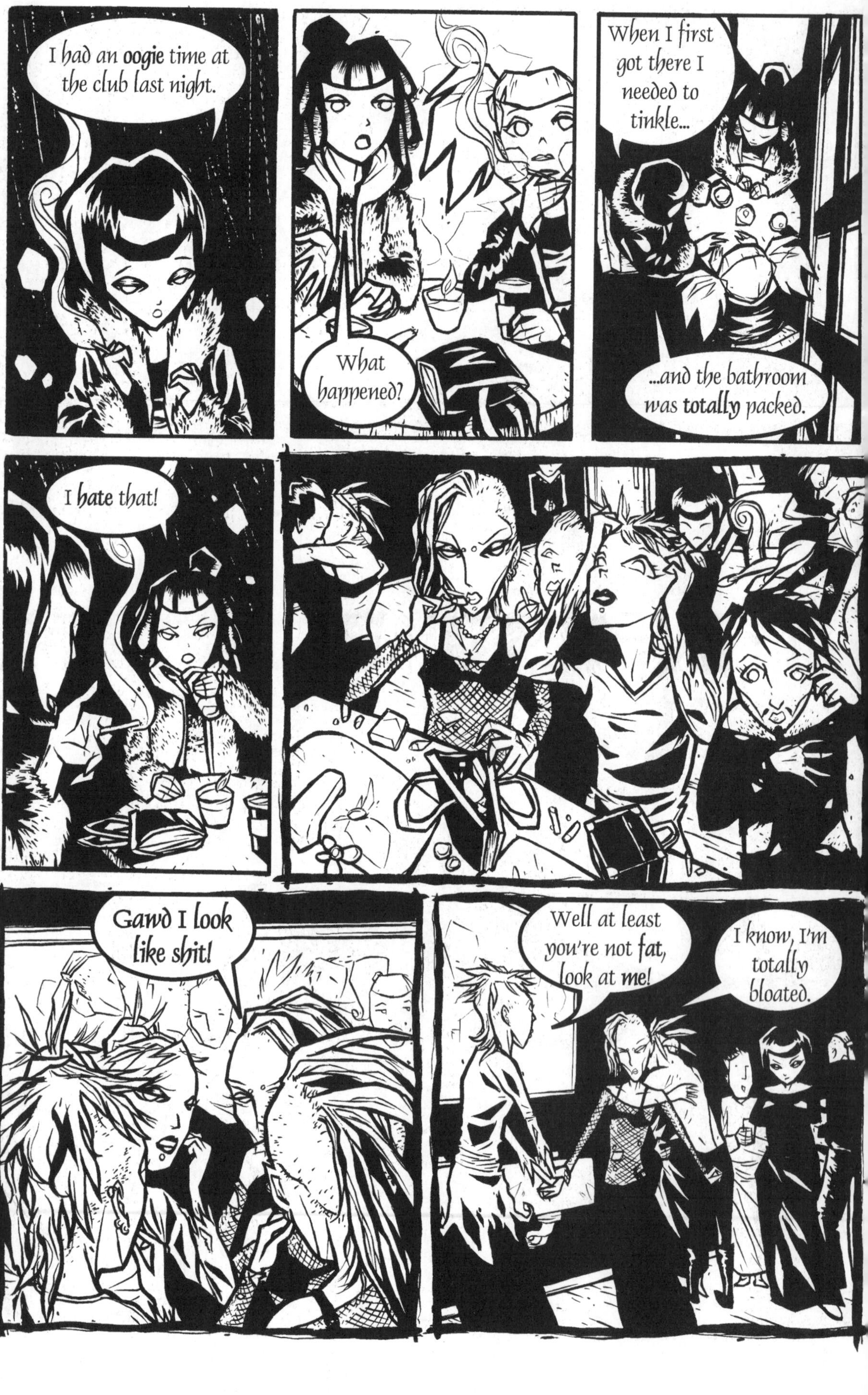
I had an **oogie** time at the club last night.
What happened?
When I first got there I needed to tinkle...
...and the bathroom was **totally** packed.
I **hate** that!
Gawd I look like shit!
Well at least you're not **fat**, look at **me**!
I know, I'm totally bloated.

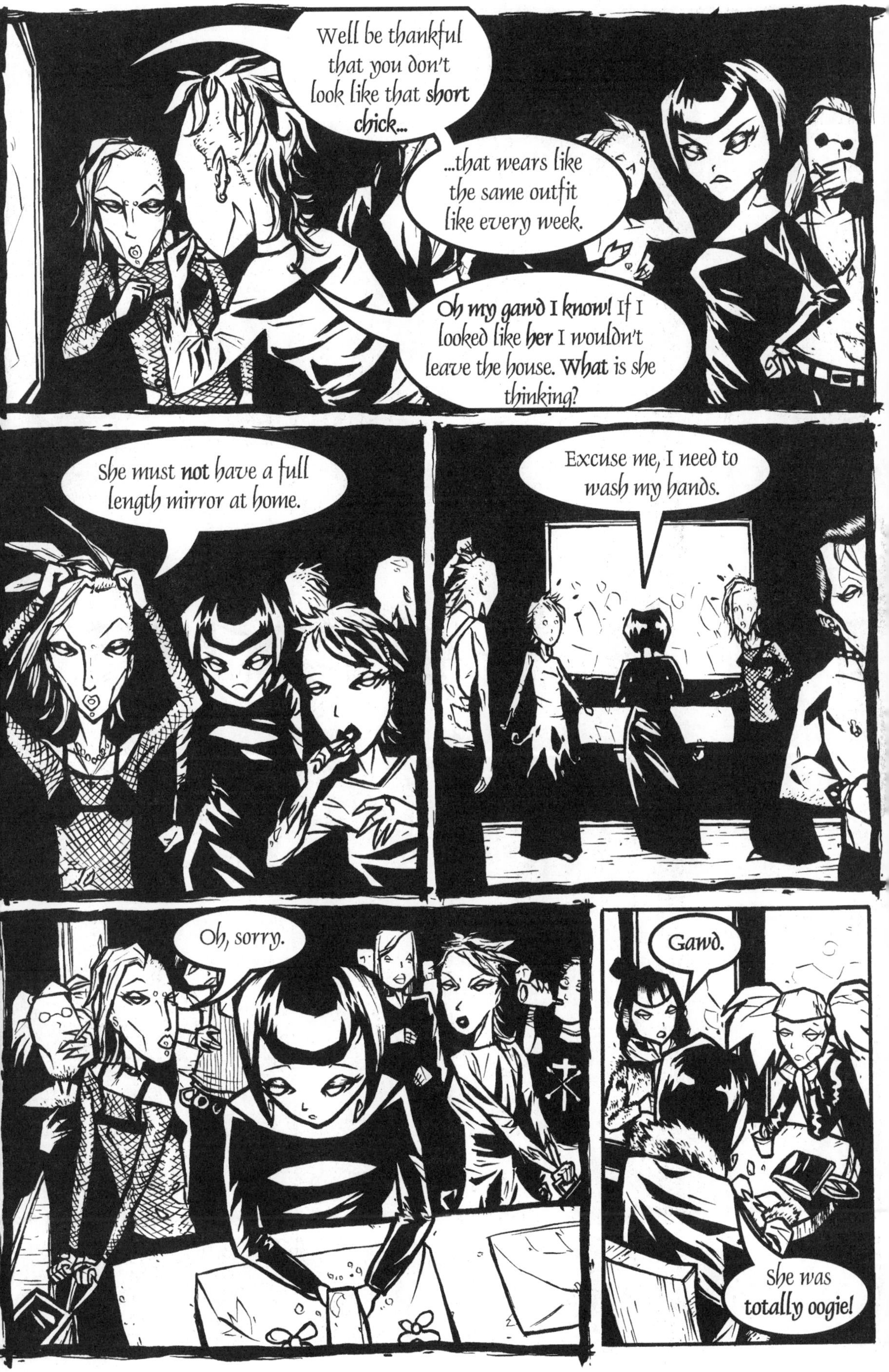
Well be thankful that you don't look like that **short chick...**
...that wears like the same outfit like every week.
Oh my gawd I know! If I looked like **her** I wouldn't leave the house. **What** is she thinking?
She must **not** have a full length mirror at home.
Excuse me, I need to wash my hands.
Oh, sorry.
Gawd.
She was **totally oogie!**

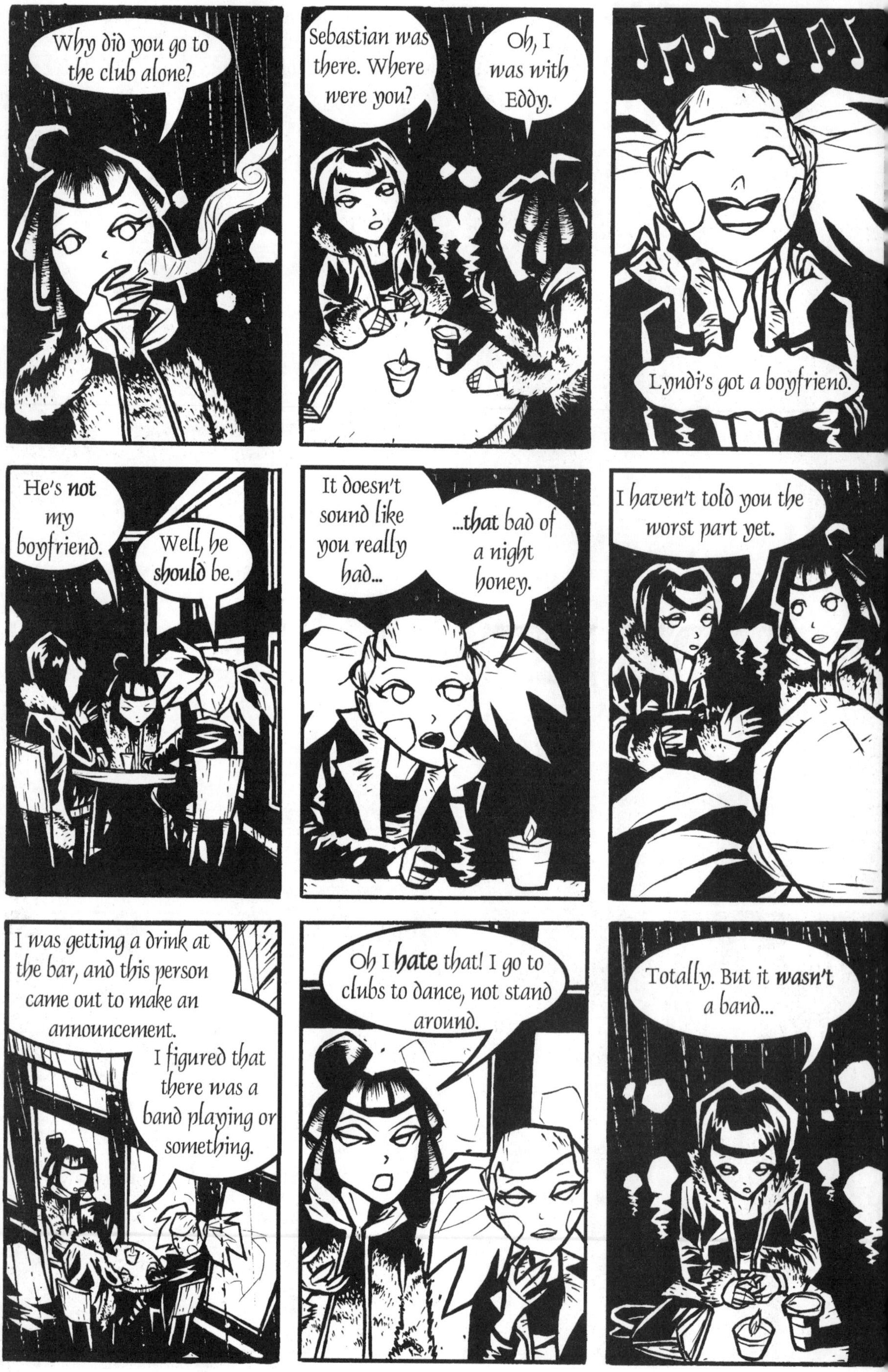

Why did you go to the club alone?
Sebastian was there. Where were you?
Oh, I was with Eddy.
Lyndi's got a boyfriend.
He's **not** my boyfriend.
Well, he **should** be.
It doesn't sound like you really had...
...**that** bad of a night honey.
I haven't told you the worst part yet.
I was getting a drink at the bar, and this person came out to make an announcement.
I figured that there was a band playing or something.
Oh I **hate** that! I go to clubs to dance, not stand around.
Totally. But it **wasn't** a band...

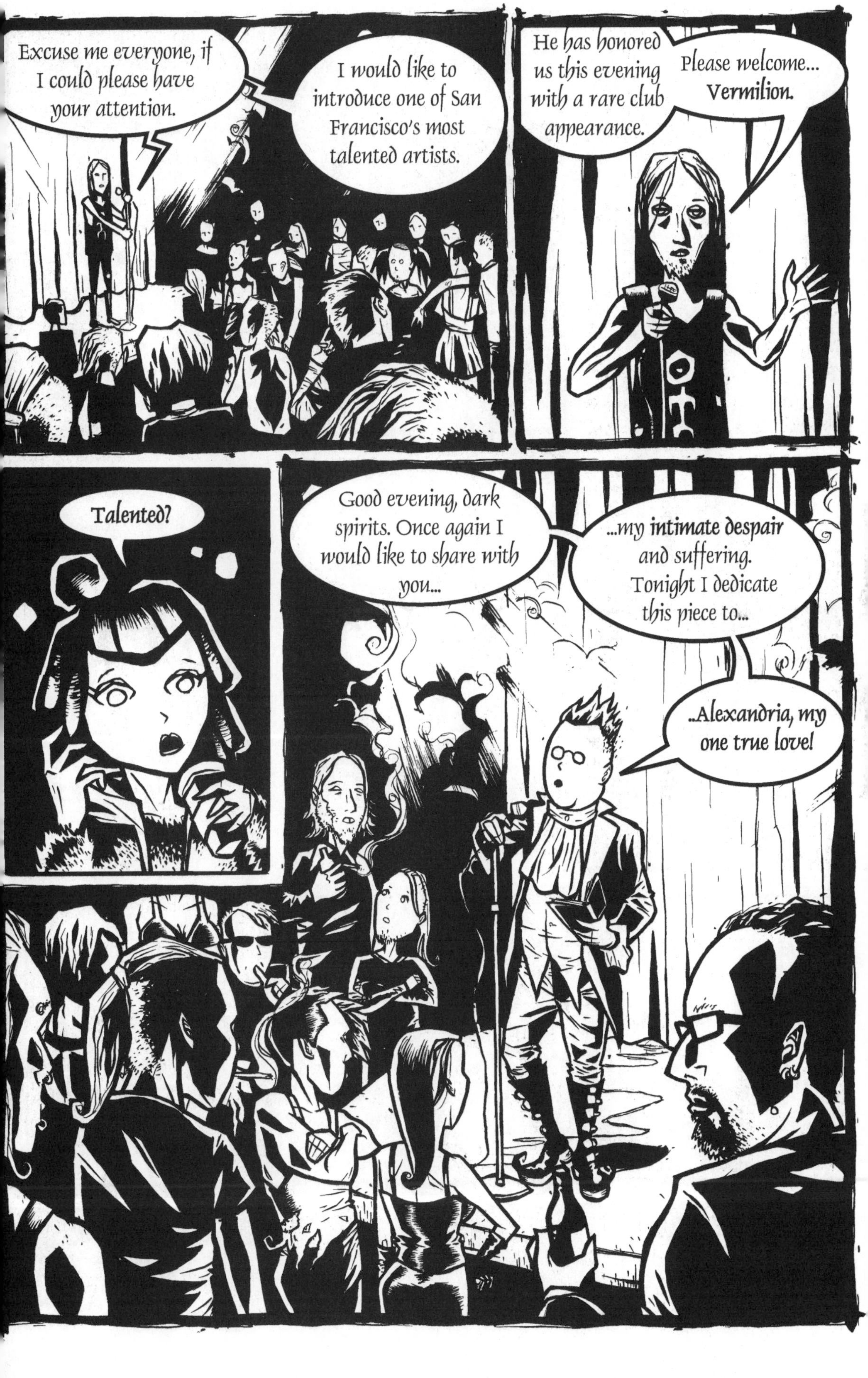
Excuse me everyone, if I could please have your attention.
I would like to introduce one of San Francisco's most talented artists.
He has honored us this evening with a rare club appearance.
Please welcome... Vermilion.
Talented?
Good evening, dark spirits. Once again I would like to share with you...
...my intimate despair and suffering. Tonight I dedicate this piece to...
..Alexandria, my one true love!

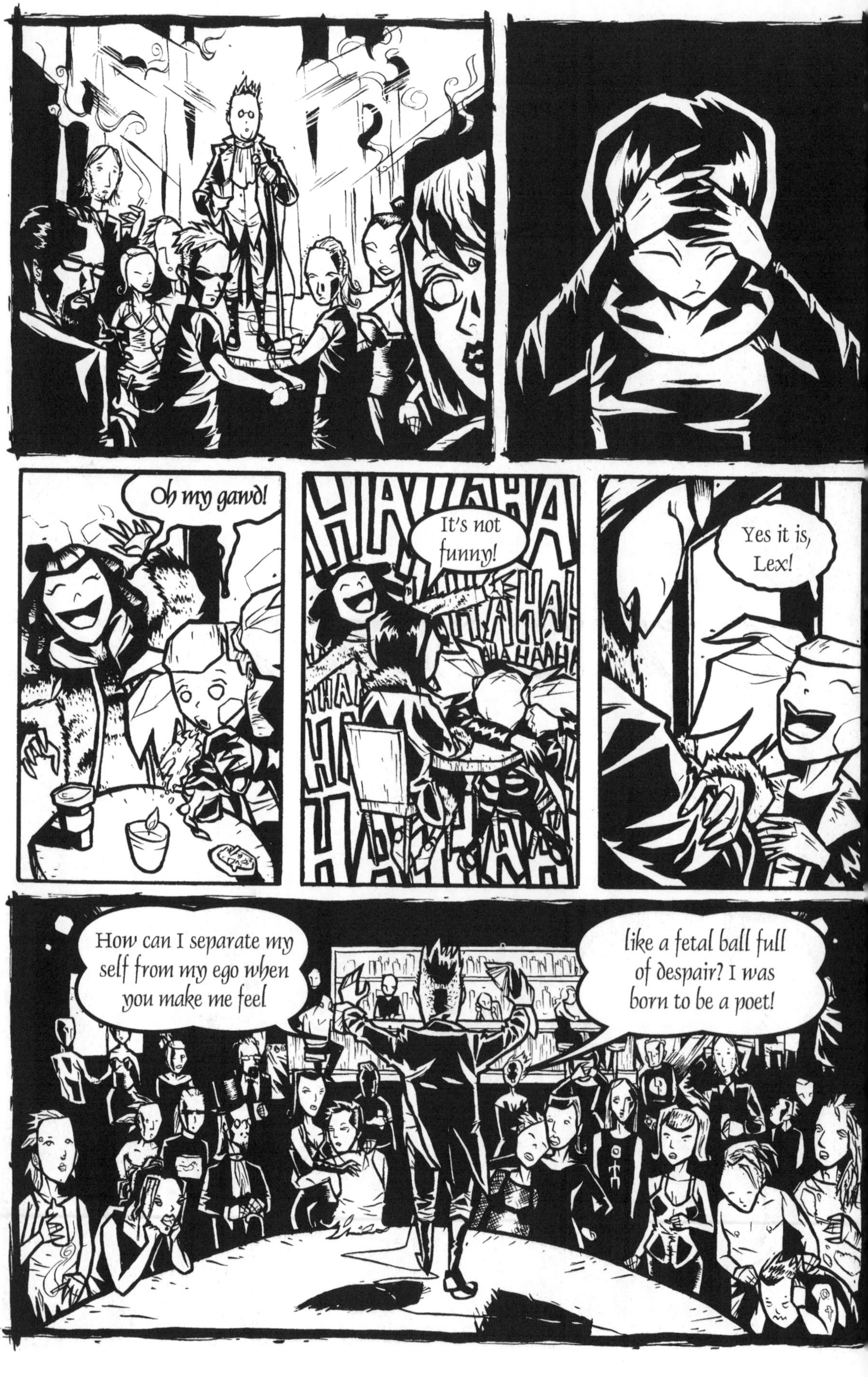
Oh my gawd!
HAHAHA
It's not funny!
HAHAHA
Yes it is, Lex!
How can I separate my self from my ego when you make me feel
like a fetal ball full of despair? I was born to be a poet!

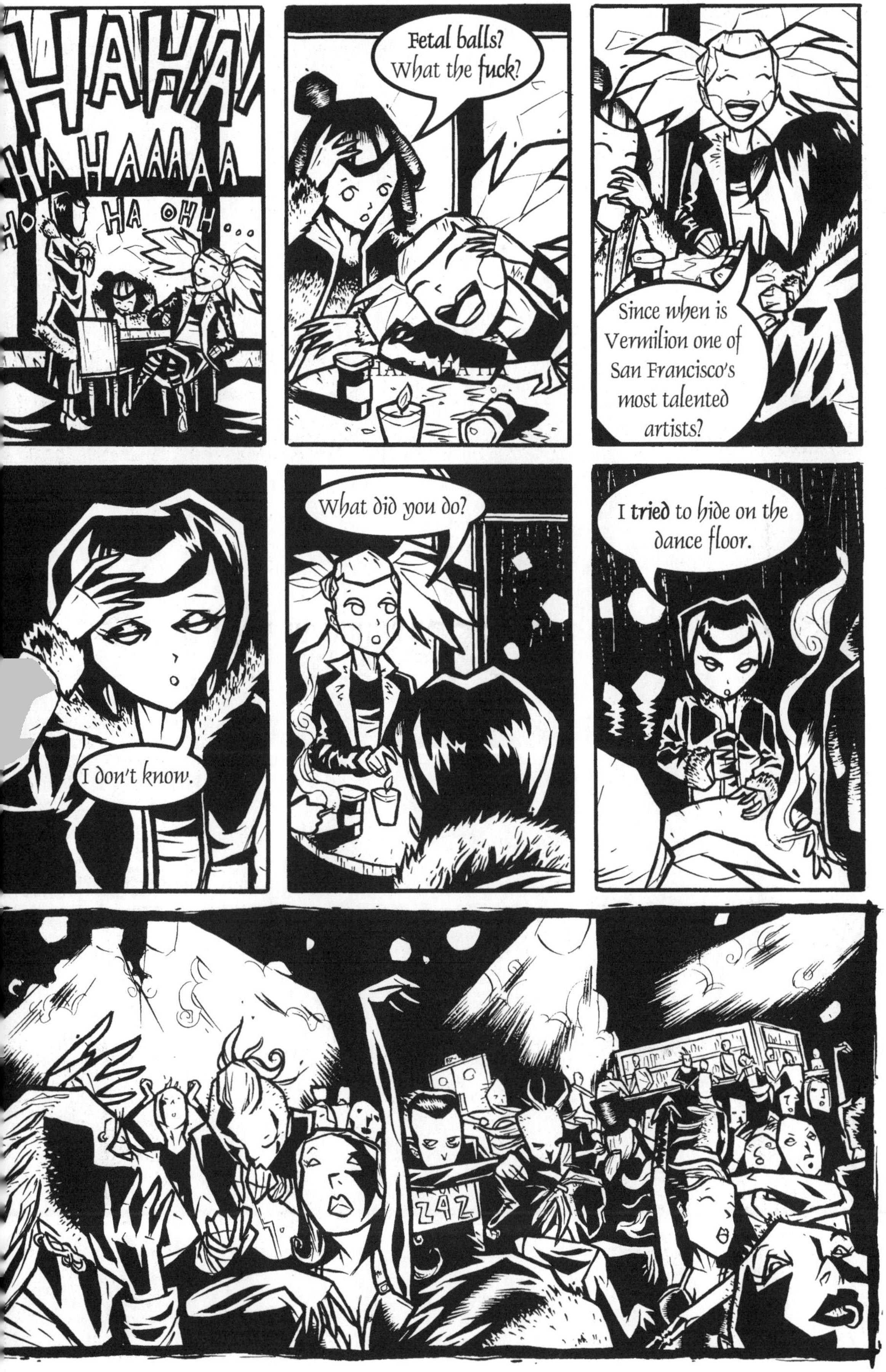
HAHA
HAHAAAAA
HA
OHH...
Fetal balls? What the fuck?
Since when is Vermilion one of San Francisco's most talented artists?
I don't know.
What did you do?
I **tried** to hide on the dance floor.
242

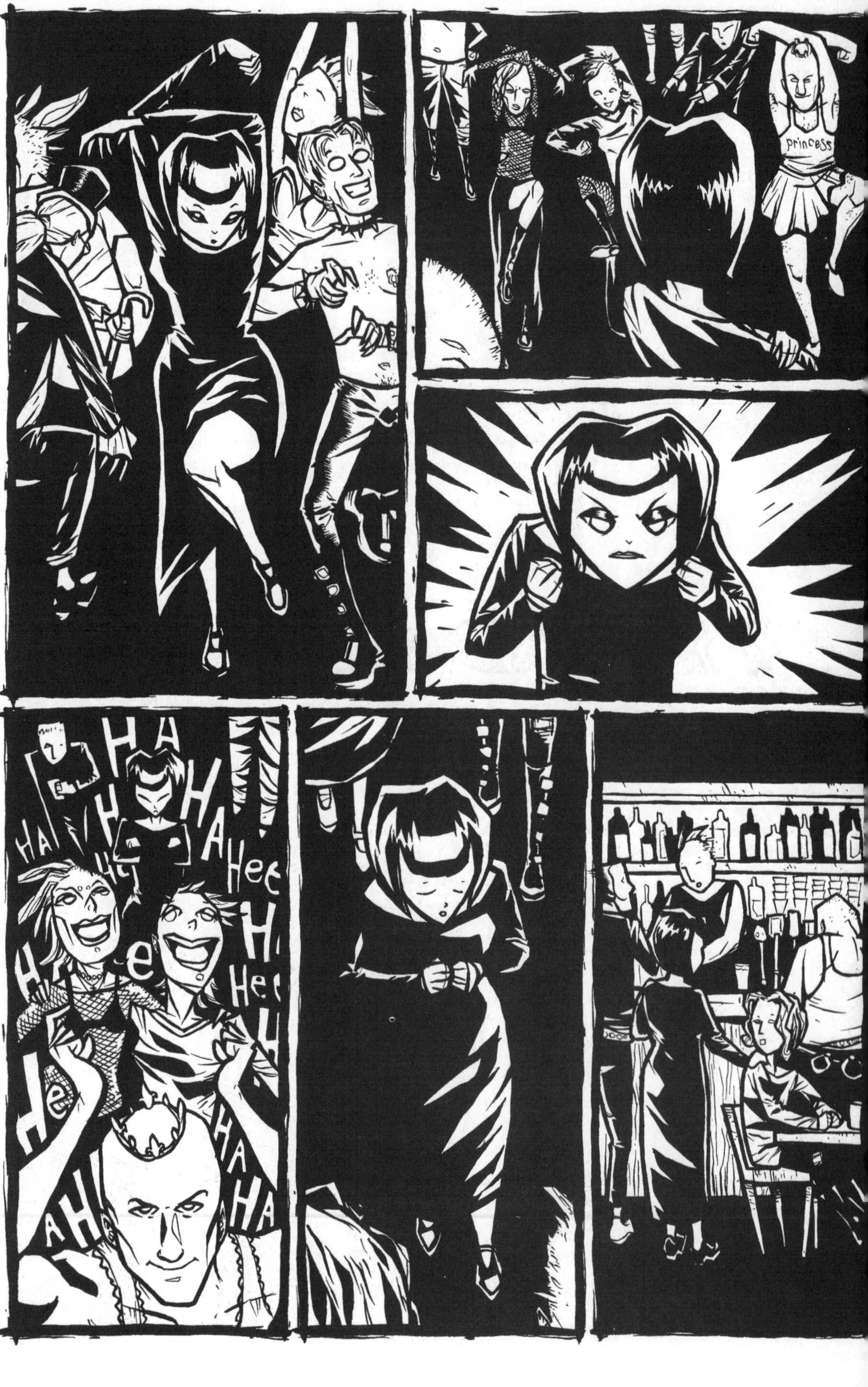
princess
HA HA HA HA HA
Hee He He Hee He
HA HA HA AH

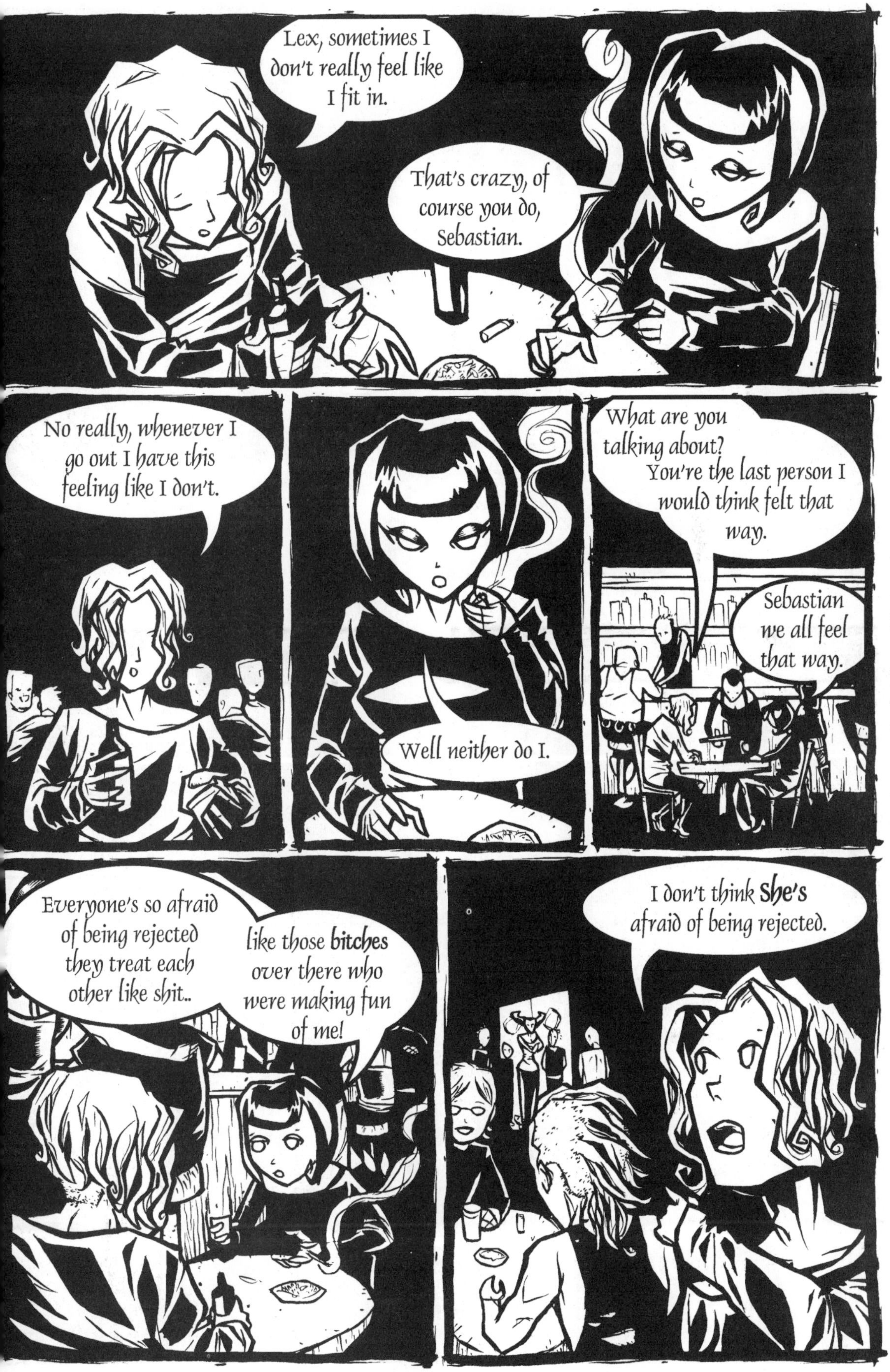

Lex, sometimes I don't really feel like I fit in.
That's crazy, of course you do, Sebastian.
No really, whenever I go out I have this feeling like I don't.
Well neither do I.
What are you talking about?
You're the last person I would think felt that way.
Sebastian we all feel that way.
Everyone's so afraid of being rejected they treat each other like shit..
like those **bitches** over there who were making fun of me!
I don't think **she's** afraid of being rejected.

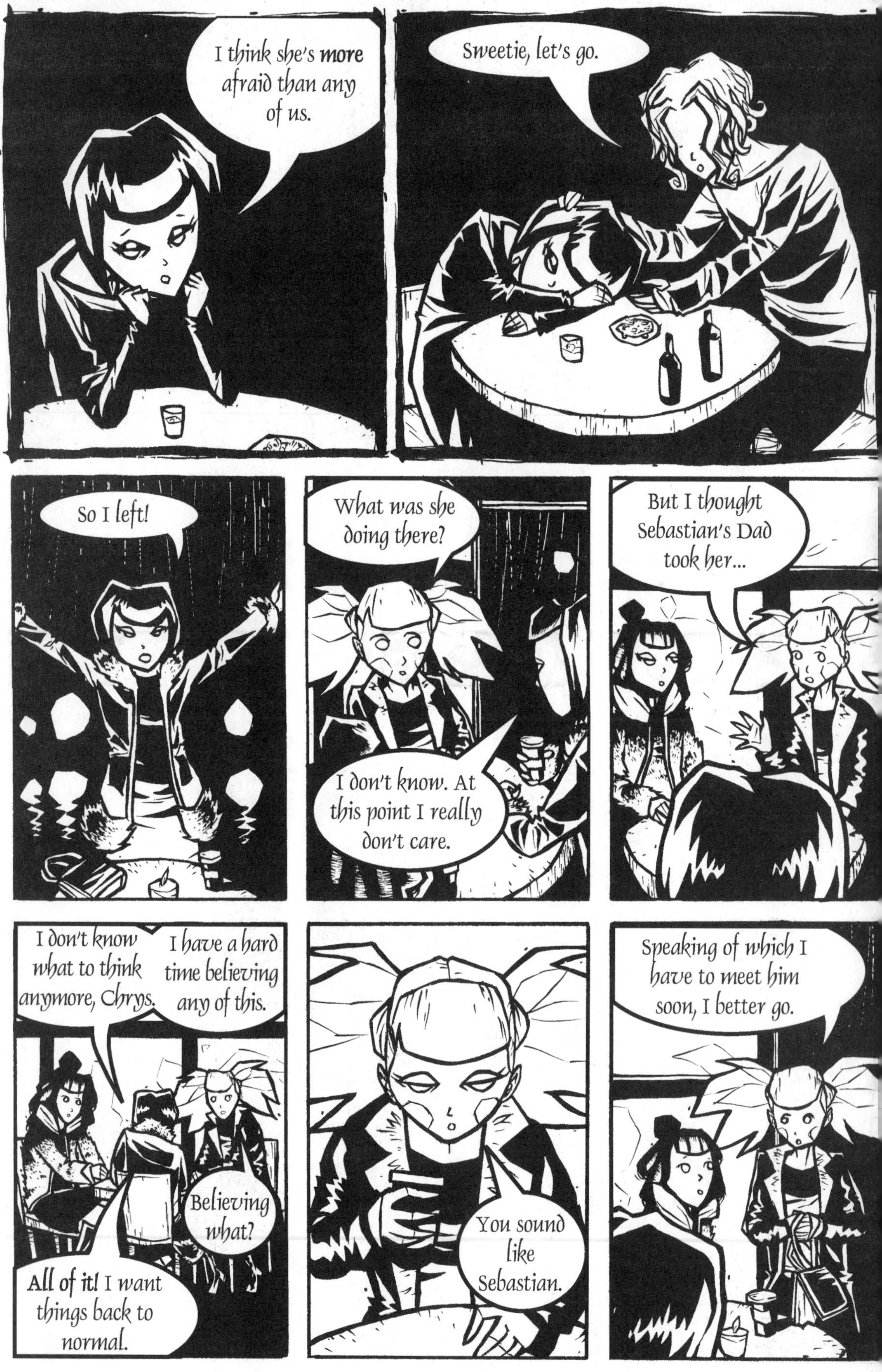
I think she's **more** afraid than any of us.
Sweetie, let's go.
So I left!
What was she doing there?
I don't know. At this point I really don't care.
But I thought Sebastian's Dad took her...
I don't know what to think anymore, Chrys.
I have a hard time believing any of this.
Believing what?
All of it! I want things back to normal.
You sound like Sebastian.
Speaking of which I have to meet him soon, I better go.

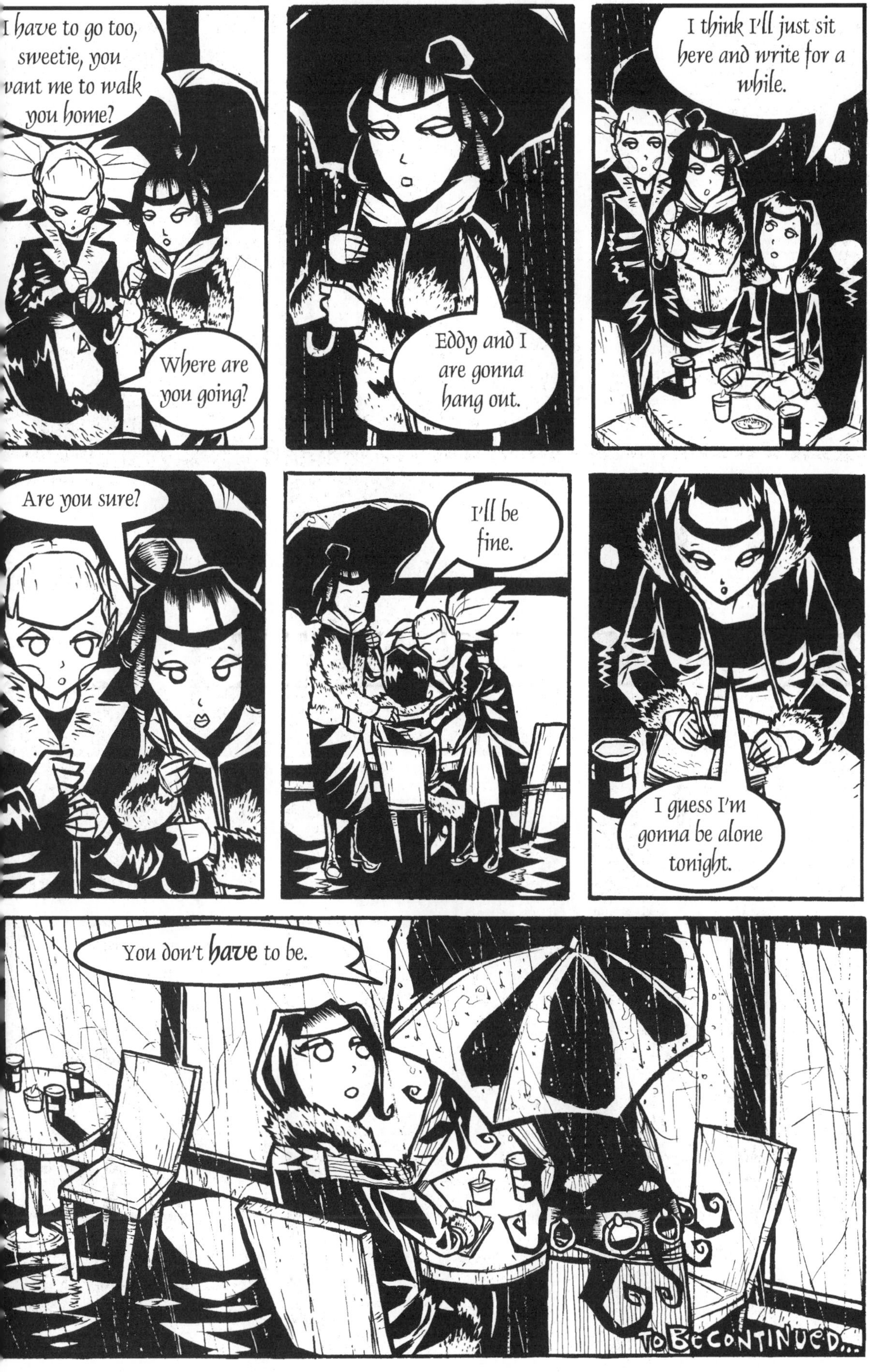
I have to go too, sweetie, you vant me to walk you home?
Where are you going?
Eddy and I are gonna hang out.
I think I'll just sit here and write for a while.
Are you sure?
I'll be fine.
I guess I'm gonna be alone tonight.
You don't **have** to be.
TO BE CONTINUED...

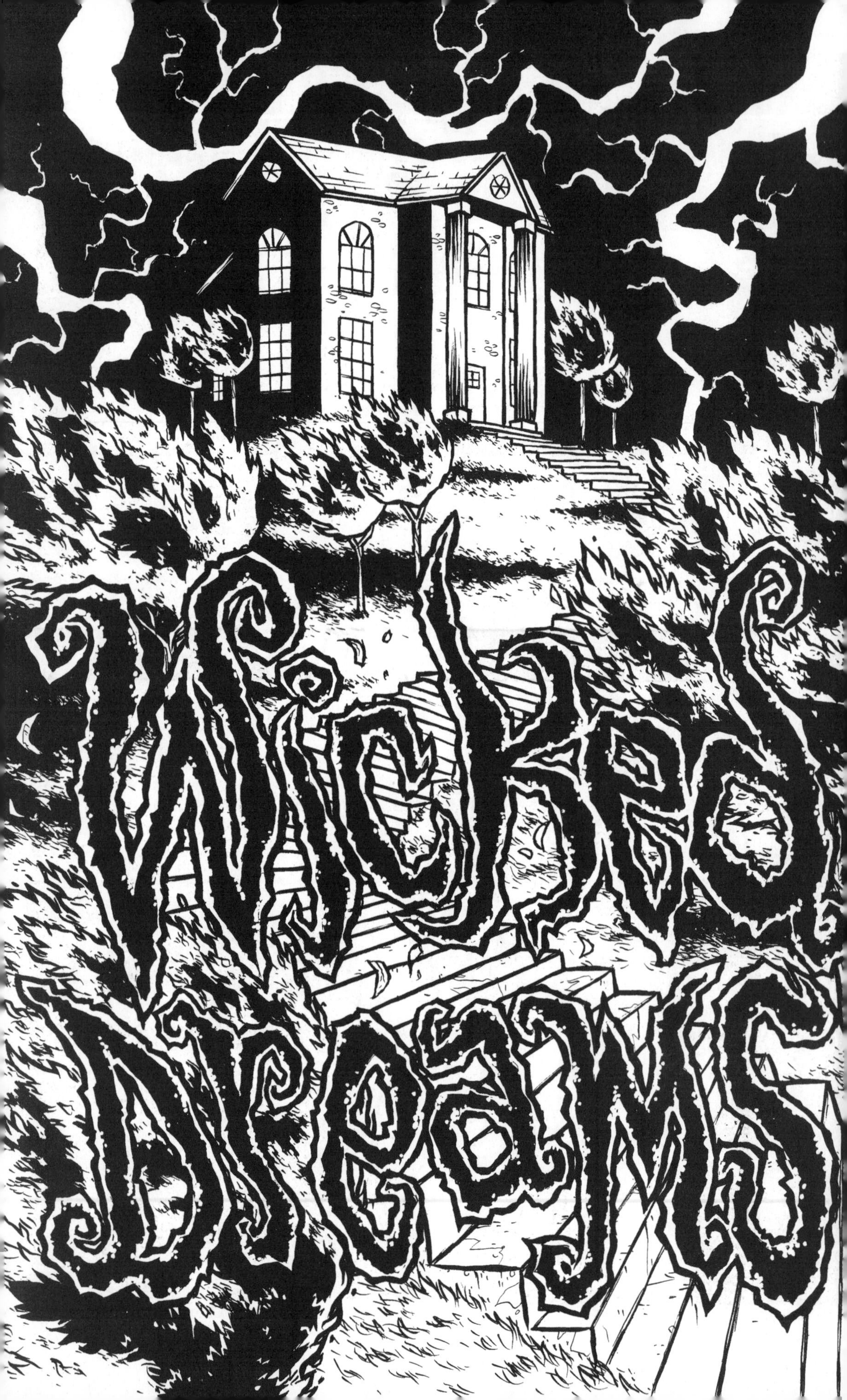
Wicked Dreams

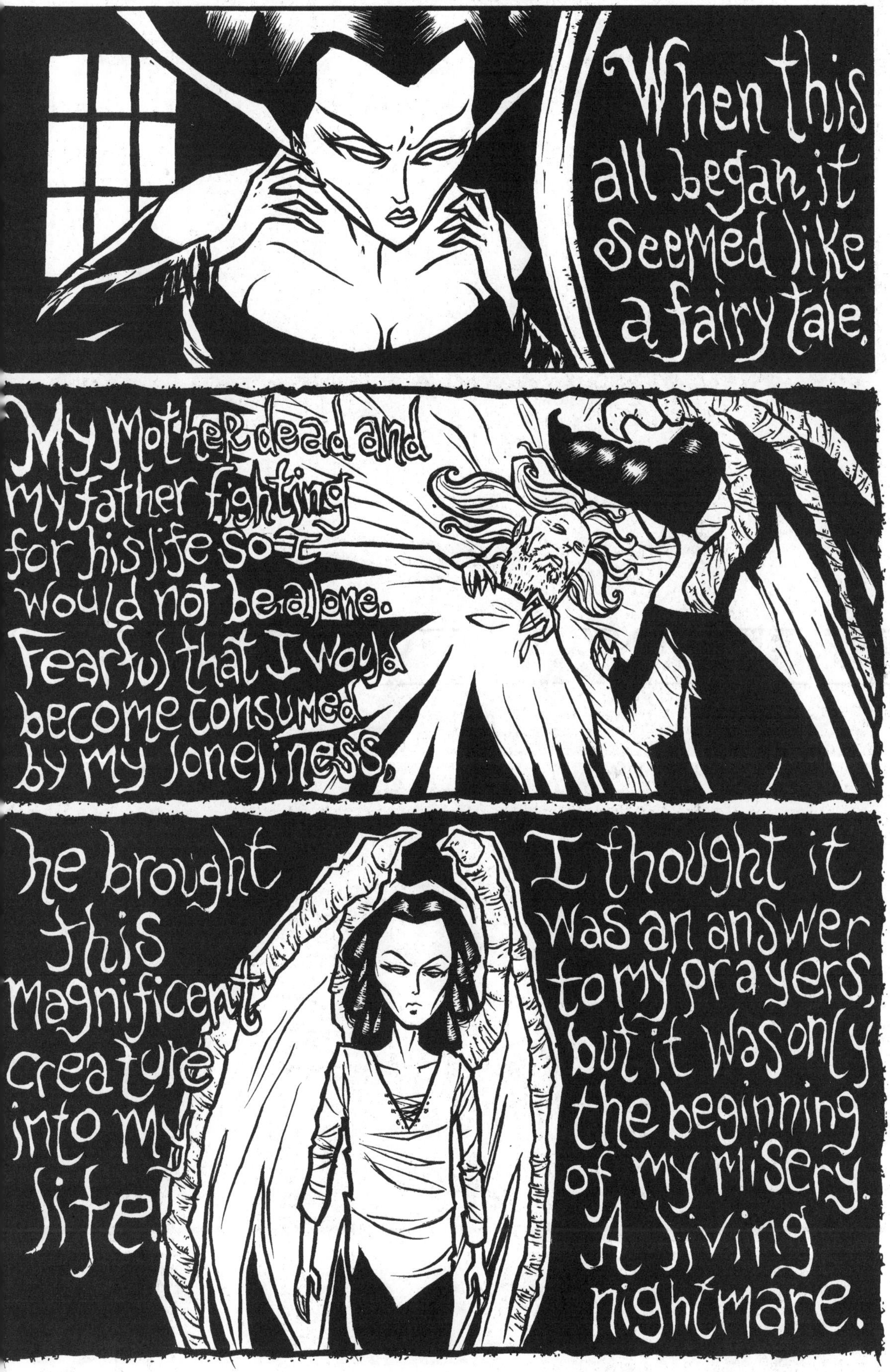
When this all began, it seemed like a fairy tale.
My mother dead and my father fighting for his life so I would not be alone. Fearful that I would become consumed by my loneliness,
he brought this magnificent creature into my life.
I thought it was an answer to my prayers, but it was only the beginning of my misery. A living nightmare.

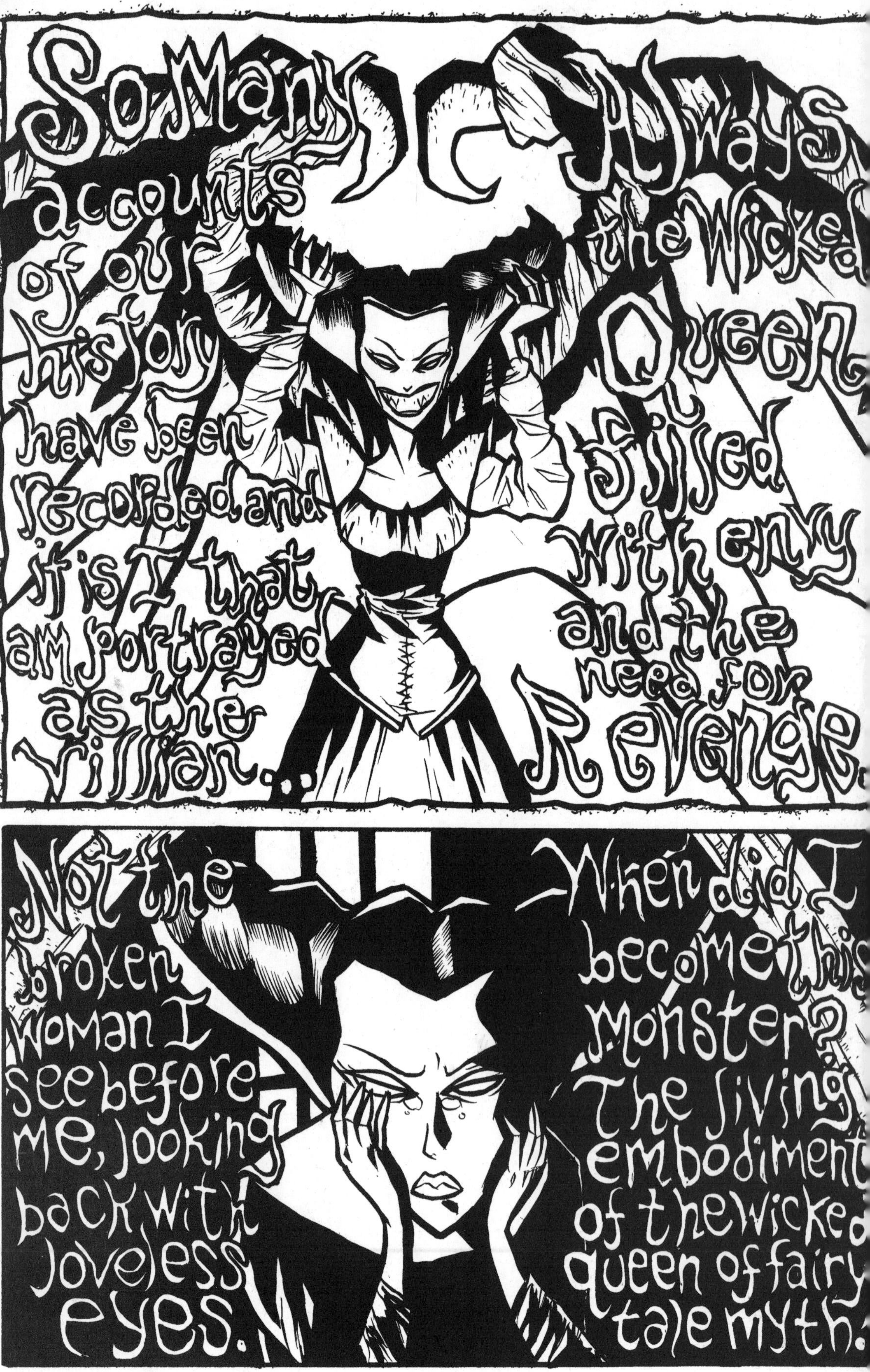
So Many accounts of our history have been recorded and it is I that am portrayed as the villian...
Always the Wicked Queen filled with envy and the need for Revenge.
Not the broken woman I see before me, looking back with loveless eyes.
When did I become this monster? The living embodiment of the wicked queen of fairy tale myth.

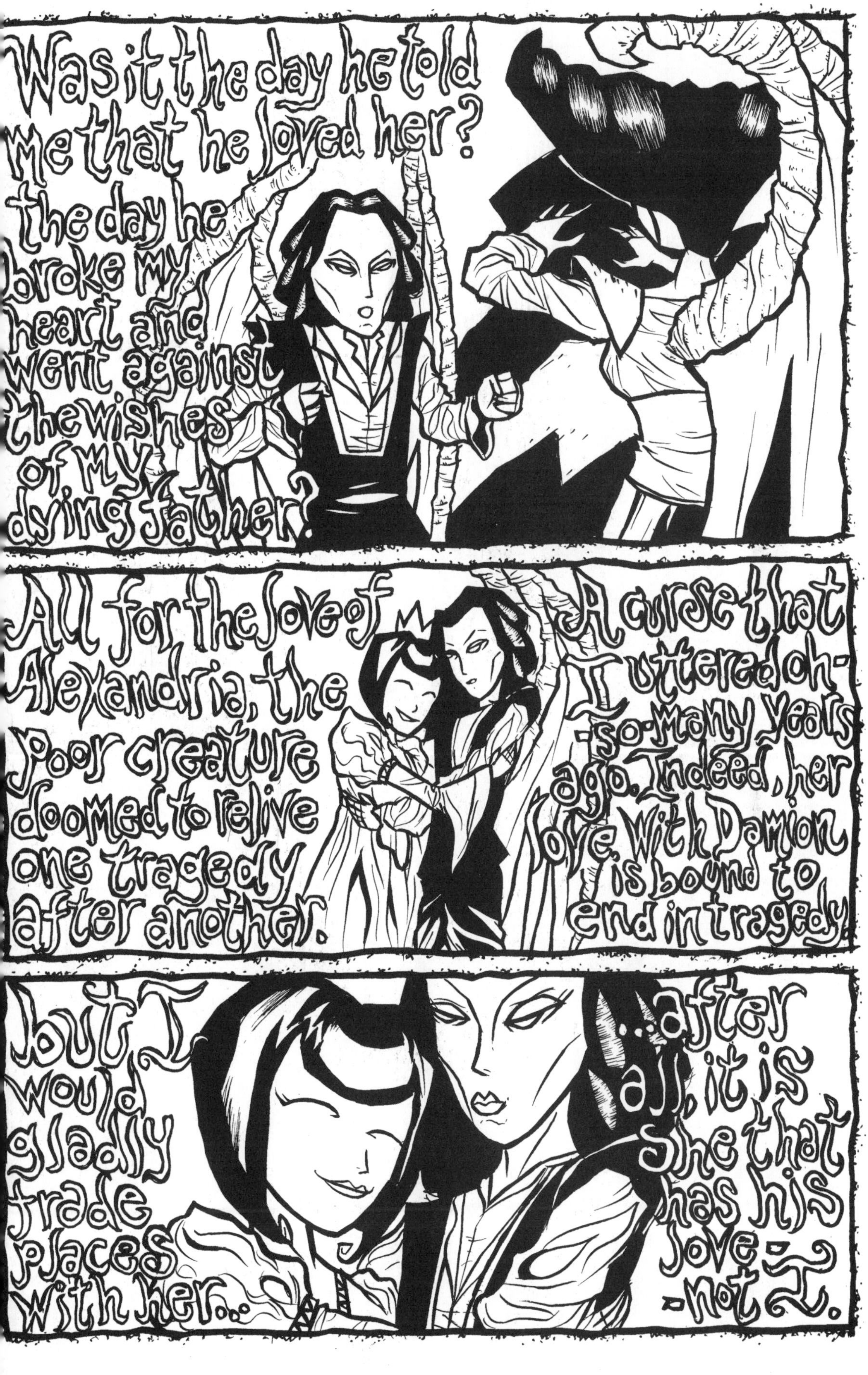
Was it the day he told me that he loved her?
the day he broke my heart and went against the wishes of my dying father?
All for the love of Alexandria, the poor creature doomed to relive one tragedy after another.
A curse that I uttered oh-so-many years ago. Indeed, her love with Damion is bound to end in tragedy.
but I would gladly trade places with her...
...after all, it is she that has his love--not I.

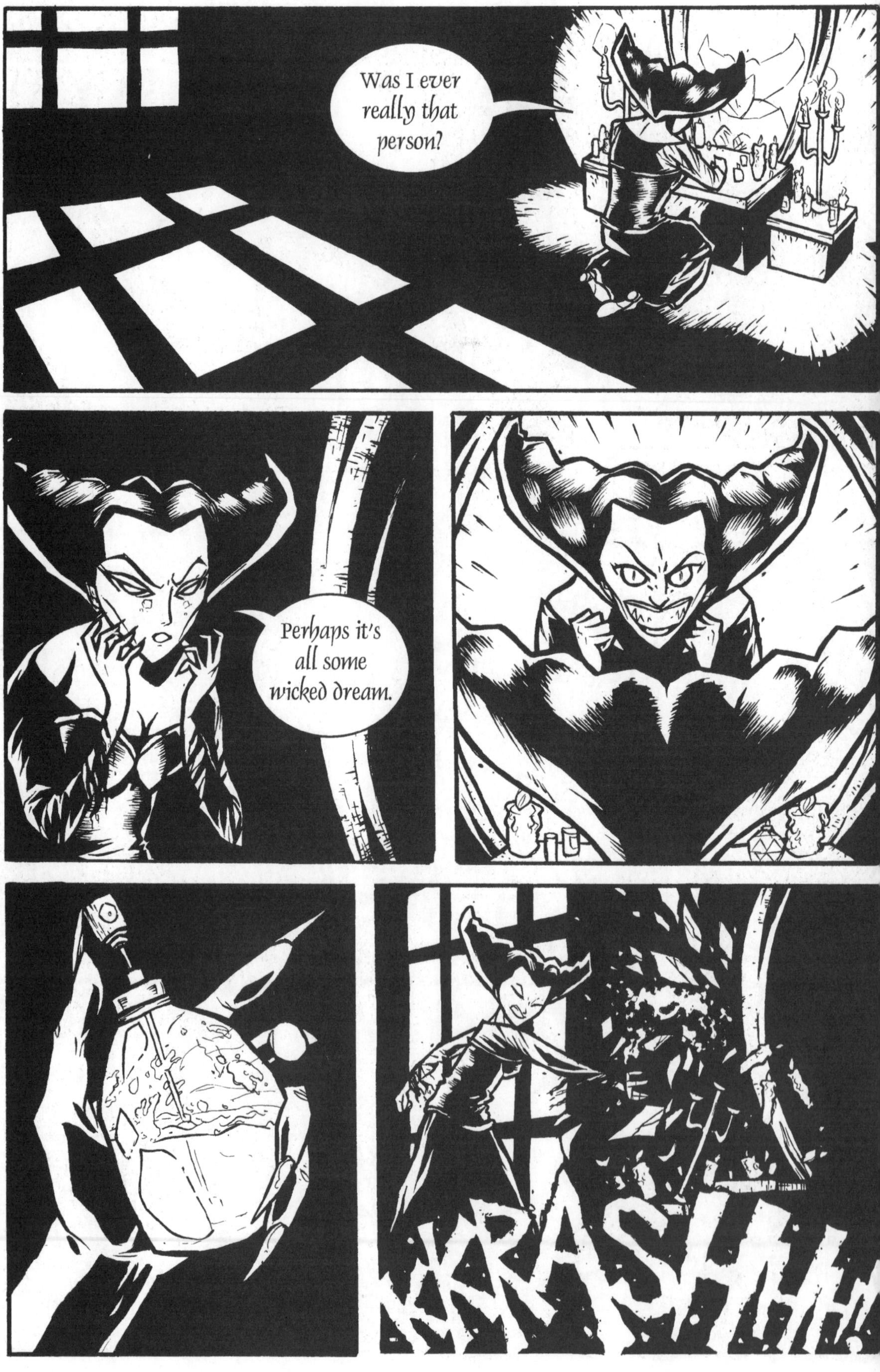
Was I ever really that person?
Perhaps it's all some wicked dream.
KRASHH!

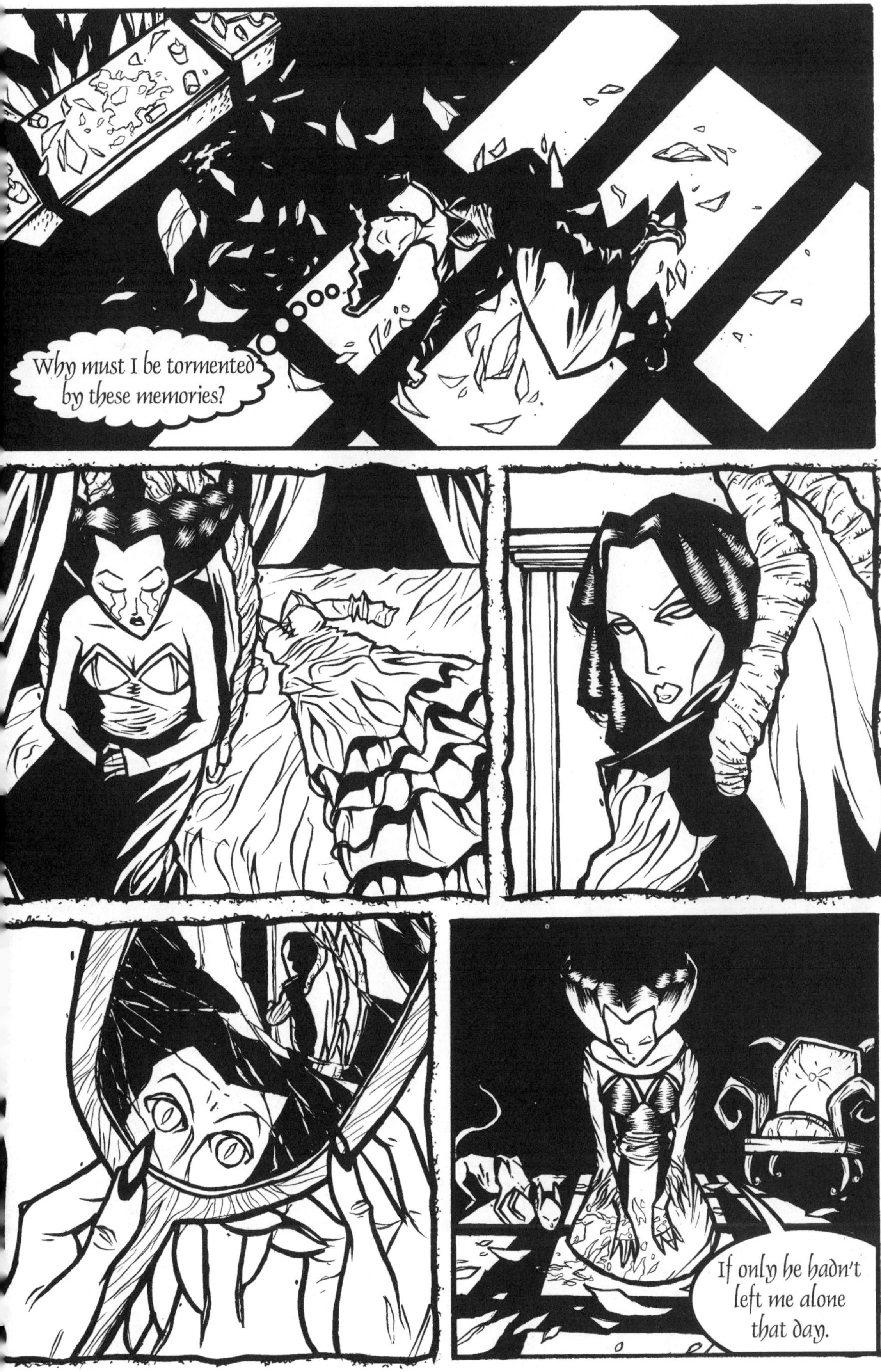
Why must I be tormented by these memories?
If only he hadn't left me alone that day.

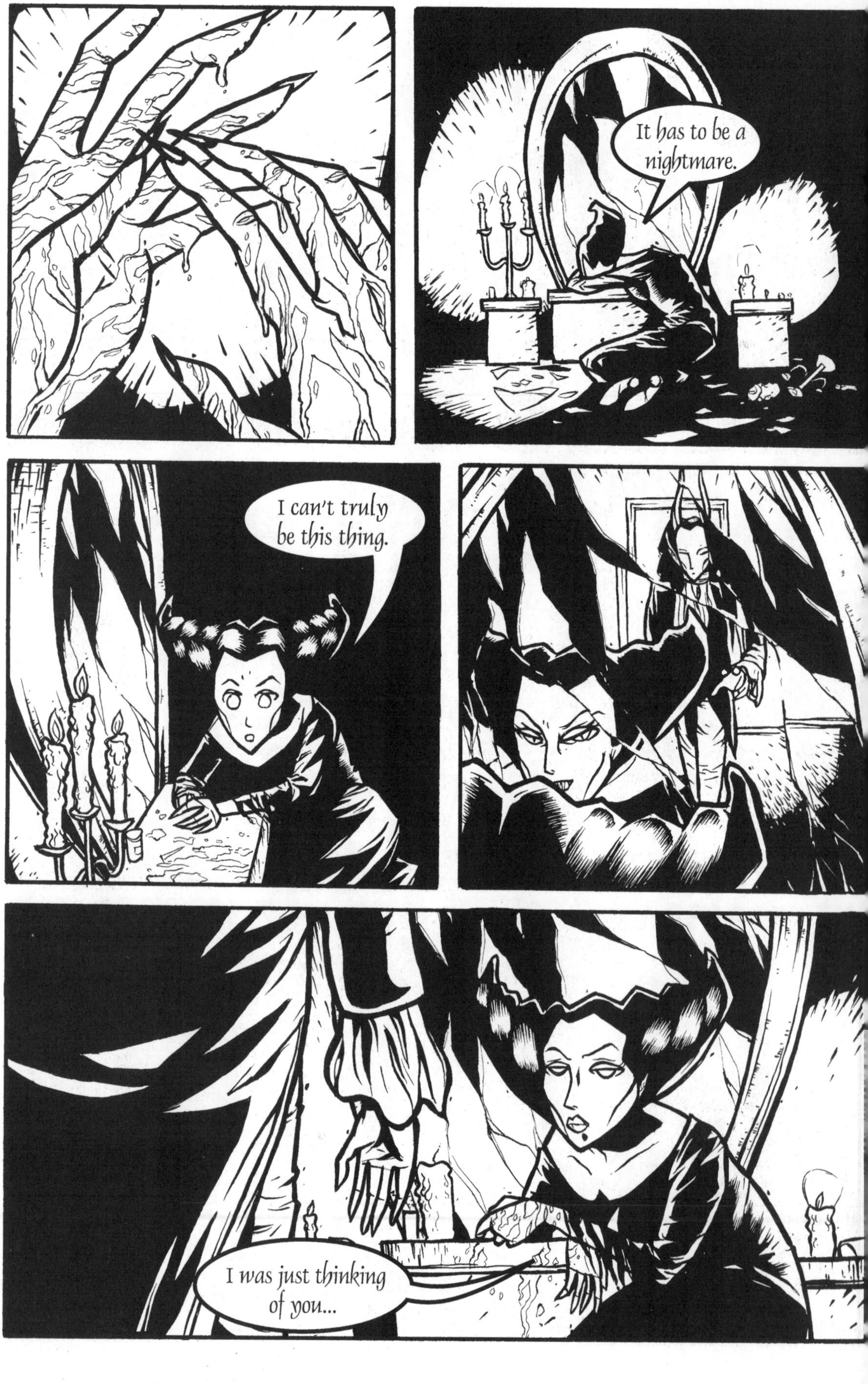
It has to be a nightmare.
I can't truly be this thing.
I was just thinking of you...

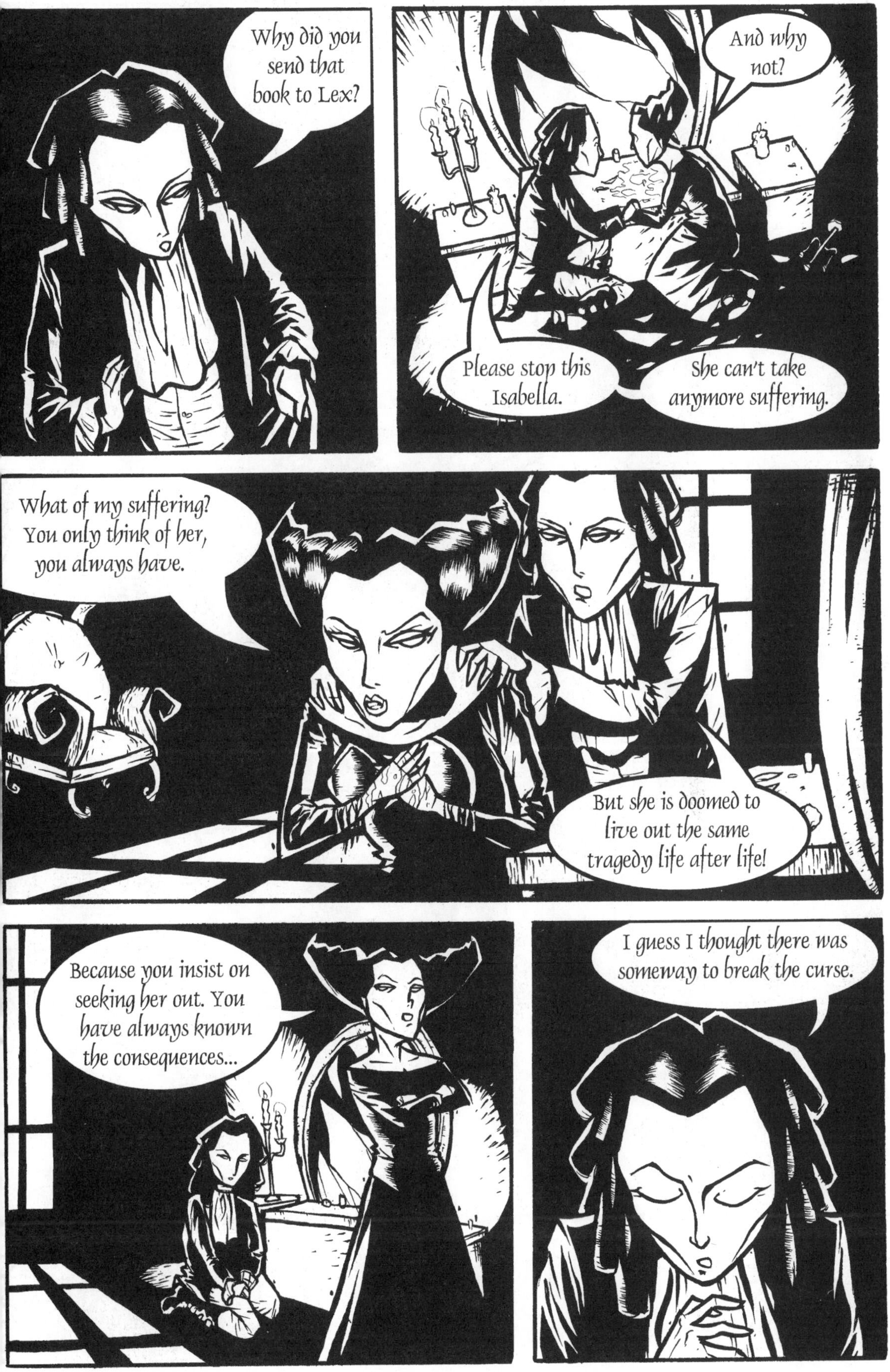
Why did you send that book to Lex?
And why not?
Please stop this Isabella.
She can't take anymore suffering.
What of my suffering? You only think of her, you always have.
But she is doomed to live out the same tragedy life after life!
Because you insist on seeking her out. You have always known the consequences...
I guess I thought there was someway to break the curse.

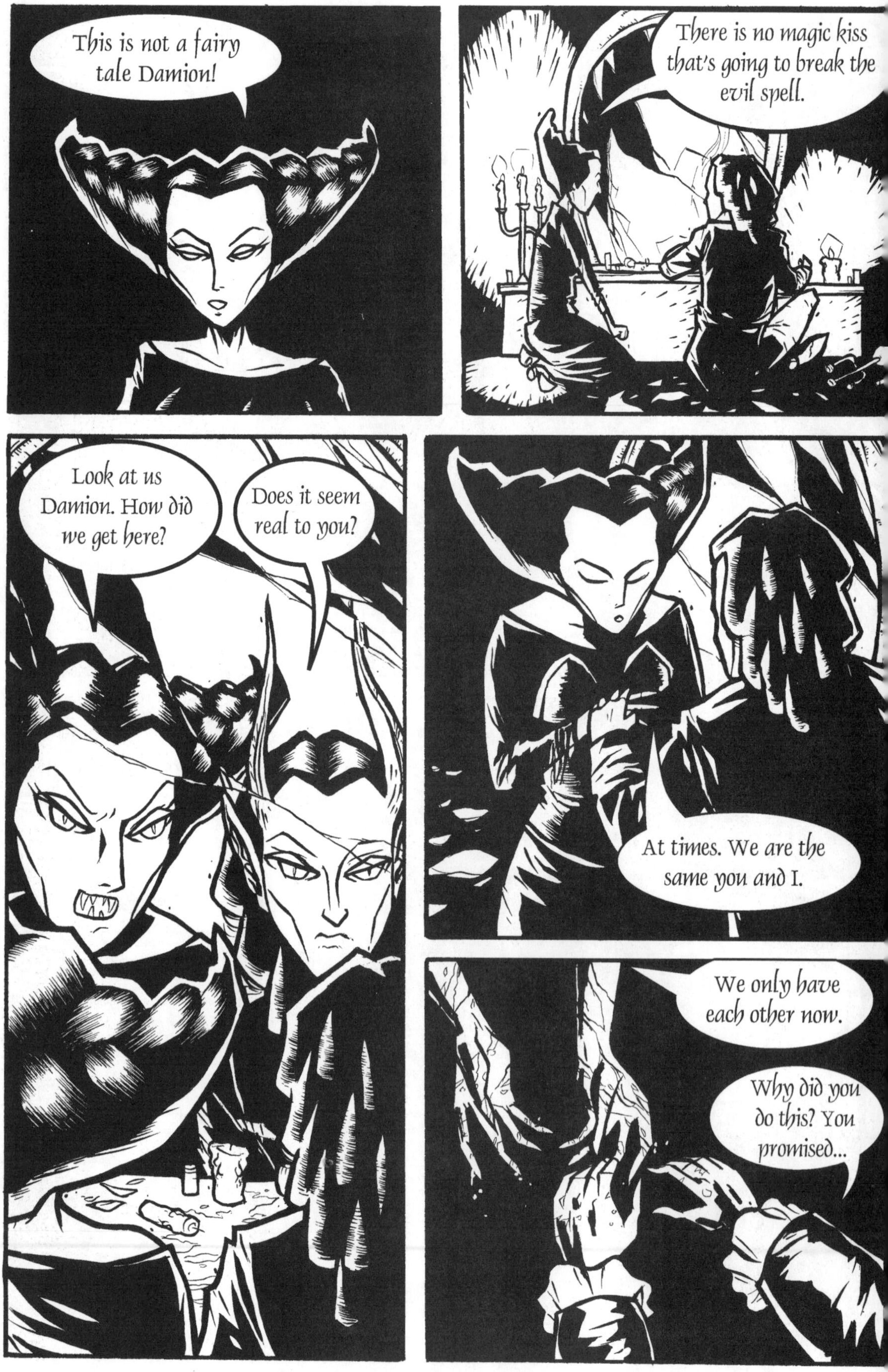
This is not a fairy tale Damion!
There is no magic kiss that's going to break the evil spell.
Look at us Damion. How did we get here?
Does it seem real to you?
At times. We are the same you and I.
We only have each other now.
Why did you do this? You promised...

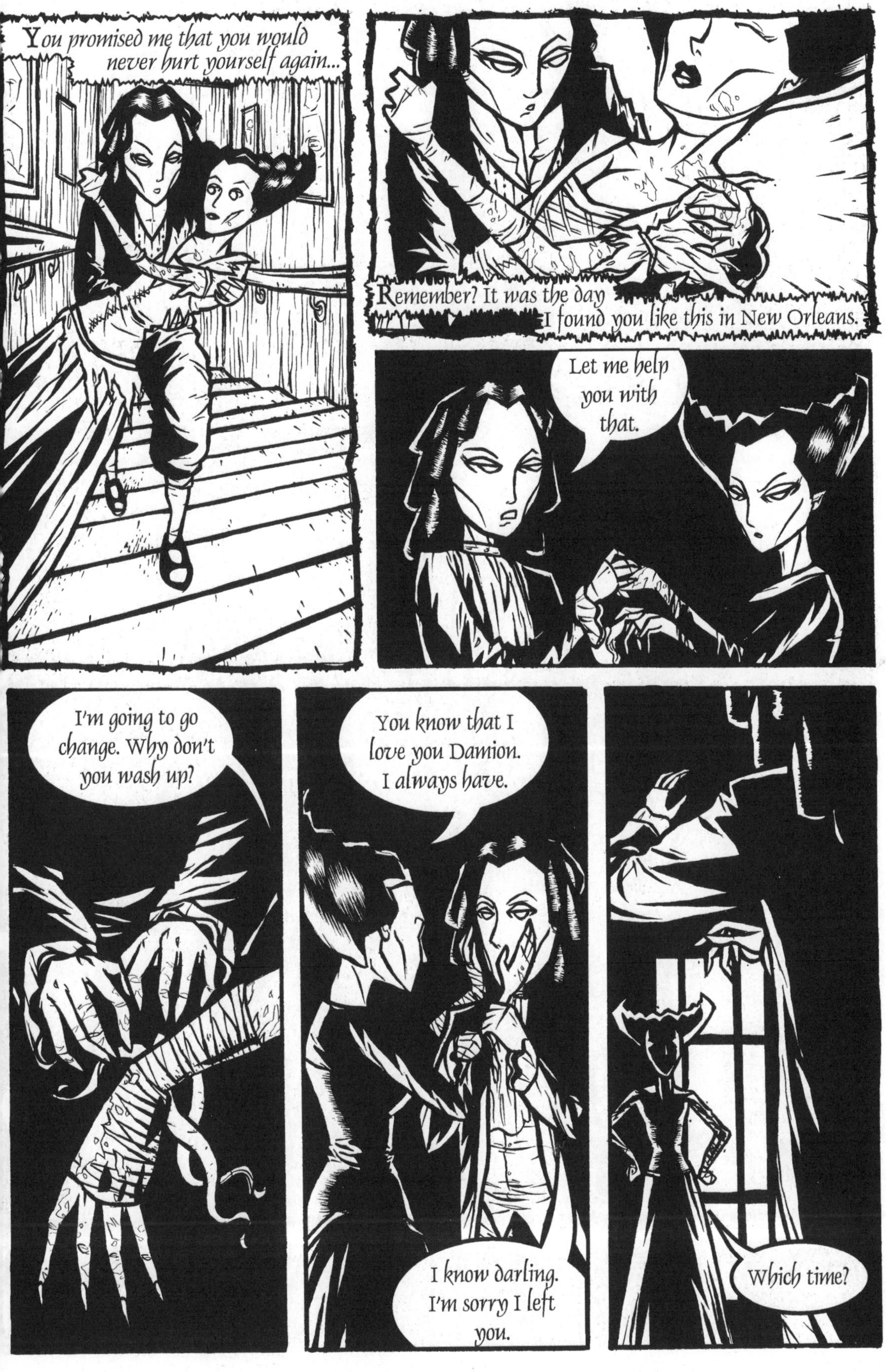
You promised me that you would never hurt yourself again...
Remember? It was the day I found you like this in New Orleans.
Let me help you with that.
I'm going to go change. Why don't you wash up?
You know that I love you Damion. I always have.
I know darling. I'm sorry I left you.
Which time?

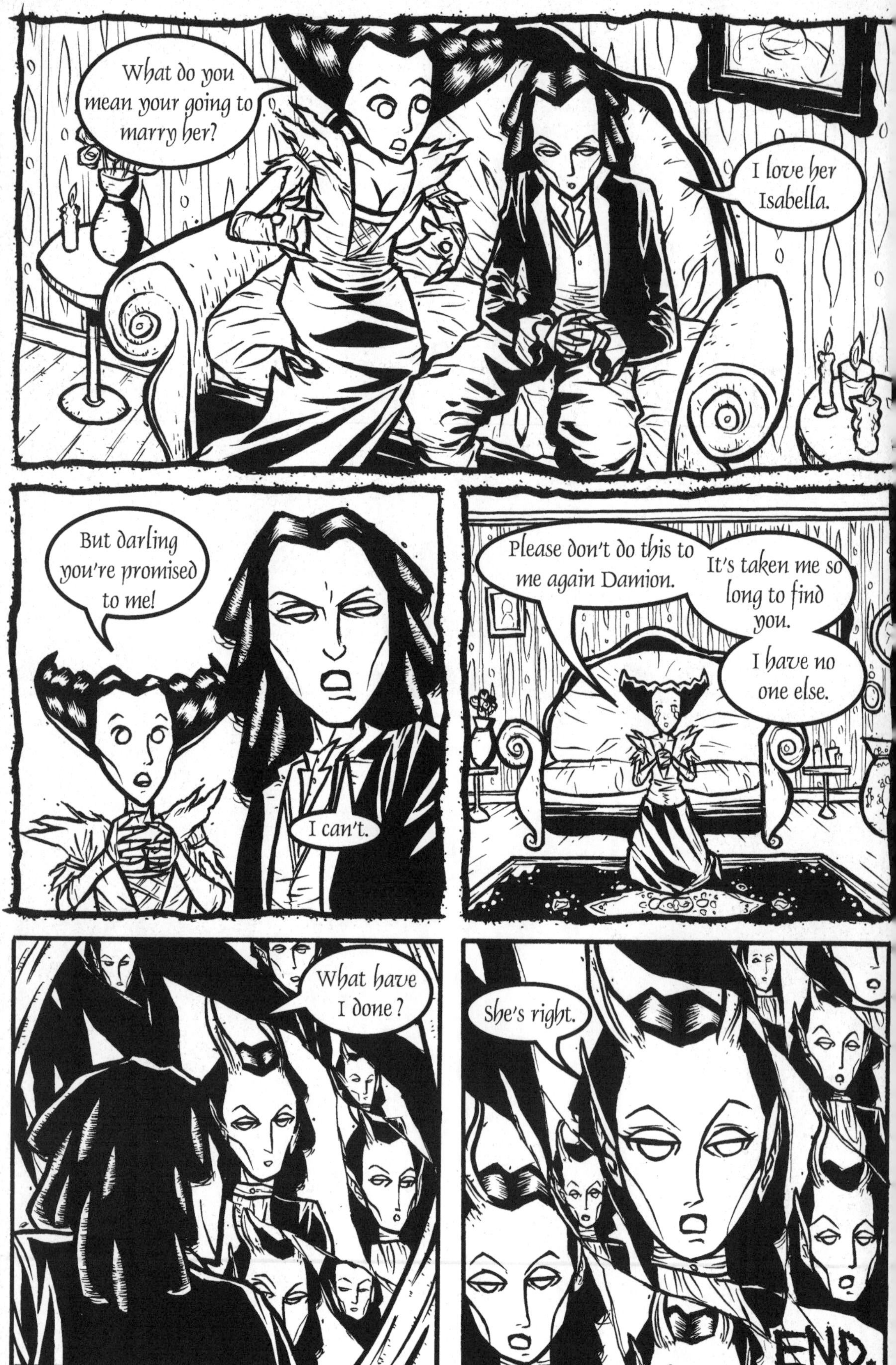
What do you mean your going to marry her?
I love her Isabella.
But darling you're promised to me!
I can't.
Please don't do this to me again Damion.
It's taken me so long to find you.
I have no one else.
What have I done?
She's right.
END.

Chapter 9

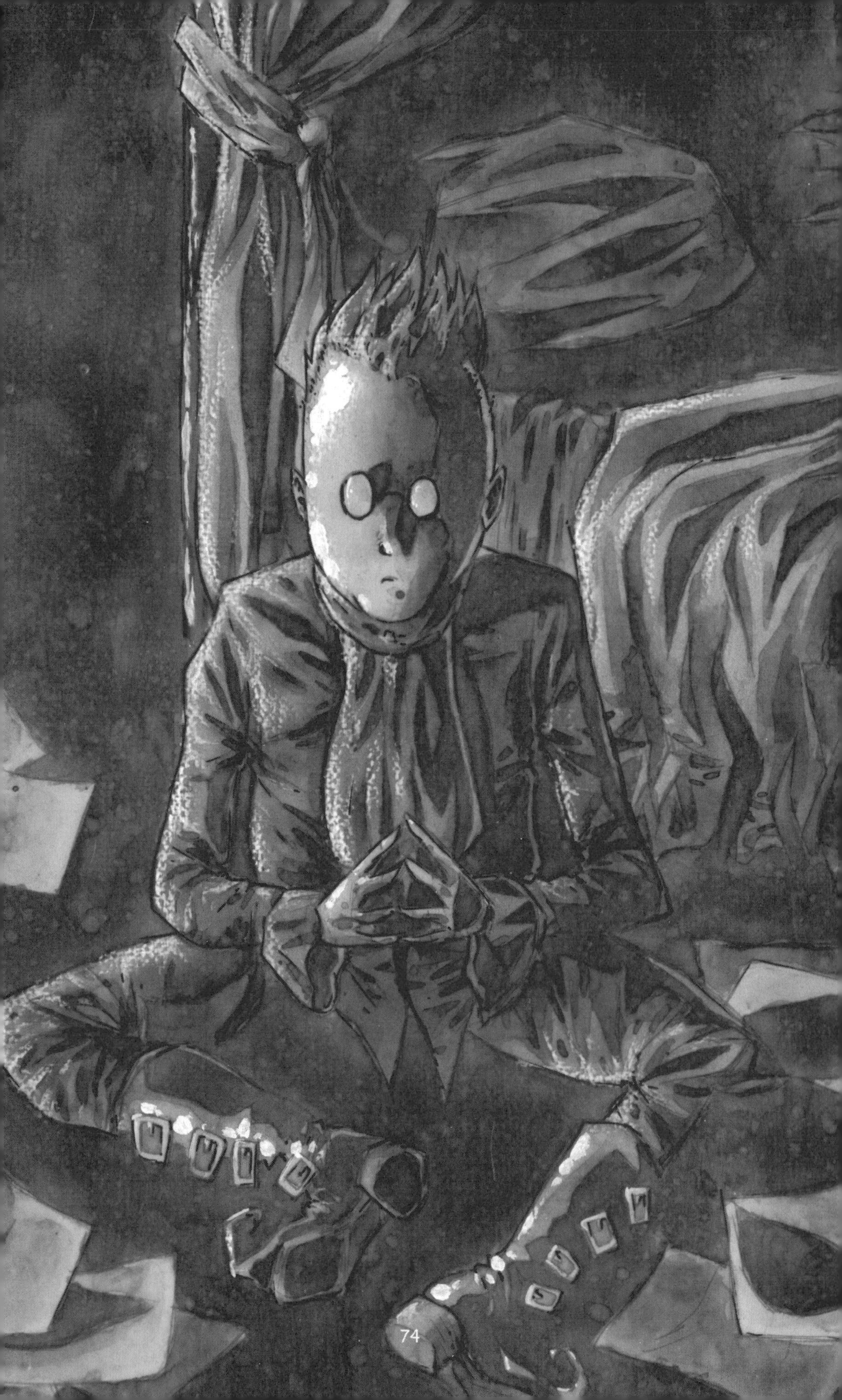

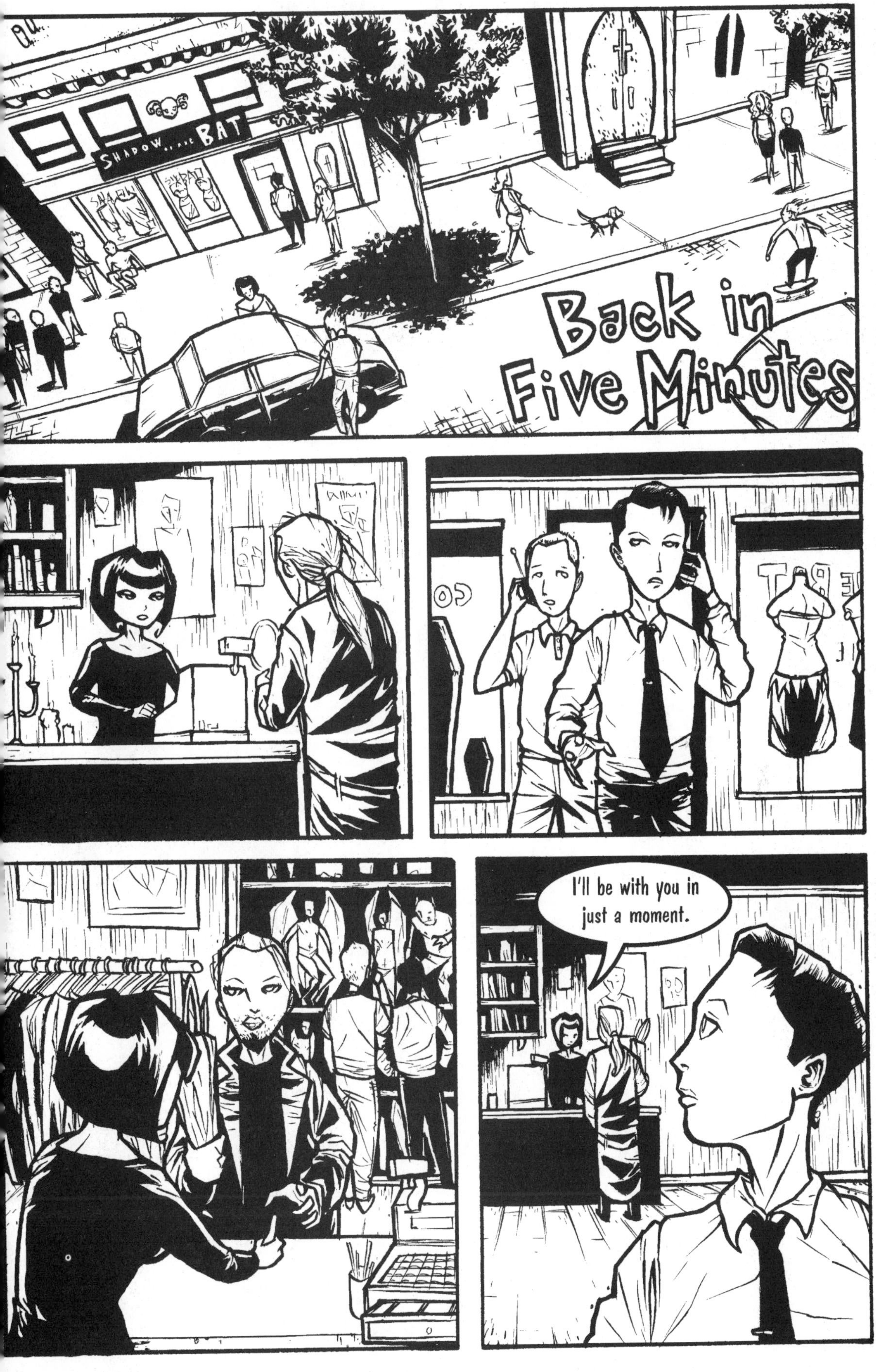
Back in Five Minutes
I'll be with you in just a moment.

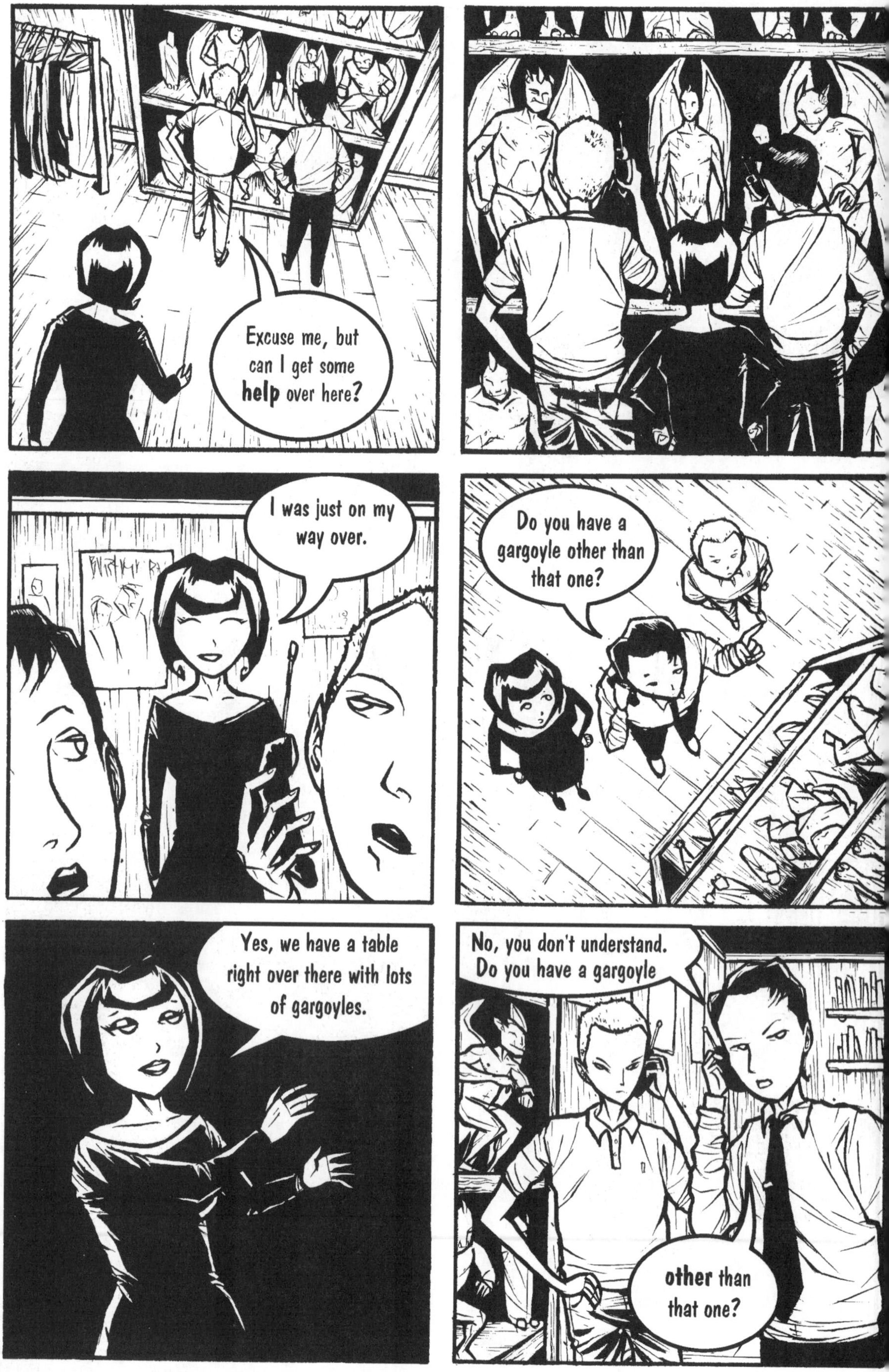
Excuse me, but can I get some **help** over here?
I was just on my way over.
Do you have a gargoyle other than that one?
Yes, we have a table right over there with lots of gargoyles.
No, you don't understand. Do you have a gargoyle
other than that one?

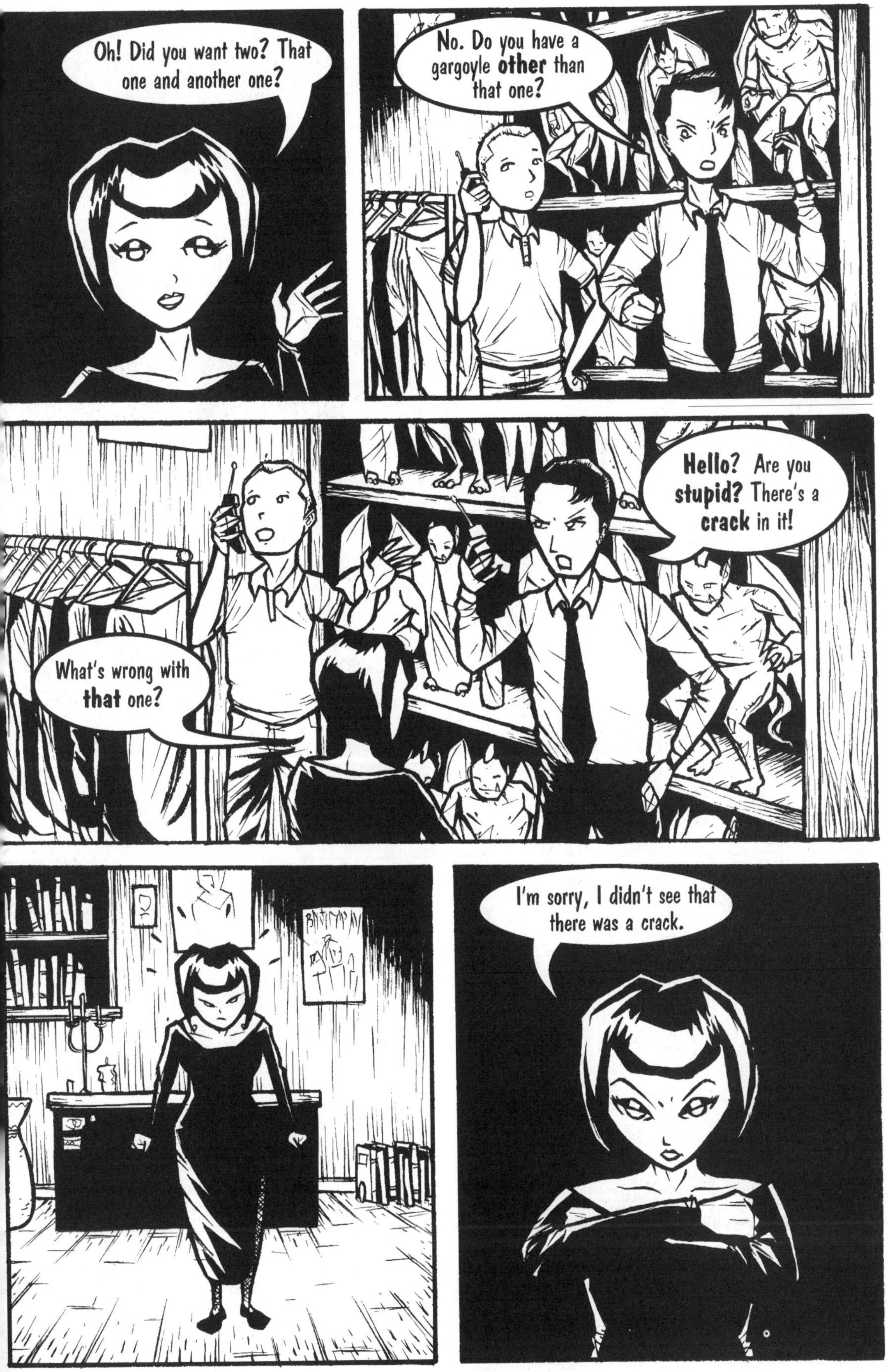
Oh! Did you want two? That one and another one?
No. Do you have a gargoyle **other** than that one?
Hello? Are you **stupid?** There's a **crack** in it!
What's wrong with **that** one?
I'm sorry, I didn't see that there was a crack.

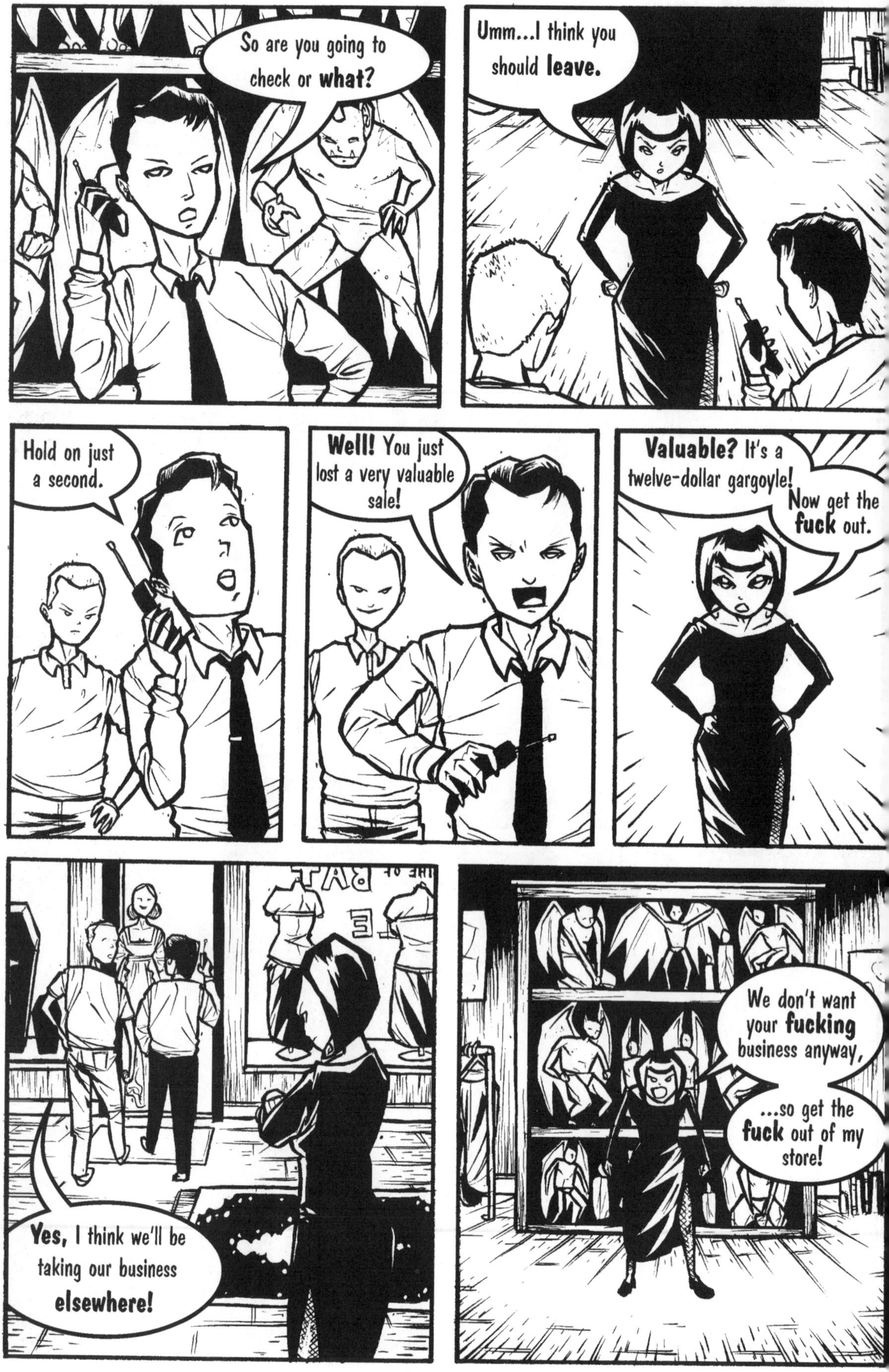
So are you going to check or **what?**
Umm...I think you should **leave.**
Hold on just a second.
Well! You just lost a very valuable sale!
Valuable? It's a twelve-dollar gargoyle!
Now get the **fuck** out.
Yes, I think we'll be taking our business **elsewhere!**
We don't want your **fucking** business anyway,
...so get the **fuck** out of my store!

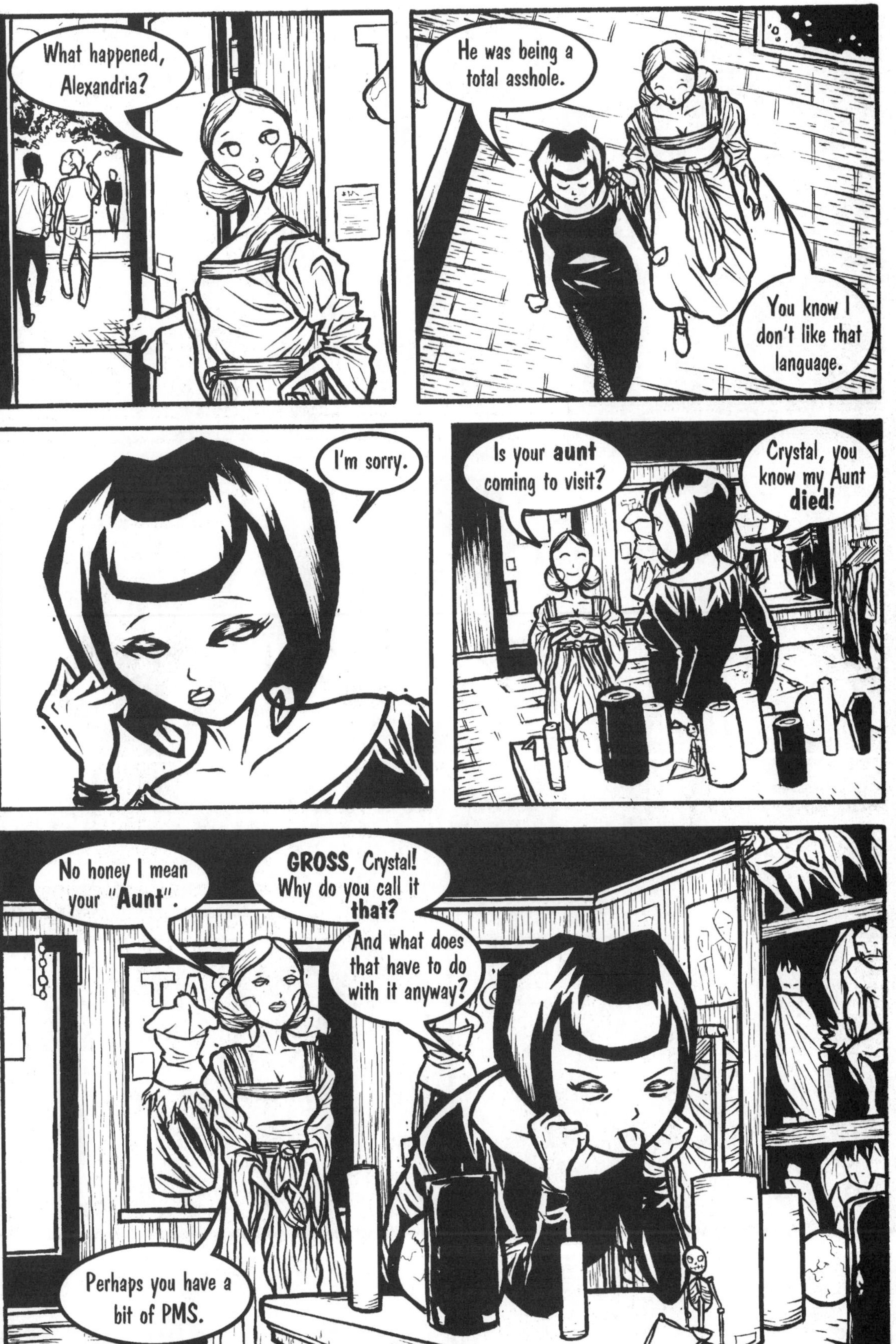
What happened, Alexandria?
He was being a total asshole.
You know I don't like that language.
I'm sorry.
Is your **aunt** coming to visit?
Crystal, you know my Aunt **died!**
No honey I mean your "**Aunt**".
GROSS, Crystal! Why do you call it **that?**
And what does that have to do with it anyway?
Perhaps you have a bit of PMS.

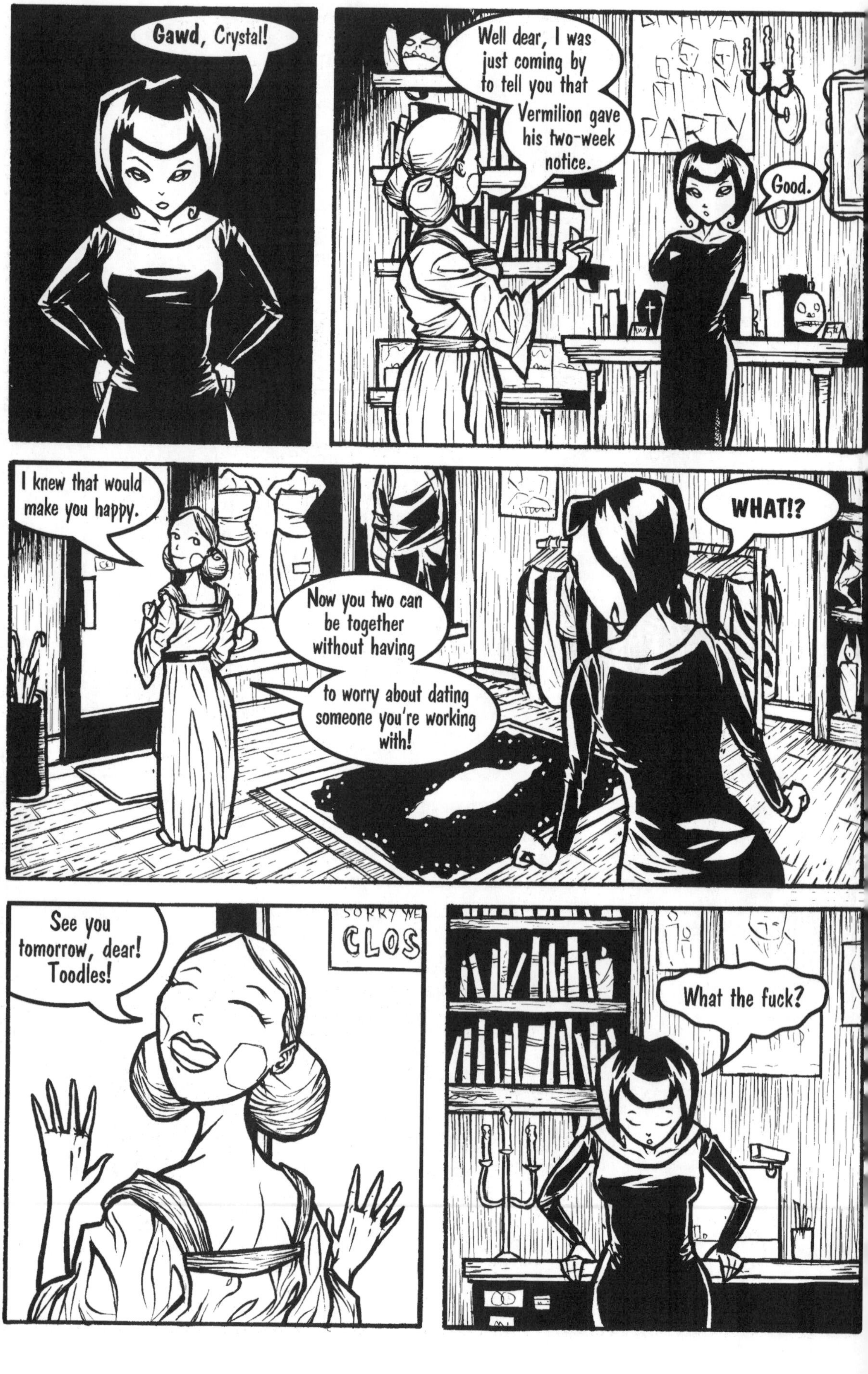
Gawd, Crystal!
Well dear, I was just coming by to tell you that Vermilion gave his two-week notice.
PARTY
Good.
I knew that would make you happy.
WHAT!?
Now you two can be together without having
to worry about dating someone you're working with!
See you tomorrow, dear! Toodles!
SORRY WE
CLOS
What the fuck?

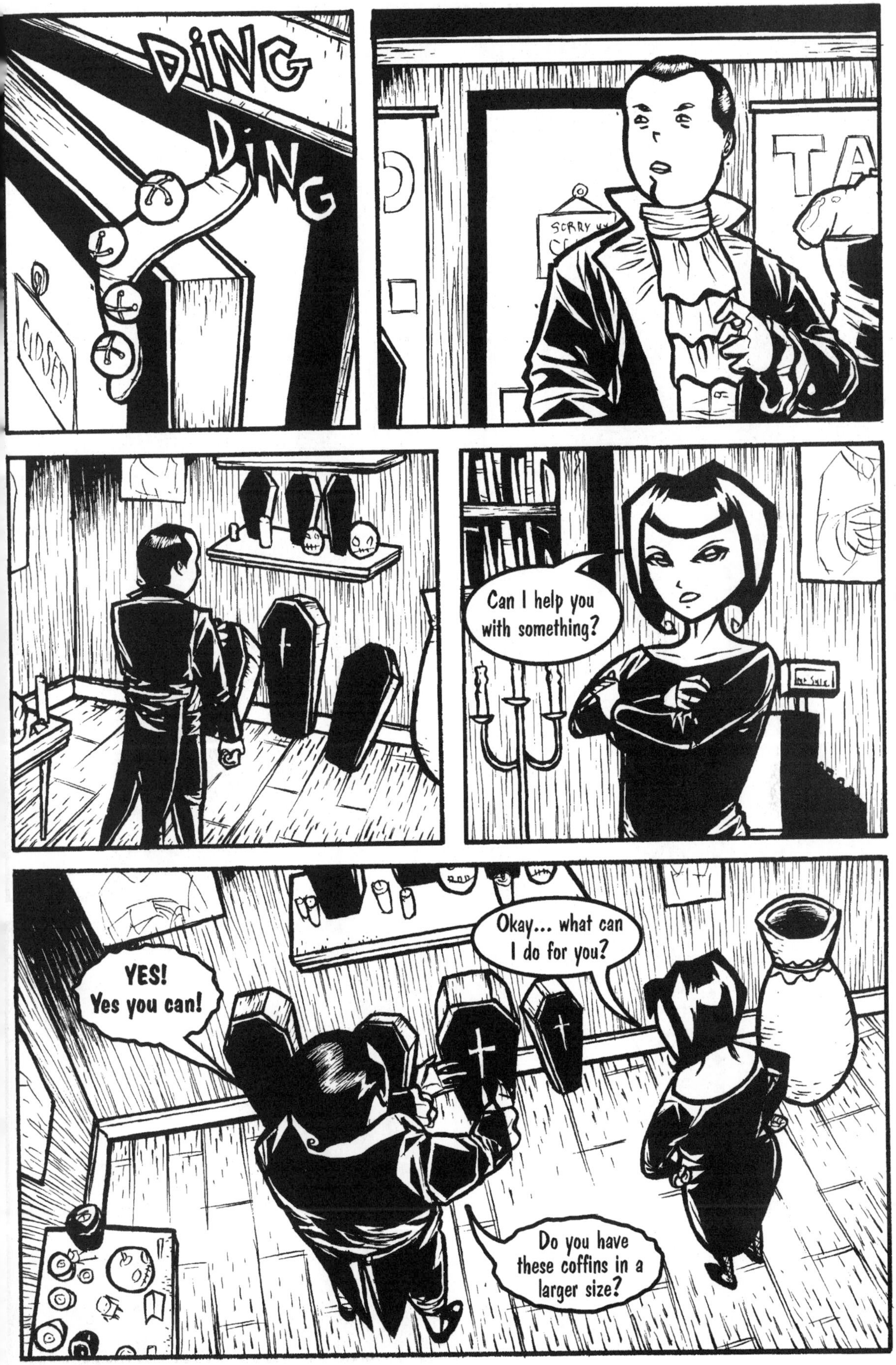
DING
DING
DING
CLOSED
SORRY
TA
Can I help you with something?
Okay... what can I do for you?
YES! Yes you can!
Do you have these coffins in a larger size?

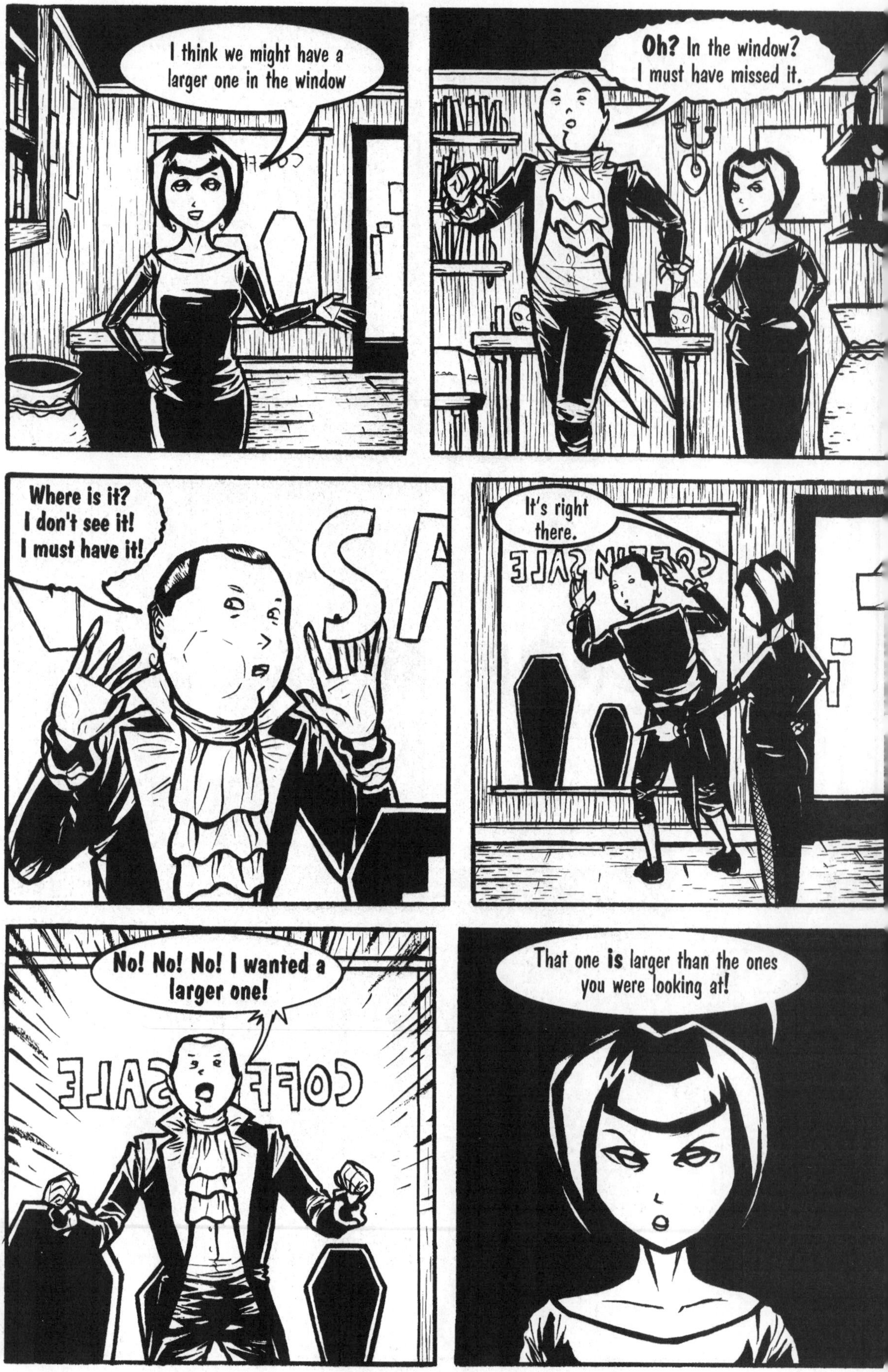
I think we might have a larger one in the window
Oh? In the window? I must have missed it.
Where is it? I don't see it! I must have it!
It's right there.
No! No! No! I wanted a larger one!
That one is larger than the ones you were looking at!

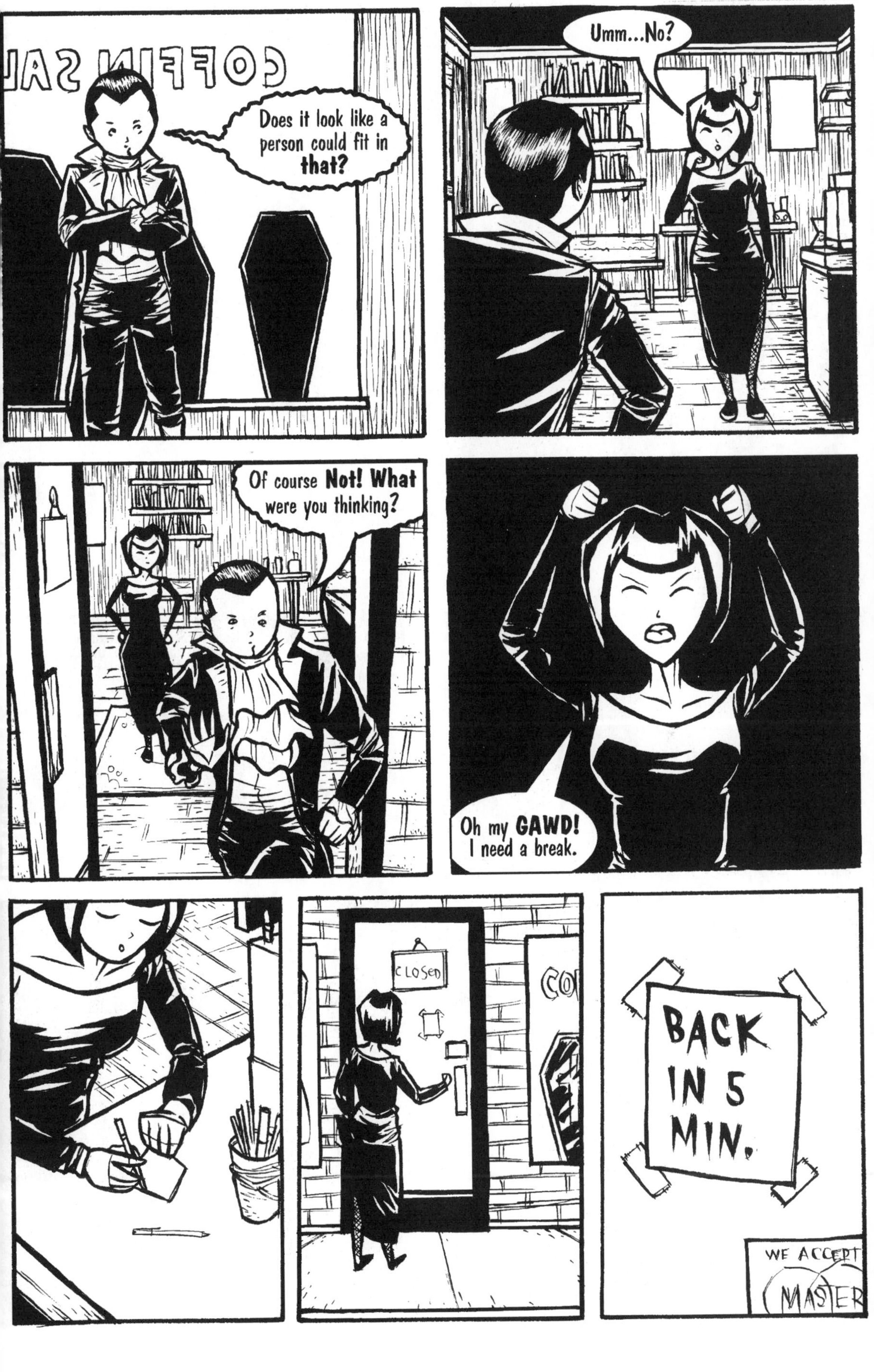
Does it look like a person could fit in **that?**
Umm...No?
Of course **Not! What** were you thinking?
Oh my **GAWD!** I need a break.
CLOSED
BACK IN 5 MIN.
WE ACCEPT
MASTER

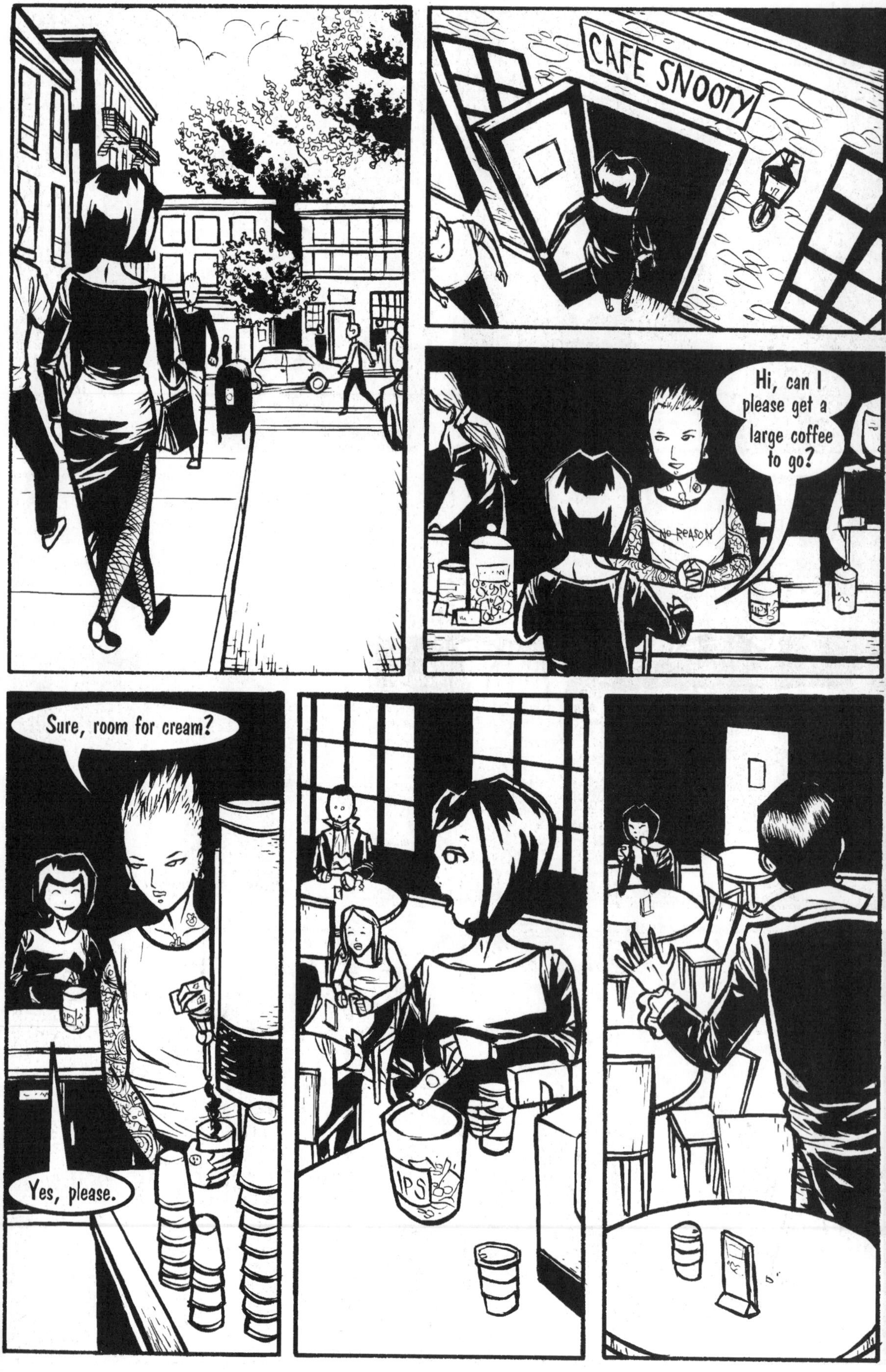
CAFE SNOOTY
Hi, can I please get a large coffee to go?
NO REASON
Sure, room for cream?
Yes, please.
TIPS

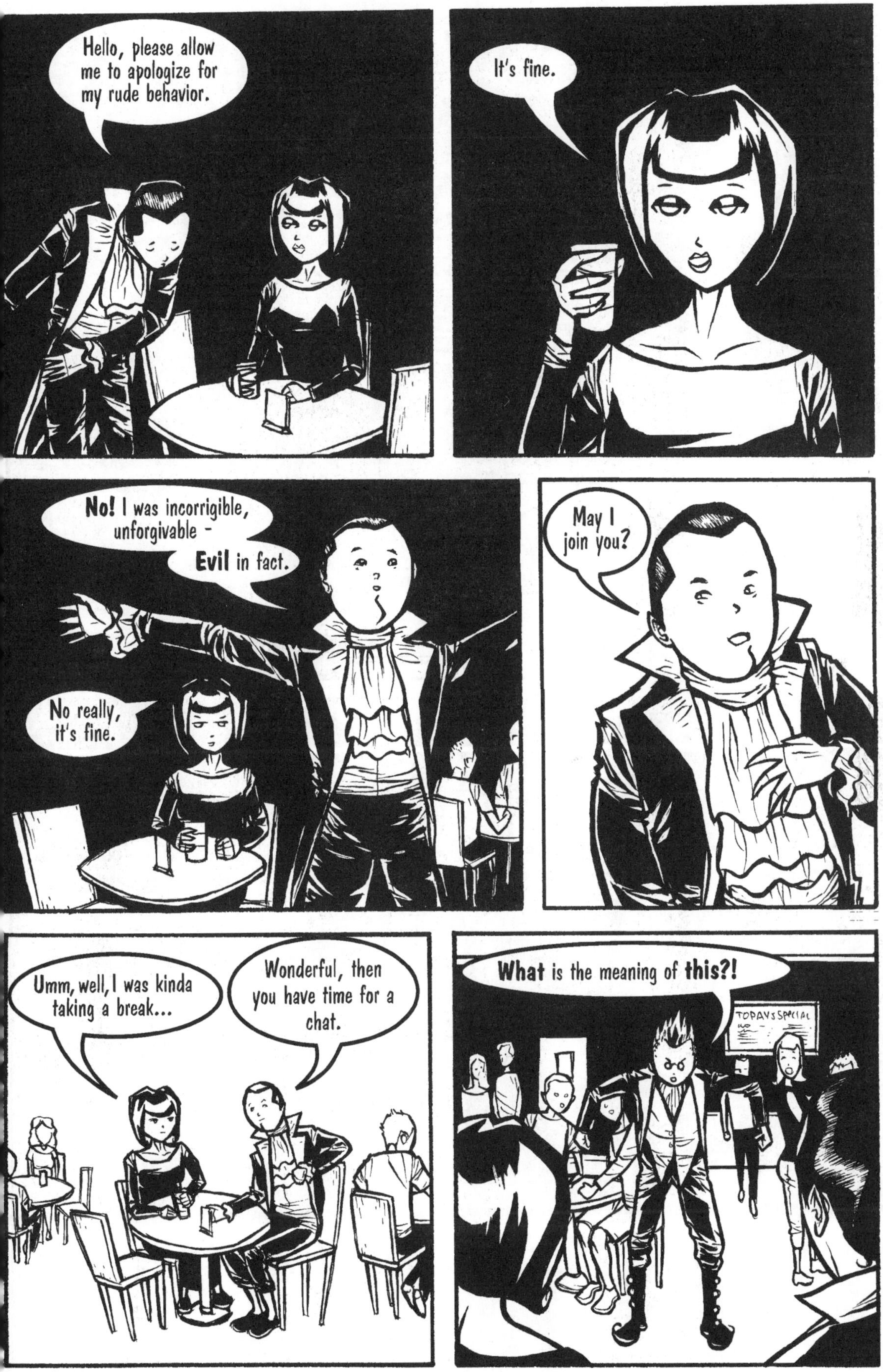
Hello, please allow me to apologize for my rude behavior.
It's fine.
No! I was incorrigible, unforgivable -
Evil in fact.
No really, it's fine.
May I join you?
Umm, well, I was kinda taking a break...
Wonderful, then you have time for a chat.
What is the meaning of this?!

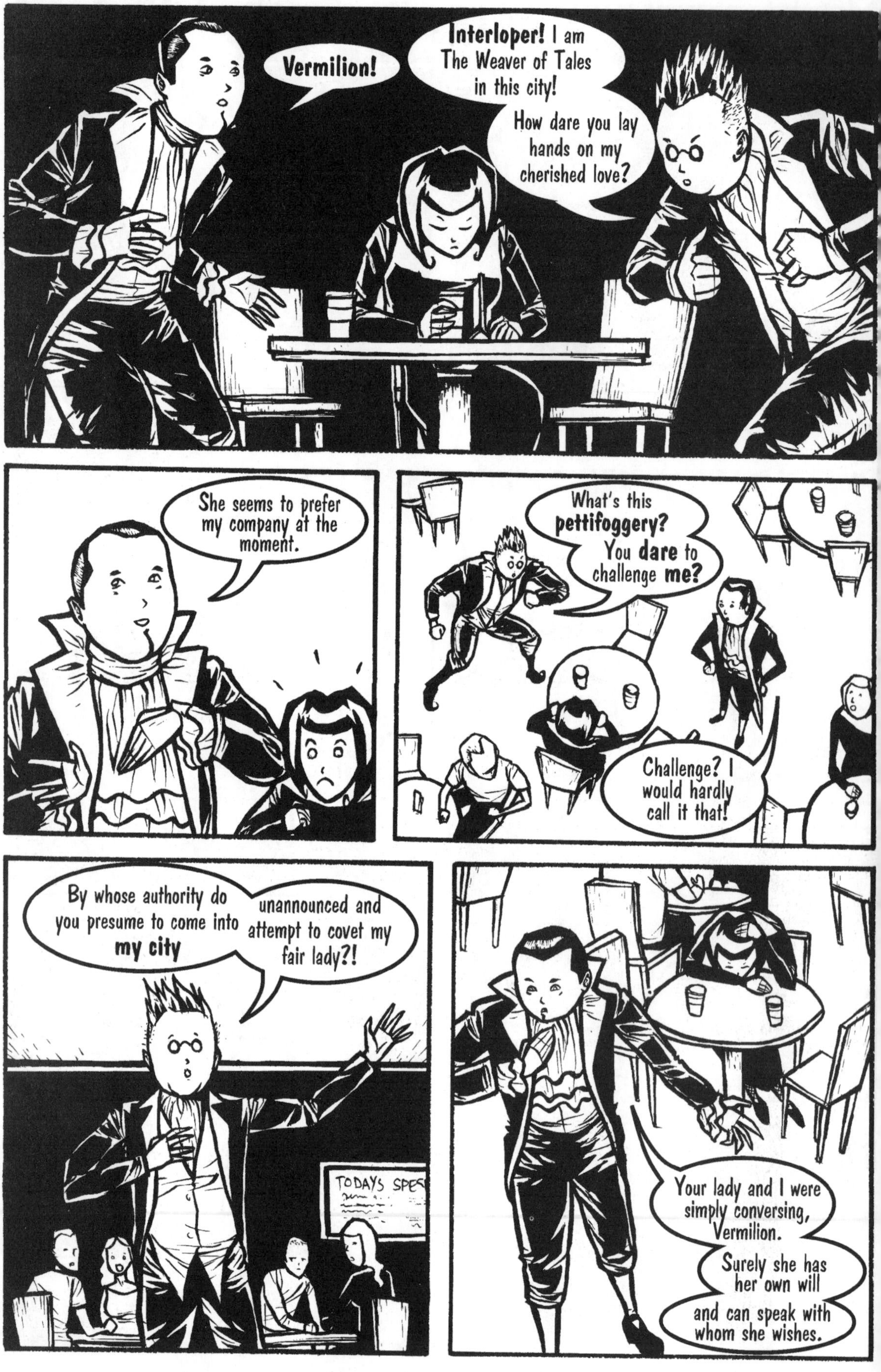
Vermilion!
Interloper! I am The Weaver of Tales in this city!
How dare you lay hands on my cherished love?
She seems to prefer my company at the moment.
What's this pettifoggery?
You dare to challenge me?
Challenge? I would hardly call it that!
By whose authority do you presume to come into my city unannounced and attempt to covet my fair lady?!
TODAYS SPE
Your lady and I were simply conversing, Vermilion.
Surely she has her own will
and can speak with whom she wishes.

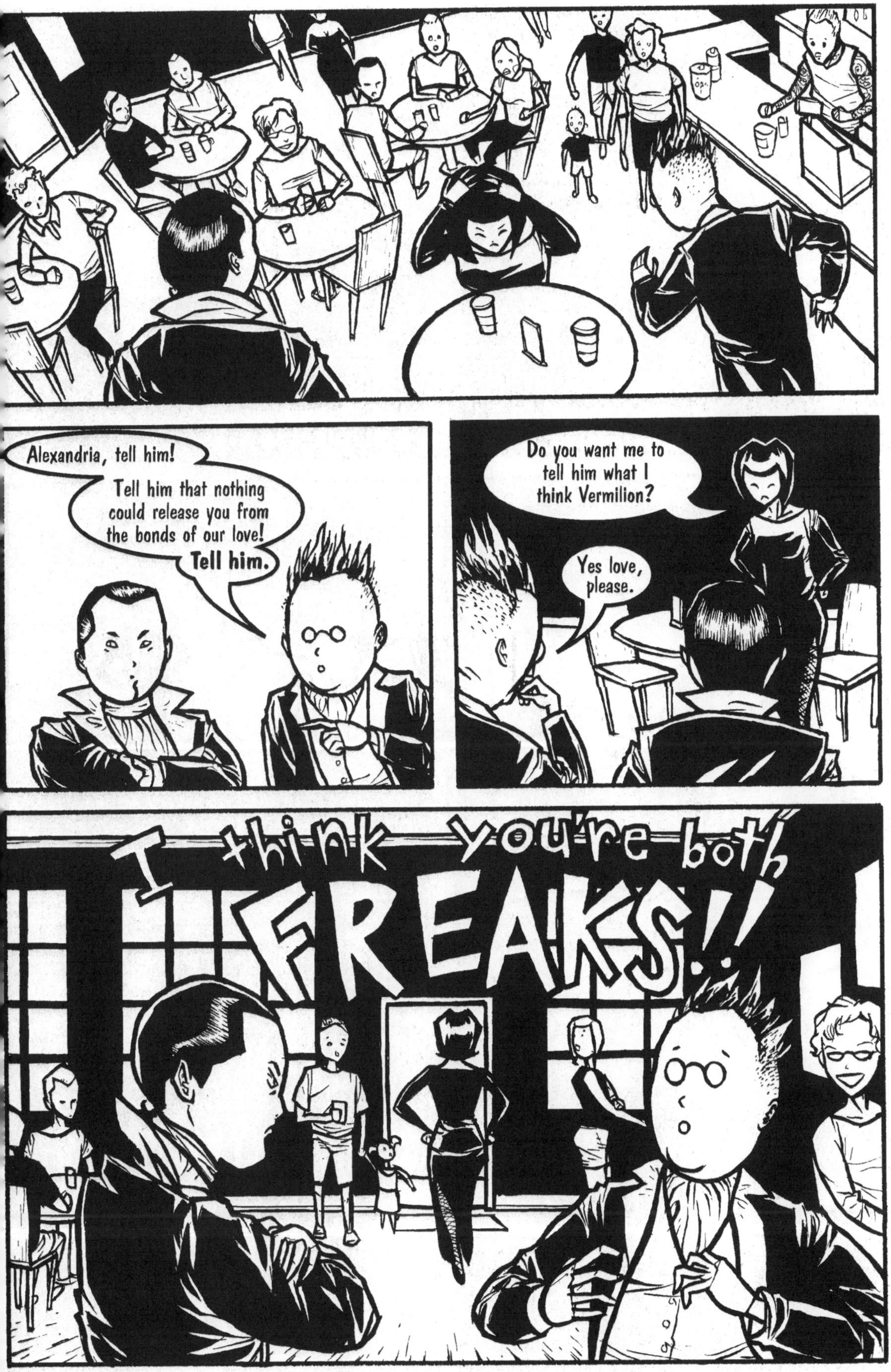
Alexandria, tell him!
Tell him that nothing could release you from the bonds of our love! Tell him.
Do you want me to tell him what I think Vermilion?
Yes love, please.
I think you're both FREAKS!!

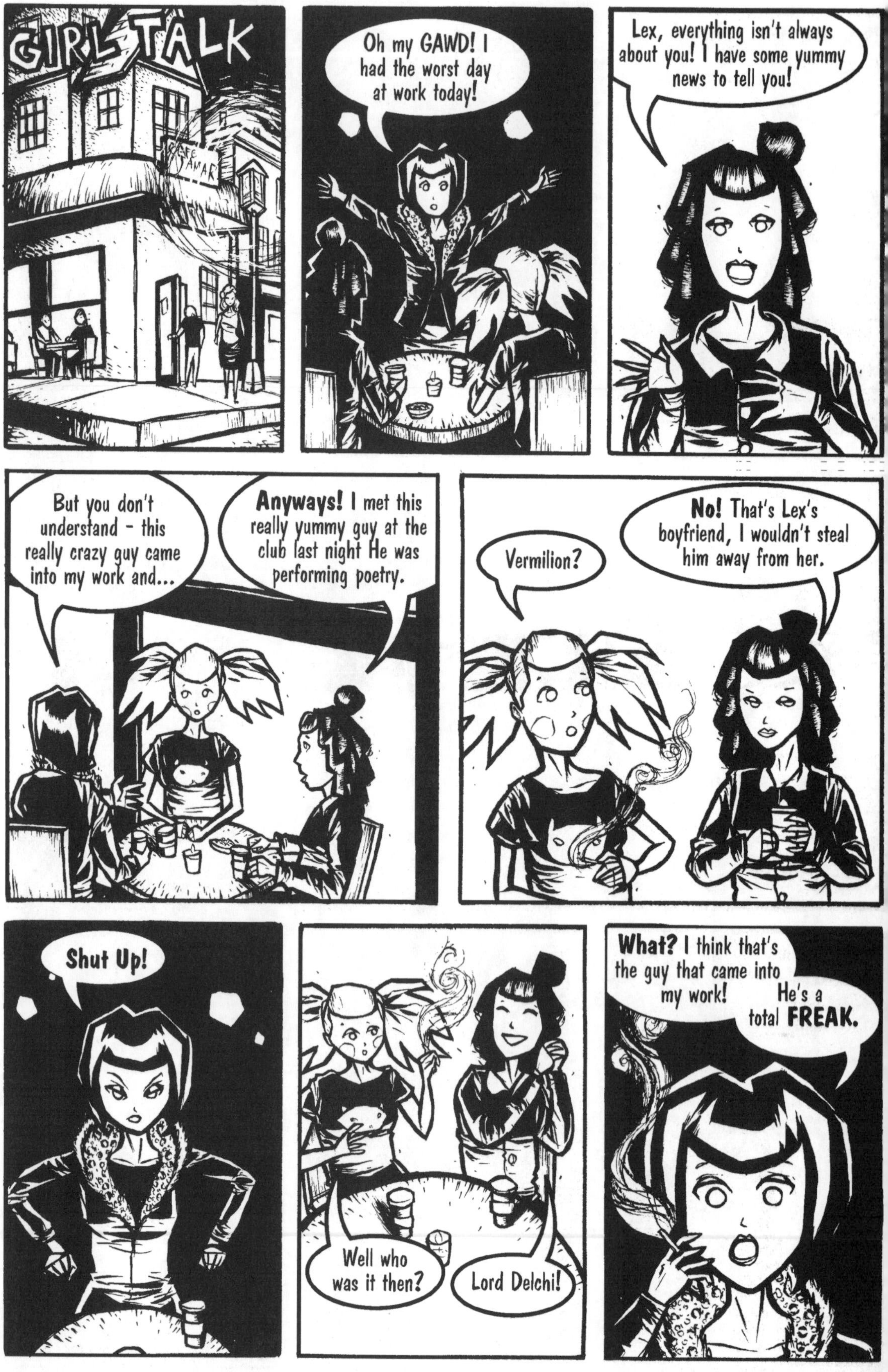
GIRL TALK
CAFE JAMAR
Oh my GAWD! I had the worst day at work today!
Lex, everything isn't always about you! I have some yummy news to tell you!
But you don't understand - this really crazy guy came into my work and...
Anyways! I met this really yummy guy at the club last night He was performing poetry.
Vermilion?
No! That's Lex's boyfriend, I wouldn't steal him away from her.
Shut Up!
Well who was it then?
Lord Delchi!
What? I think that's the guy that came into my work!
He's a total **FREAK.**

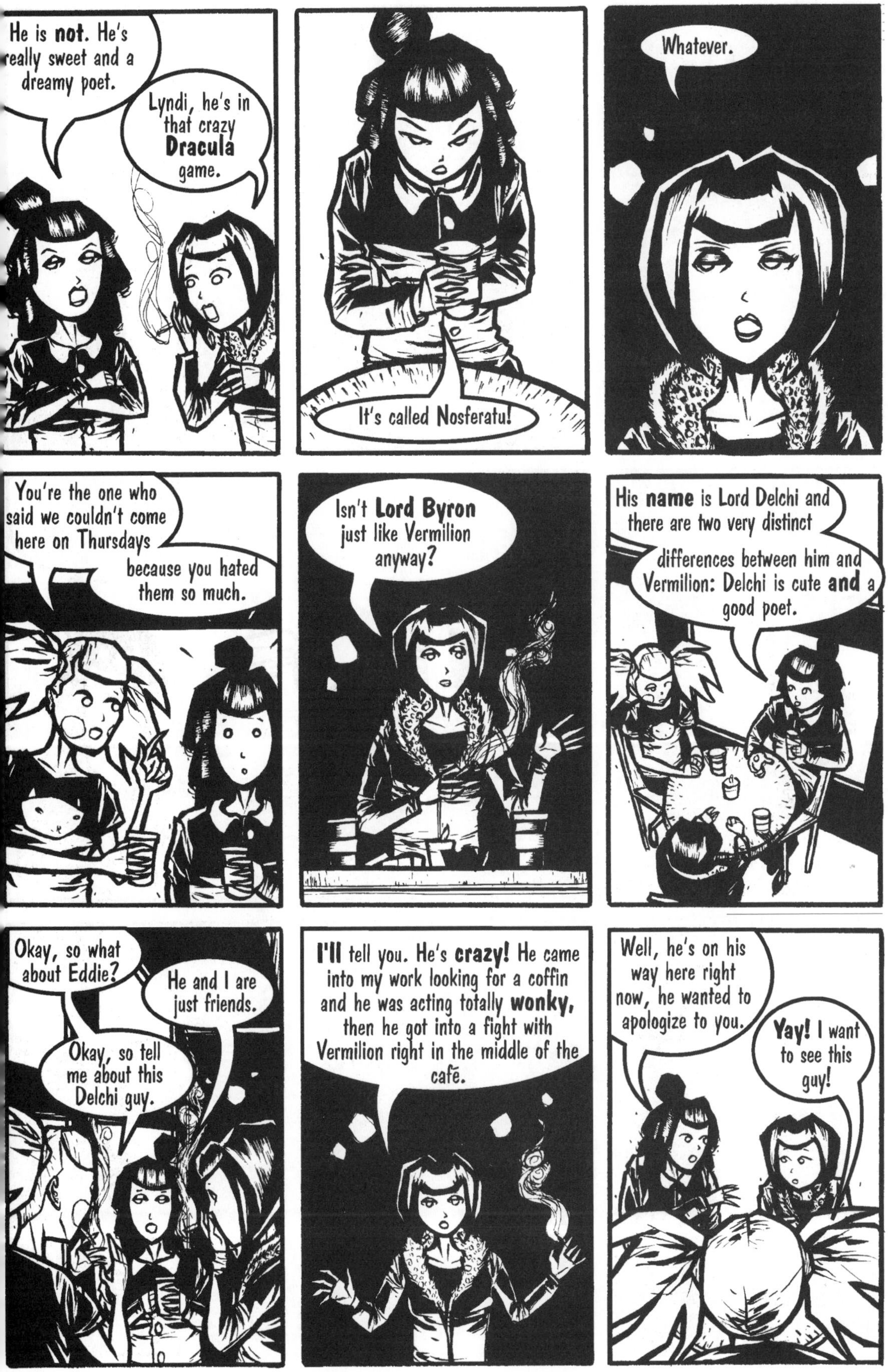
He is not. He's really sweet and a dreamy poet.
Lyndi, he's in that crazy Dracula game.
It's called Nosferatu!
Whatever.
You're the one who said we couldn't come here on Thursdays
because you hated them so much.
Isn't Lord Byron just like Vermilion anyway?
His name is Lord Delchi and there are two very distinct
differences between him and Vermilion: Delchi is cute and a good poet.
Okay, so what about Eddie?
He and I are just friends.
Okay, so tell me about this Delchi guy.
I'll tell you. He's crazy! He came into my work looking for a coffin and he was acting totally wonky, then he got into a fight with Vermilion right in the middle of the café.
Well, he's on his way here right now, he wanted to apologize to you.
Yay! I want to see this guy!

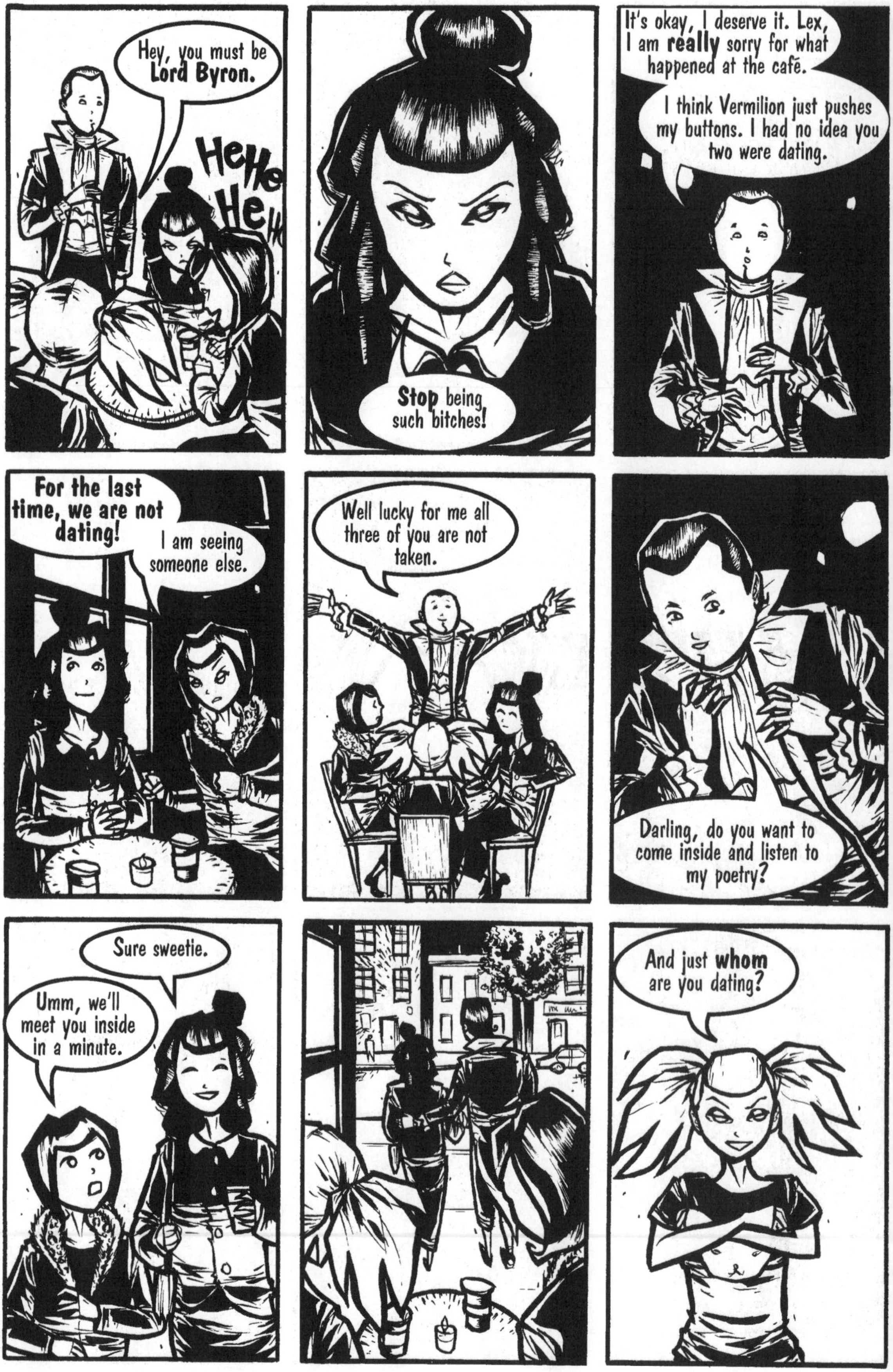
Hey, you must be Lord Byron.
HeHe HeHe
Stop being such bitches!
It's okay, I deserve it. Lex, I am really sorry for what happened at the café.
I think Vermilion just pushes my buttons. I had no idea you two were dating.
For the last time, we are not dating!
I am seeing someone else.
Well lucky for me all three of you are not taken.
Darling, do you want to come inside and listen to my poetry?
Sure sweetie.
Umm, we'll meet you inside in a minute.
And just whom are you dating?

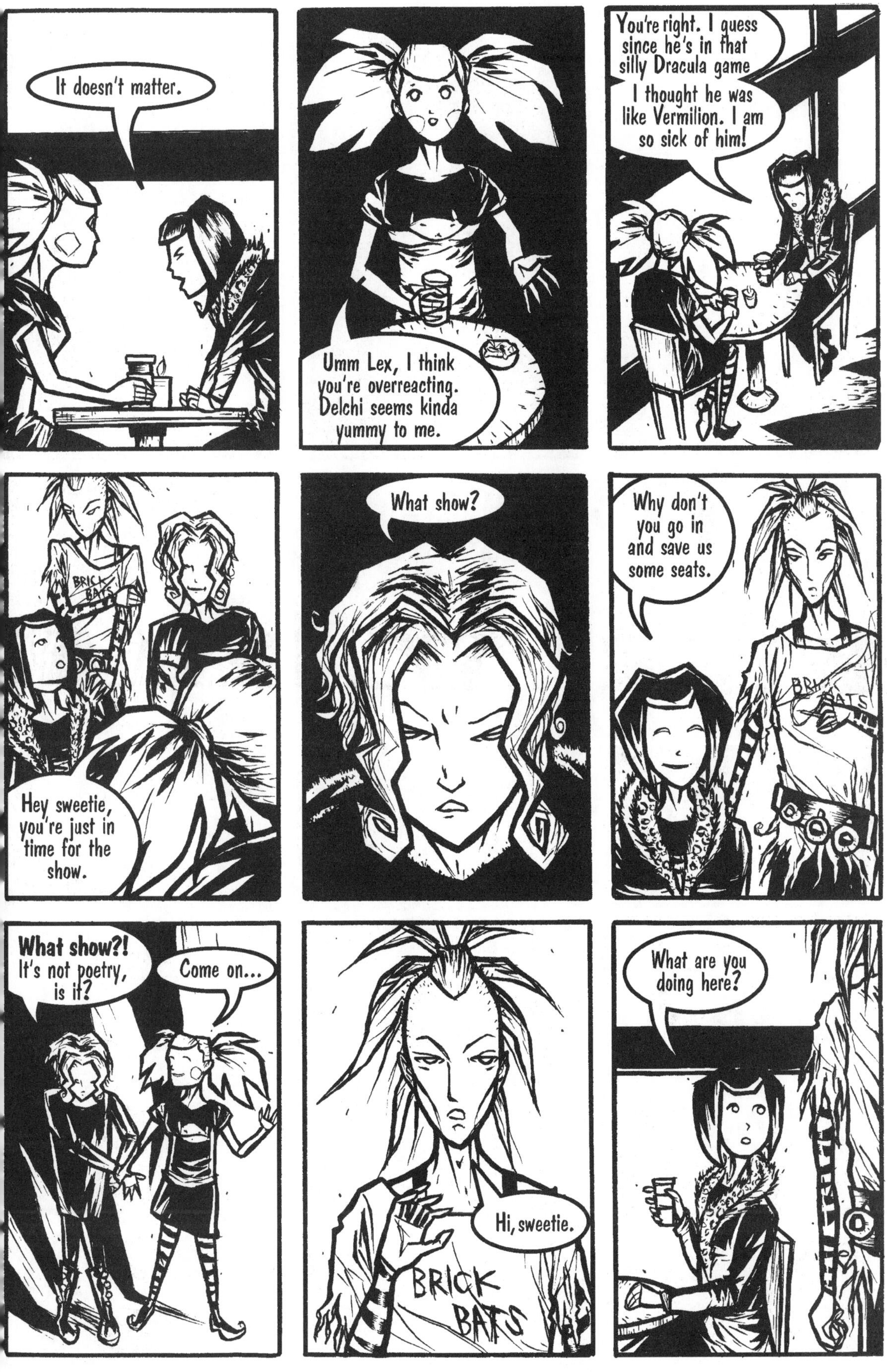
It doesn't matter.
Umm Lex, I think you're overreacting. Delchi seems kinda yummy to me.
You're right. I guess since he's in that silly Dracula game
I thought he was like Vermilion. I am so sick of him!
BRICK BATS
Hey sweetie, you're just in time for the show.
What show?
Why don't you go in and save us some seats.
What show?! It's not poetry, is it?
Come on...
Hi, sweetie.
BRICK BATS
What are you doing here?

Aren't you happy to see me?

Sure, but I really haven't had that much time to think since last night.

But I thought...

I need some time, Max.

CLAP CLAP CLAP CLAP CLAP CLAP CLAP

Latte Mocha

CLAP CLAP CLAP CLAP CLAP CLA AP

Wow! It looks like everyone loved him.

Yeah, he was great.

CLAP CLAP CLAP CLA

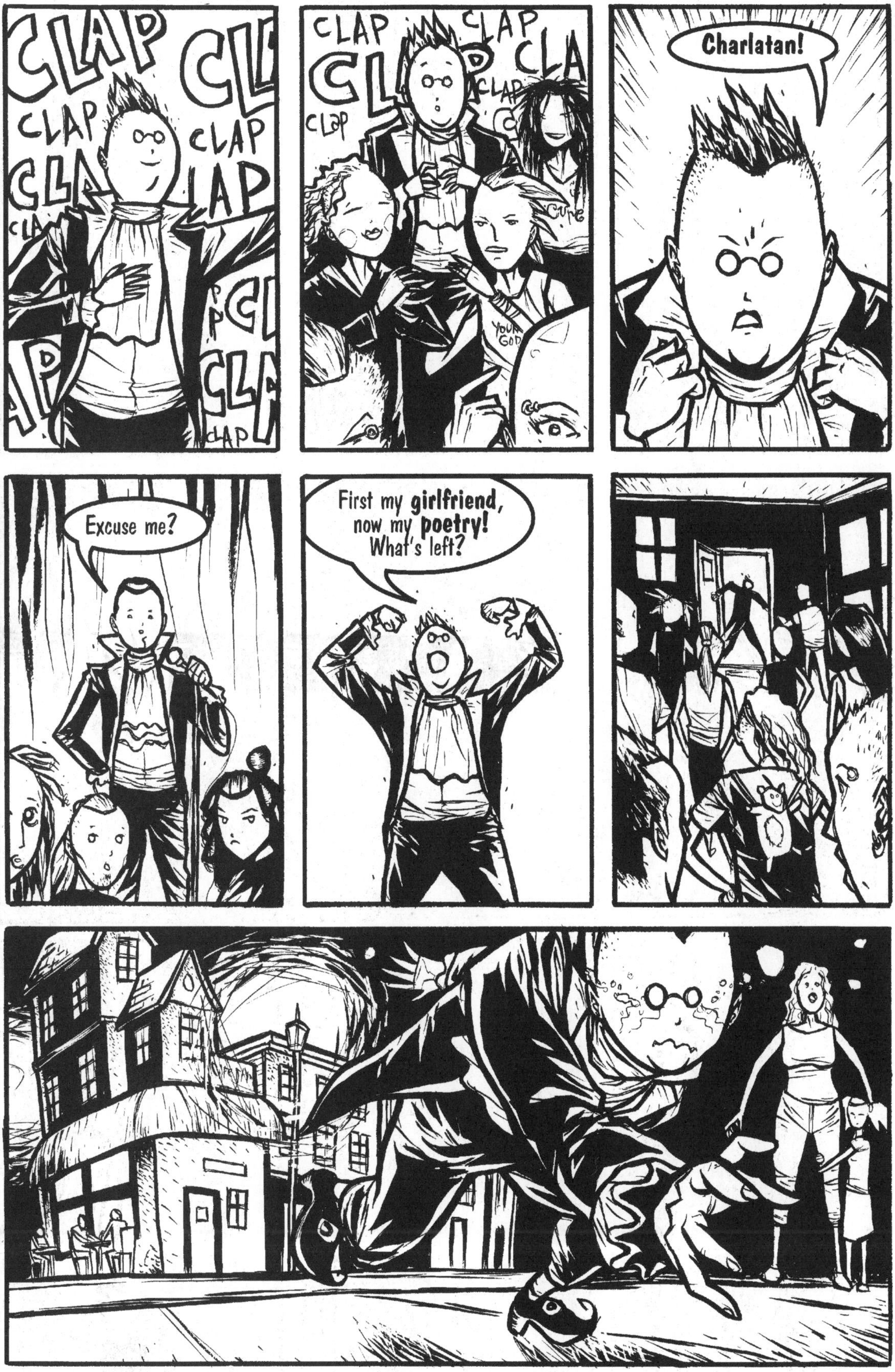
CLAP CLAP CLAP CLAP
CLAP CLAP CLAP
Charlatan!
Excuse me?
First my girlfriend, now my poetry! What's left?

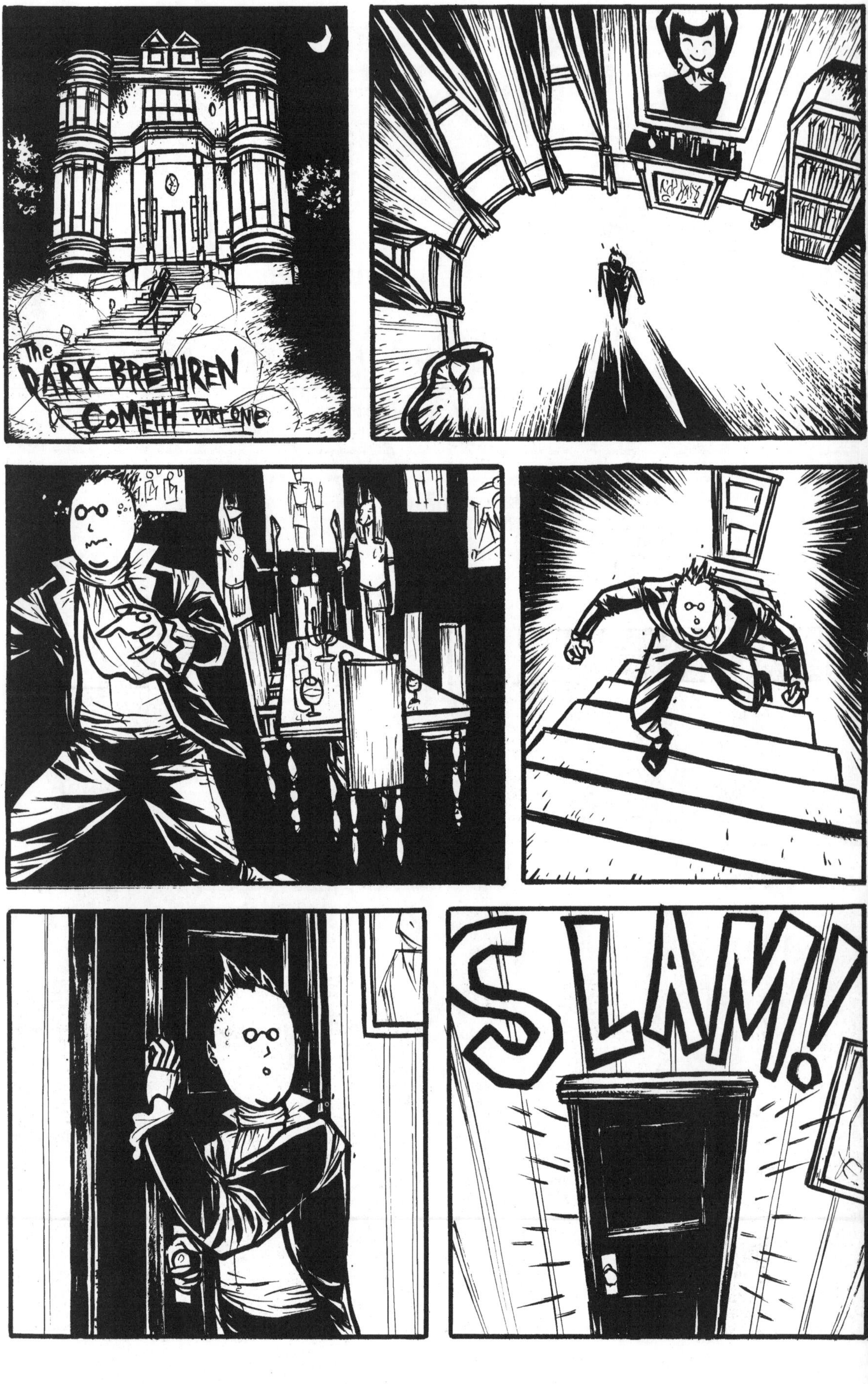
The DARK BRETHREN COMETH - PART ONE
SLAM!

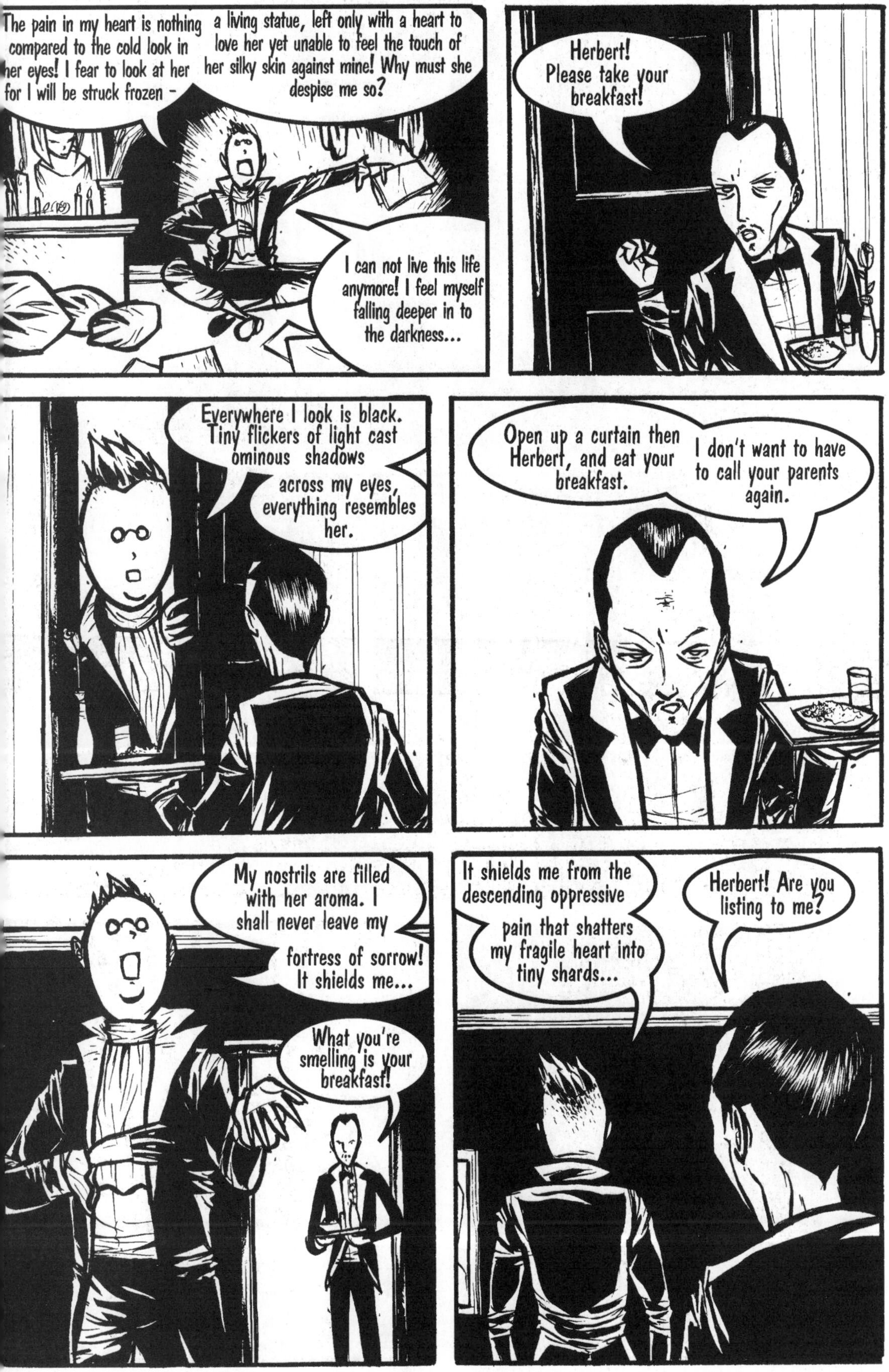
The pain in my heart is nothing compared to the cold look in her eyes! I fear to look at her for I will be struck frozen -
a living statue, left only with a heart to love her yet unable to feel the touch of her silky skin against mine! Why must she despise me so?
I can not live this life anymore! I feel myself falling deeper in to the darkness...
Herbert! Please take your breakfast!
Everywhere I look is black. Tiny flickers of light cast ominous shadows
across my eyes, everything resembles her.
Open up a curtain then Herbert, and eat your breakfast.
I don't want to have to call your parents again.
My nostrils are filled with her aroma. I shall never leave my
fortress of sorrow! It shields me...
What you're smelling is your breakfast!
It shields me from the descending oppressive
pain that shatters my fragile heart into tiny shards...
Herbert! Are you listing to me?

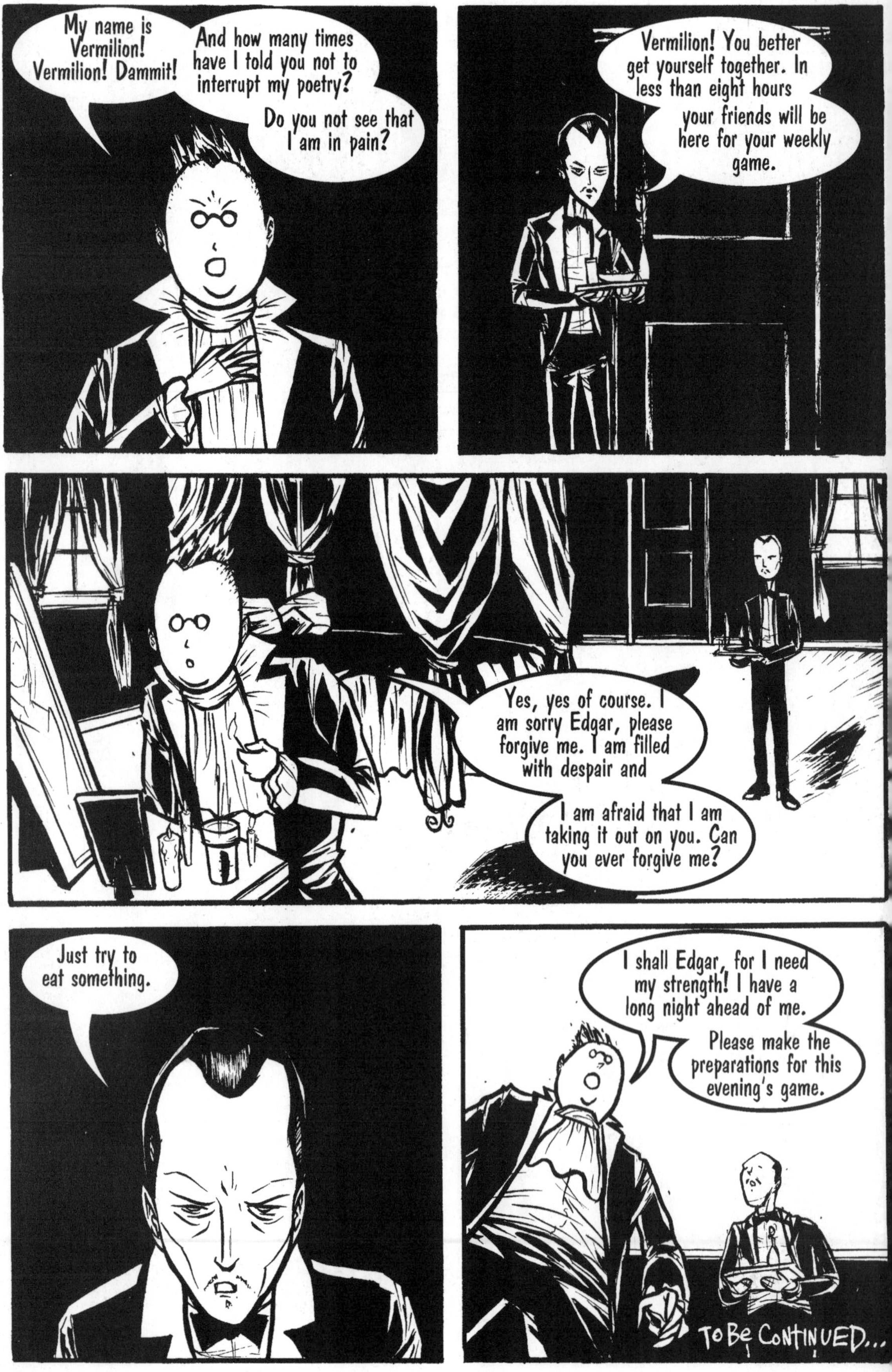
My name is Vermilion! Vermilion! Dammit!
And how many times have I told you not to interrupt my poetry?
Do you not see that I am in pain?
Vermilion! You better get yourself together. In less than eight hours
your friends will be here for your weekly game.
Yes, yes of course. I am sorry Edgar, please forgive me. I am filled with despair and
I am afraid that I am taking it out on you. Can you ever forgive me?
Just try to eat something.
I shall Edgar, for I need my strength! I have a long night ahead of me.
Please make the preparations for this evening's game.
TO BE CONTINUED...

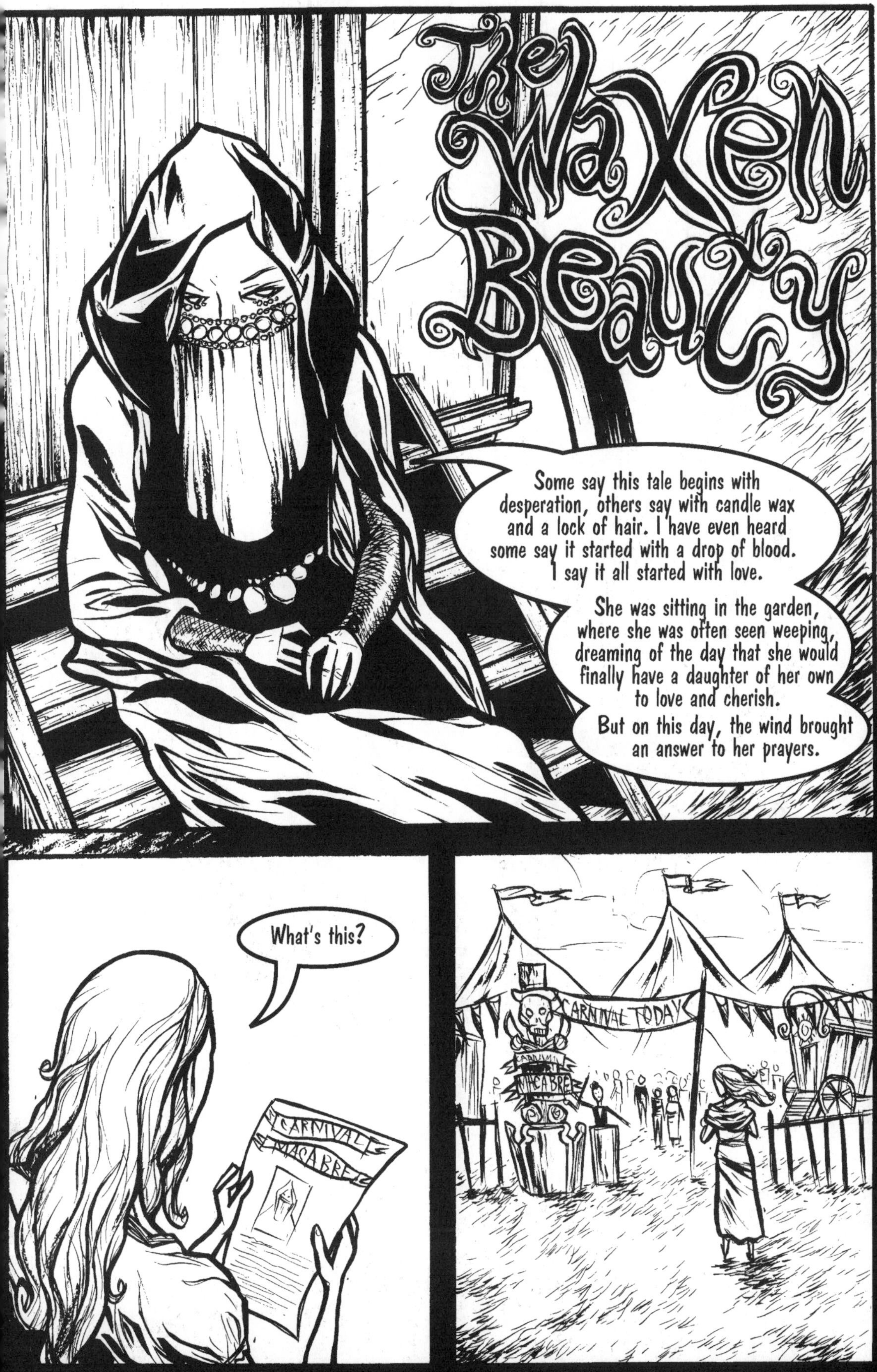
The Waxen Beauty
Some say this tale begins with desperation, others say with candle wax and a lock of hair. I have even heard some say it started with a drop of blood. I say it all started with love.
She was sitting in the garden, where she was often seen weeping, dreaming of the day that she would finally have a daughter of her own to love and cherish.
But on this day, the wind brought an answer to her prayers.
What's this?
CARNIVALE
MACABRE
CARNIVAL TODAY
MACABRE

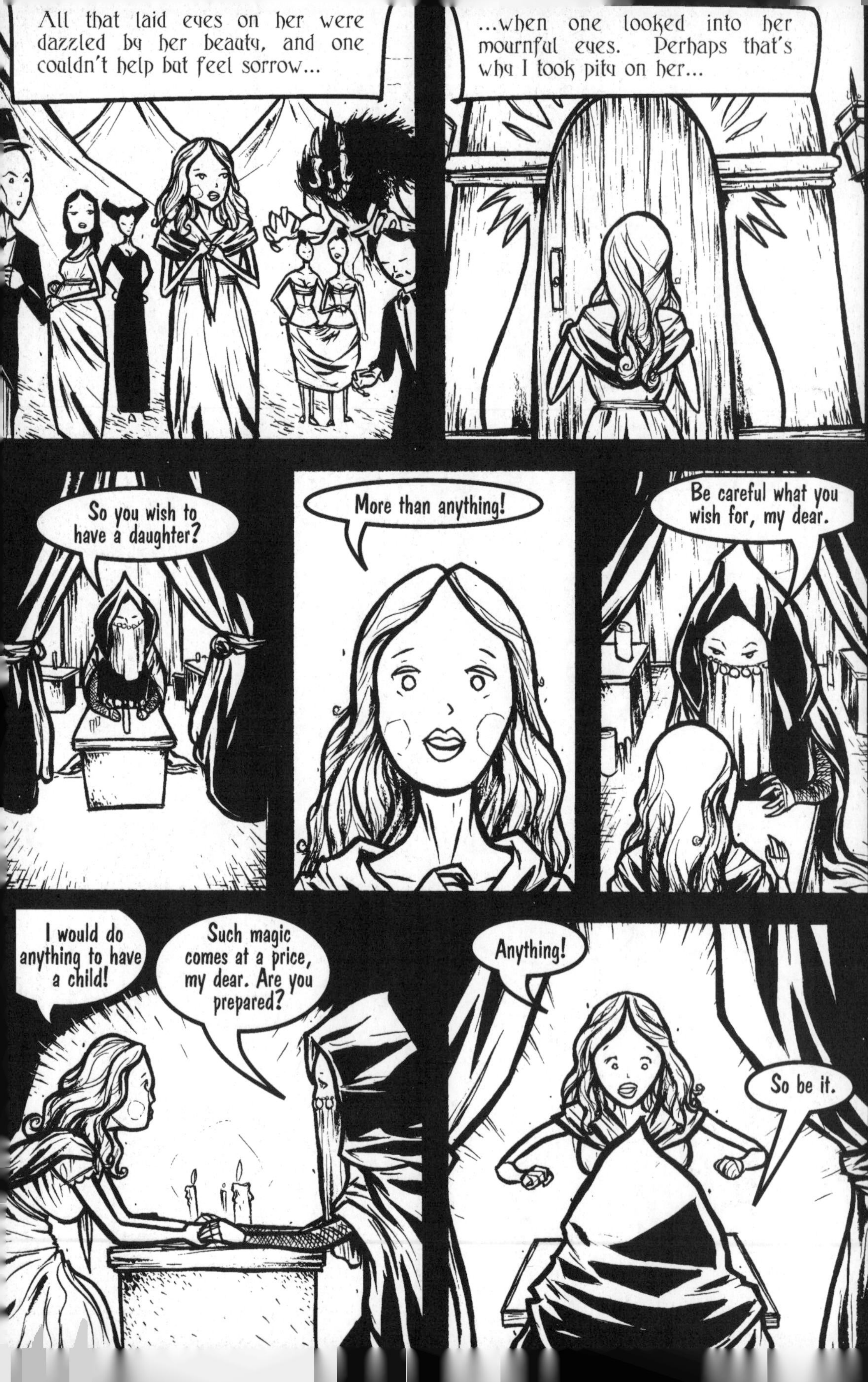
All that laid eyes on her were dazzled by her beauty, and one couldn't help but feel sorrow...
...when one looked into her mournful eyes. Perhaps that's why I took pity on her...
So you wish to have a daughter?
More than anything!
Be careful what you wish for, my dear.
I would do anything to have a child!
Such magic comes at a price, my dear. Are you prepared?
Anything!
So be it.

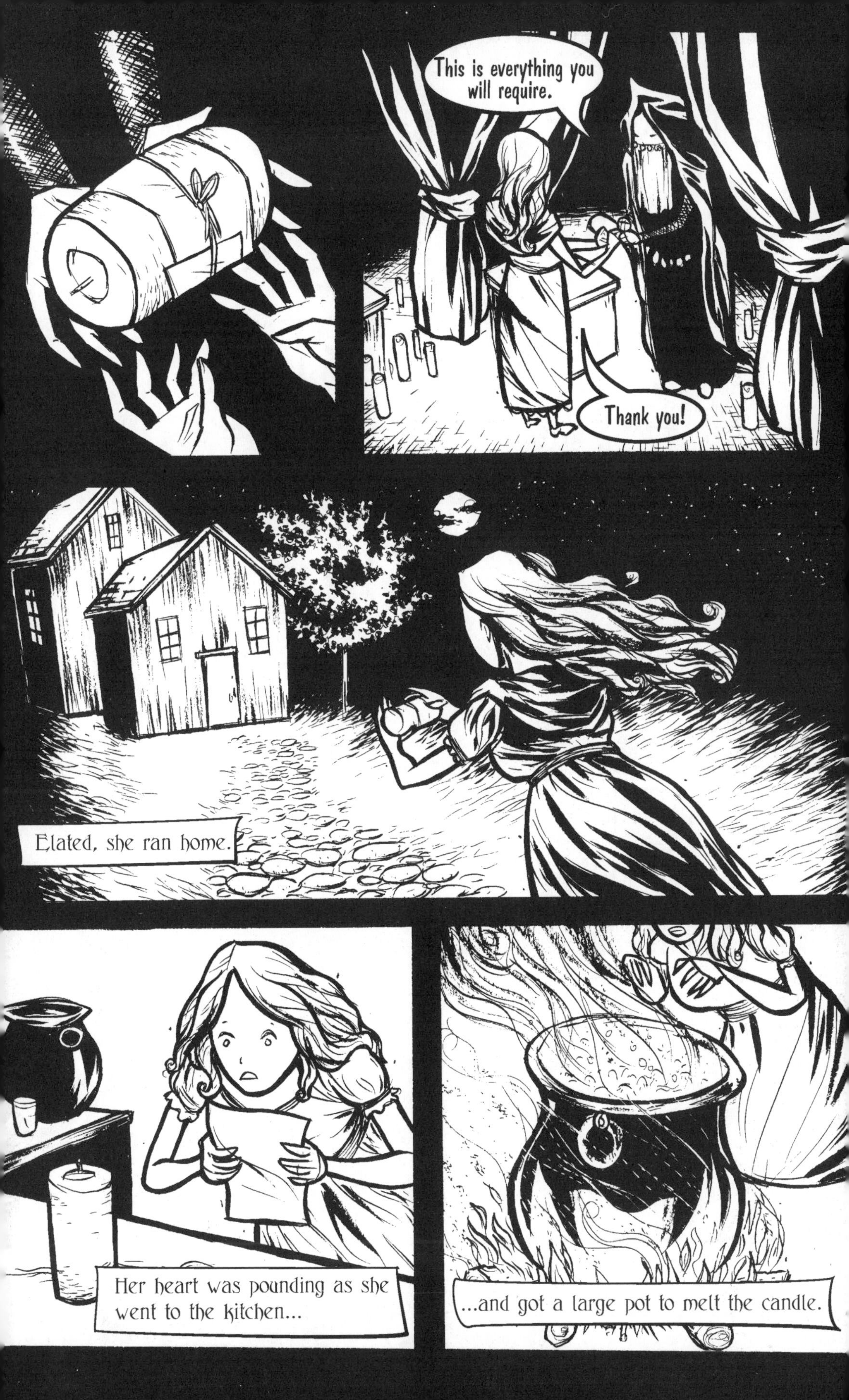
This is everything you will require.
Thank you!
Elated, she ran home.
Her heart was pounding as she went to the kitchen...
...and got a large pot to melt the candle.

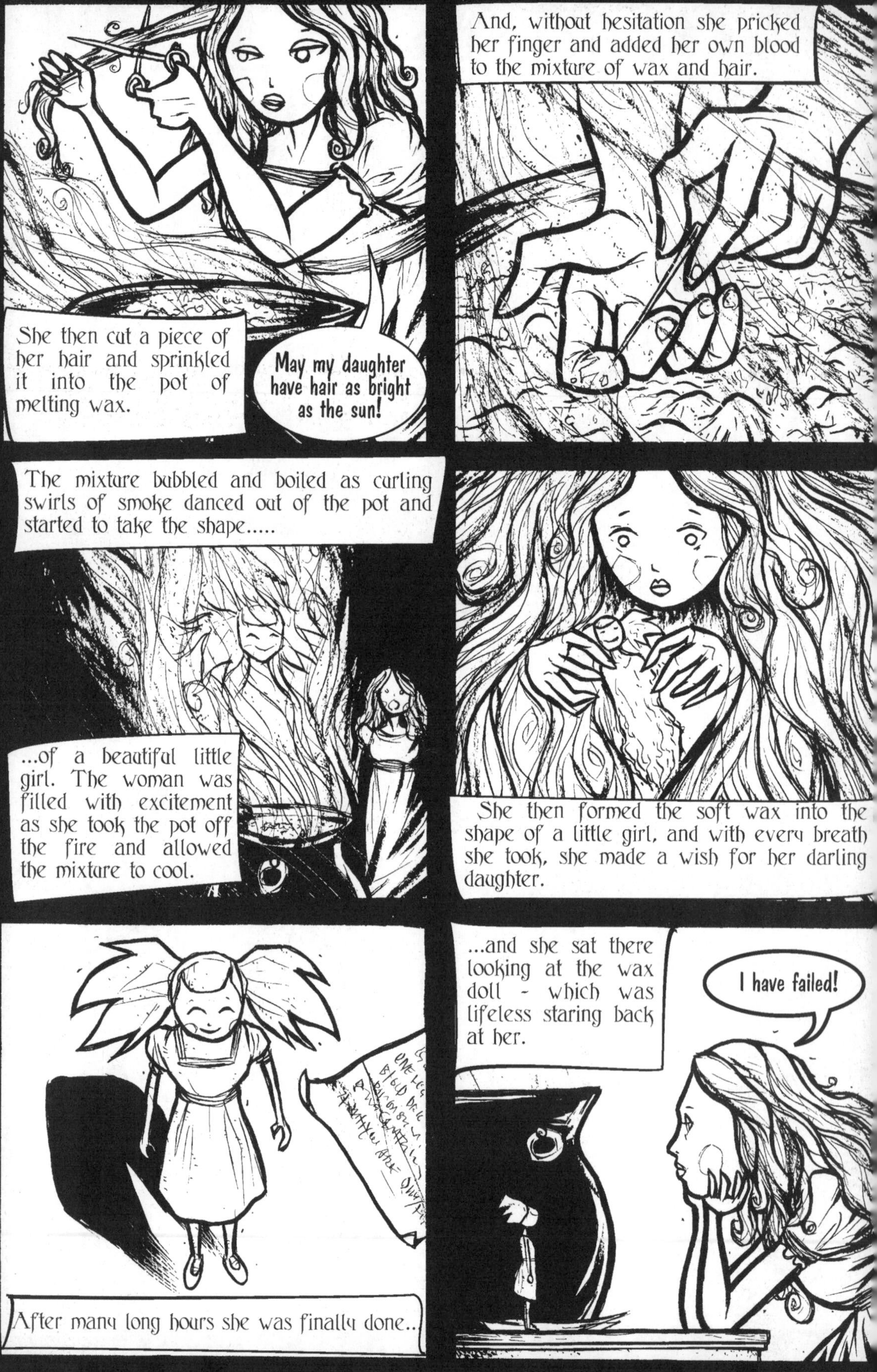
She then cut a piece of her hair and sprinkled it into the pot of melting wax.
May my daughter have hair as bright as the sun!
And, without hesitation she pricked her finger and added her own blood to the mixture of wax and hair.
The mixture bubbled and boiled as curling swirls of smoke danced out of the pot and started to take the shape.....
...of a beautiful little girl. The woman was filled with excitement as she took the pot off the fire and allowed the mixture to cool.
She then formed the soft wax into the shape of a little girl, and with every breath she took, she made a wish for her darling daughter.
After many long hours she was finally done..
...and she sat there looking at the wax doll - which was lifeless staring back at her.
I have failed!

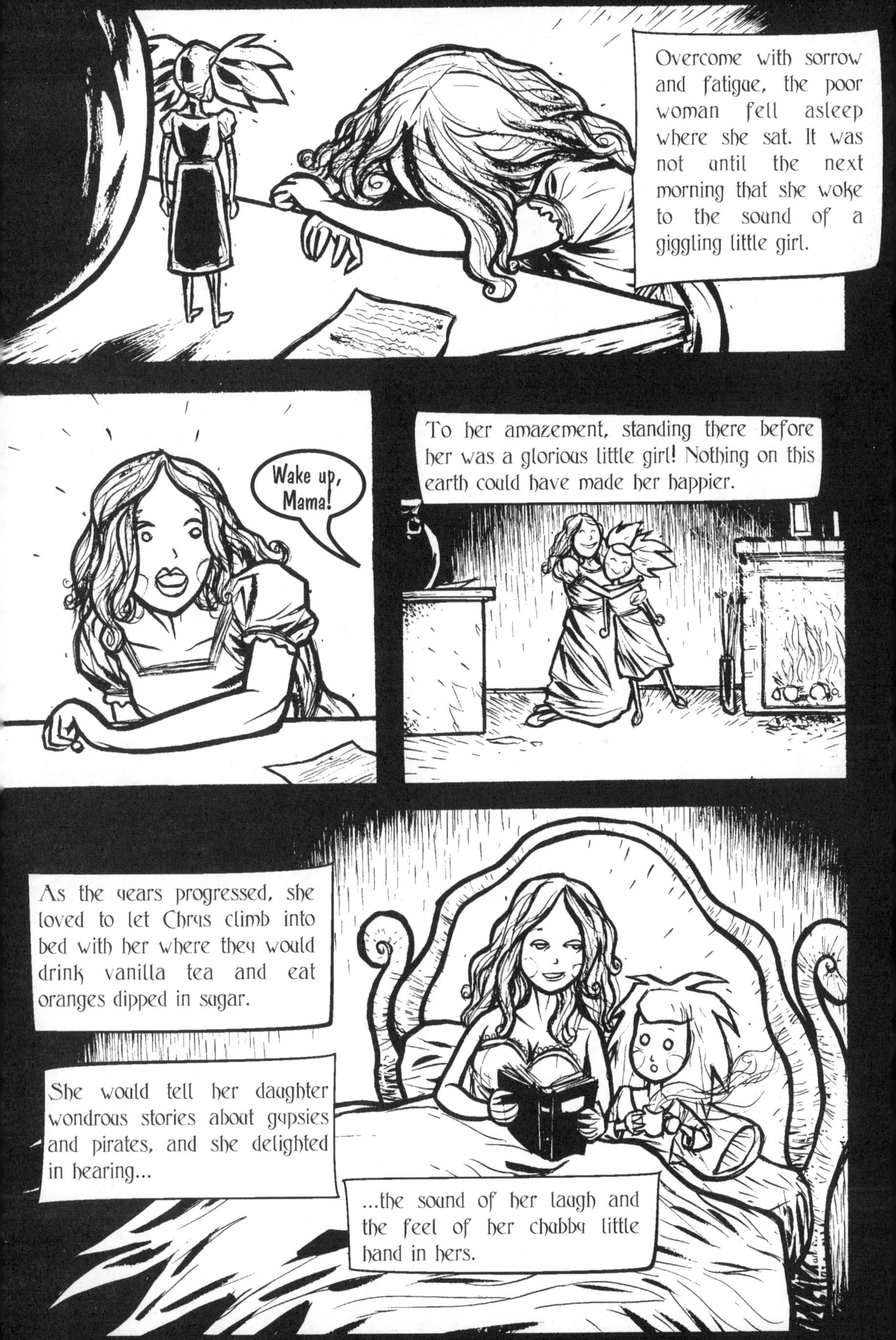
Overcome with sorrow and fatigue, the poor woman fell asleep where she sat. It was not until the next morning that she woke to the sound of a giggling little girl.
Wake up, Mama!
To her amazement, standing there before her was a glorious little girl! Nothing on this earth could have made her happier.
As the years progressed, she loved to let Chrys climb into bed with her where they would drink vanilla tea and eat oranges dipped in sugar.
She would tell her daughter wondrous stories about gypsies and pirates, and she delighted in hearing...
...the sound of her laugh and the feel of her chubby little hand in hers.

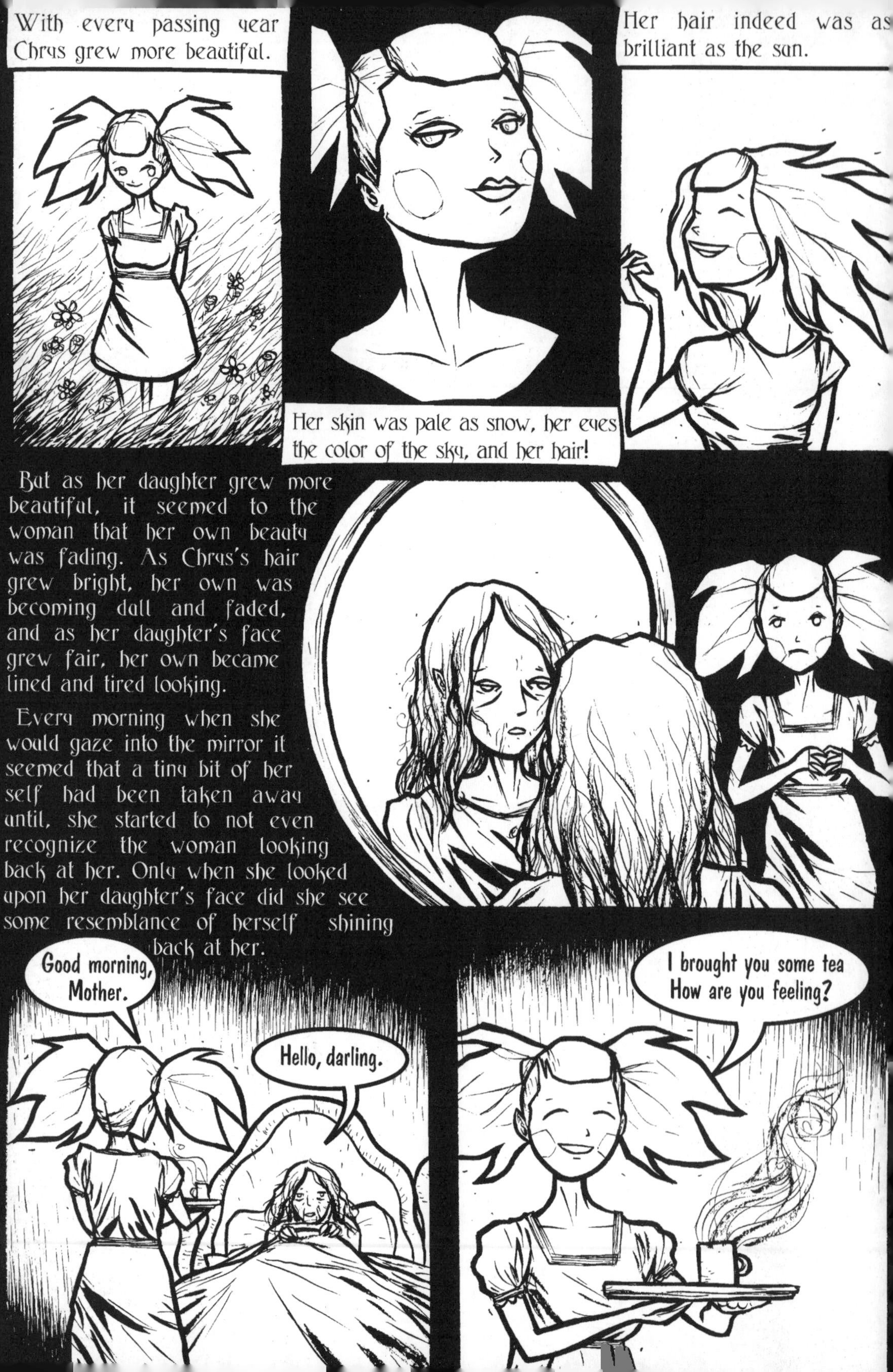
With every passing year Chrys grew more beautiful.
Her skin was pale as snow, her eyes the color of the sky, and her hair!
Her hair indeed was as brilliant as the sun.
But as her daughter grew more beautiful, it seemed to the woman that her own beauty was fading. As Chrys's hair grew bright, her own was becoming dull and faded, and as her daughter's face grew fair, her own became lined and tired looking.
Every morning when she would gaze into the mirror it seemed that a tiny bit of her self had been taken away until, she started to not even recognize the woman looking back at her. Only when she looked upon her daughter's face did she see some resemblance of herself shining back at her.
Good morning, Mother.
Hello, darling.
I brought you some tea How are you feeling?

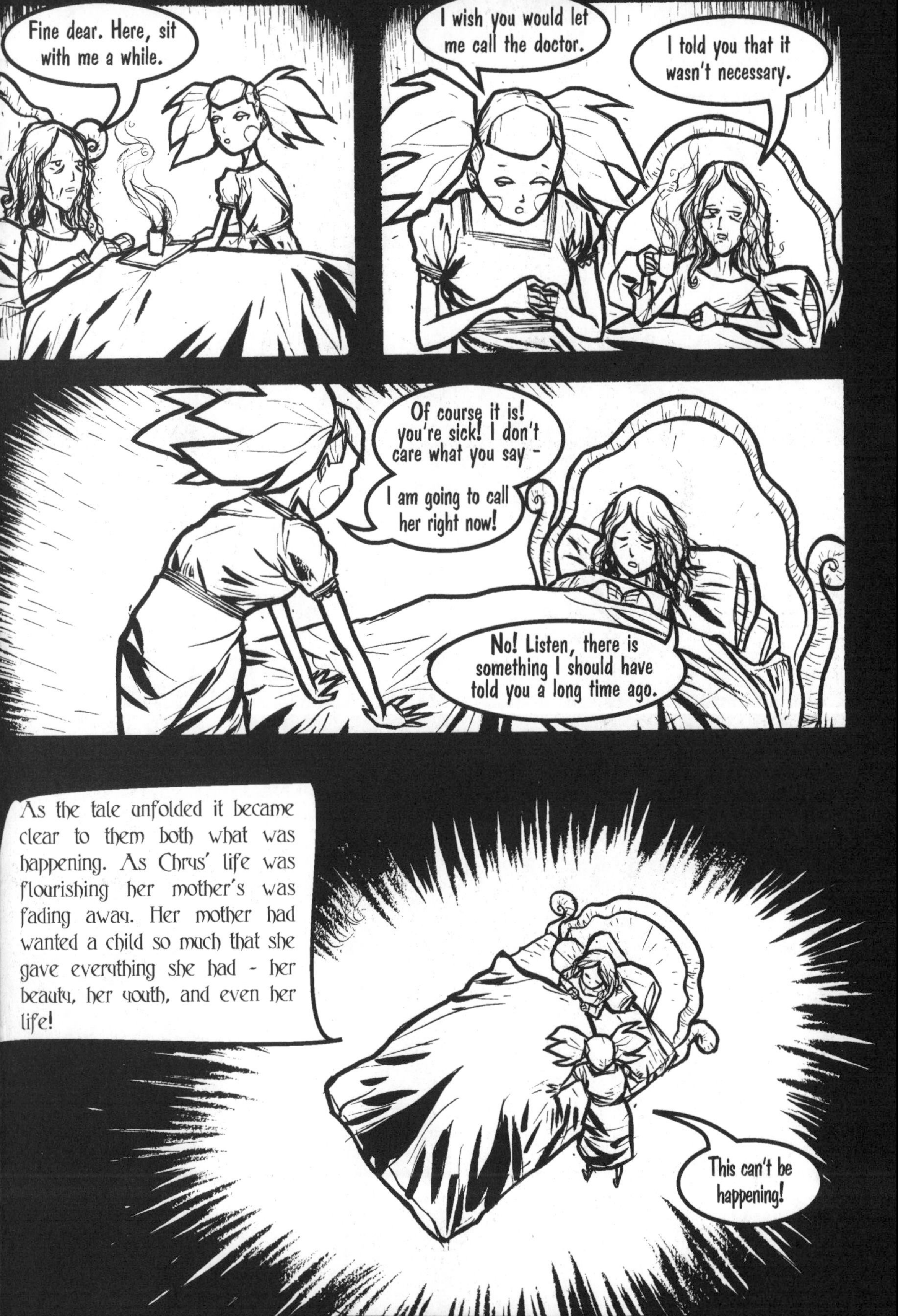

Fine dear. Here, sit with me a while.
I wish you would let me call the doctor.
I told you that it wasn't necessary.
Of course it is! you're sick! I don't care what you say -
I am going to call her right now!
No! Listen, there is something I should have told you a long time ago.
As the tale unfolded it became clear to them both what was happening. As Chrys' life was flourishing her mother's was fading away. Her mother had wanted a child so much that she gave everything she had - her beauty, her youth, and even her life!
This can't be happening!

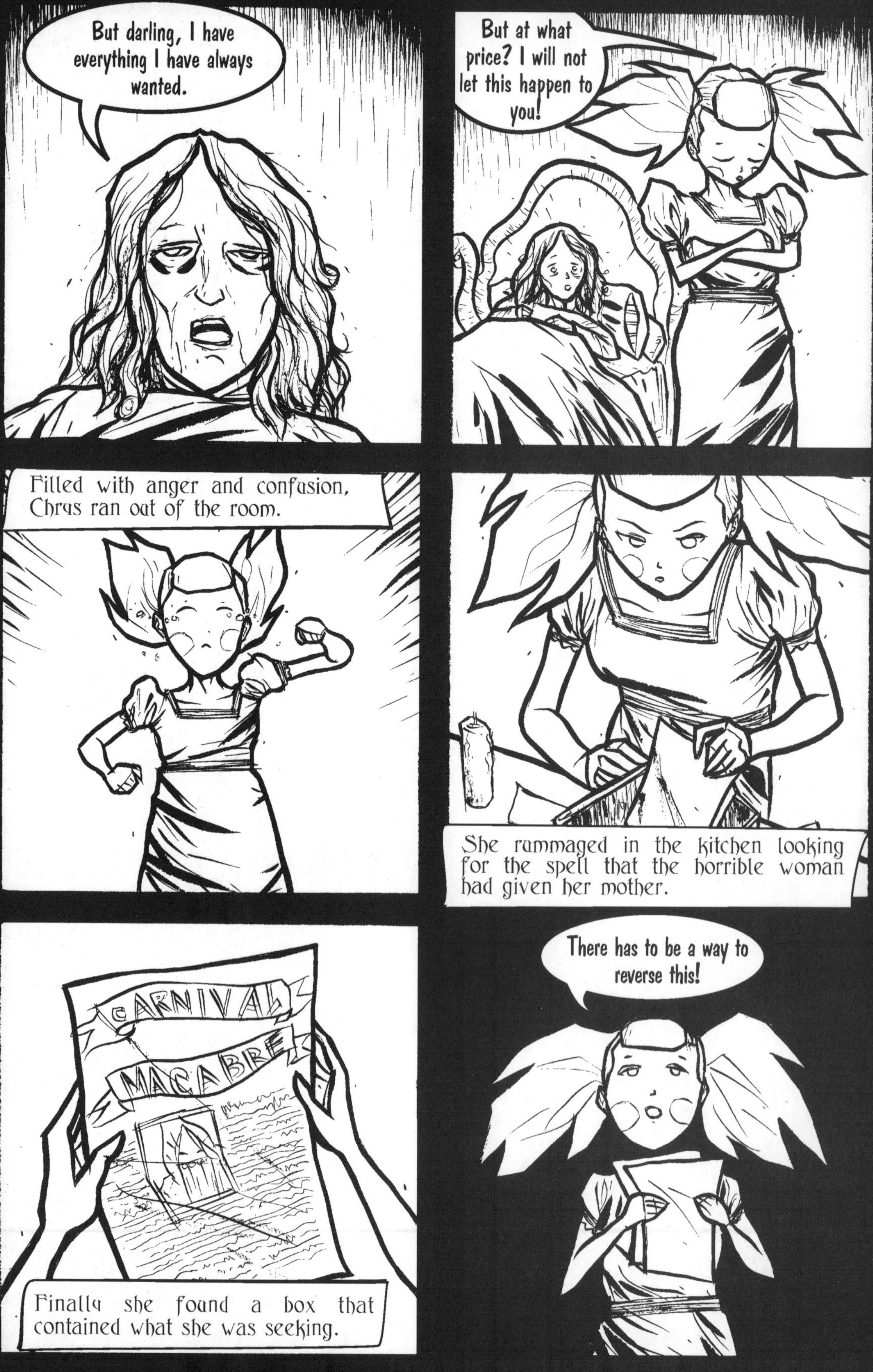
But darling, I have everything I have always wanted.
But at what price? I will not let this happen to you!
Filled with anger and confusion, Chrys ran out of the room.
She rummaged in the kitchen looking for the spell that the horrible woman had given her mother.
CARNIVAL MACABRE
Finally she found a box that contained what she was seeking.
There has to be a way to reverse this!

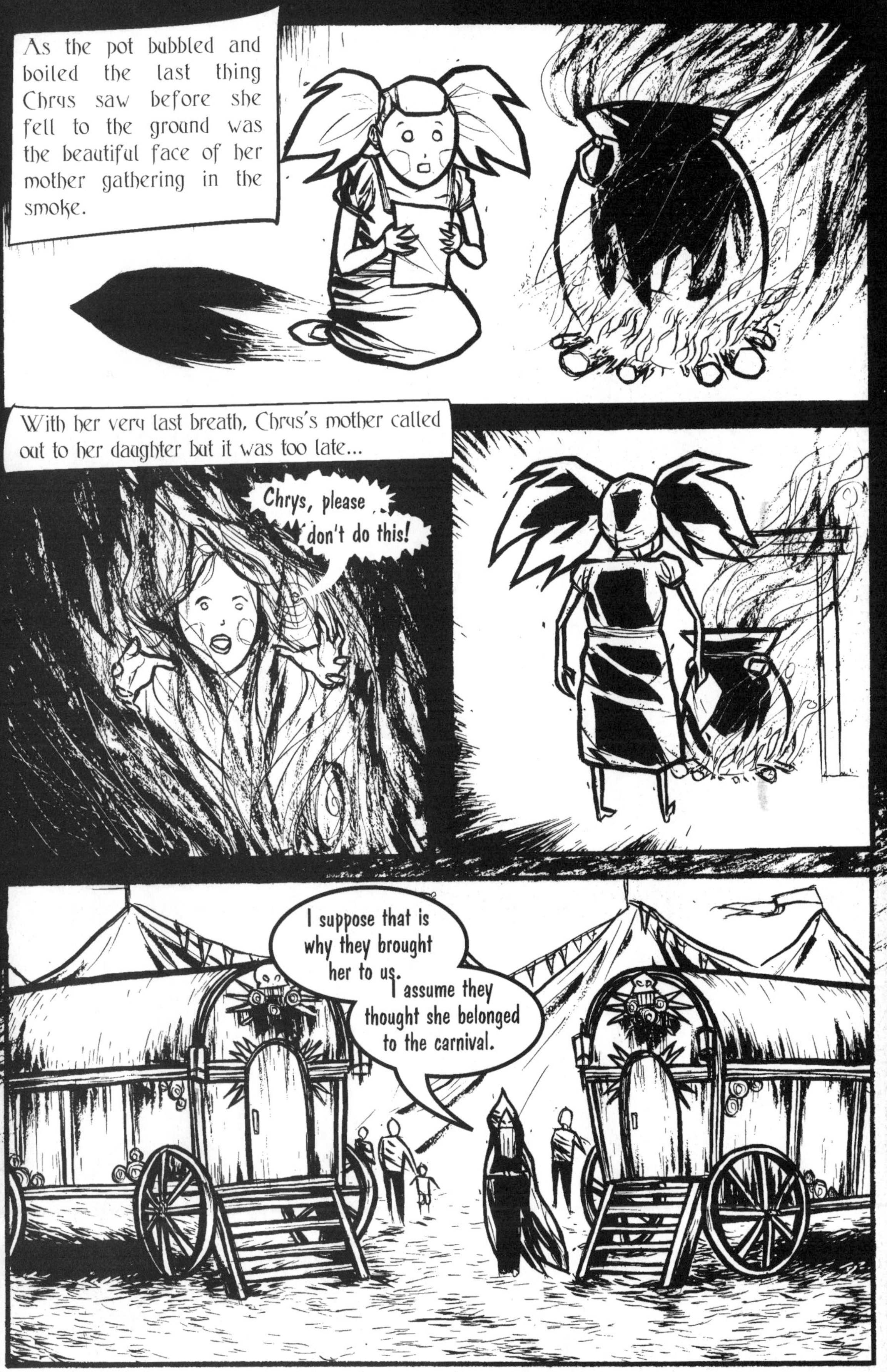

As the pot bubbled and boiled the last thing Chrys saw before she fell to the ground was the beautiful face of her mother gathering in the smoke.
With her very last breath, Chrys's mother called out to her daughter but it was too late...
Chrys, please don't do this!
I suppose that is why they brought her to us.
I assume they thought she belonged to the carnival.

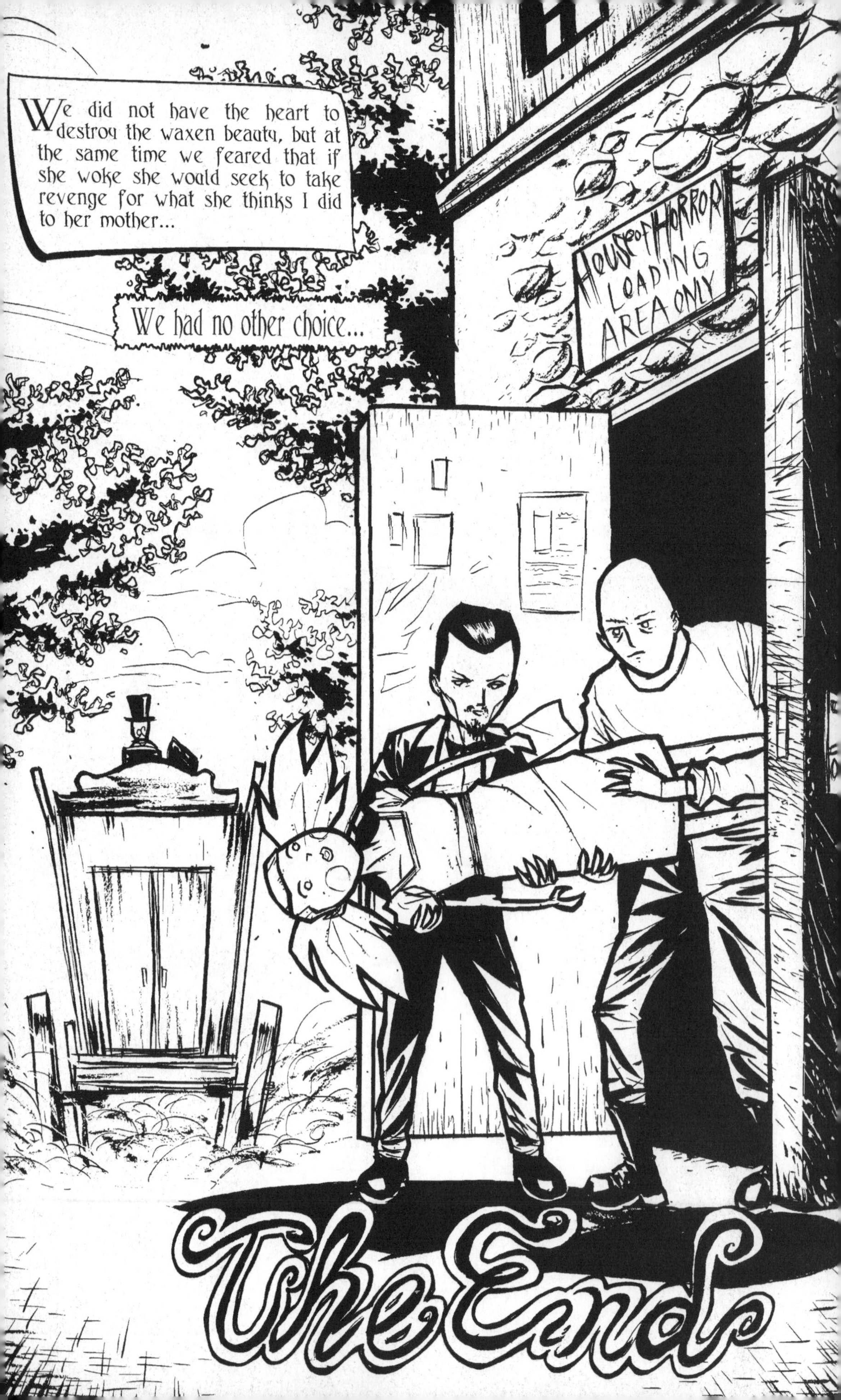

We did not have the heart to destroy the waxen beauty, but at the same time we feared that if she woke she would seek to take revenge for what she thinks I did to her mother...
We had no other choice...
House of Horror
LOADING AREA ONLY
The End

Chapter 10

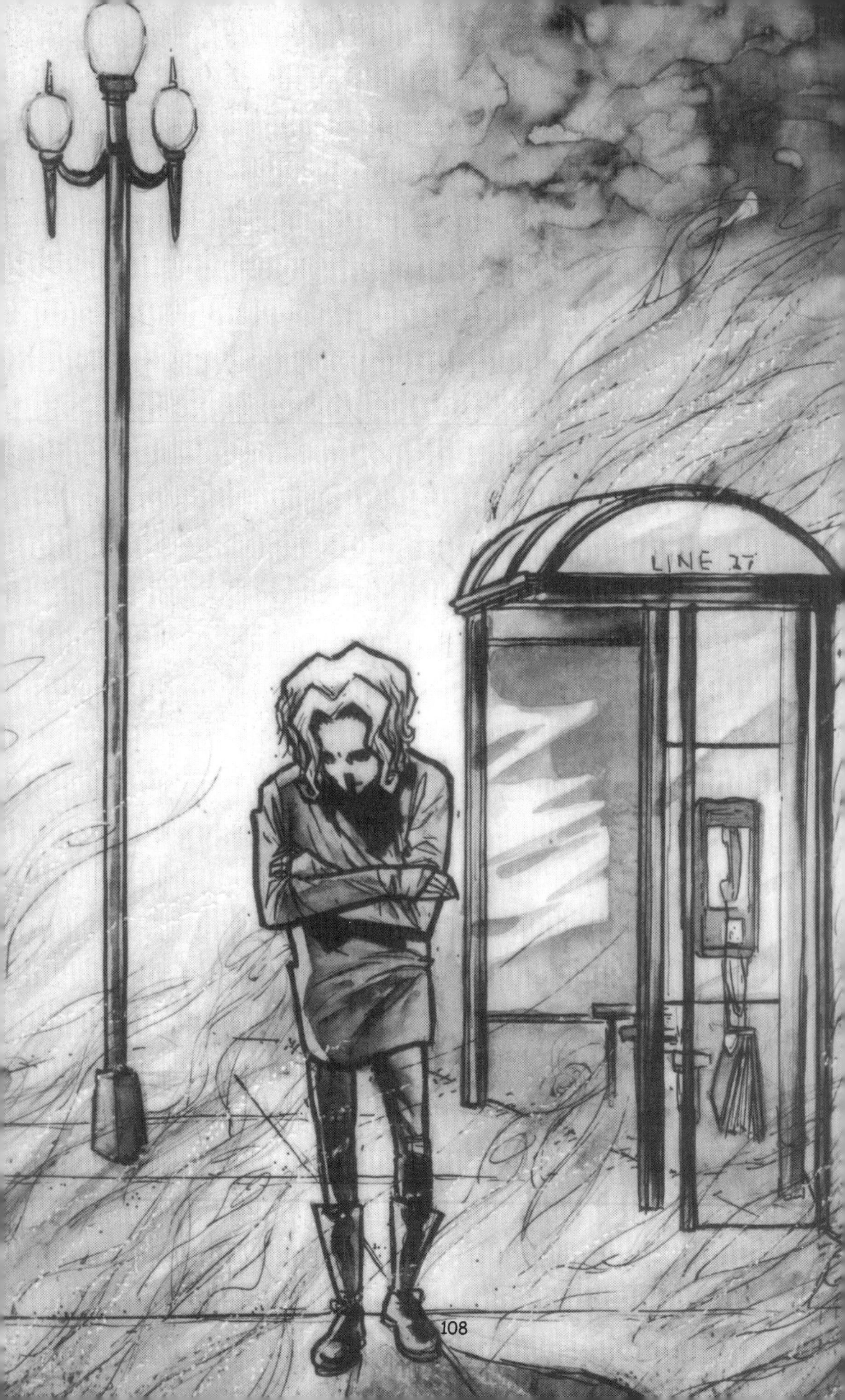
LINE 27

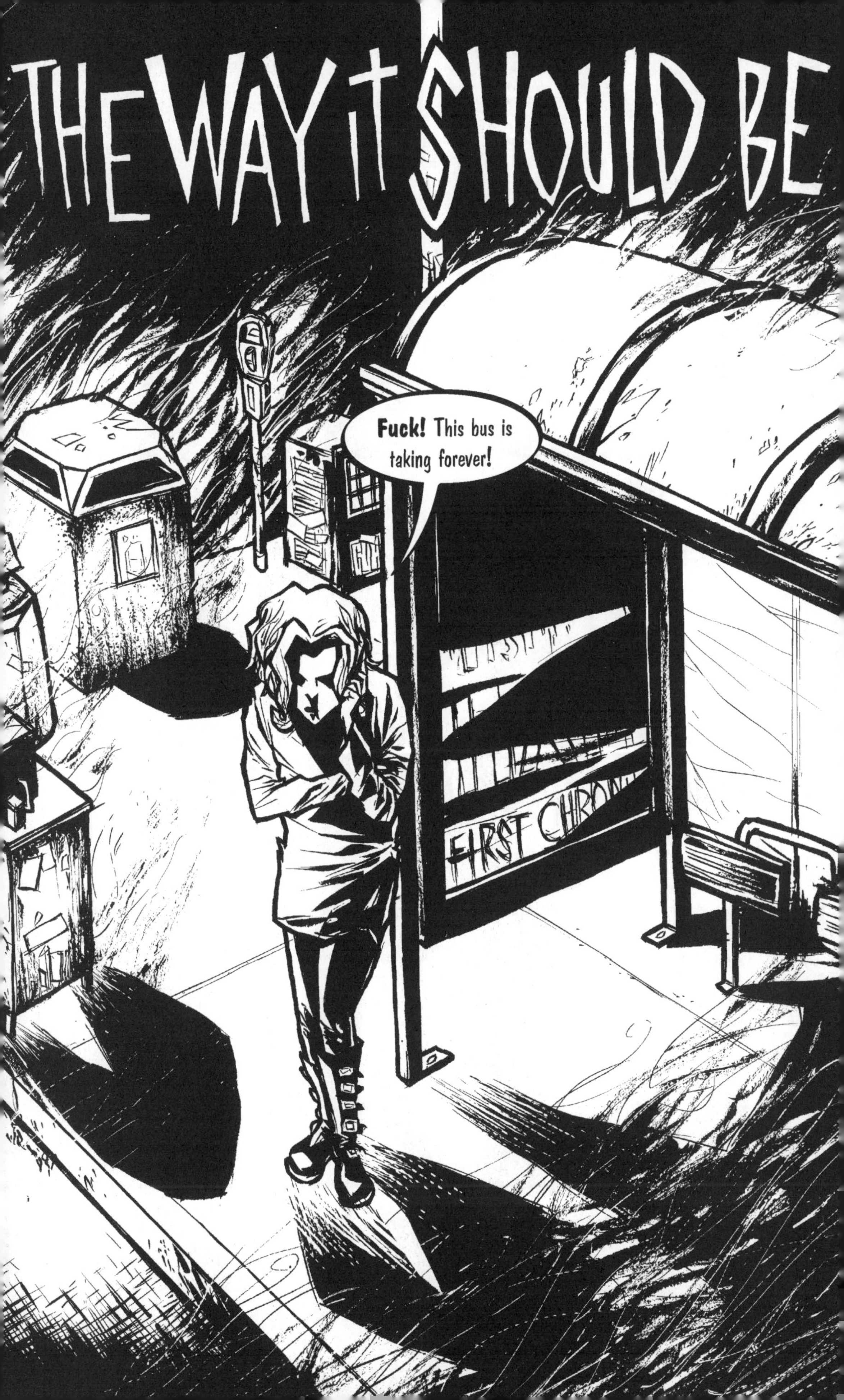
THE WAY IT SHOULD BE
Fuck! This bus is taking forever!

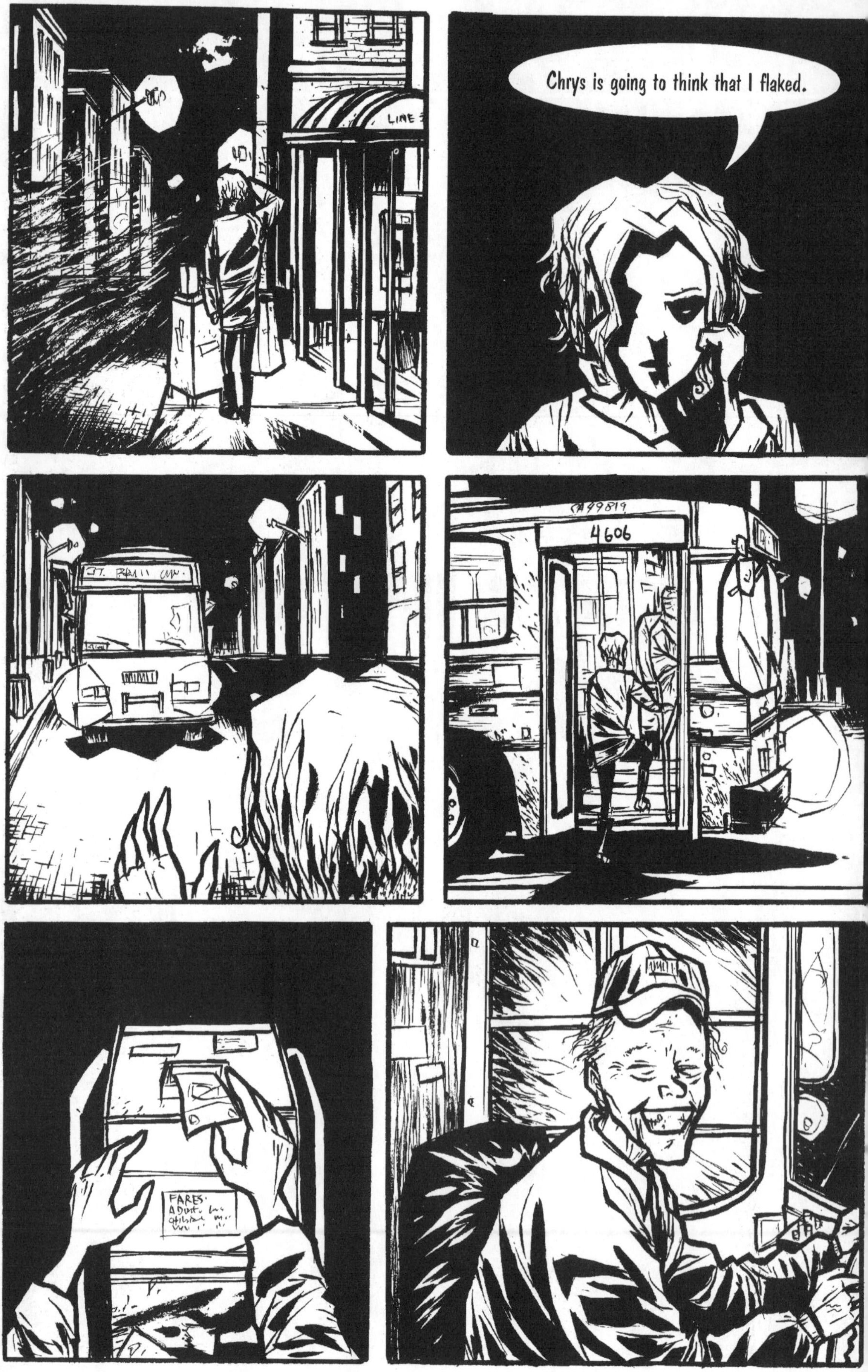
Chrys is going to think that I flaked.

Excuse me?

Yes?

Does this bus go to 3rd and Market?

Going to that club over there?

Yeah.

What kind of club is that? vampire club?

No.

It's just that I see all these freaks dressed up like vampires standing out front smoking. I didn't know vampires smoke!

HA HA HA HA HA HeHAHe HA He HE

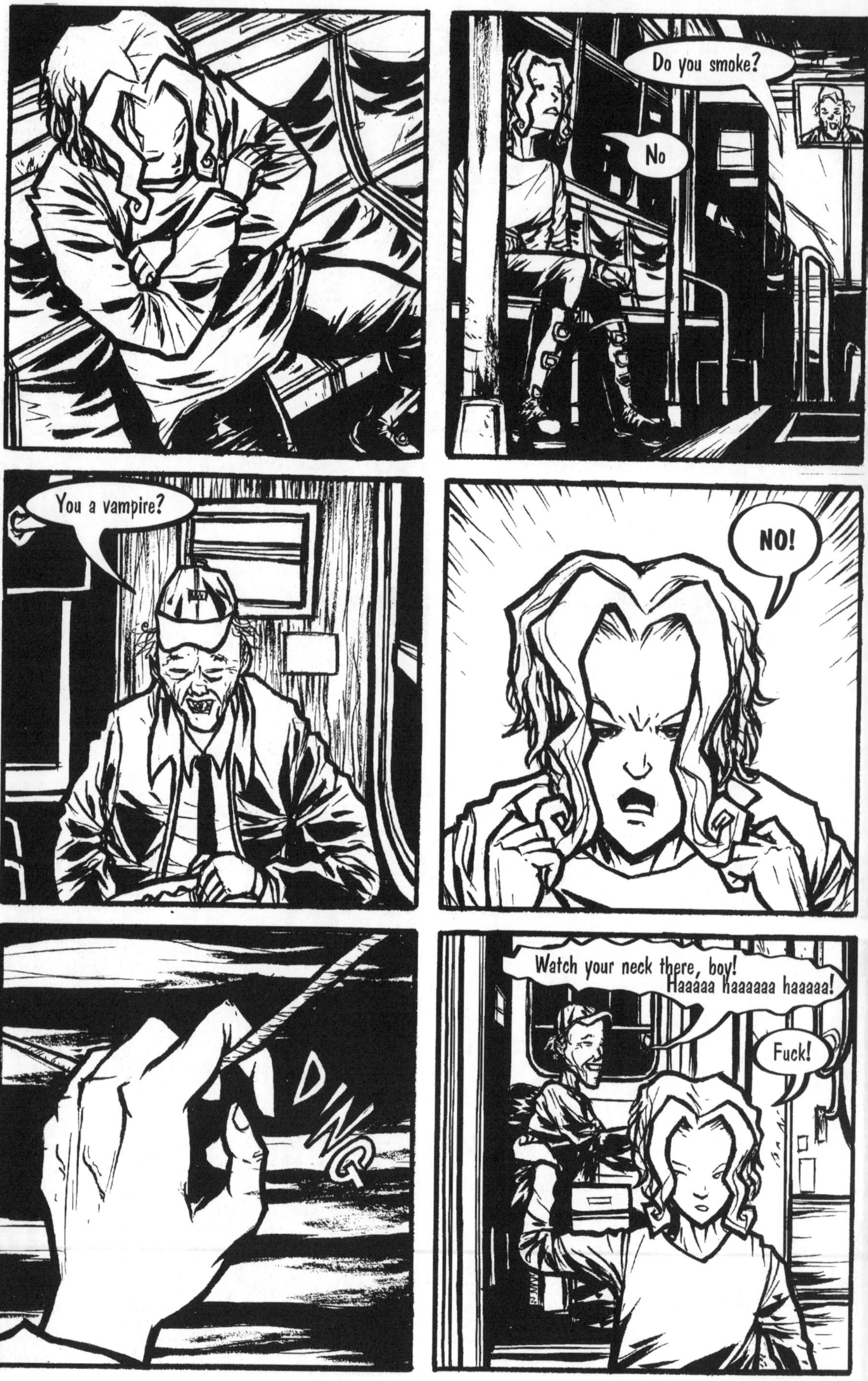
Do you smoke?
No
You a vampire?
NO!
DING
Watch your neck there, boy!
Haaaaa haaaaaa haaaaa!
Fuck!

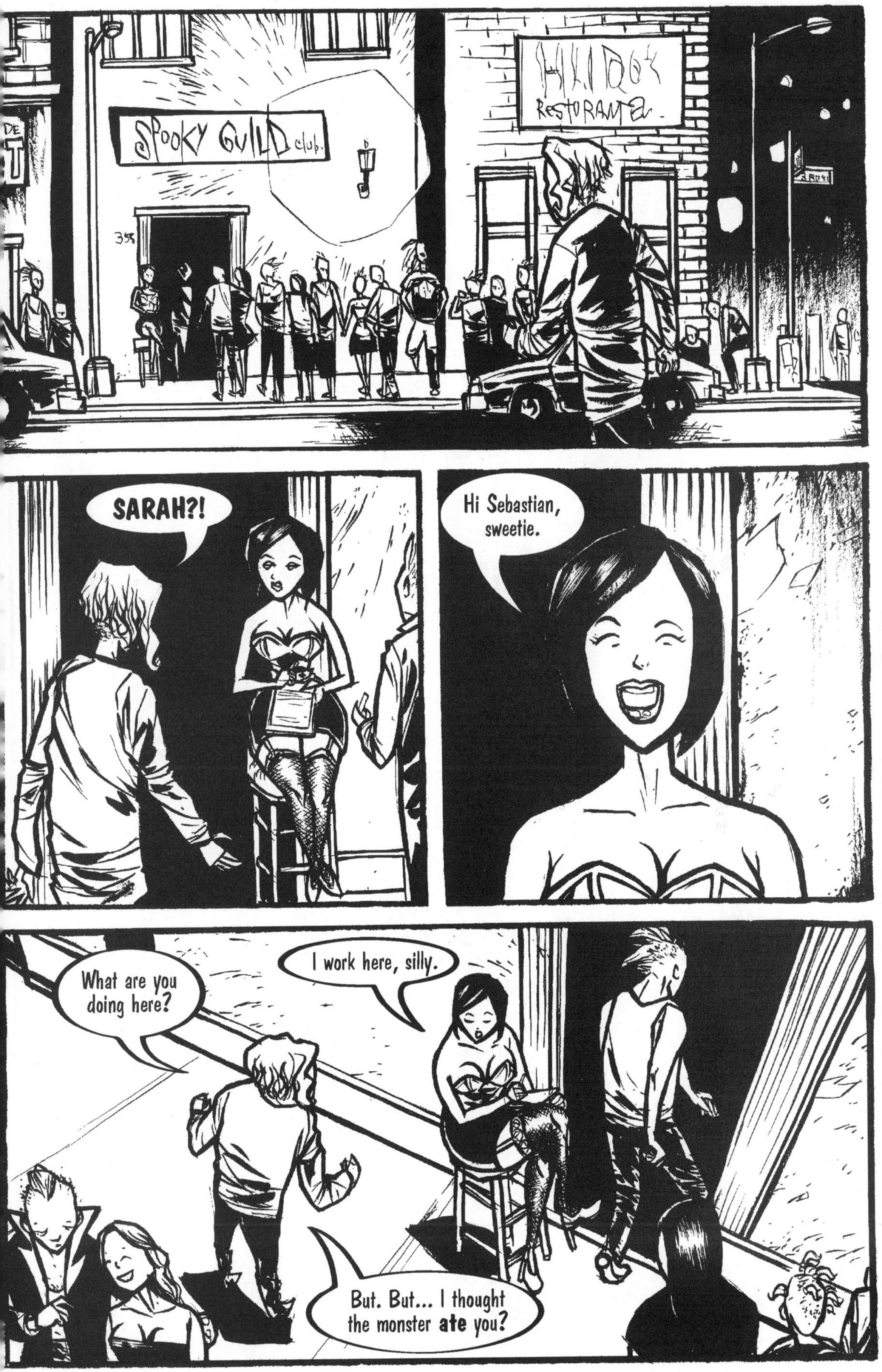
SPOOKY GUILD club.
RESTORANTE
SARAH?!
Hi Sebastian, sweetie.
What are you doing here?
I work here, silly.
But. But... I thought the monster ate you?

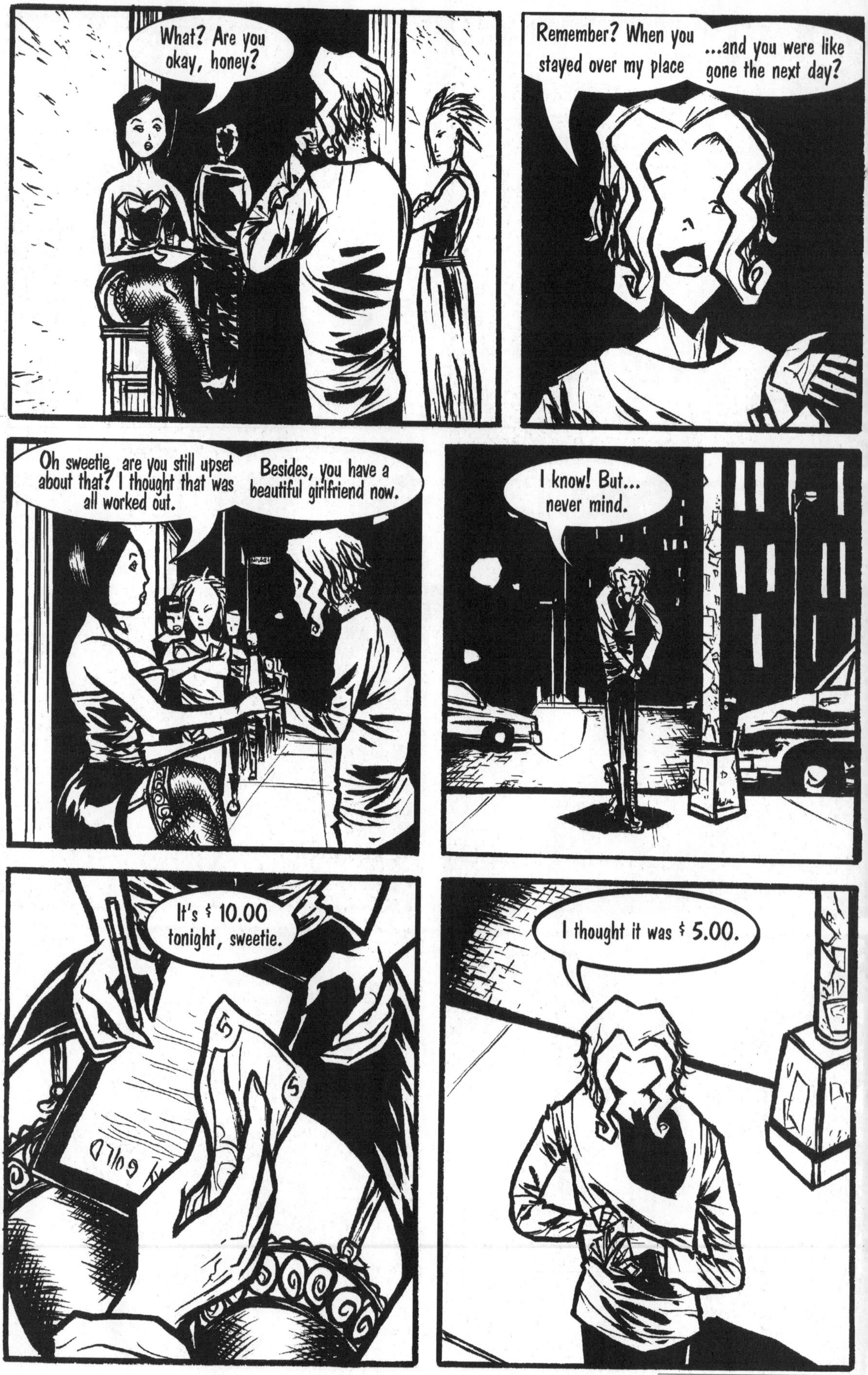
What? Are you okay, honey?
Remember? When you stayed over my place
...and you were like gone the next day?
Oh sweetie, are you still upset about that? I thought that was all worked out.
Besides, you have a beautiful girlfriend now.
I know! But... never mind.
It's $ 10.00 tonight, sweetie.
GOLD
I thought it was $ 5.00.

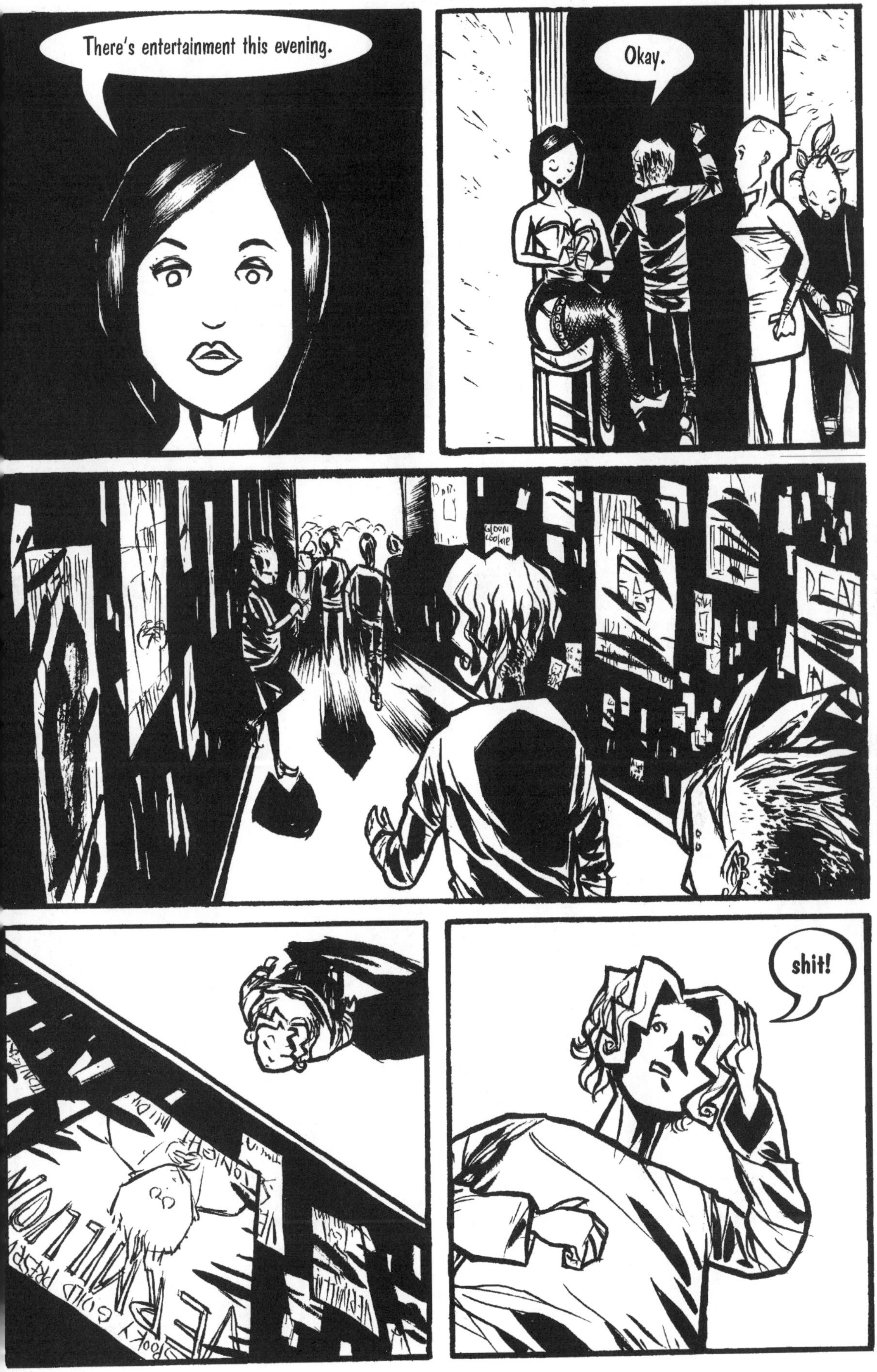
There's entertainment this evening.
Okay.
shit!

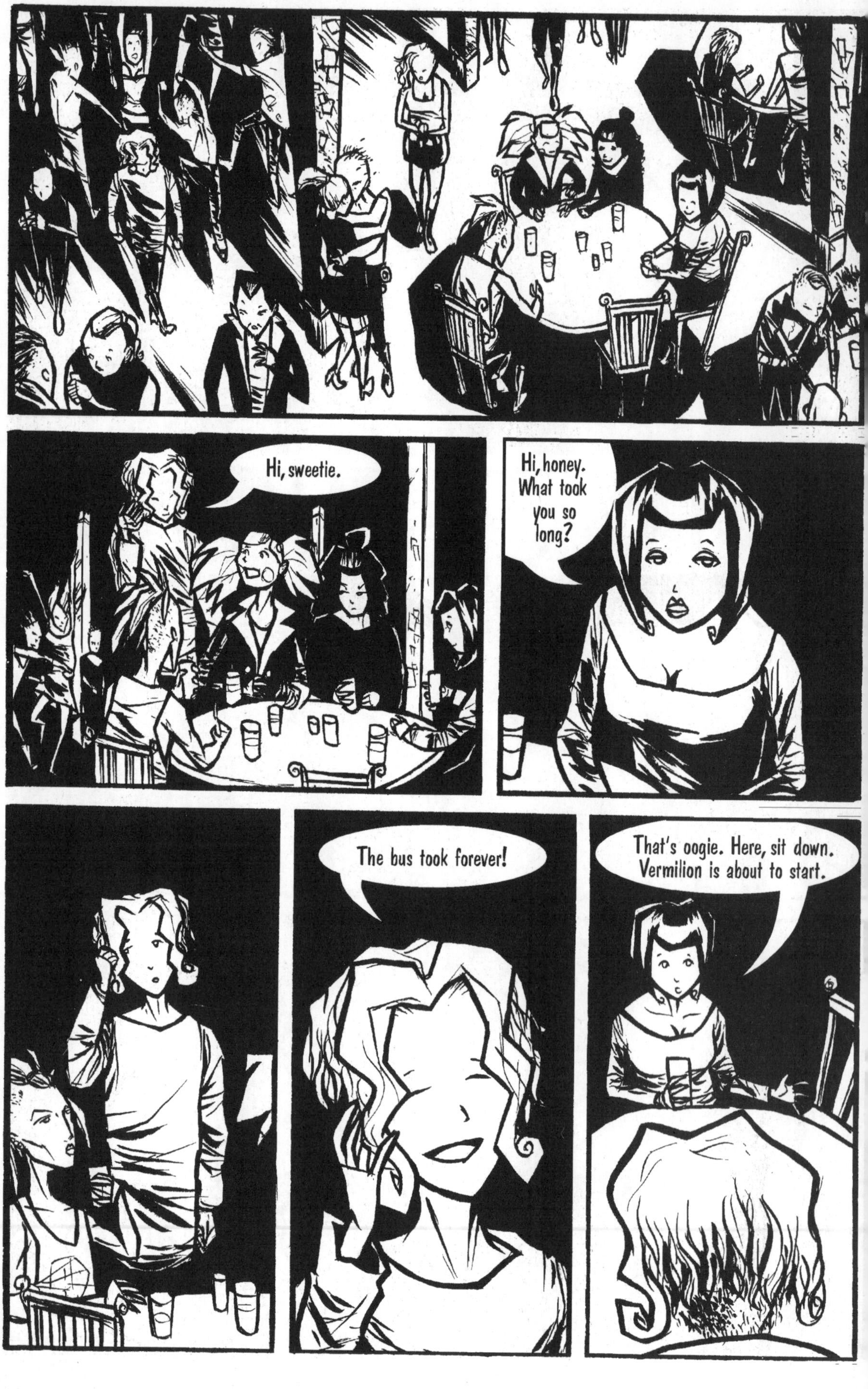
Hi, sweetie.
Hi, honey. What took you so long?
The bus took forever!
That's oogie. Here, sit down. Vermilion is about to start.

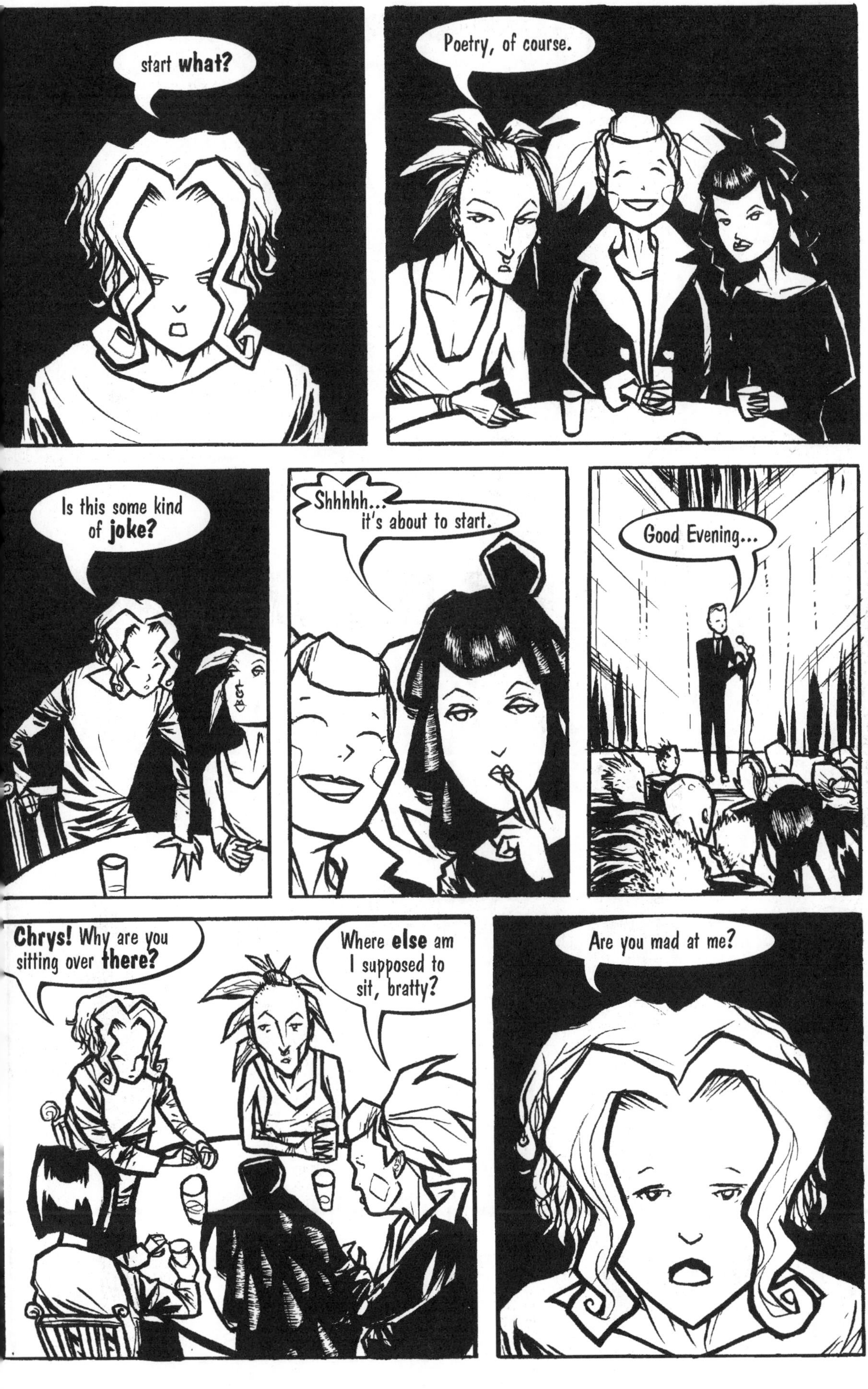
start **what?**
Poetry, of course.
Is this some kind of **joke?**
Shhhhh... it's about to start.
Good Evening...
Chrys! Why are you sitting over **there?**
Where **else** am I supposed to sit, bratty?
Are you mad at me?

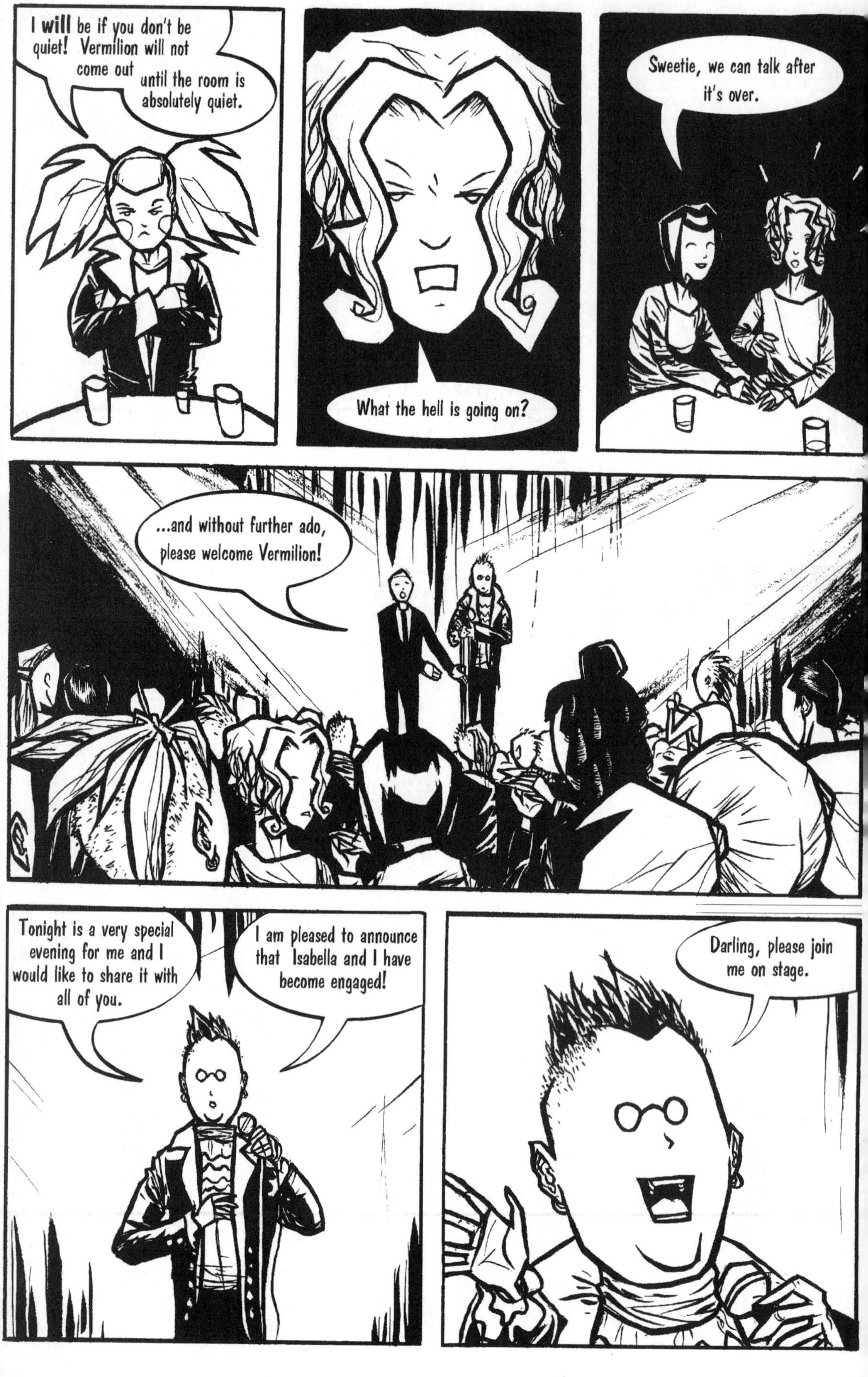

I will be if you don't be quiet! Vermilion will not come out
until the room is absolutely quiet.
What the hell is going on?
Sweetie, we can talk after it's over.
...and without further ado, please welcome Vermilion!
Tonight is a very special evening for me and I would like to share it with all of you.
I am pleased to announce that Isabella and I have become engaged!
Darling, please join me on stage.

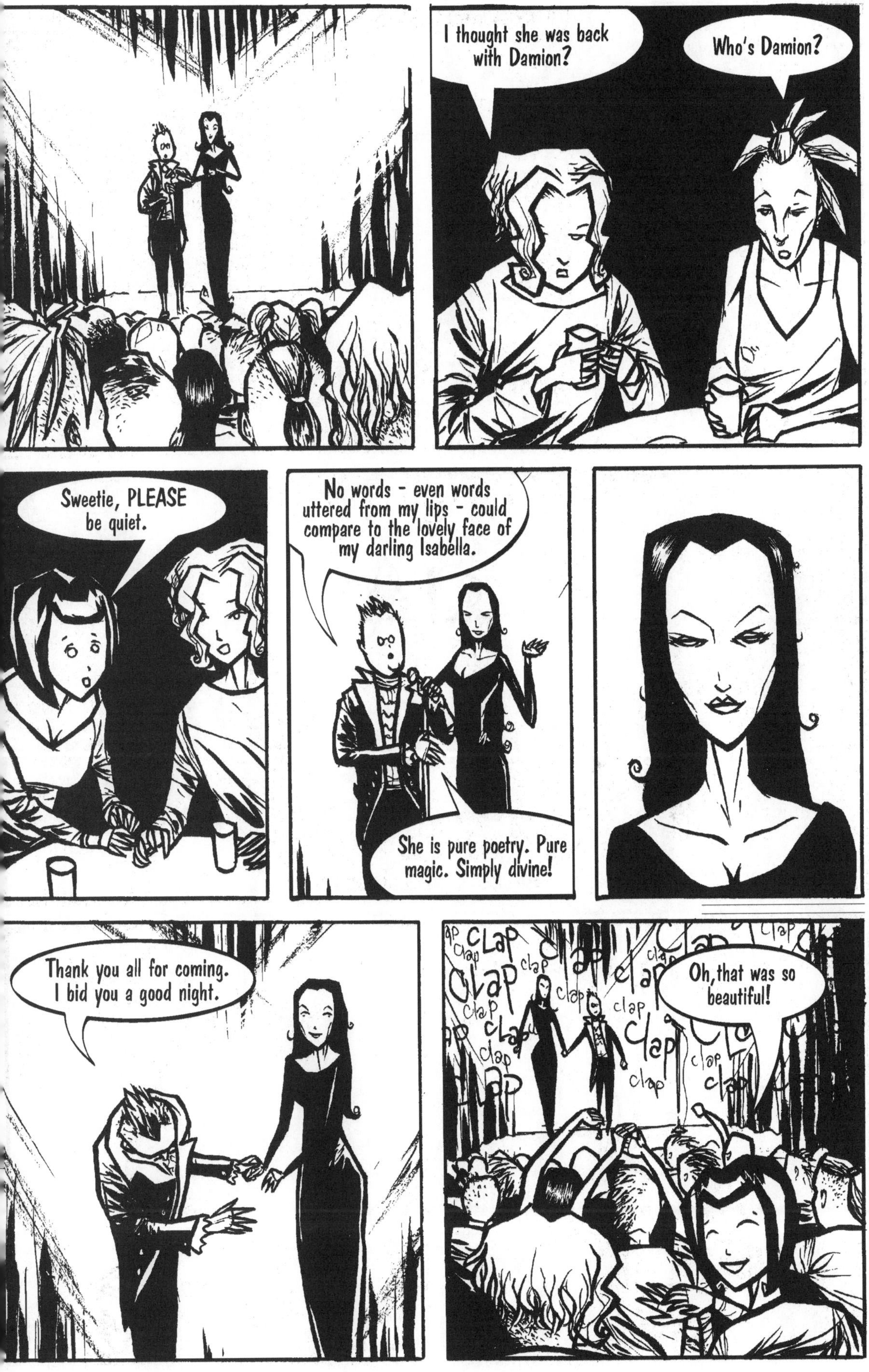
I thought she was back with Damion?
Who's Damion?
Sweetie, PLEASE be quiet.
No words - even words uttered from my lips - could compare to the lovely face of my darling Isabella.
She is pure poetry. Pure magic. Simply divine!
Thank you all for coming. I bid you a good night.
clap clap clap clap clap clap clap clap clap clap clap clap clap
Oh, that was so beautiful!

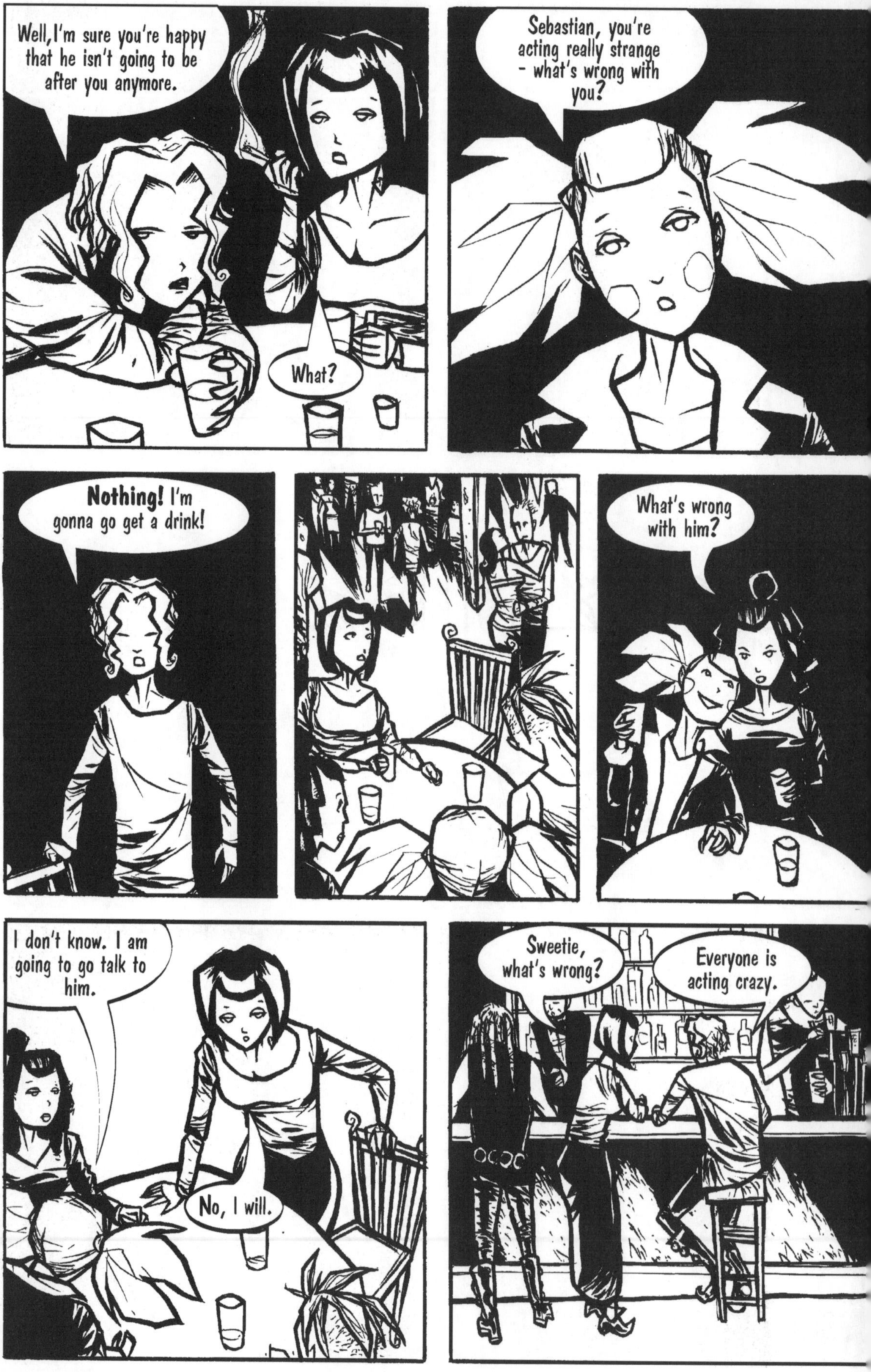
Well, I'm sure you're happy that he isn't going to be after you anymore.
What?
Sebastian, you're acting really strange - what's wrong with you?
Nothing! I'm gonna go get a drink!
What's wrong with him?
I don't know. I am going to go talk to him.
No, I will.
Sweetie, what's wrong?
Everyone is acting crazy.

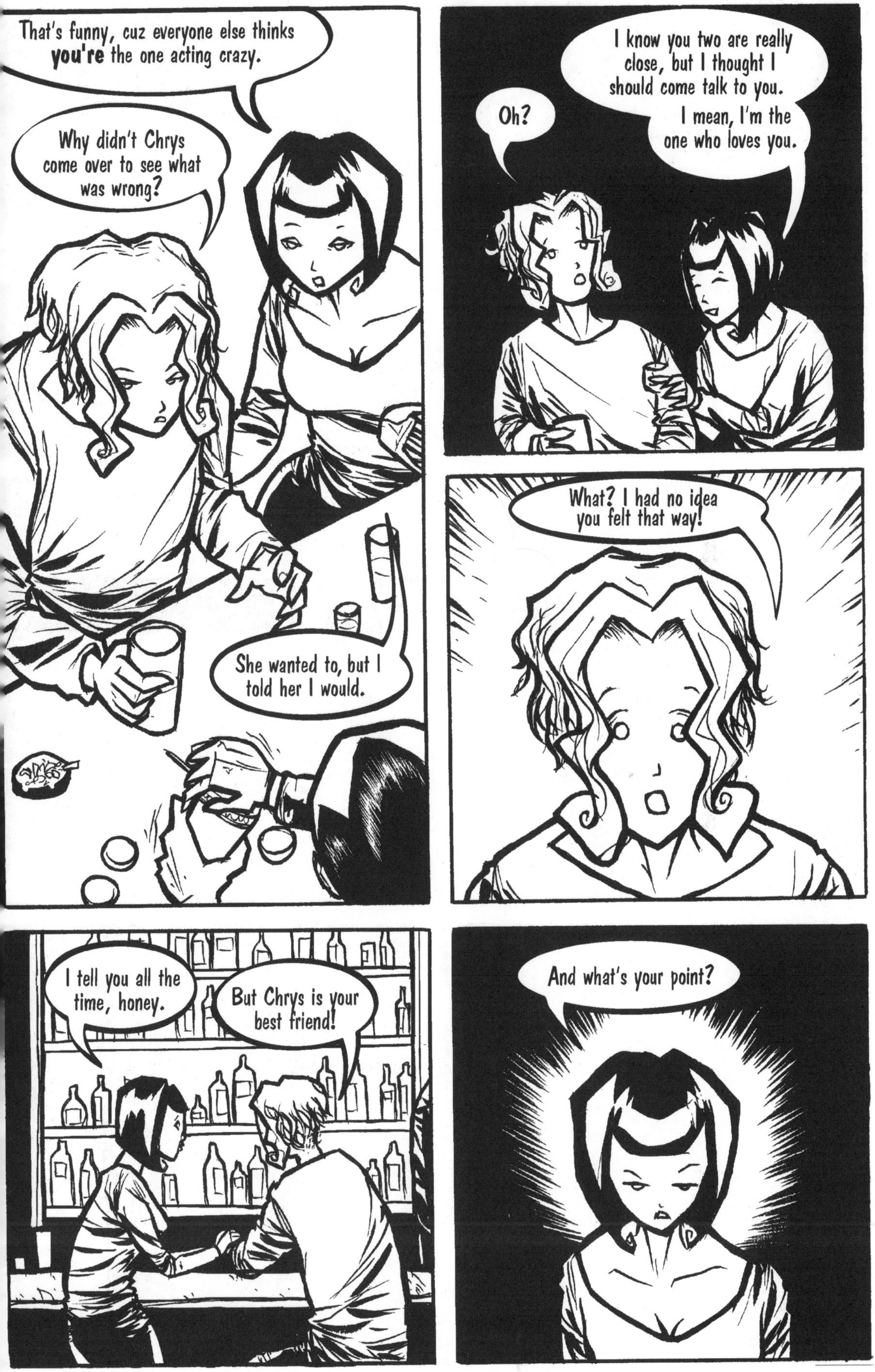
That's funny, cuz everyone else thinks **you're** the one acting crazy.
Why didn't Chrys come over to see what was wrong?
She wanted to, but I told her I would.
I know you two are really close, but I thought I should come talk to you.
Oh?
I mean, I'm the one who loves you.
What? I had no idea you felt that way!
I tell you all the time, honey.
But Chrys is your best friend!
And what's your point?

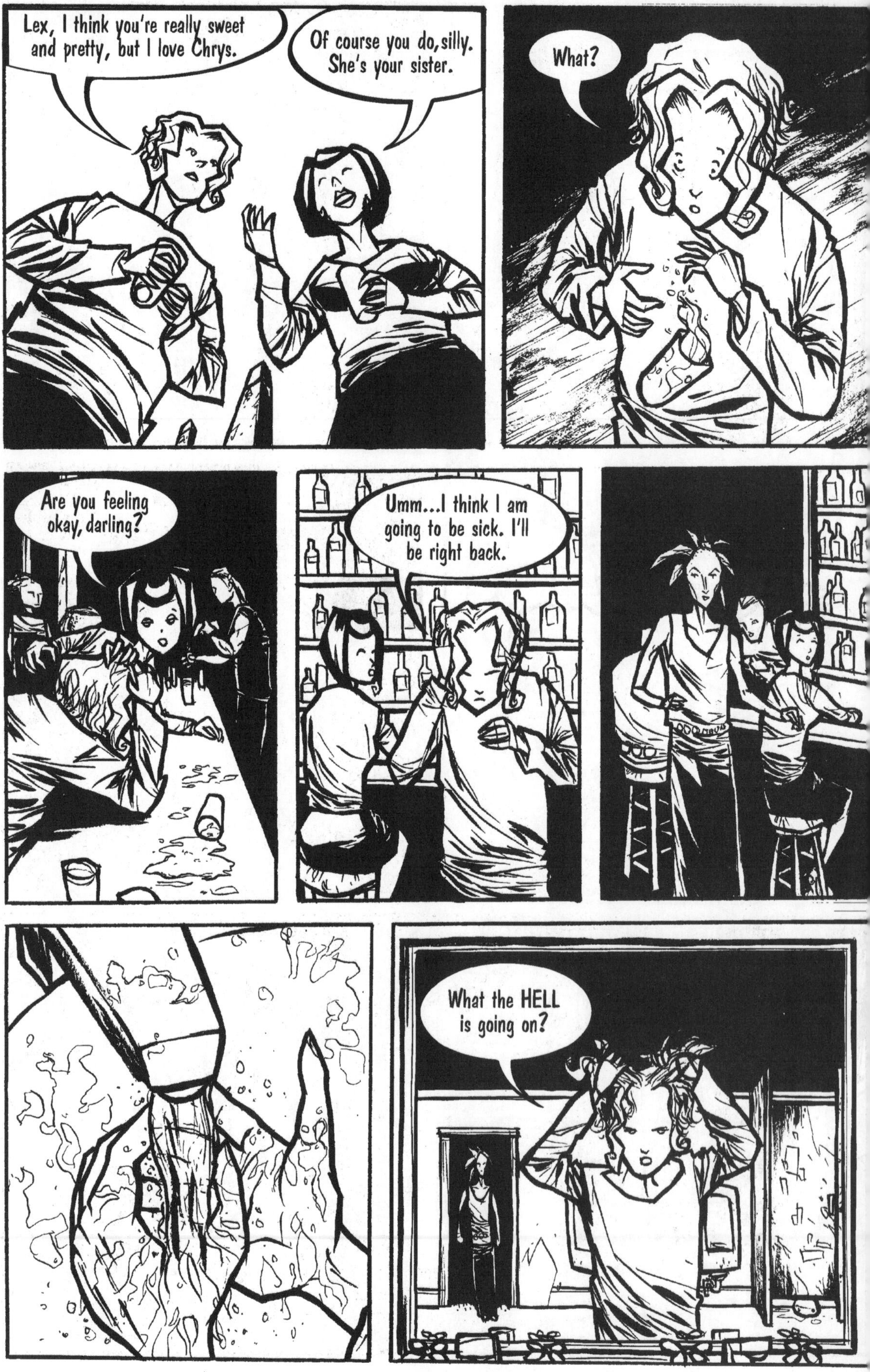
Lex, I think you're really sweet and pretty, but I love Chrys.
Of course you do, silly. She's your sister.
What?
Are you feeling okay, darling?
Umm...I think I am going to be sick. I'll be right back.
What the HELL is going on?

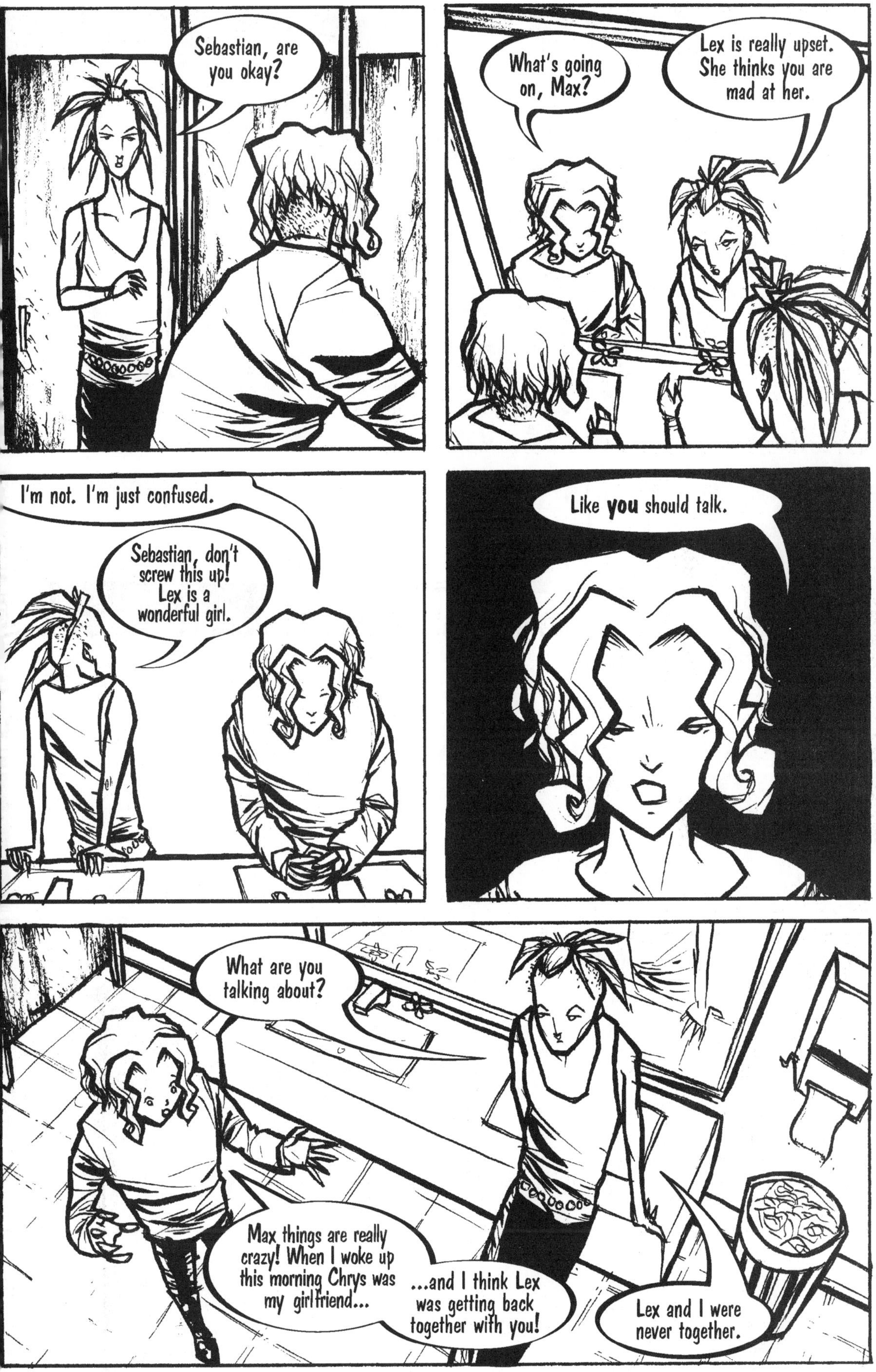
Sebastian, are you okay?
What's going on, Max?
Lex is really upset. She thinks you are mad at her.
I'm not. I'm just confused.
Sebastian, don't screw this up! Lex is a wonderful girl.
Like **you** should talk.
What are you talking about?
Max things are really crazy! When I woke up this morning Chrys was my girlfriend...
...and I think Lex was getting back together with you!
Lex and I were never together.

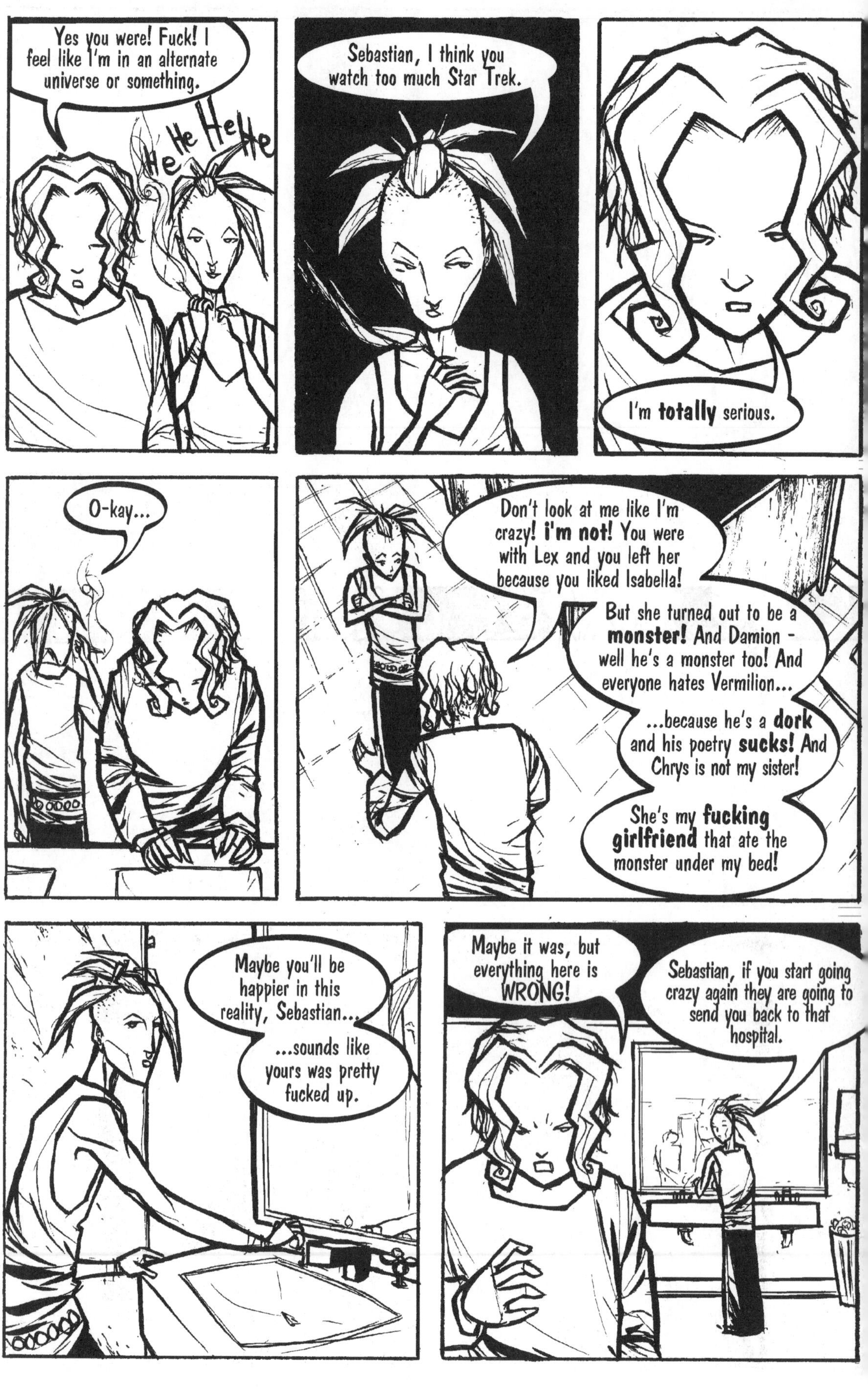
Yes you were! Fuck! I feel like I'm in an alternate universe or something.
He He He He He
Sebastian, I think you watch too much Star Trek.
I'm **totally** serious.
O-kay...
Don't look at me like I'm crazy! **i'm not!** You were with Lex and you left her because you liked Isabella!
But she turned out to be a **monster!** And Damion - well he's a monster too! And everyone hates Vermilion...
...because he's a **dork** and his poetry **sucks!** And Chrys is not my sister!
She's my **fucking girlfriend** that ate the monster under my bed!
Maybe you'll be happier in this reality, Sebastian...
...sounds like yours was pretty fucked up.
Maybe it was, but everything here is WRONG!
Sebastian, if you start going crazy again they are going to send you back to that hospital.

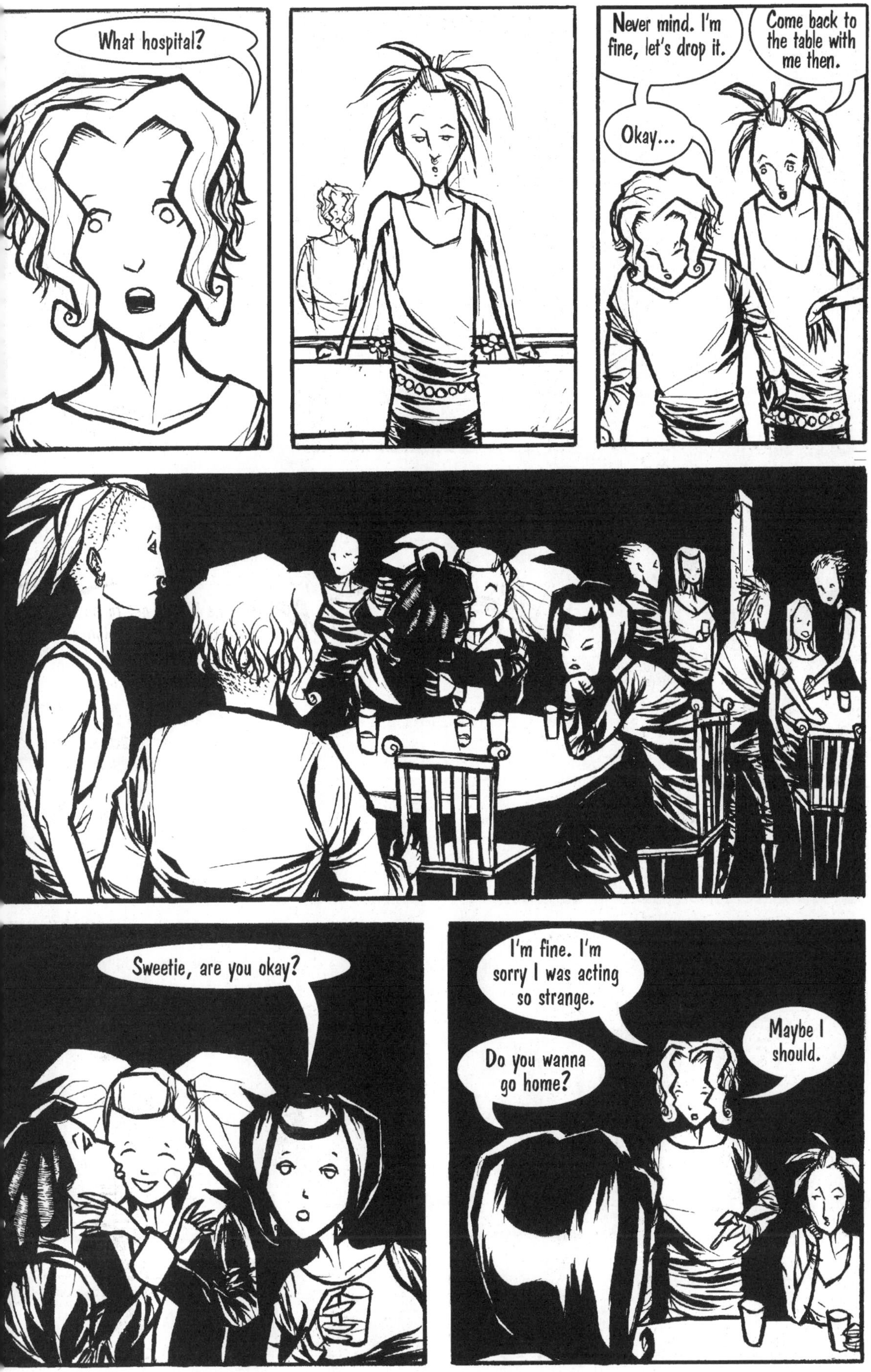

What hospital?
Never mind. I'm fine, let's drop it.
Come back to the table with me then.
Okay...
Sweetie, are you okay?
I'm fine. I'm sorry I was acting so strange.
Do you wanna go home?
Maybe I should.

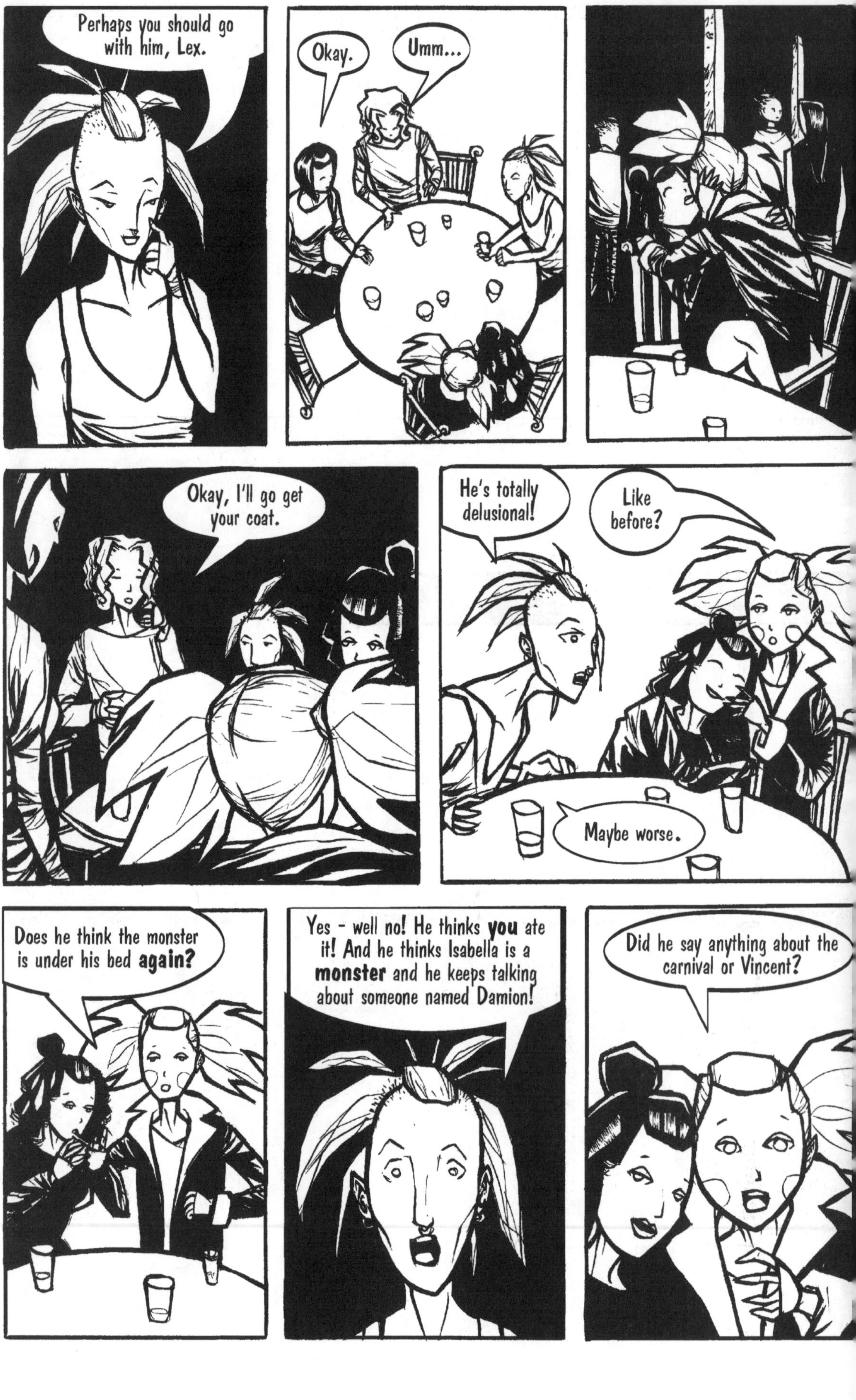
Perhaps you should go with him, Lex.
Okay.
Umm...
Okay, I'll go get your coat.
He's totally delusional!
Like before?
Maybe worse.
Does he think the monster is under his bed again?
Yes - well no! He thinks you ate it! And he thinks Isabella is a monster and he keeps talking about someone named Damion!
Did he say anything about the carnival or Vincent?

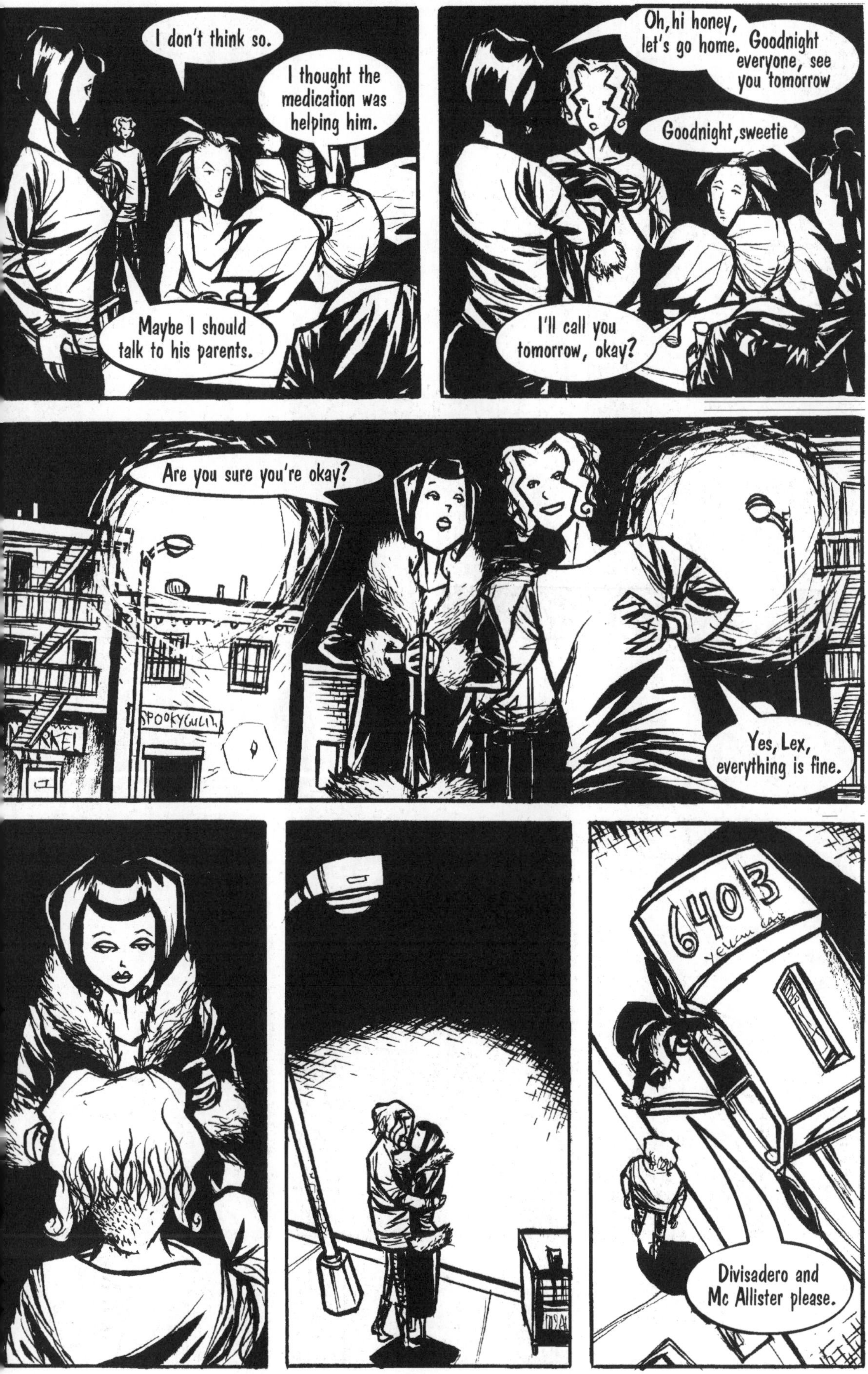

I don't think so.
I thought the medication was helping him.
Maybe I should talk to his parents.
Oh, hi honey, let's go home.
Goodnight everyone, see you tomorrow
Goodnight, sweetie
I'll call you tomorrow, okay?
Are you sure you're okay?
SPOOKYGULCH
Yes, Lex, everything is fine.
6403
Divisadero and Mc Allister please.

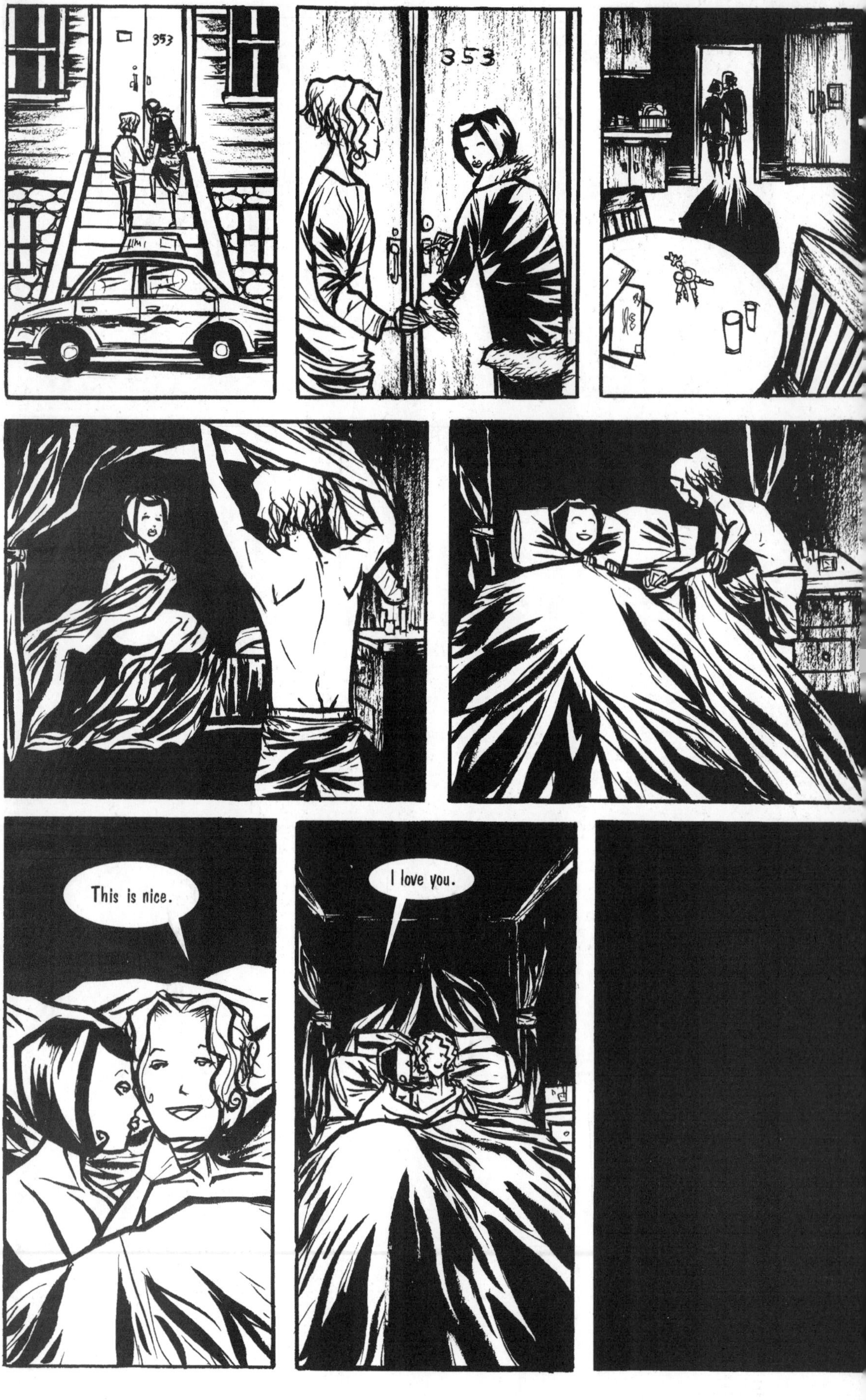
353
353
This is nice.
I love you.

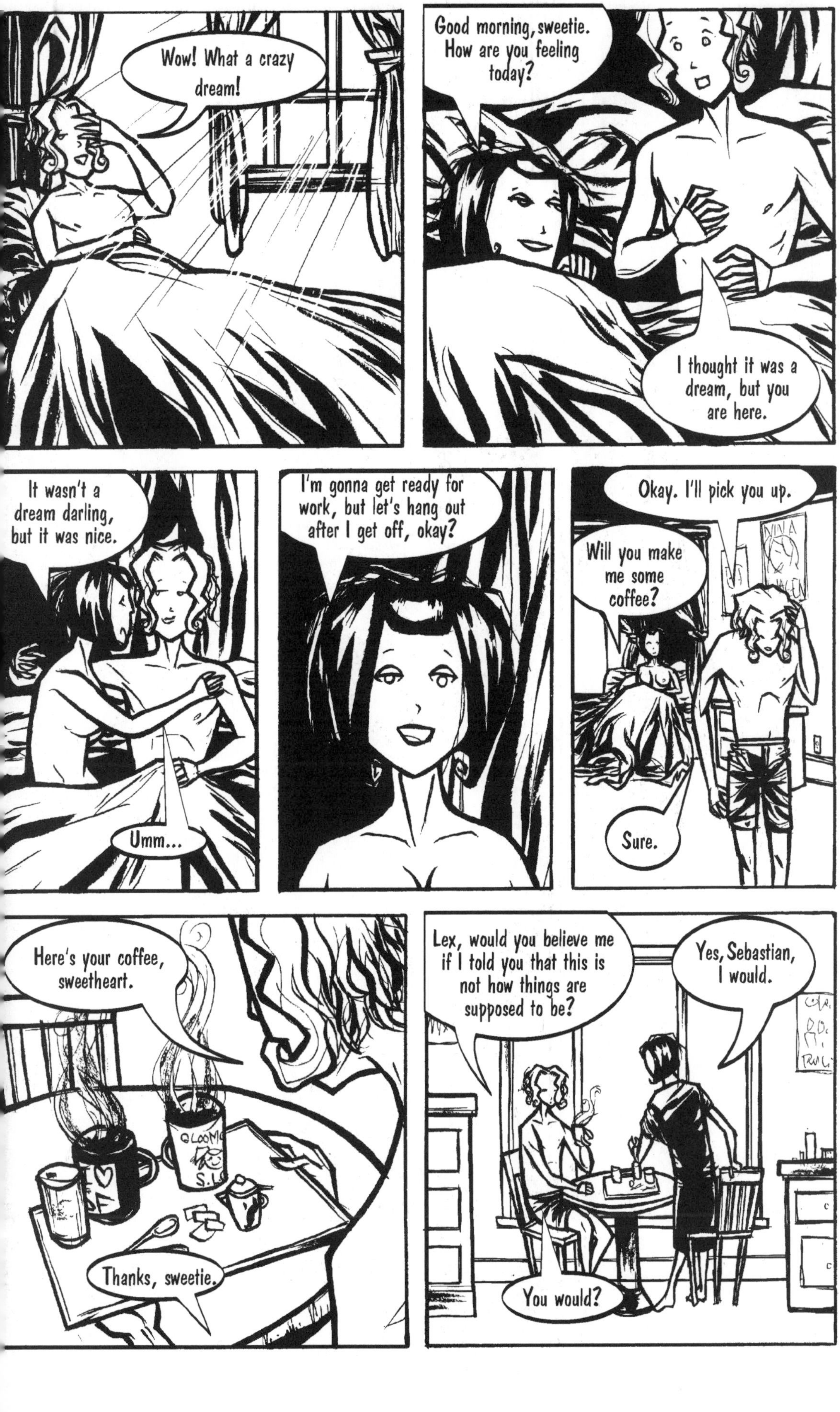
Wow! What a crazy dream!
Good morning, sweetie. How are you feeling today?
I thought it was a dream, but you are here.
It wasn't a dream darling, but it was nice.
Umm...
I'm gonna get ready for work, but let's hang out after I get off, okay?
Okay. I'll pick you up.
Will you make me some coffee?
Sure.
Here's your coffee, sweetheart.
Thanks, sweetie.
Lex, would you believe me if I told you that this is not how things are supposed to be?
Yes, Sebastian, I would.
You would?

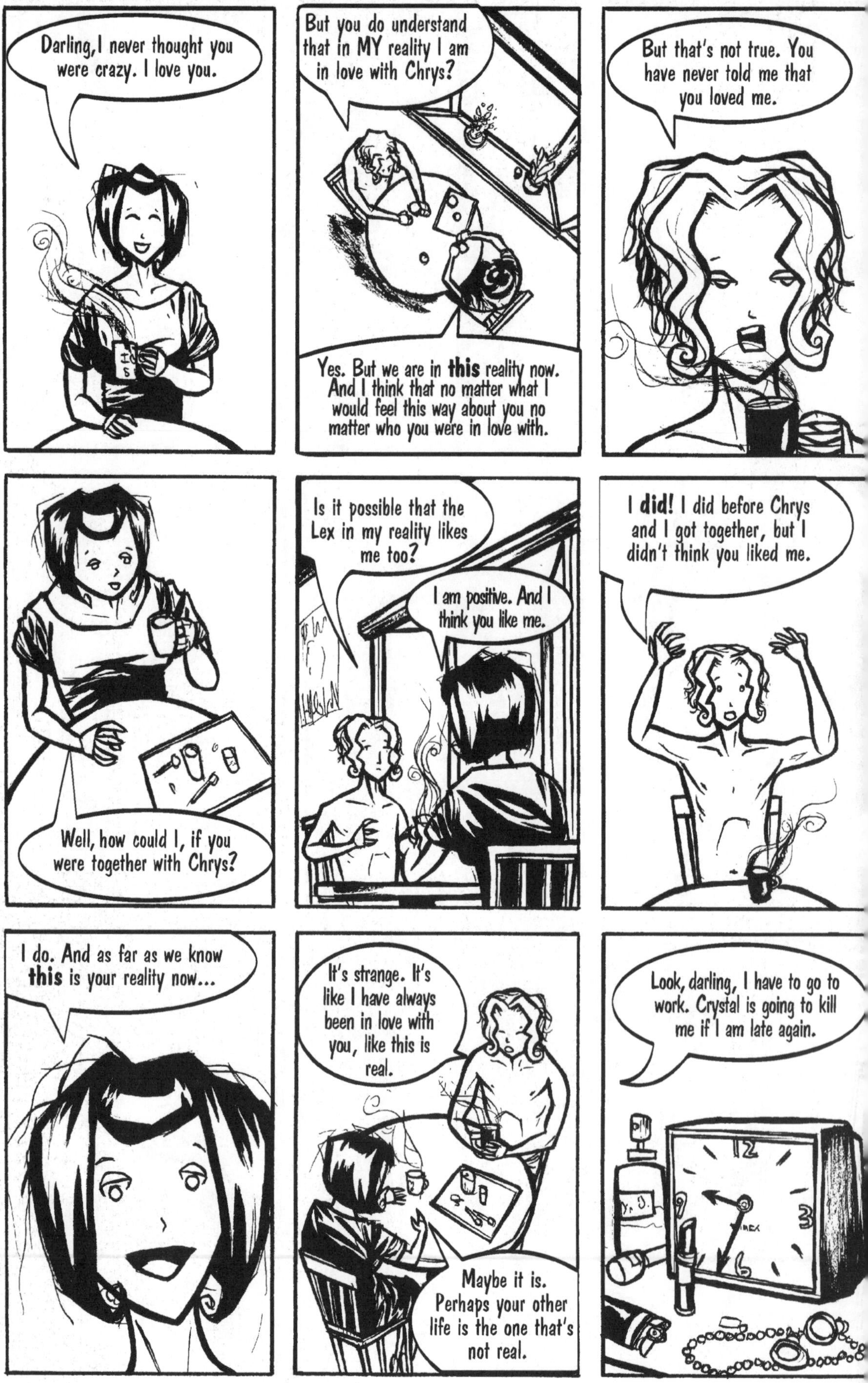

Darling, I never thought you were crazy. I love you.
But you do understand that in MY reality I am in love with Chrys?
Yes. But we are in **this** reality now. And I think that no matter what I would feel this way about you no matter who you were in love with.
But that's not true. You have never told me that you loved me.
Well, how could I, if you were together with Chrys?
Is it possible that the Lex in my reality likes me too?
I am positive. And I think you like me.
I **did!** I did before Chrys and I got together, but I didn't think you liked me.
I do. And as far as we know **this** is your reality now...
It's strange. It's like I have always been in love with you, like this is real.
Maybe it is. Perhaps your other life is the one that's not real.
Look, darling, I have to go to work. Crystal is going to kill me if I am late again.

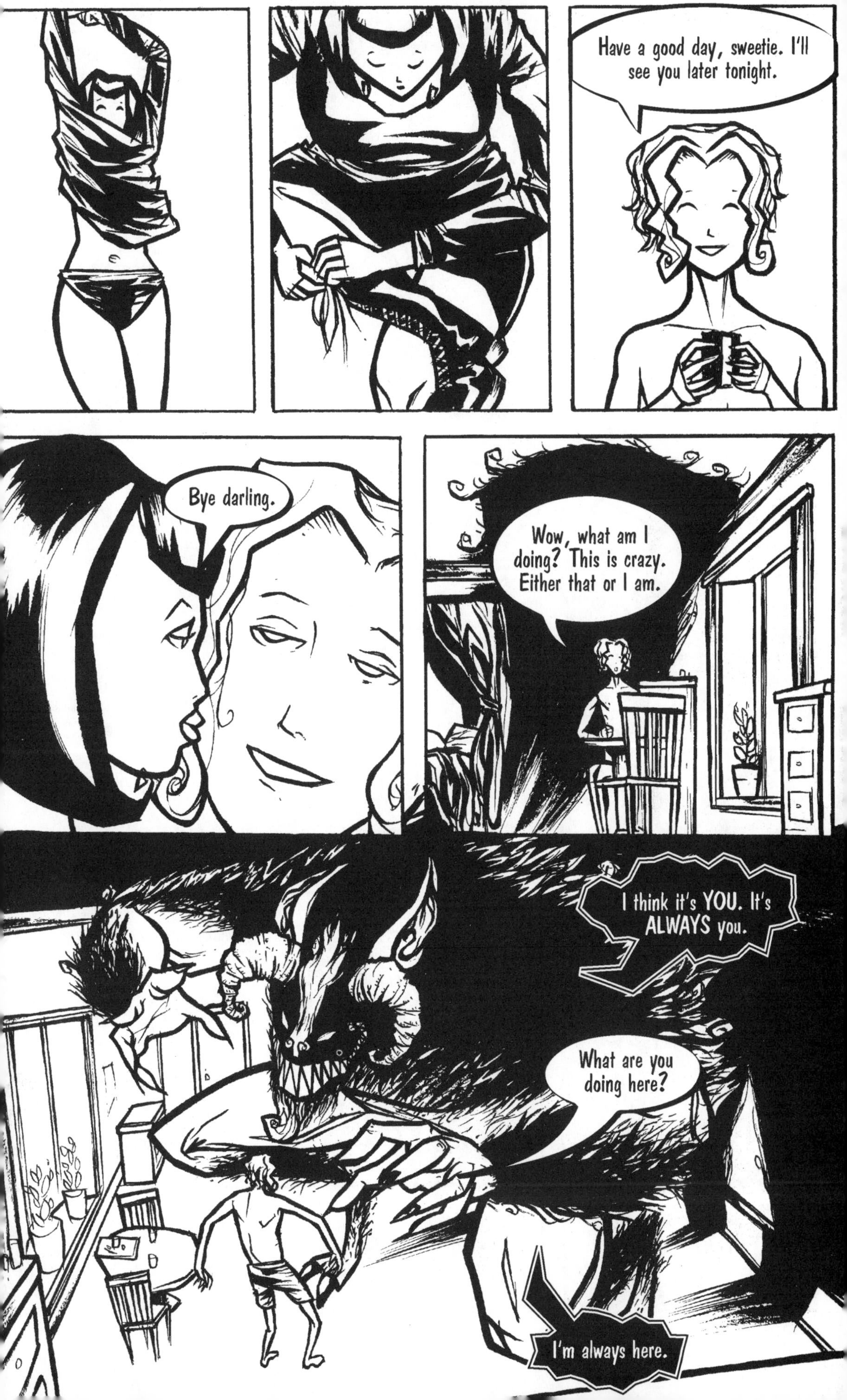
Have a good day, sweetie. I'll see you later tonight.
Bye darling.
Wow, what am I doing? This is crazy. Either that or I am.
I think it's YOU. It's ALWAYS you.
What are you doing here?
I'm always here.

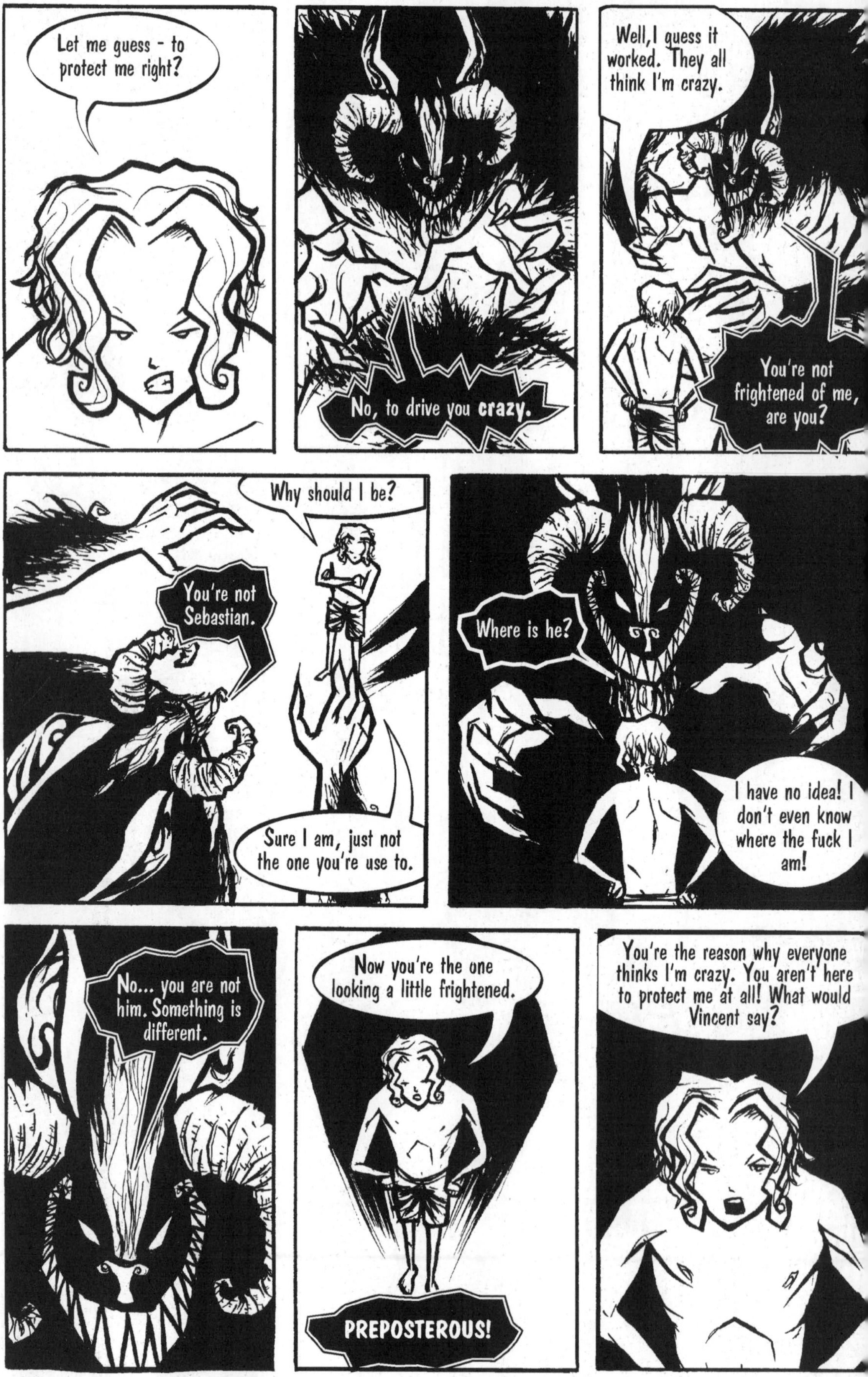

Let me guess - to protect me right?
No, to drive you crazy.
Well, I guess it worked. They all think I'm crazy.
You're not frightened of me, are you?
Why should I be?
You're not Sebastian.
Sure I am, just not the one you're use to.
Where is he?
I have no idea! I don't even know where the fuck I am!
No... you are not him. Something is different.
Now you're the one looking a little frightened.
PREPOSTEROUS!
You're the reason why everyone thinks I'm crazy. You aren't here to protect me at all! What would Vincent say?

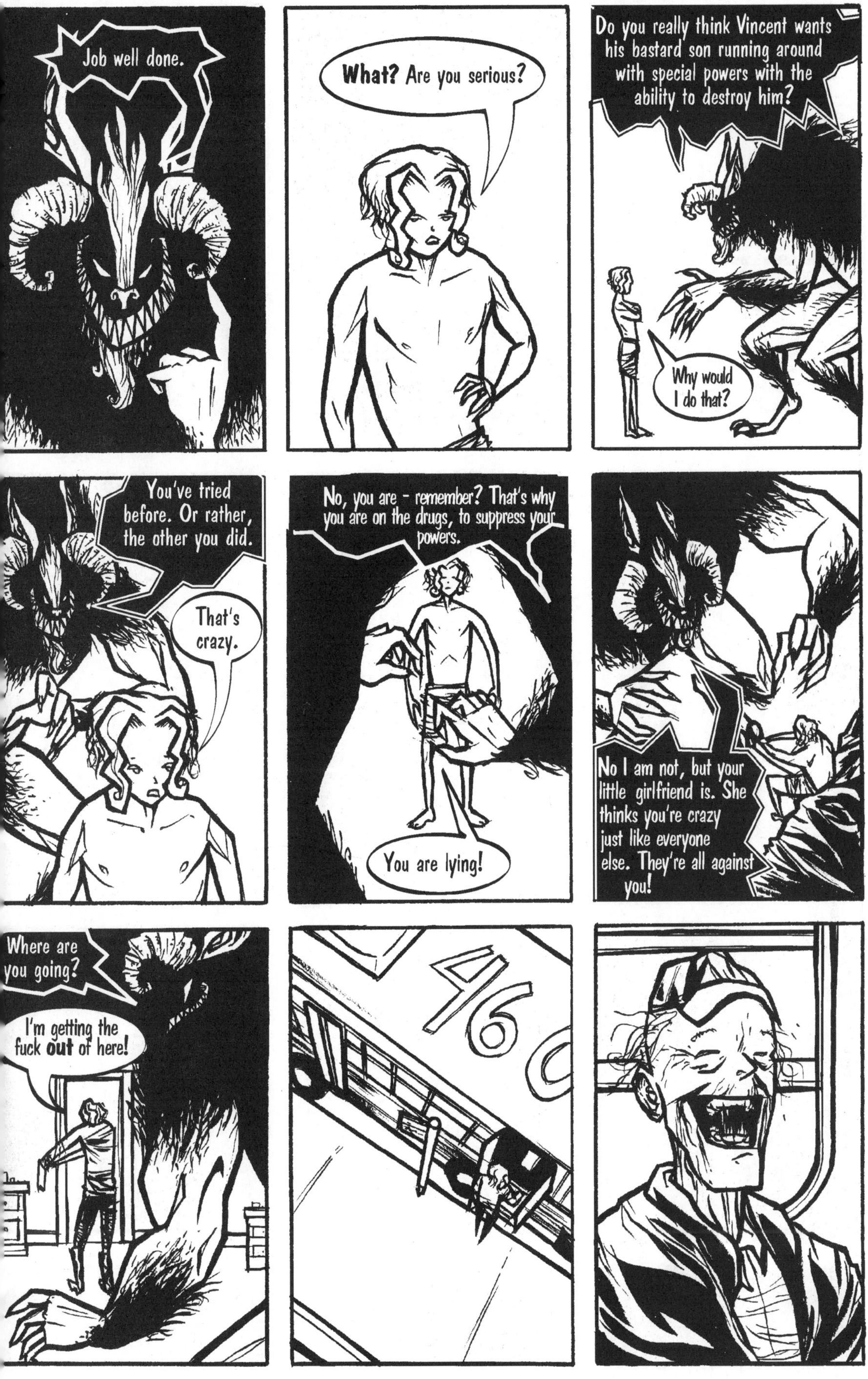
Job well done.
What? Are you serious?
Do you really think Vincent wants his bastard son running around with special powers with the ability to destroy him?
Why would I do that?
You've tried before. Or rather, the other you did.
That's crazy.
No, you are - remember? That's why you are on the drugs, to suppress your powers.
You are lying!
No I am not, but your little girlfriend is. She thinks you're crazy just like everyone else. They're all against you!
Where are you going?
I'm getting the fuck out of here!
960

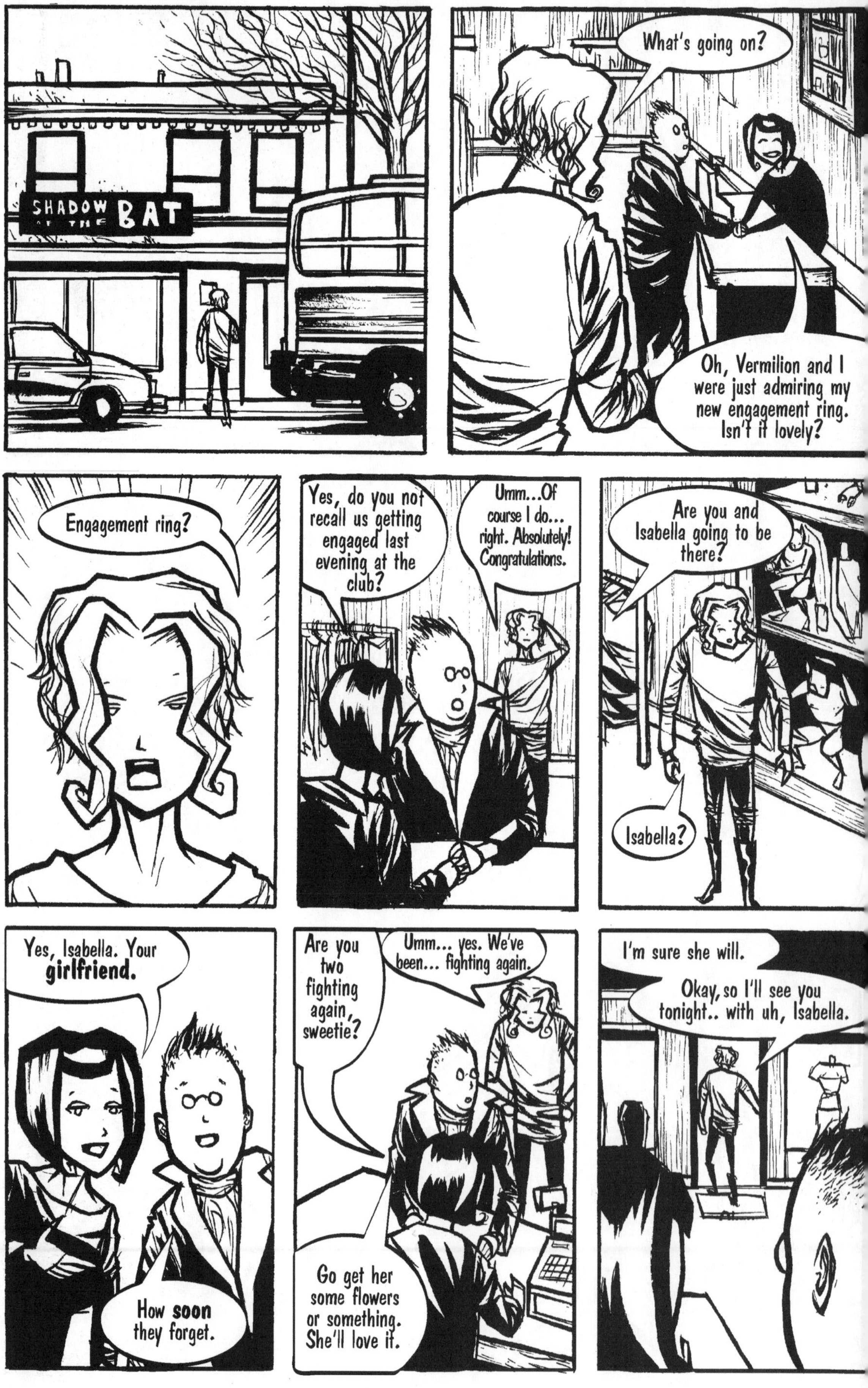
SHADOW OF THE BAT
What's going on?
Oh, Vermilion and I were just admiring my new engagement ring. Isn't it lovely?
Engagement ring?
Yes, do you not recall us getting engaged last evening at the club?
Umm...Of course I do... right. Absolutely! Congratulations.
Are you and Isabella going to be there?
Isabella?
Yes, Isabella. Your **girlfriend.**
How **soon** they forget.
Are you two fighting again, sweetie?
Umm... yes. We've been... fighting again.
Go get her some flowers or something. She'll love it.
I'm sure she will.
Okay, so I'll see you tonight.. with uh, Isabella.

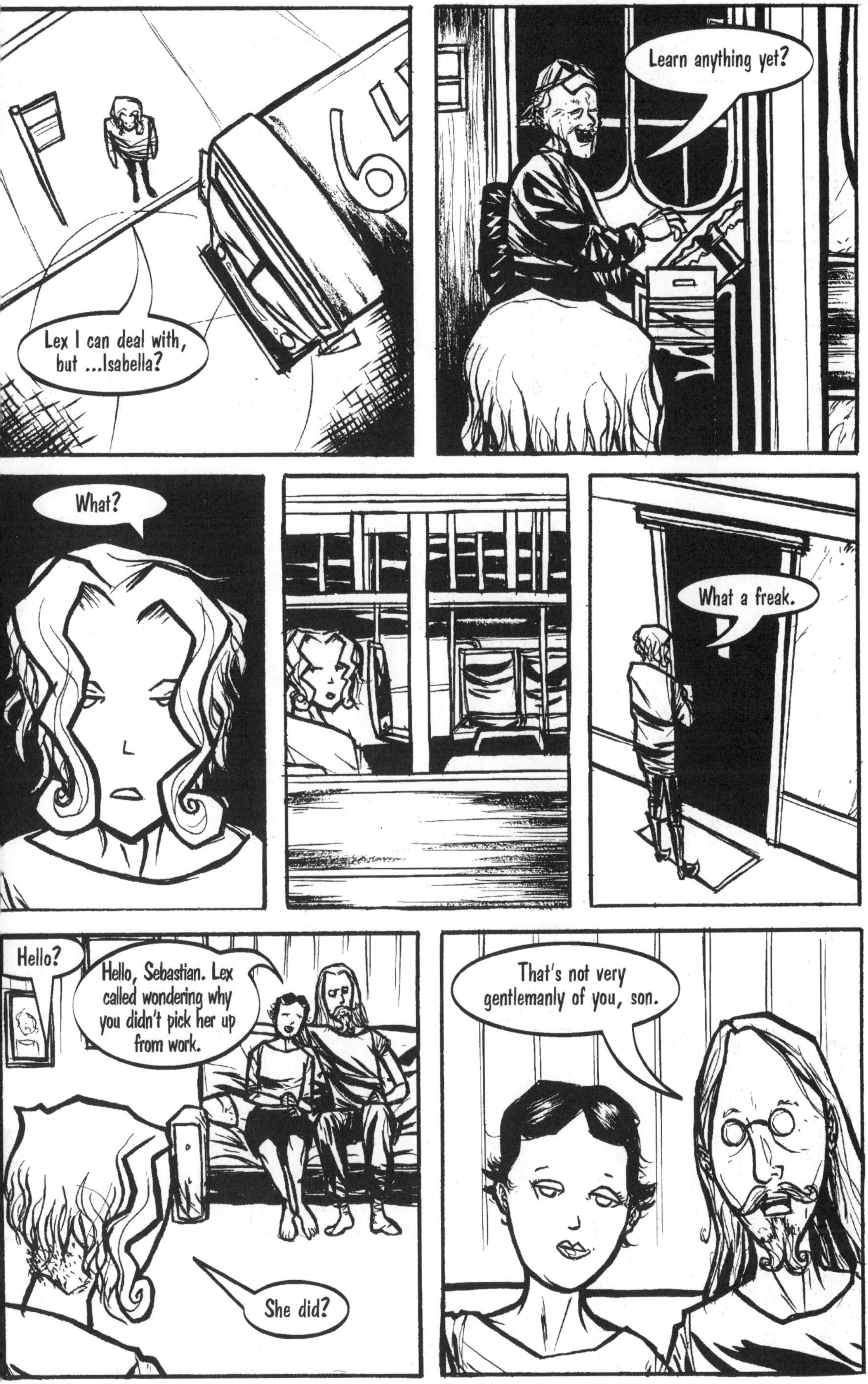
Lex I can deal with, but ...Isabella?
Learn anything yet?
What?
What a freak.
Hello?
Hello, Sebastian. Lex called wondering why you didn't pick her up from work.
She did?
That's not very gentlemanly of you, son.

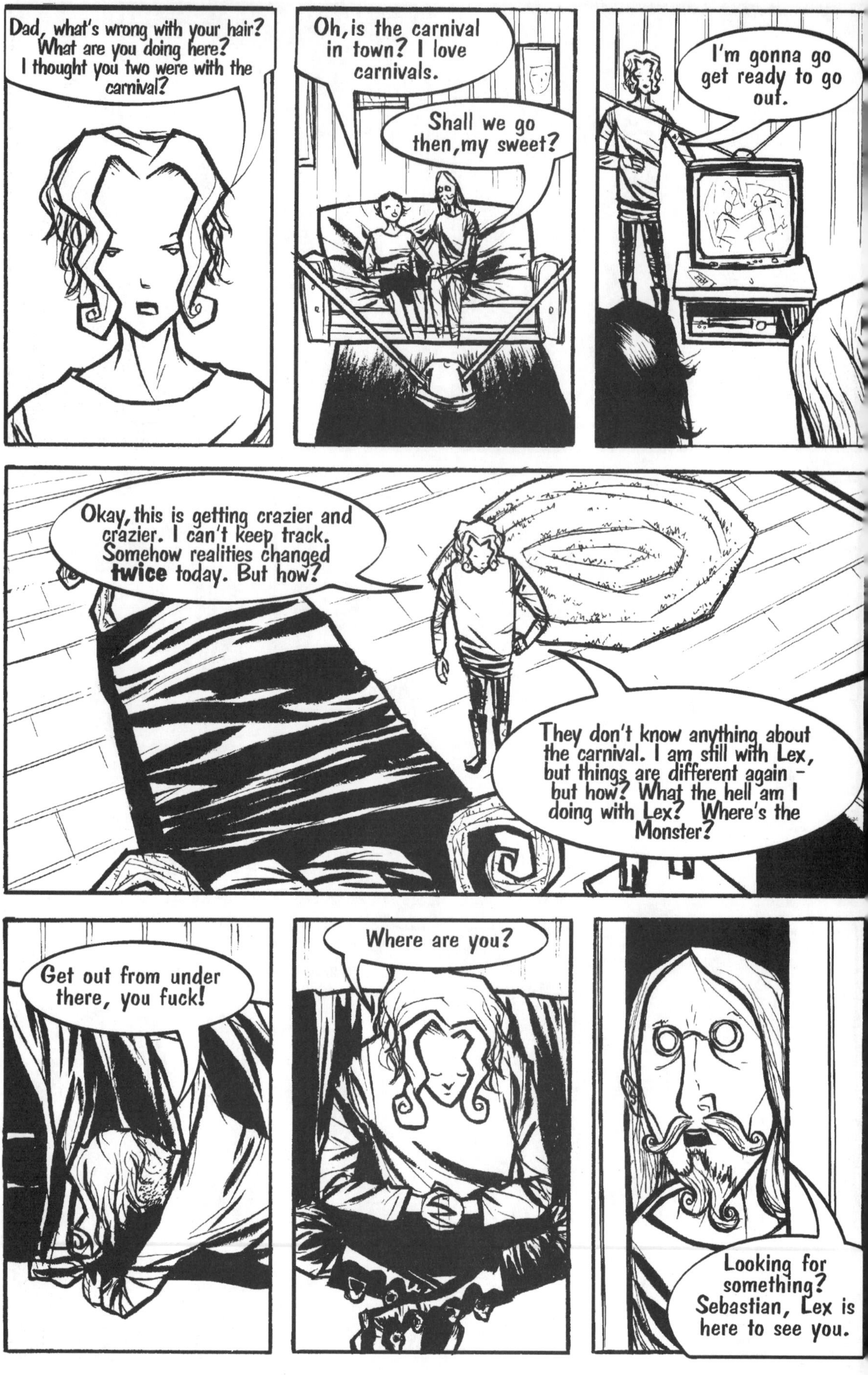
Dad, what's wrong with your hair? What are you doing here? I thought you two were with the carnival?
Oh, is the carnival in town? I love carnivals.
Shall we go then, my sweet?
I'm gonna go get ready to go out.
Okay, this is getting crazier and crazier. I can't keep track. Somehow realities changed twice today. But how?
They don't know anything about the carnival. I am still with Lex, but things are different again - but how? What the hell am I doing with Lex? Where's the Monster?
Get out from under there, you fuck!
Where are you?
Looking for something? Sebastian, Lex is here to see you.

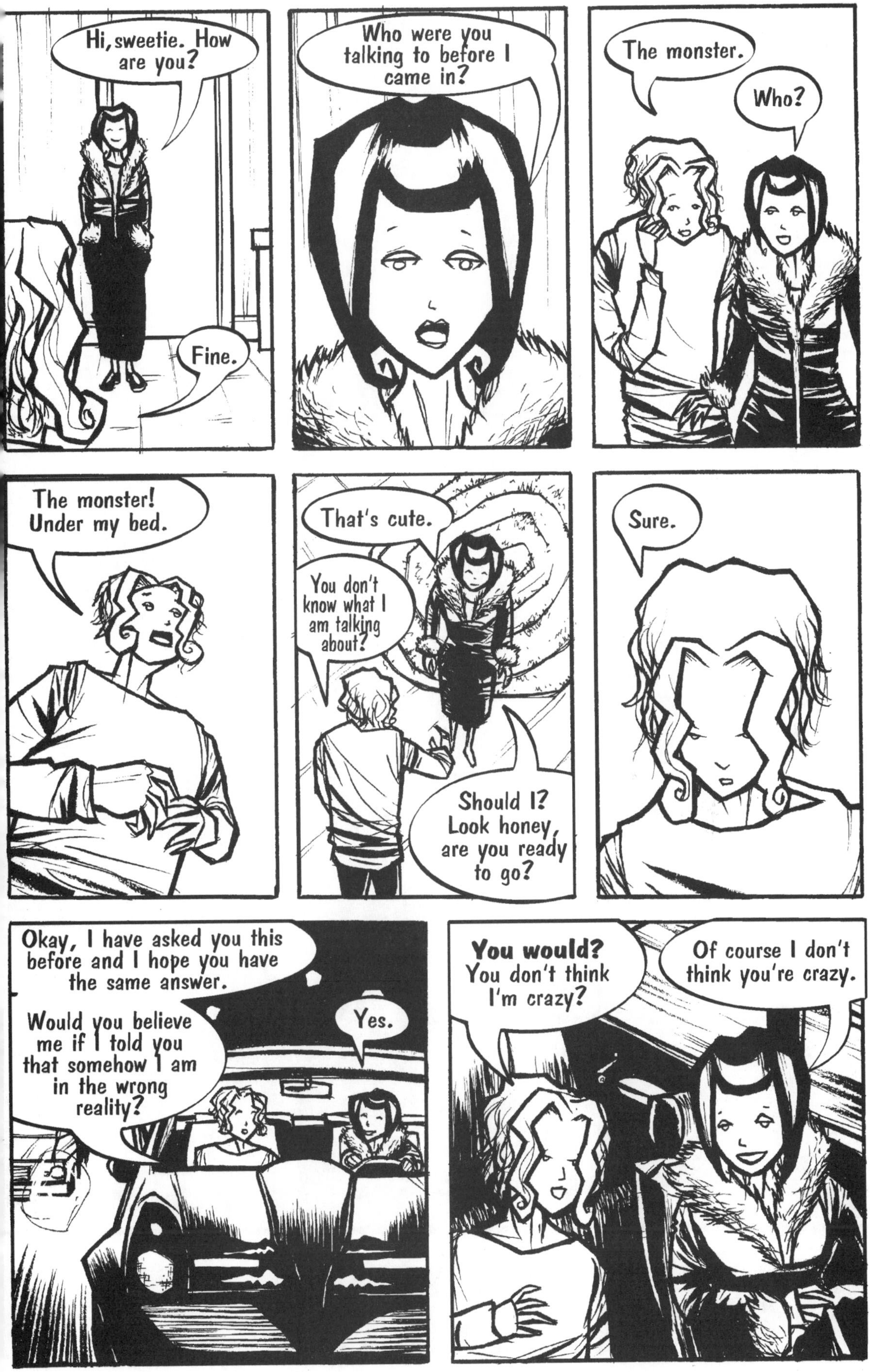

Hi, sweetie. How are you?
Fine.
Who were you talking to before I came in?
The monster.
Who?
The monster! Under my bed.
That's cute.
You don't know what I am talking about?
Should I? Look honey, are you ready to go?
Sure.
Okay, I have asked you this before and I hope you have the same answer.
Would you believe me if I told you that somehow I am in the wrong reality?
Yes.
You would? You don't think I'm crazy?
Of course I don't think you're crazy.

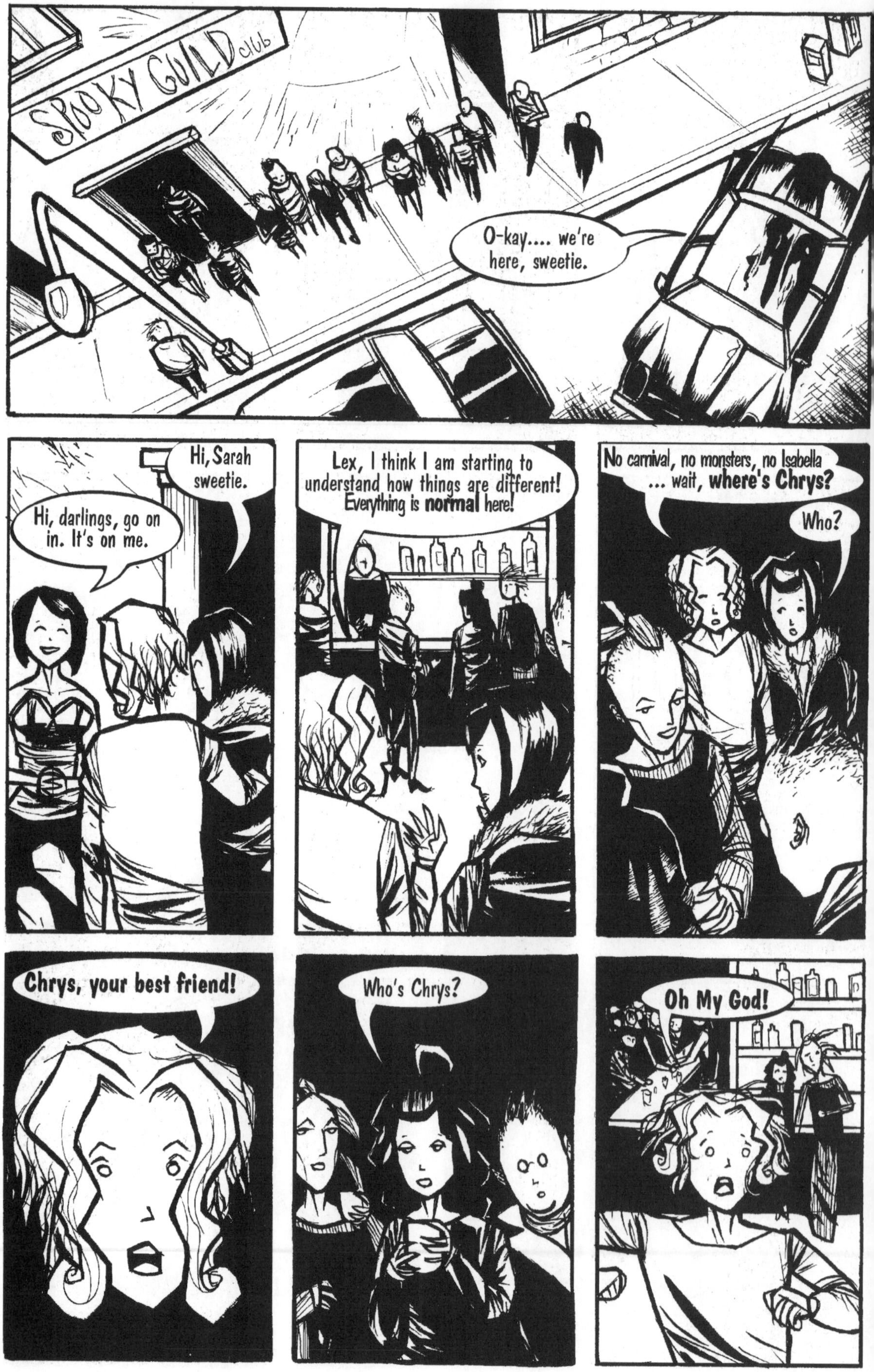
SPOOKY GUILD club
O-kay.... we're here, sweetie.
Hi, Sarah sweetie.
Hi, darlings, go on in. It's on me.
Lex, I think I am starting to understand how things are different! Everything is **normal** here!
No carnival, no monsters, no Isabella ... wait, **where's Chrys?**
Who?
Chrys, your best friend!
Who's Chrys?
Oh My God!

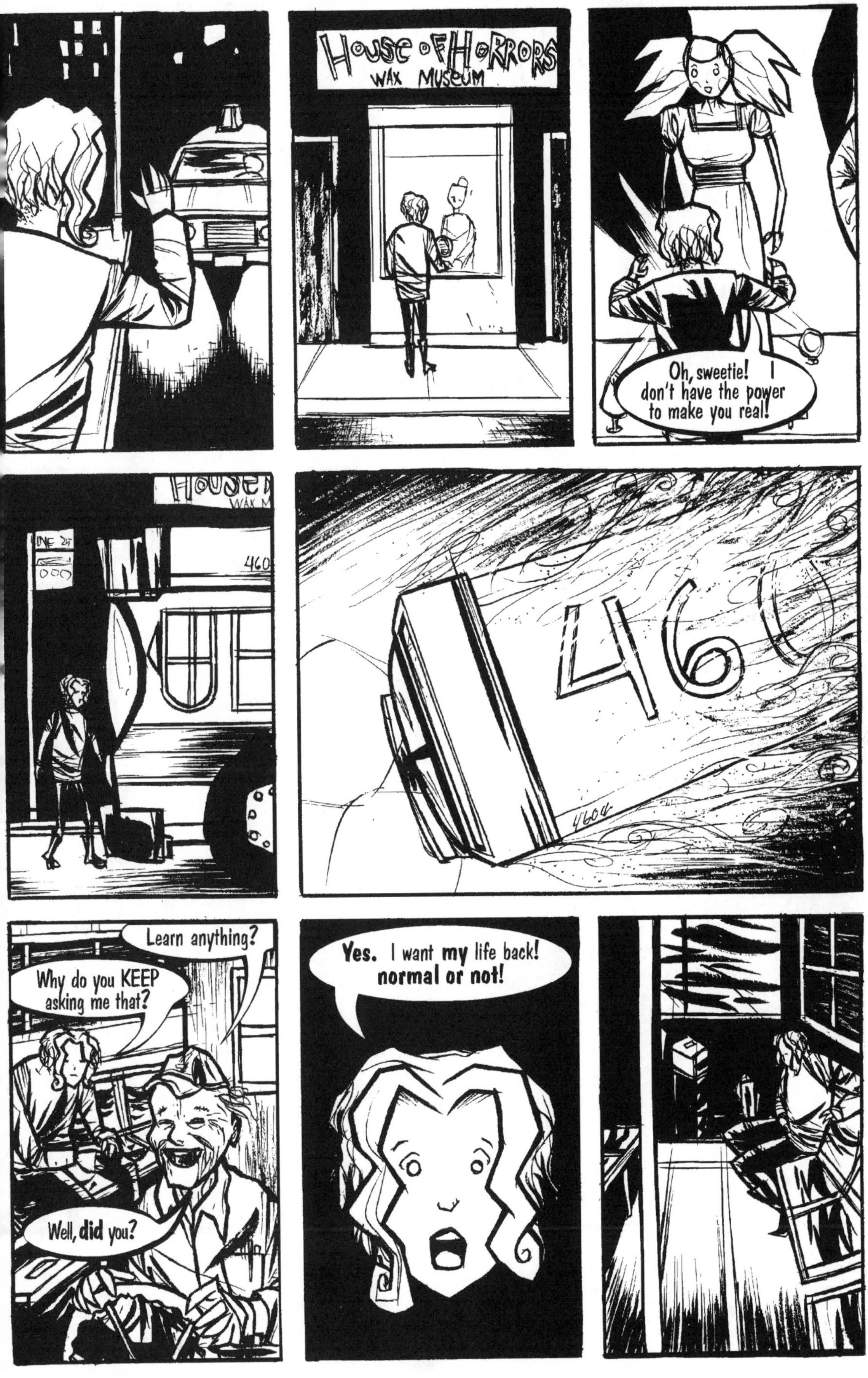
House of Horrors
Wax Museum
Oh, sweetie! I don't have the power to make you real!
4604
Learn anything?
Why do you KEEP asking me that?
Well, **did** you?
Yes. I want **my** life back! **normal or not!**

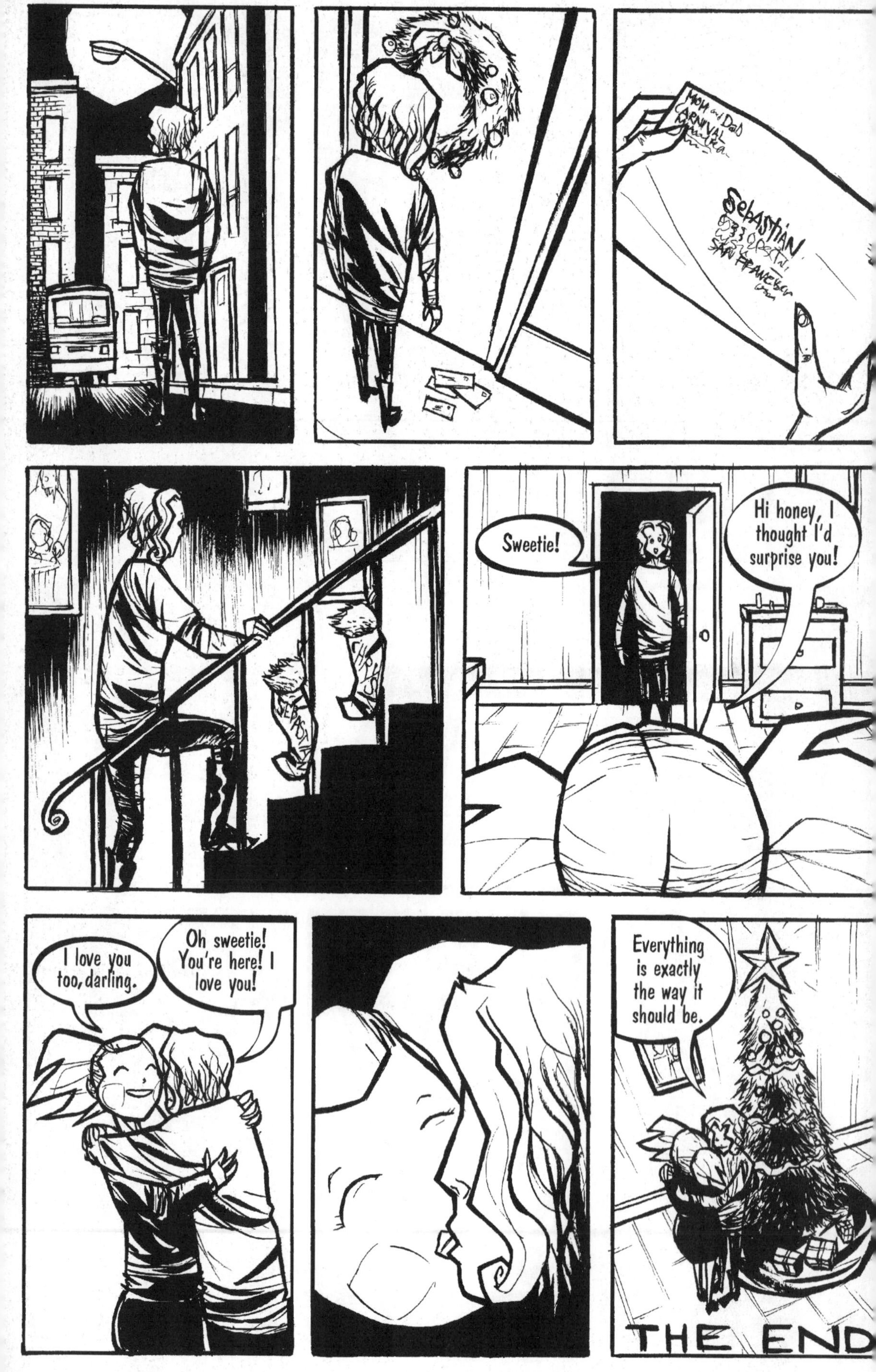
MOM and DAD
CARNIVAL
Sebastian
Sweetie!
Hi honey, I thought I'd surprise you!
I love you too, darling.
Oh sweetie! You're here! I love you!
Everything is exactly the way it should be.
THE END

Chapter 11

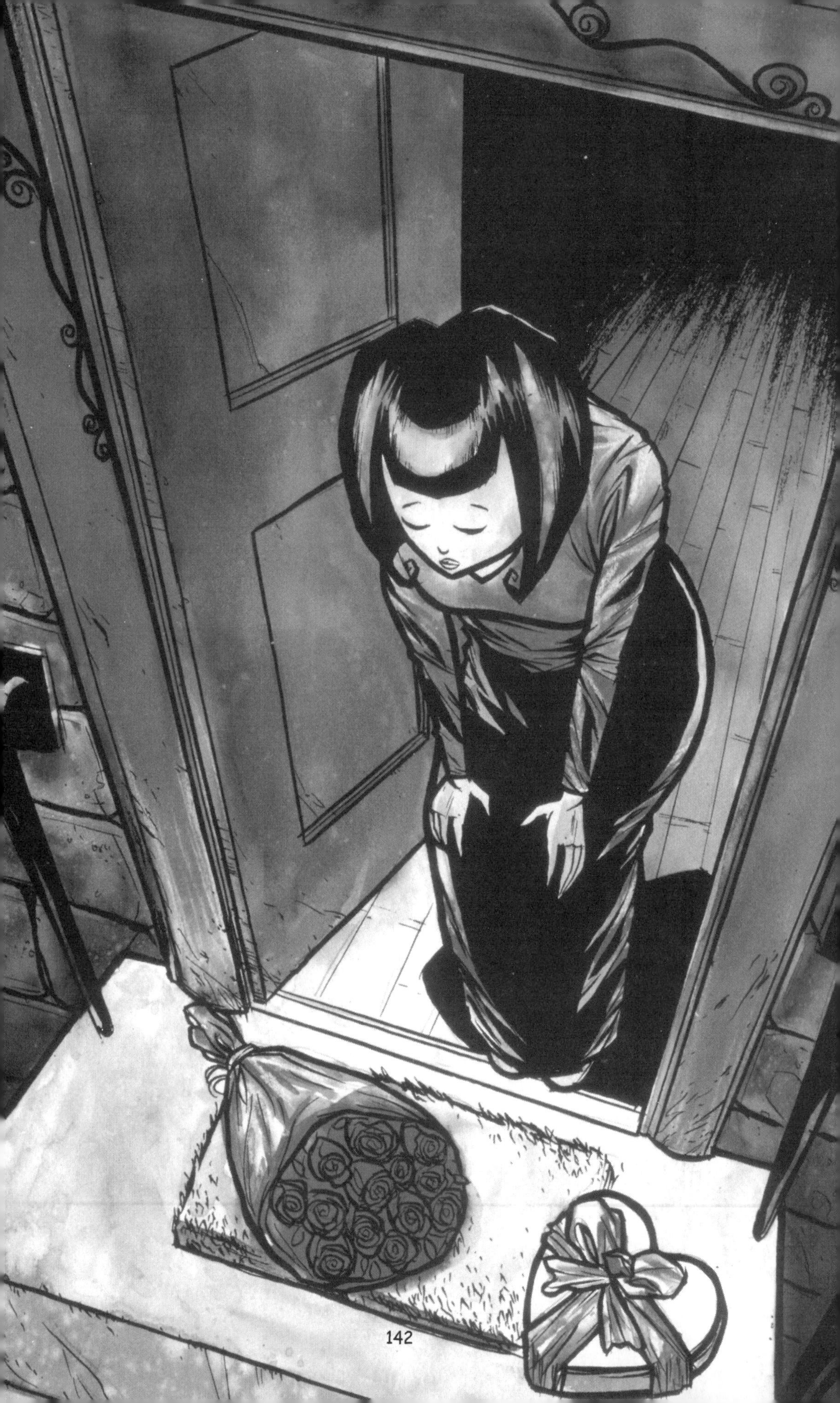

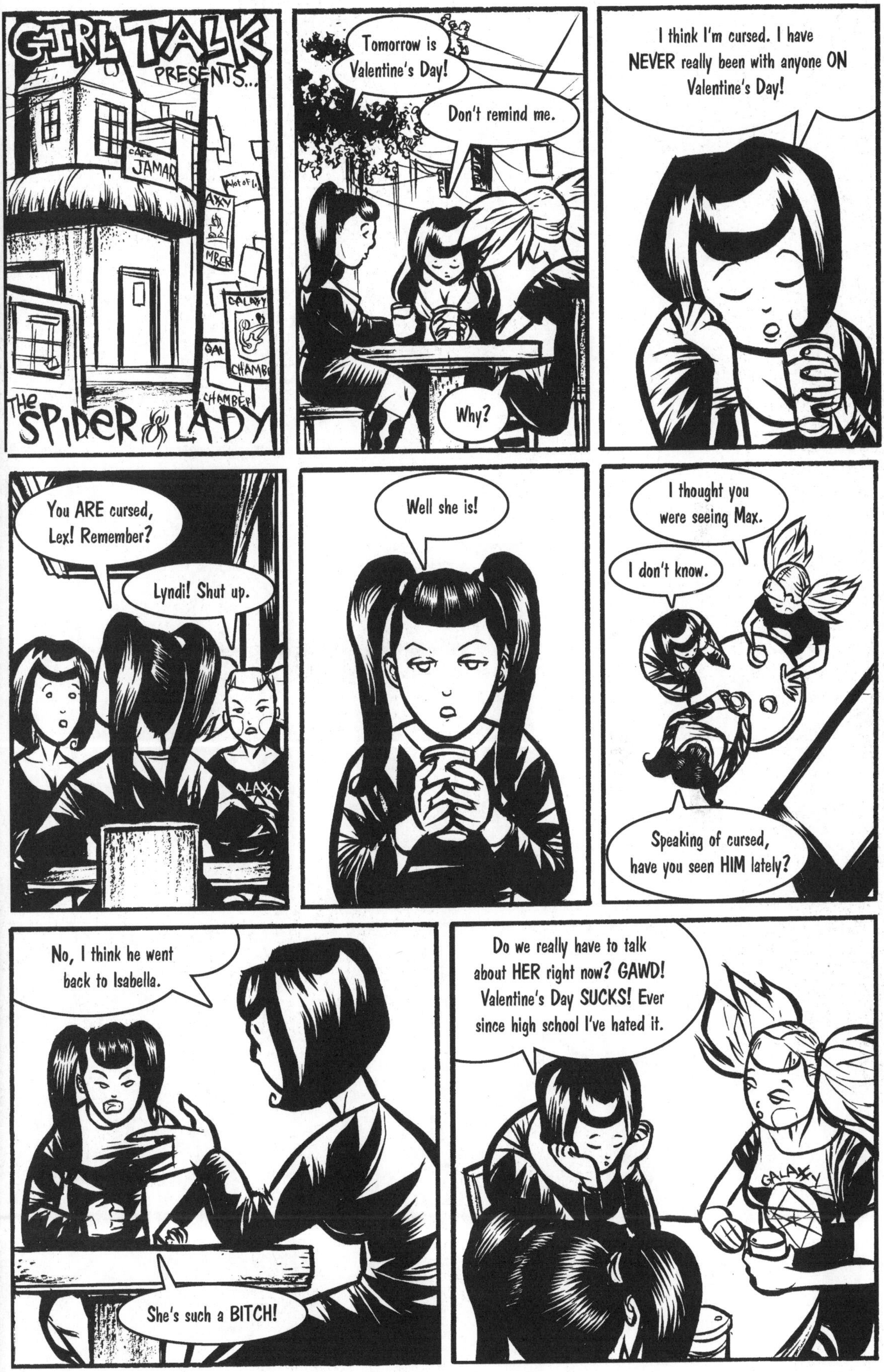
GIRL TALK
PRESENTS...
CAFE
JAMAR
GALAXY
CHAMBER
THE SPIDER LADY
Tomorrow is Valentine's Day!
Don't remind me.
Why?
I think I'm cursed. I have NEVER really been with anyone ON Valentine's Day!
You ARE cursed, Lex! Remember?
Lyndi! Shut up.
GALAXY
Well she is!
I thought you were seeing Max.
I don't know.
Speaking of cursed, have you seen HIM lately?
No, I think he went back to Isabella.
She's such a BITCH!
Do we really have to talk about HER right now? GAWD! Valentine's Day SUCKS! Ever since high school I've hated it.
GALAXY

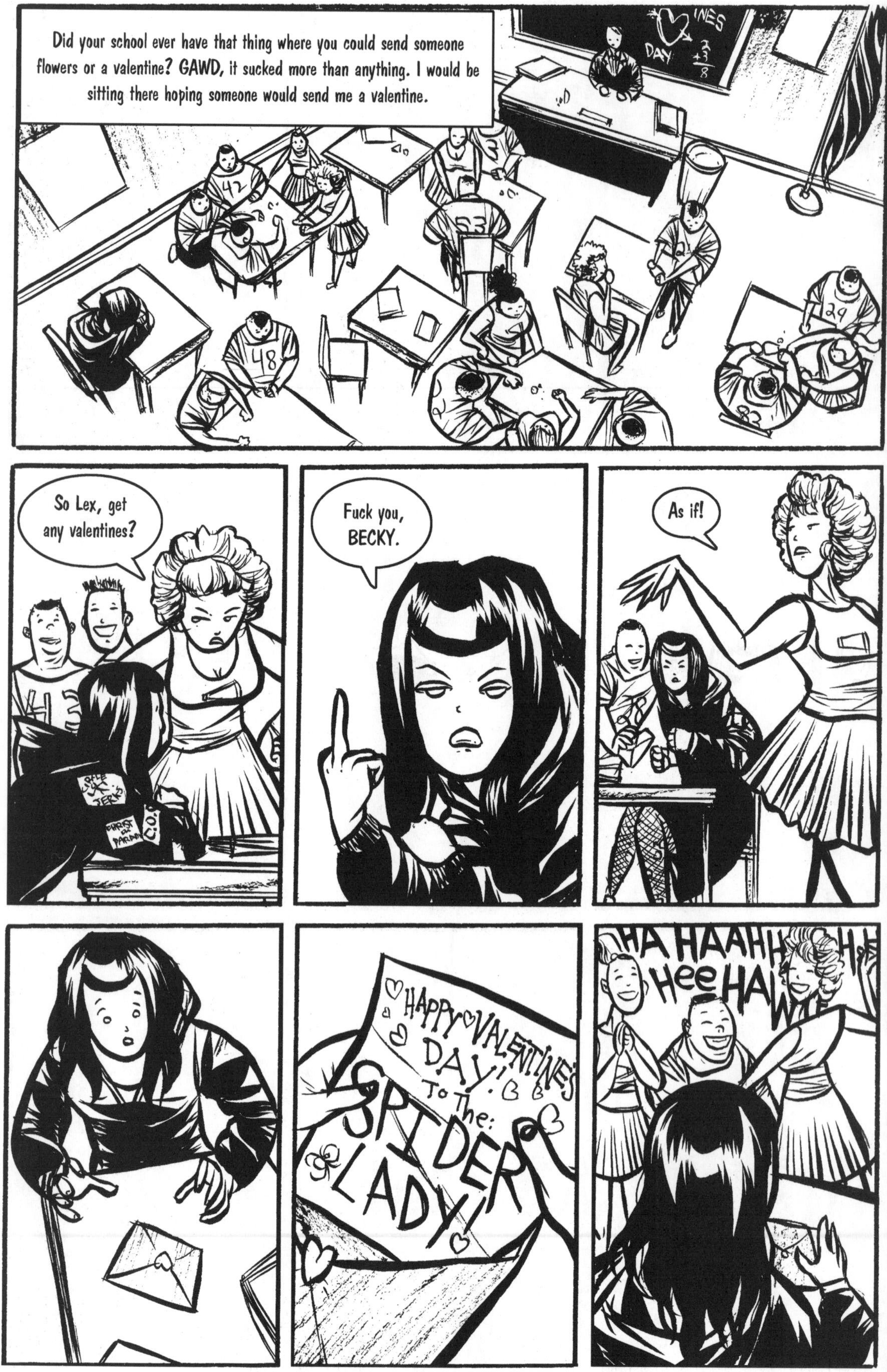
Did your school ever have that thing where you could send someone flowers or a valentine? GAWD, it sucked more than anything. I would be sitting there hoping someone would send me a valentine.
So Lex, get any valentines?
Fuck you, BECKY.
As if!
HAPPY VALENTINE'S DAY! To The: SPIDER LADY!
HA HAAHH HEE HAW

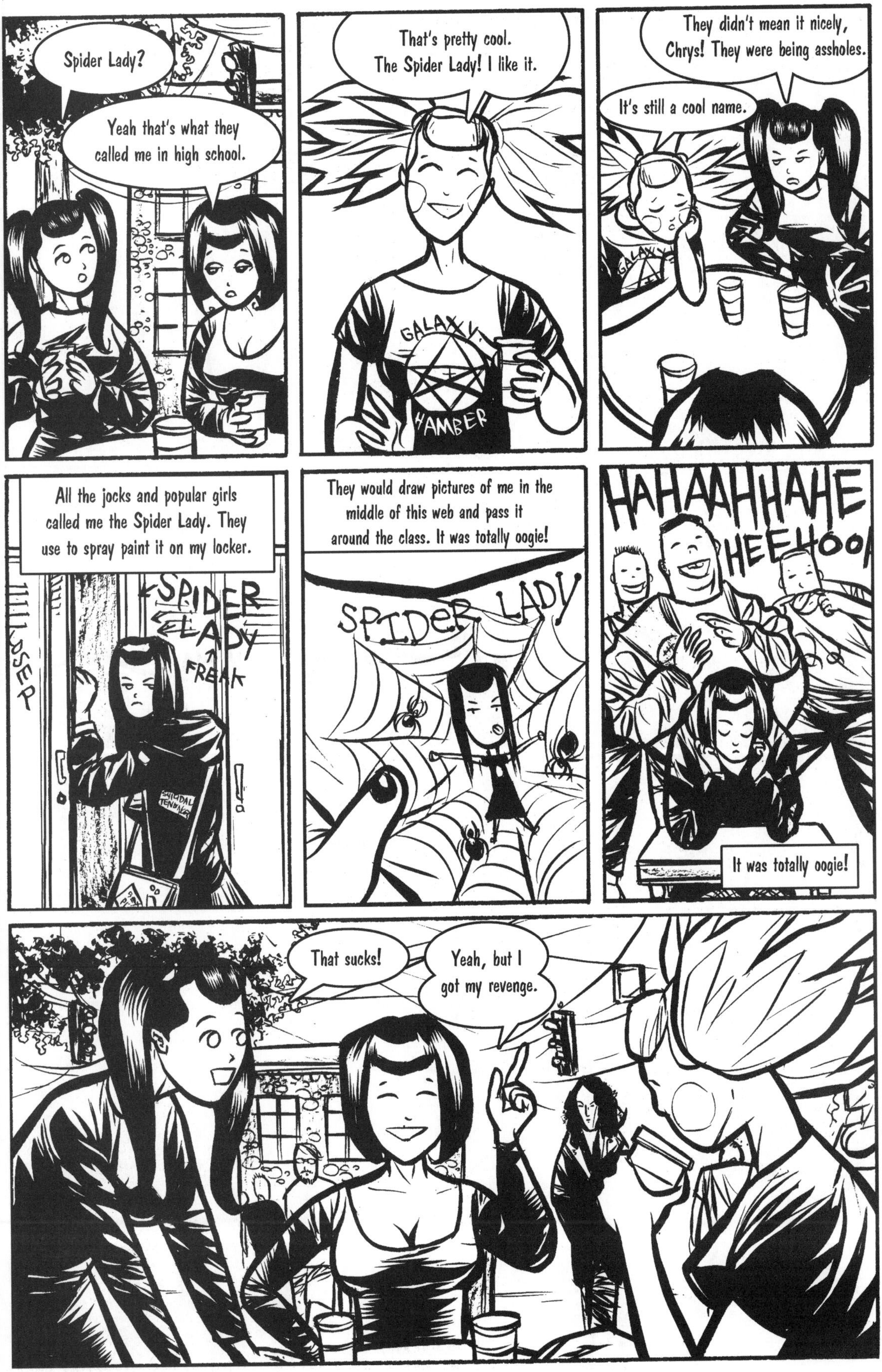
Spider Lady?
Yeah that's what they called me in high school.
That's pretty cool. The Spider Lady! I like it.
They didn't mean it nicely, Chrys! They were being assholes.
It's still a cool name.
GALAXY HAMBER
All the jocks and popular girls called me the Spider Lady. They use to spray paint it on my locker.
SPIDER LADY FREAK
LOSER
They would draw pictures of me in the middle of this web and pass it around the class. It was totally oogie!
SPIDER LADY
HAHAAHHAHE HEEHOO
It was totally oogie!
That sucks!
Yeah, but I got my revenge.

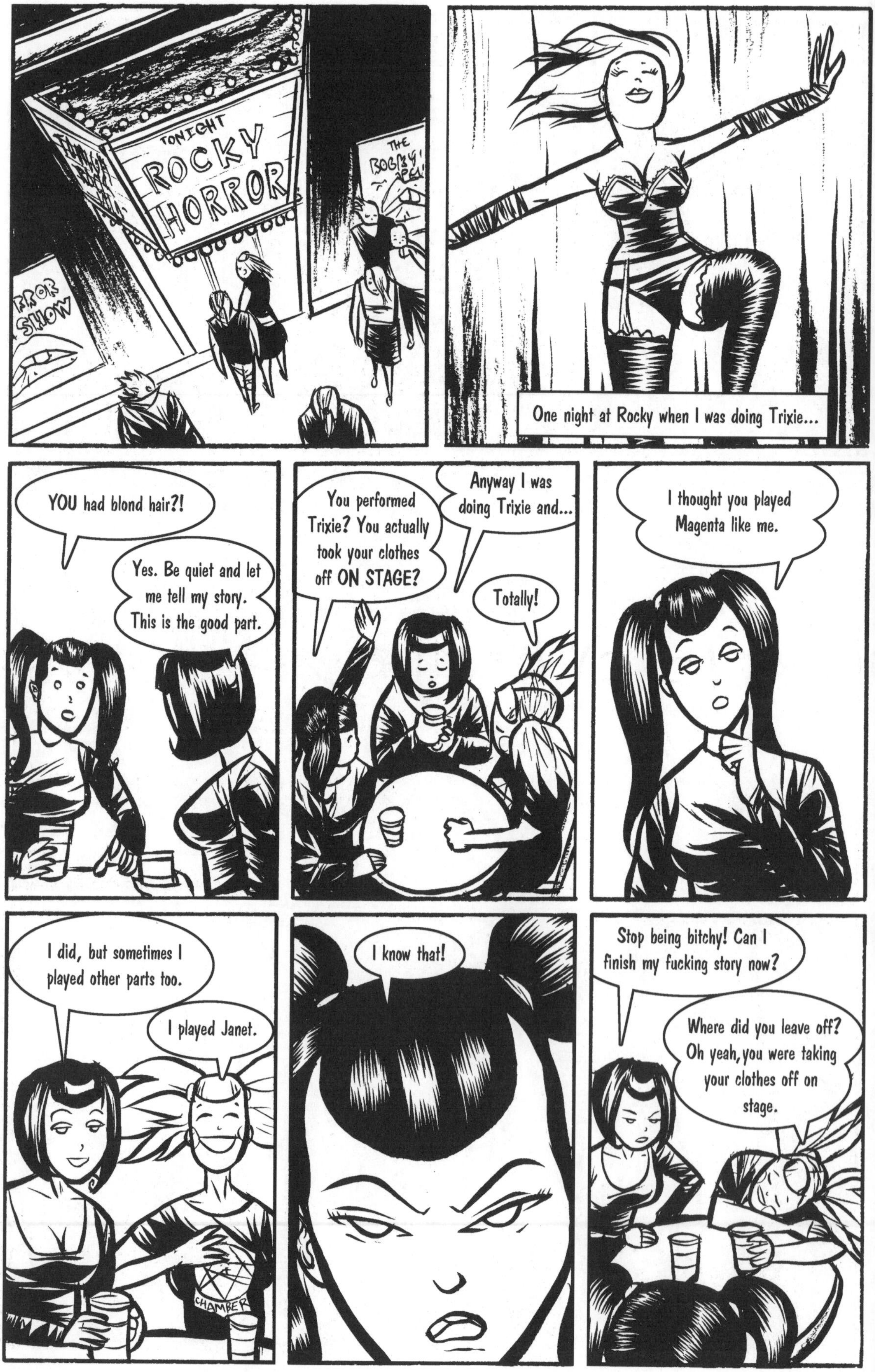
TONIGHT
ROCKY HORROR
One night at Rocky when I was doing Trixie...
YOU had blond hair?!
Yes. Be quiet and let me tell my story. This is the good part.
You performed Trixie? You actually took your clothes off ON STAGE?
Anyway I was doing Trixie and...
Totally!
I thought you played Magenta like me.
I did, but sometimes I played other parts too.
I played Janet.
I know that!
Stop being bitchy! Can I finish my fucking story now?
Where did you leave off? Oh yeah, you were taking your clothes off on stage.

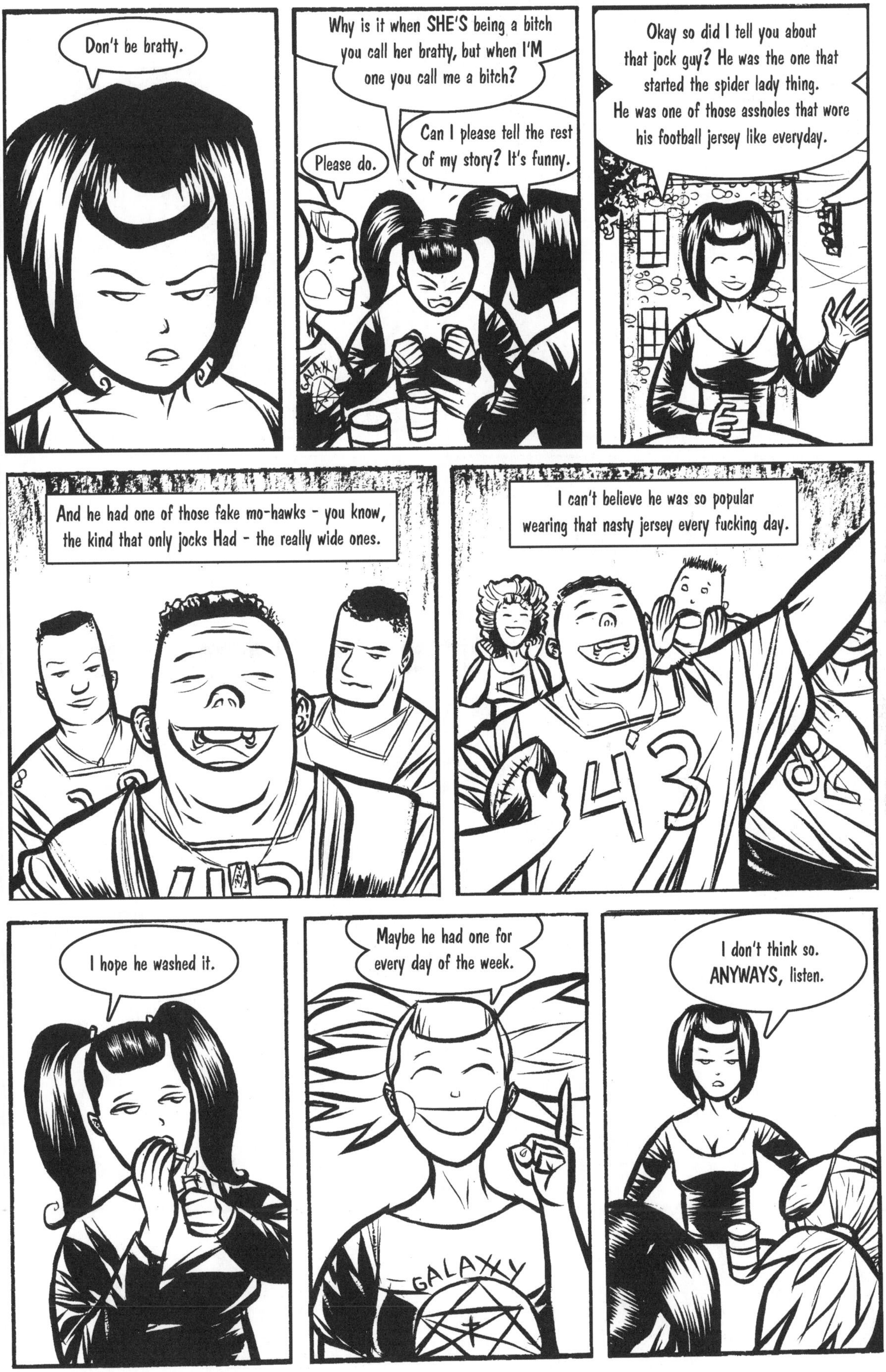
Don't be bratty.
Why is it when SHE'S being a bitch you call her bratty, but when I'M one you call me a bitch?
Please do.
Can I please tell the rest of my story? It's funny.
Okay so did I tell you about that jock guy? He was the one that started the spider lady thing. He was one of those assholes that wore his football jersey like everyday.
And he had one of those fake mo-hawks - you know, the kind that only jocks Had - the really wide ones.
I can't believe he was so popular wearing that nasty jersey every fucking day.
43
I hope he washed it.
Maybe he had one for every day of the week.
GALAXY
I don't think so. ANYWAYS, listen.

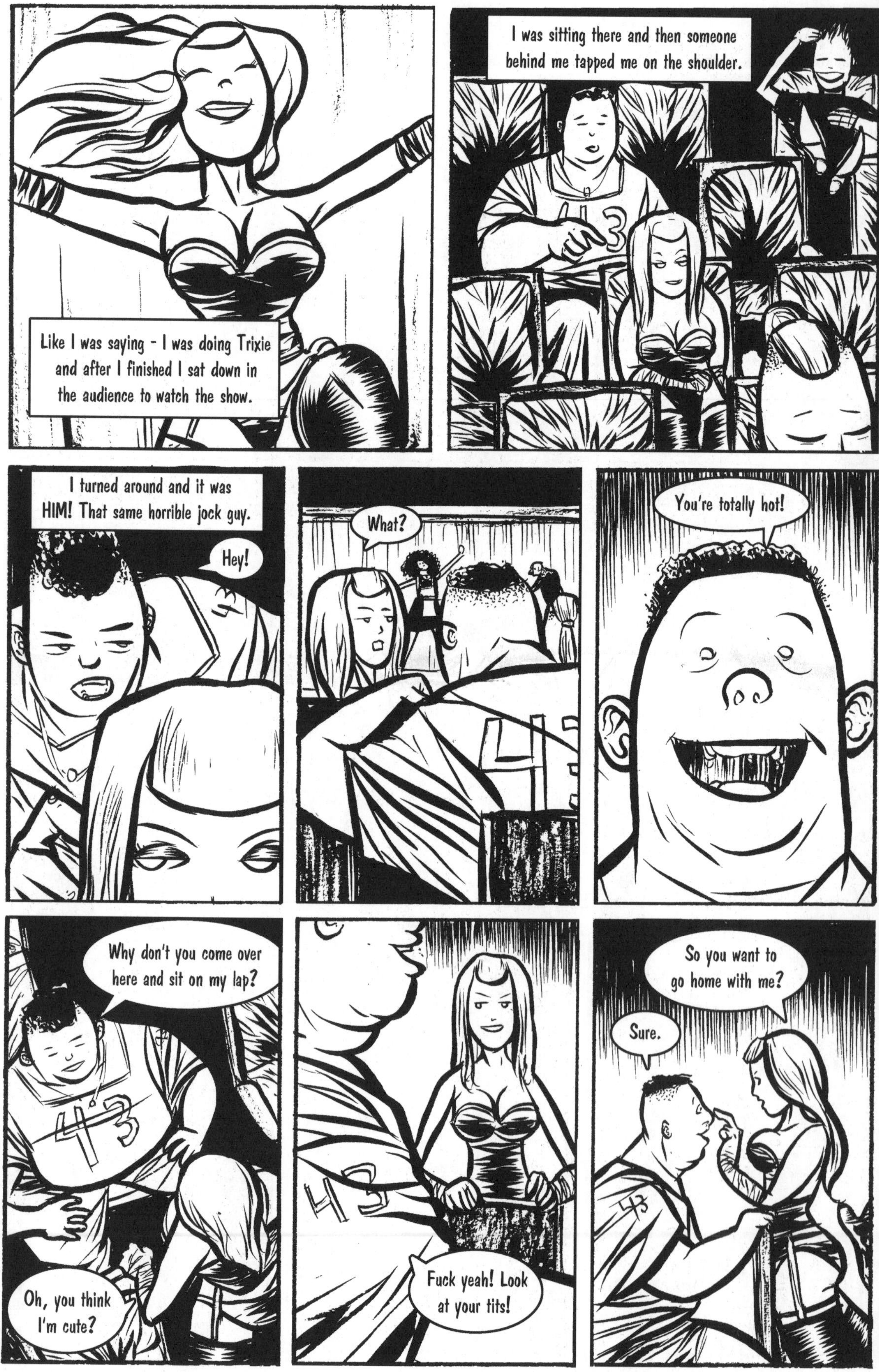

Like I was saying - I was doing Trixie and after I finished I sat down in the audience to watch the show.
I was sitting there and then someone behind me tapped me on the shoulder.
I turned around and it was HIM! That same horrible jock guy.
Hey!
What?
You're totally hot!
Why don't you come over here and sit on my lap?
Oh, you think I'm cute?
Fuck yeah! Look at your tits!
So you want to go home with me?
Sure.

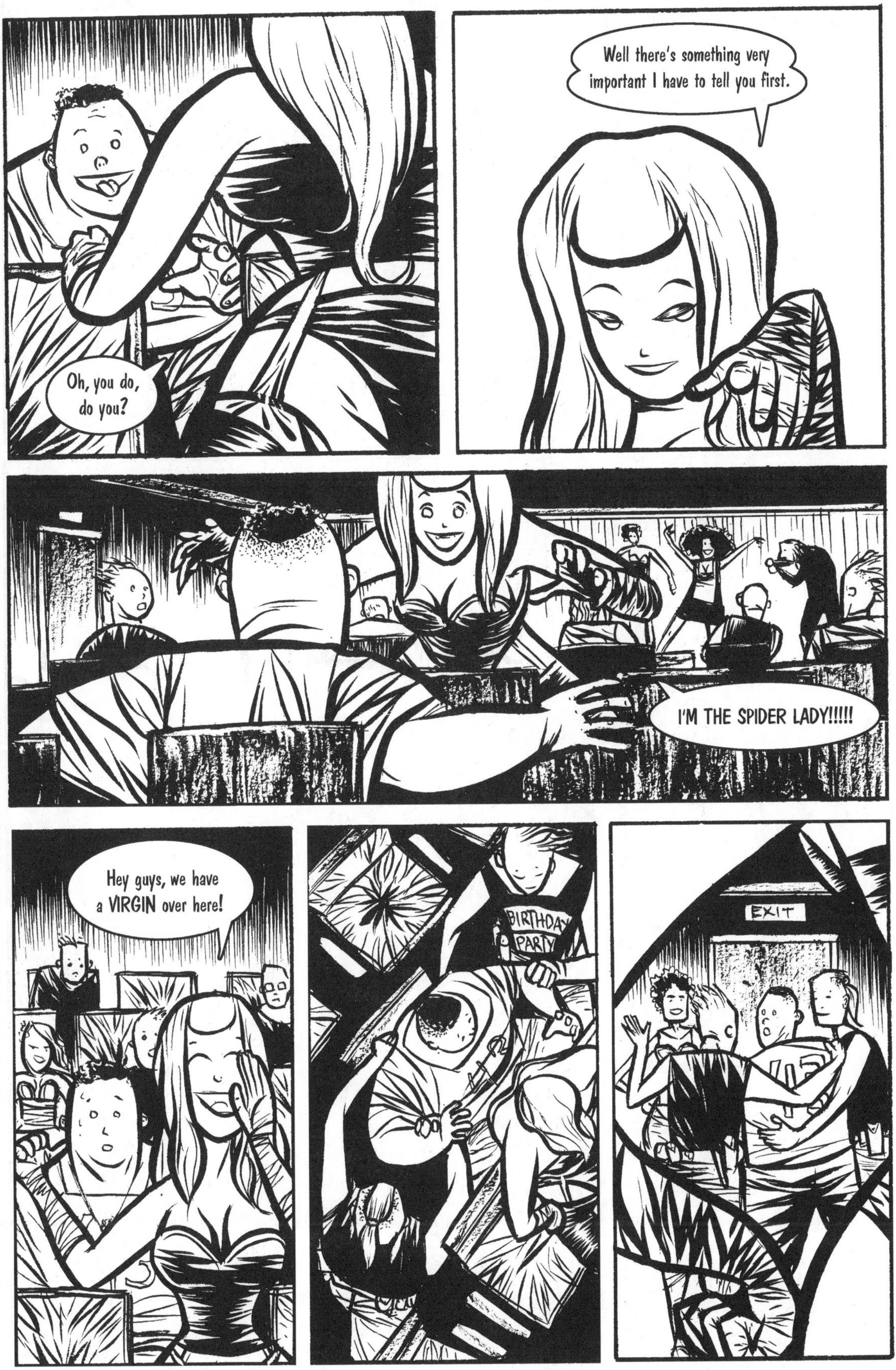
Oh, you do, do you?
Well there's something very important I have to tell you first.
I'M THE SPIDER LADY!!!!!
Hey guys, we have a VIRGIN over here!
BIRTHDAY PARTY
EXIT

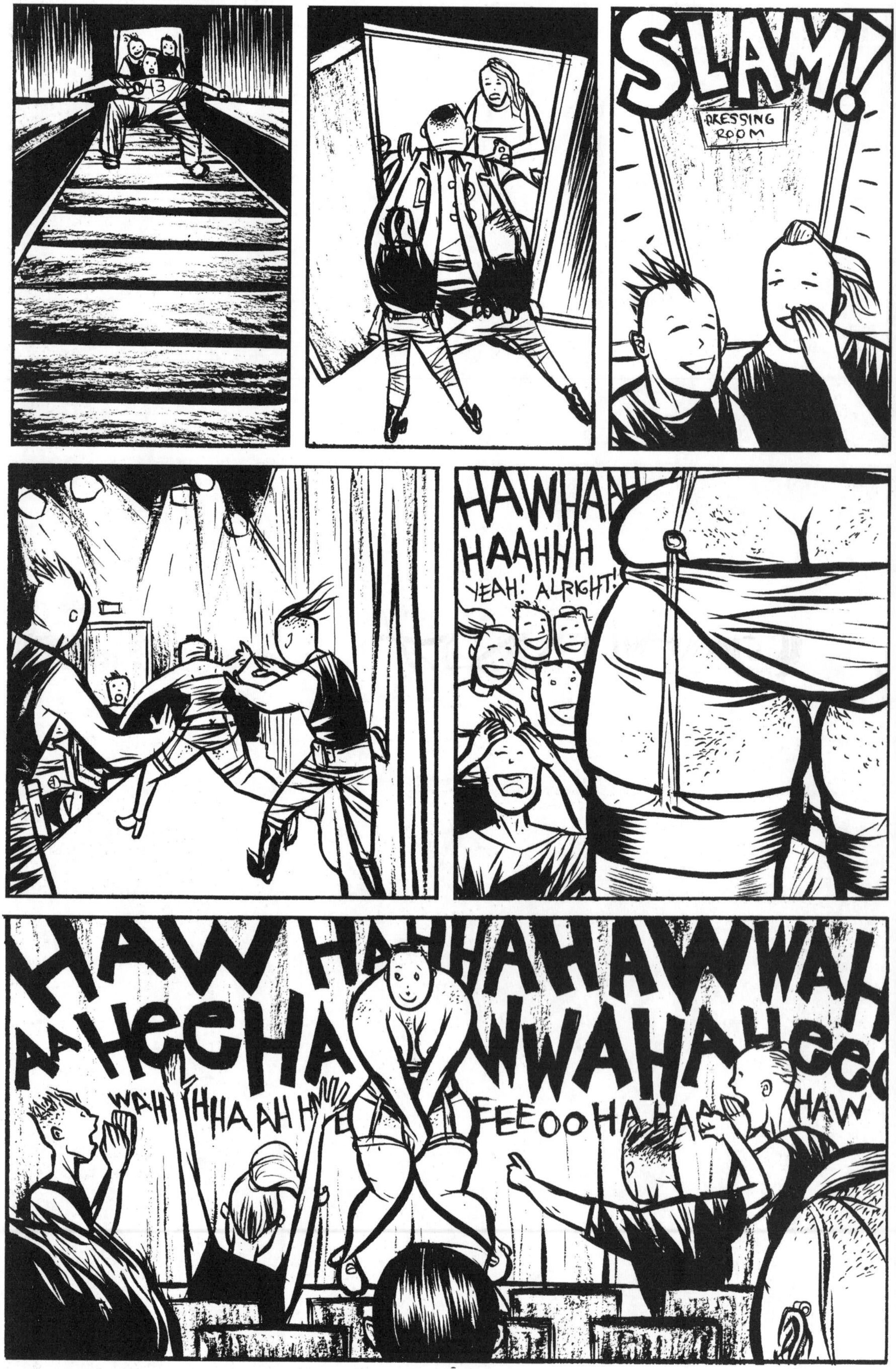
SLAM!
DRESSING ROOM
HAWHAAH
HAAHHH
YEAH! ALRIGHT!
HAW HA
AA HEEHA
WAH HHAAHH
FEEOOHAHA
HAW

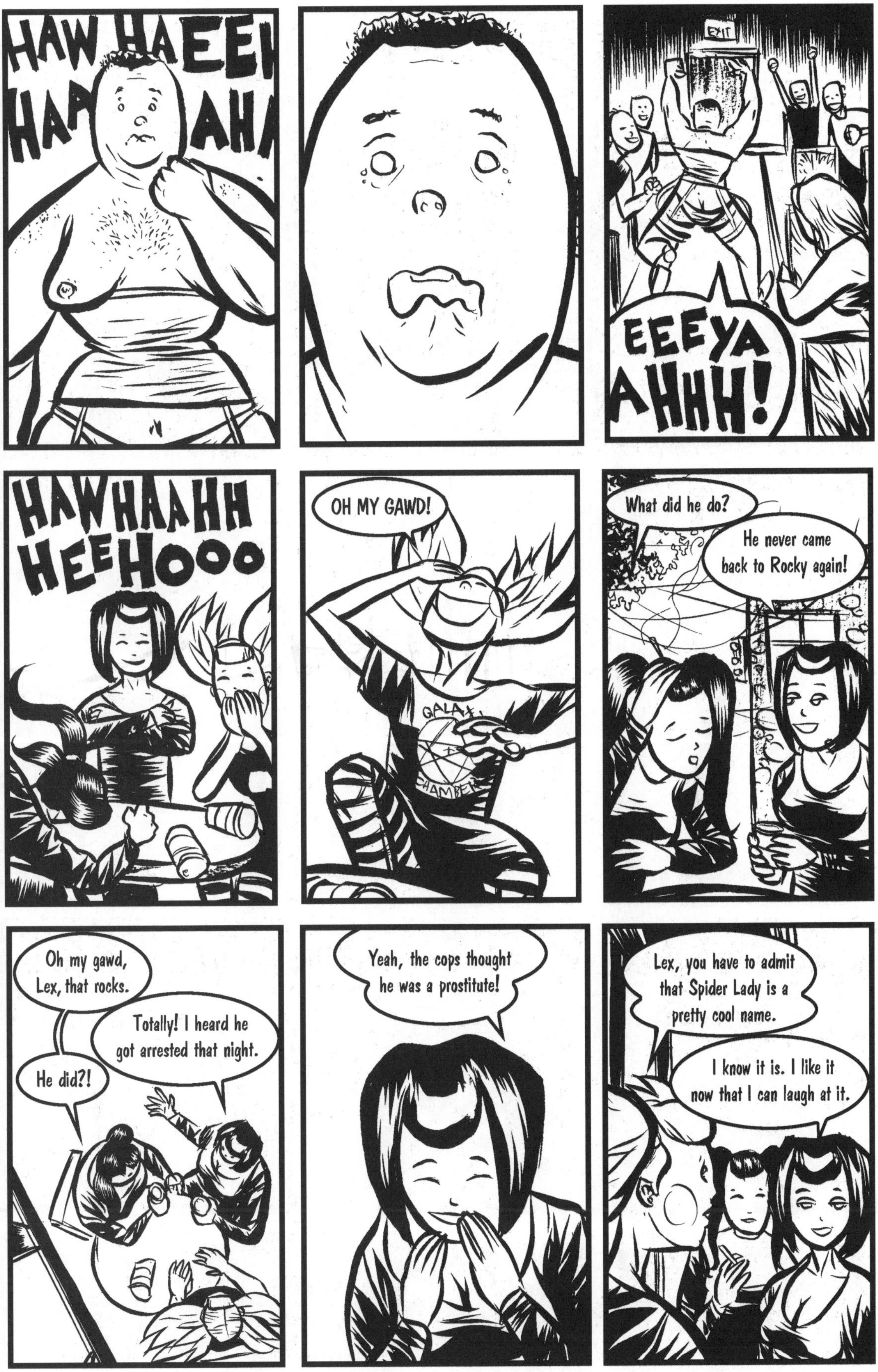
HAW HA EEK
HAP AHA
EEEYA AHHH!
HAWHAAHH HEEHOOO
OH MY GAWD!
What did he do?
He never came back to Rocky again!
Oh my gawd, Lex, that rocks.
Totally! I heard he got arrested that night.
He did?!
Yeah, the cops thought he was a prostitute!
Lex, you have to admit that Spider Lady is a pretty cool name.
I know it is. I like it now that I can laugh at it.

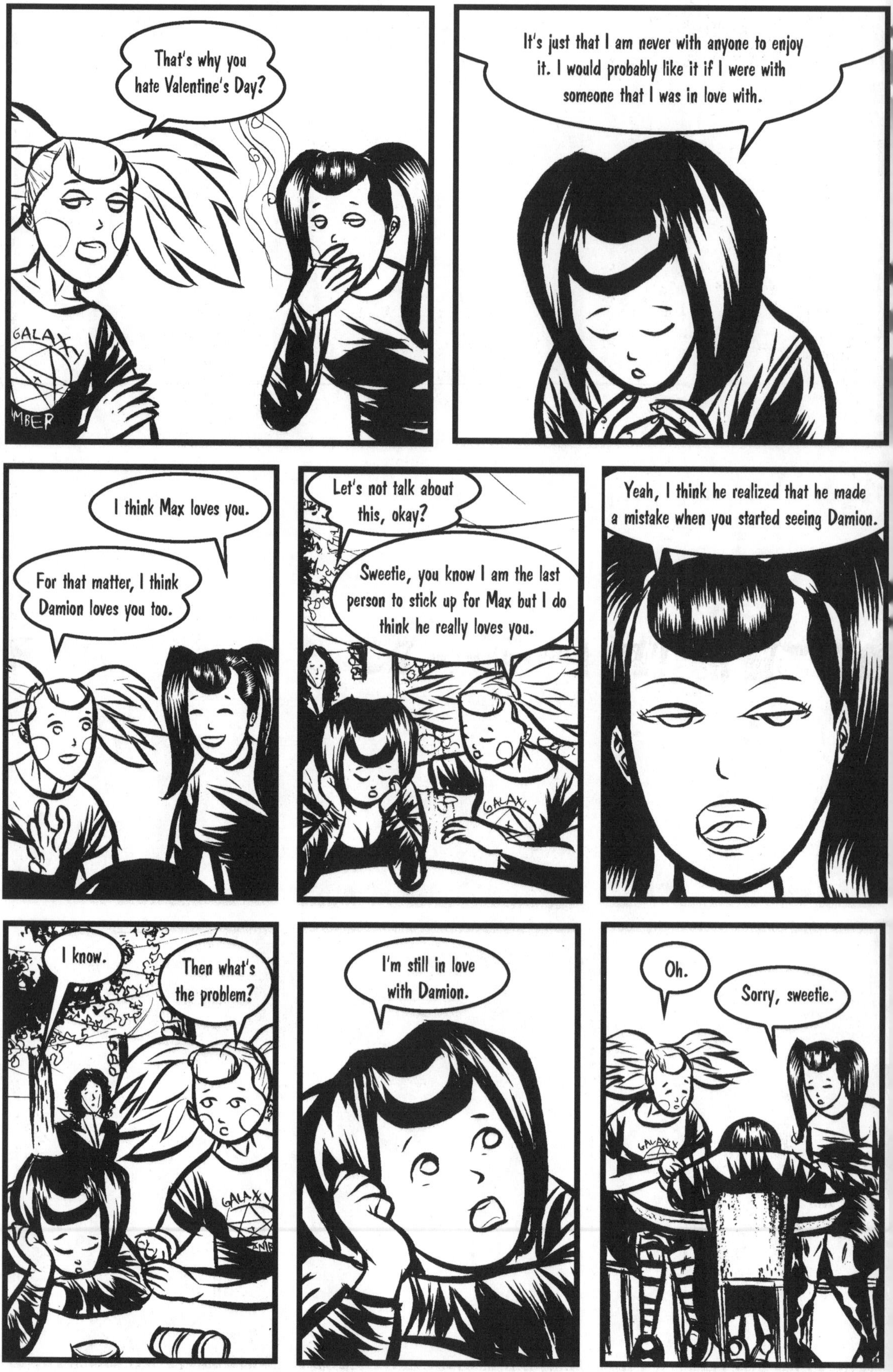
That's why you hate Valentine's Day?
GALAXY
It's just that I am never with anyone to enjoy it. I would probably like it if I were with someone that I was in love with.
I think Max loves you.
For that matter, I think Damion loves you too.
Let's not talk about this, okay?
Sweetie, you know I am the last person to stick up for Max but I do think he really loves you.
GALAXY
Yeah, I think he realized that he made a mistake when you started seeing Damion.
I know.
Then what's the problem?
GALAXY
I'm still in love with Damion.
Oh.
Sorry, sweetie.
GALAXY

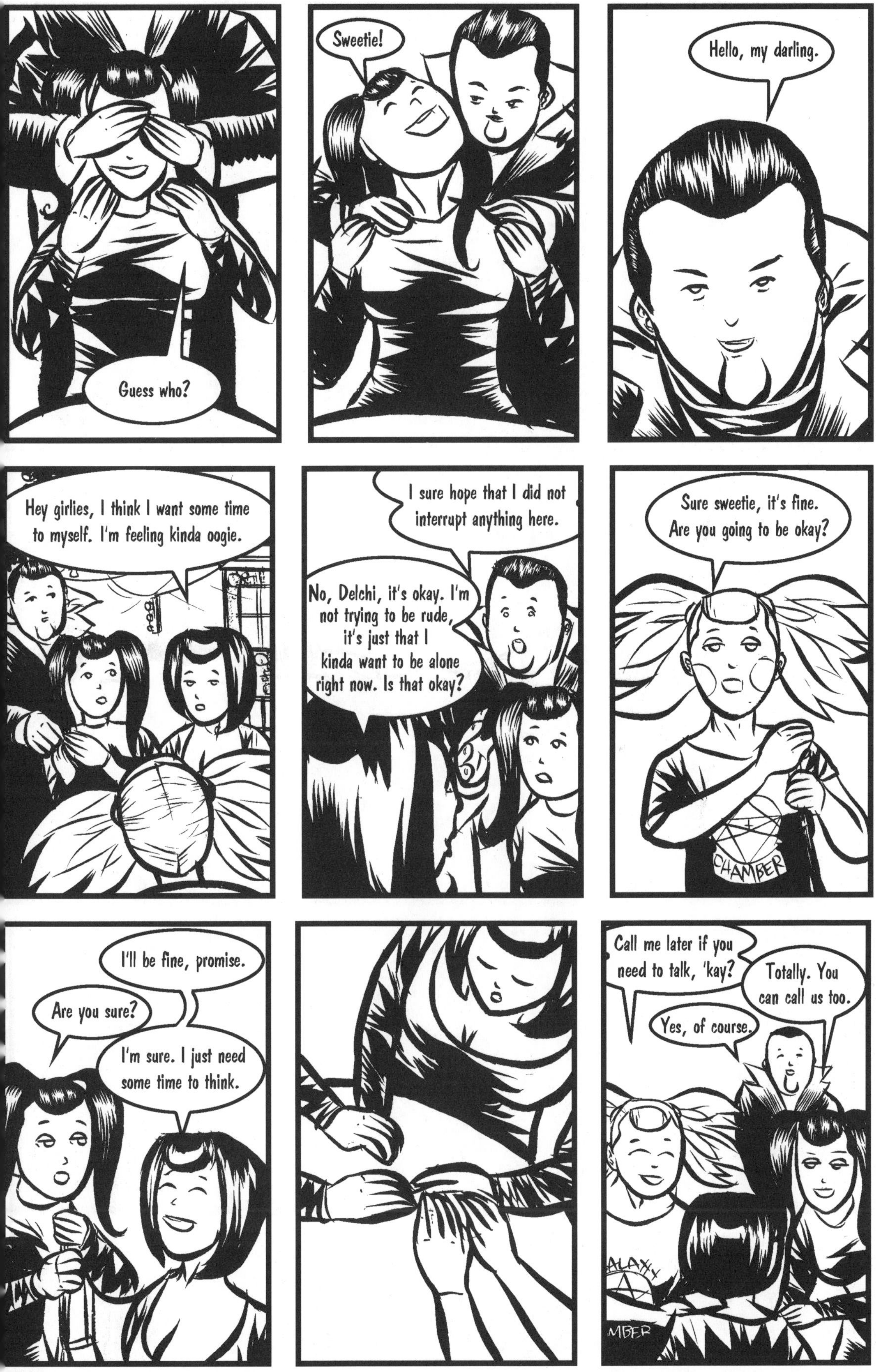
Guess who?
Sweetie!
Hello, my darling.
Hey girlies, I think I want some time to myself. I'm feeling kinda oogie.
I sure hope that I did not interrupt anything here.
No, Delchi, it's okay. I'm not trying to be rude, it's just that I kinda want to be alone right now. Is that okay?
Sure sweetie, it's fine. Are you going to be okay?
CHAMBER
Are you sure?
I'll be fine, promise.
I'm sure. I just need some time to think.
Call me later if you need to talk, 'kay?
Yes, of course.
Totally. You can call us too.

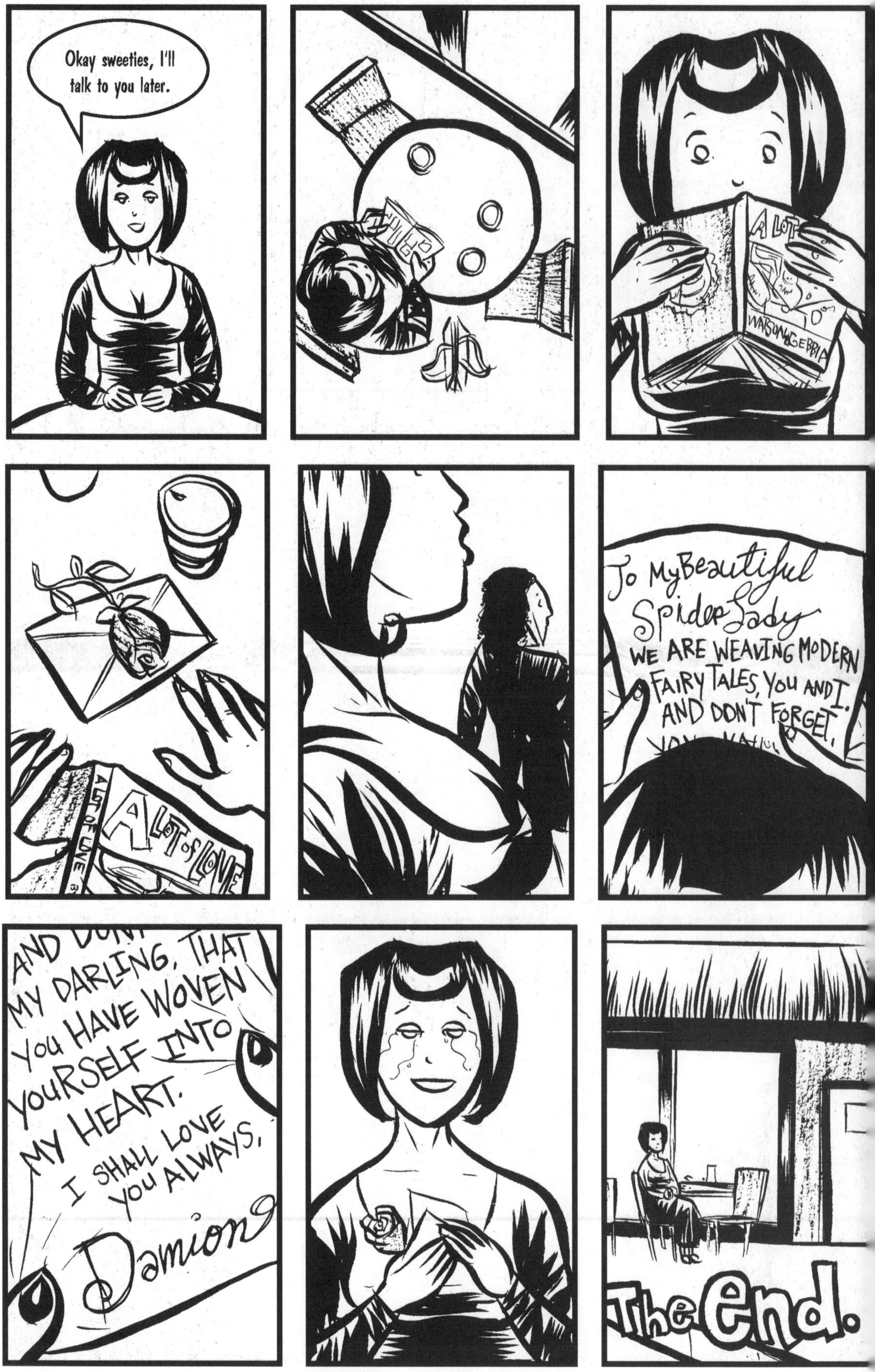
Okay sweeties, I'll talk to you later.
A LOT
A LOT of LOVE
A LOT OF LOVE
To My Beautiful Spider Lady
WE ARE WEAVING MODERN FAIRY TALES, YOU AND I. AND DON'T FORGET,
MY DARLING, THAT YOU HAVE WOVEN YOURSELF INTO MY HEART.
I SHALL LOVE YOU ALWAYS,
Damion
The end.

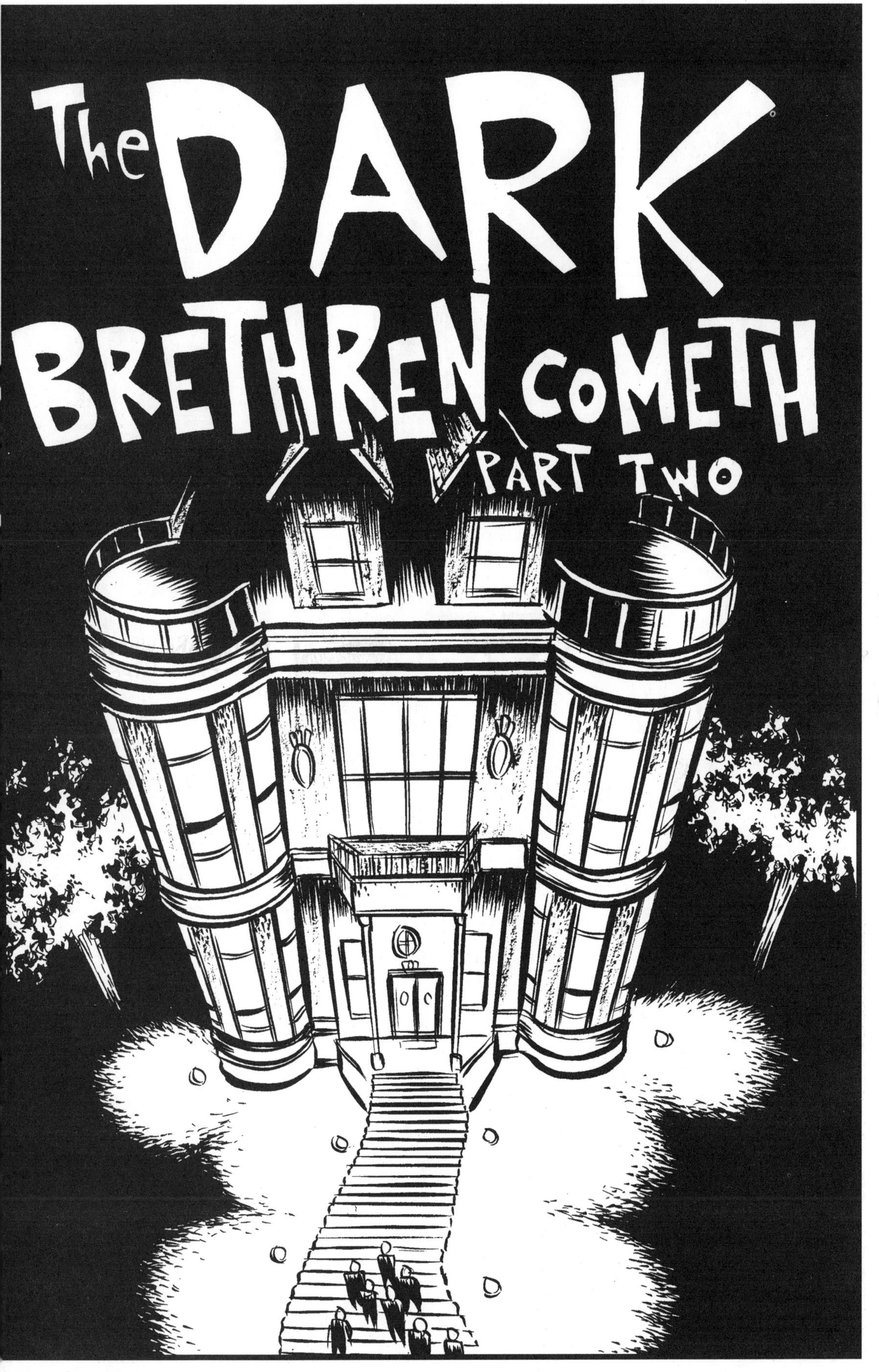
The DARK
BRETHREN COMETH
PART TWO

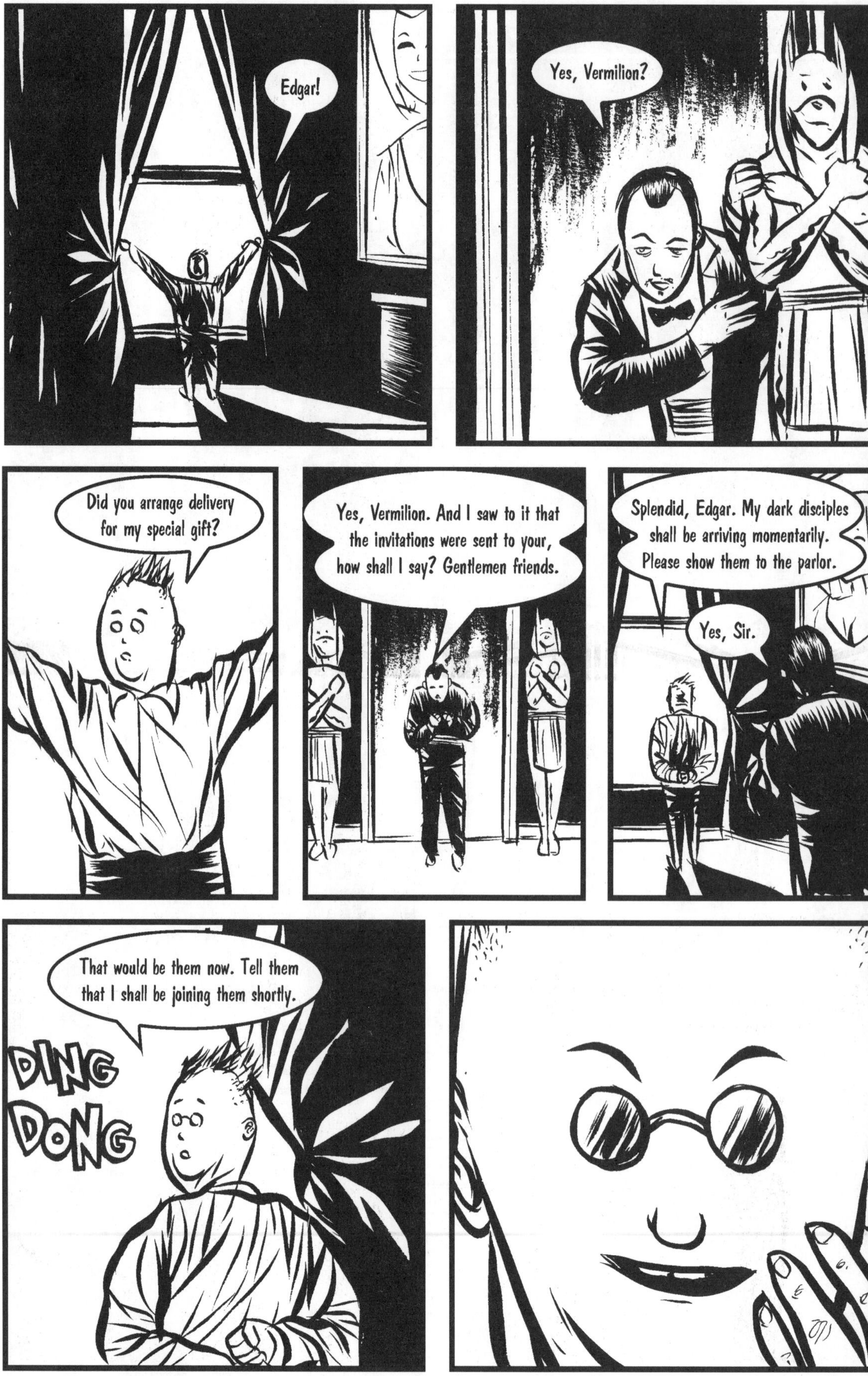
Edgar!
Yes, Vermilion?
Did you arrange delivery for my special gift?
Yes, Vermilion. And I saw to it that the invitations were sent to your, how shall I say? Gentlemen friends.
Splendid, Edgar. My dark disciples shall be arriving momentarily. Please show them to the parlor.
Yes, Sir.
That would be them now. Tell them that I shall be joining them shortly.
DING DONG

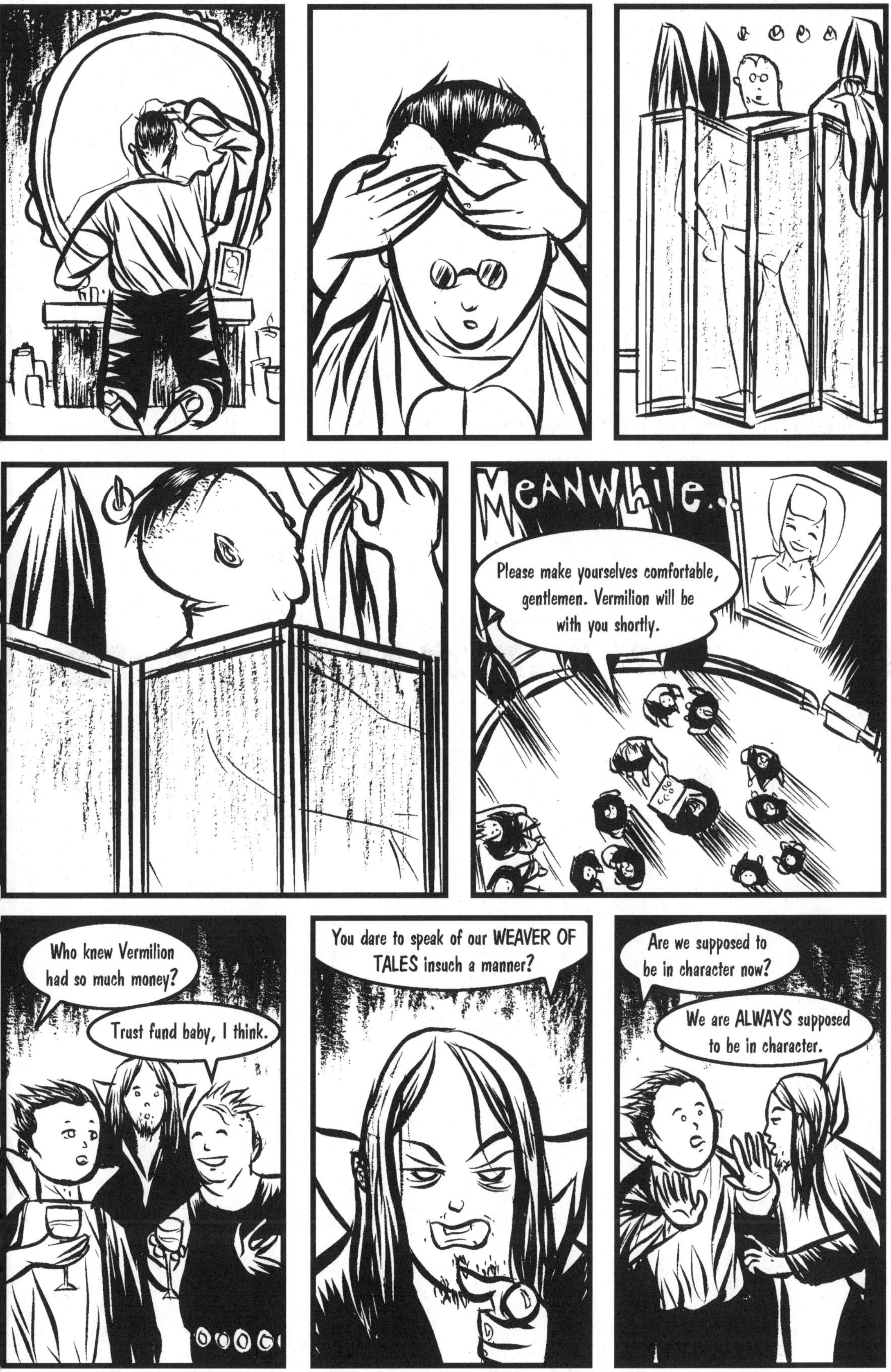
MEANWHILE...
Please make yourselves comfortable, gentlemen. Vermilion will be with you shortly.
Who knew Vermilion had so much money?
Trust fund baby, I think.
You dare to speak of our WEAVER OF TALES insuch a manner?
Are we supposed to be in character now?
We are ALWAYS supposed to be in character.

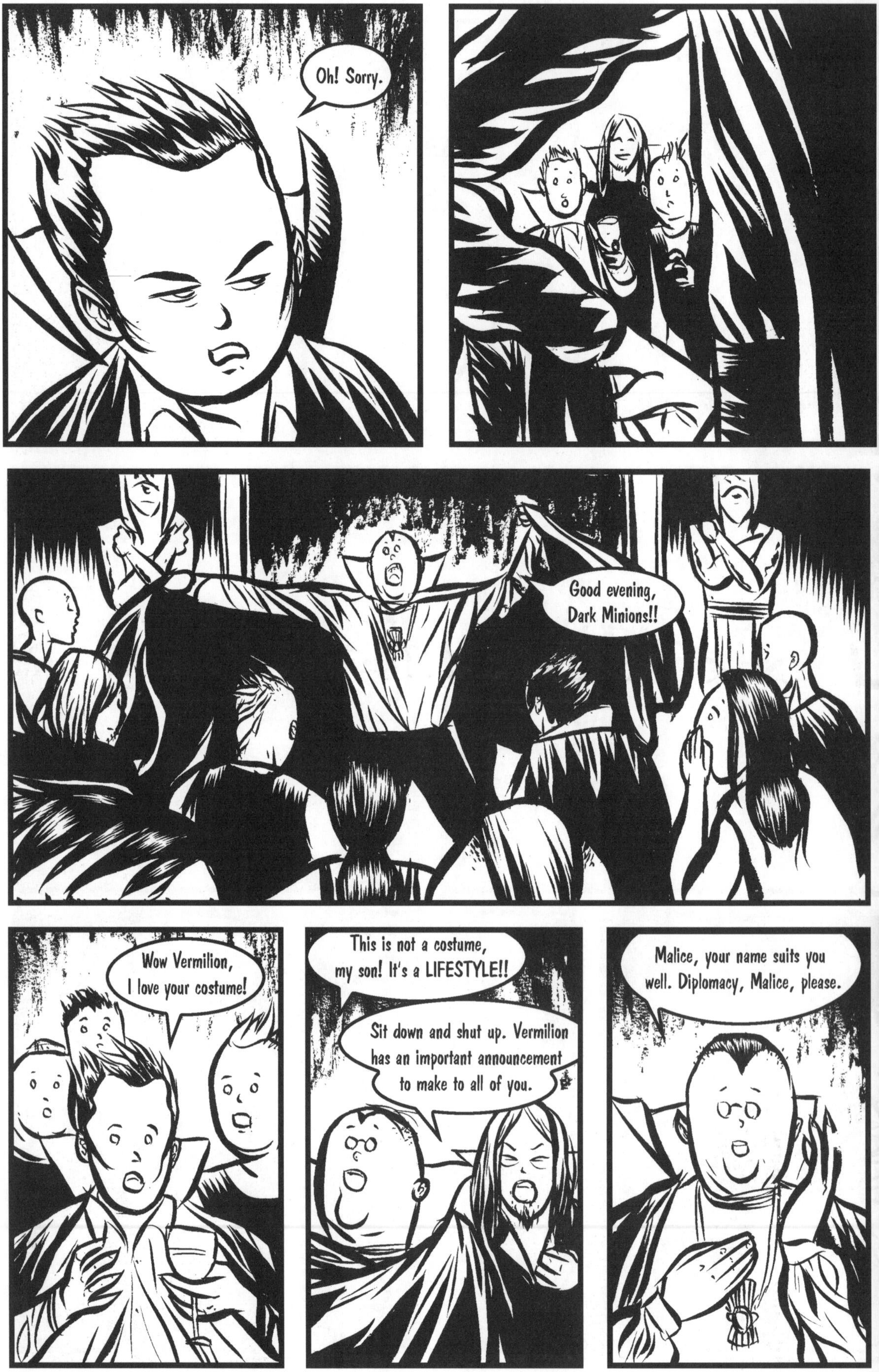
Oh! Sorry.
Good evening, Dark Minions!!
Wow Vermilion, I love your costume!
This is not a costume, my son! It's a LIFESTYLE!!
Sit down and shut up. Vermilion has an important announcement to make to all of you.
Malice, your name suits you well. Diplomacy, Malice, please.

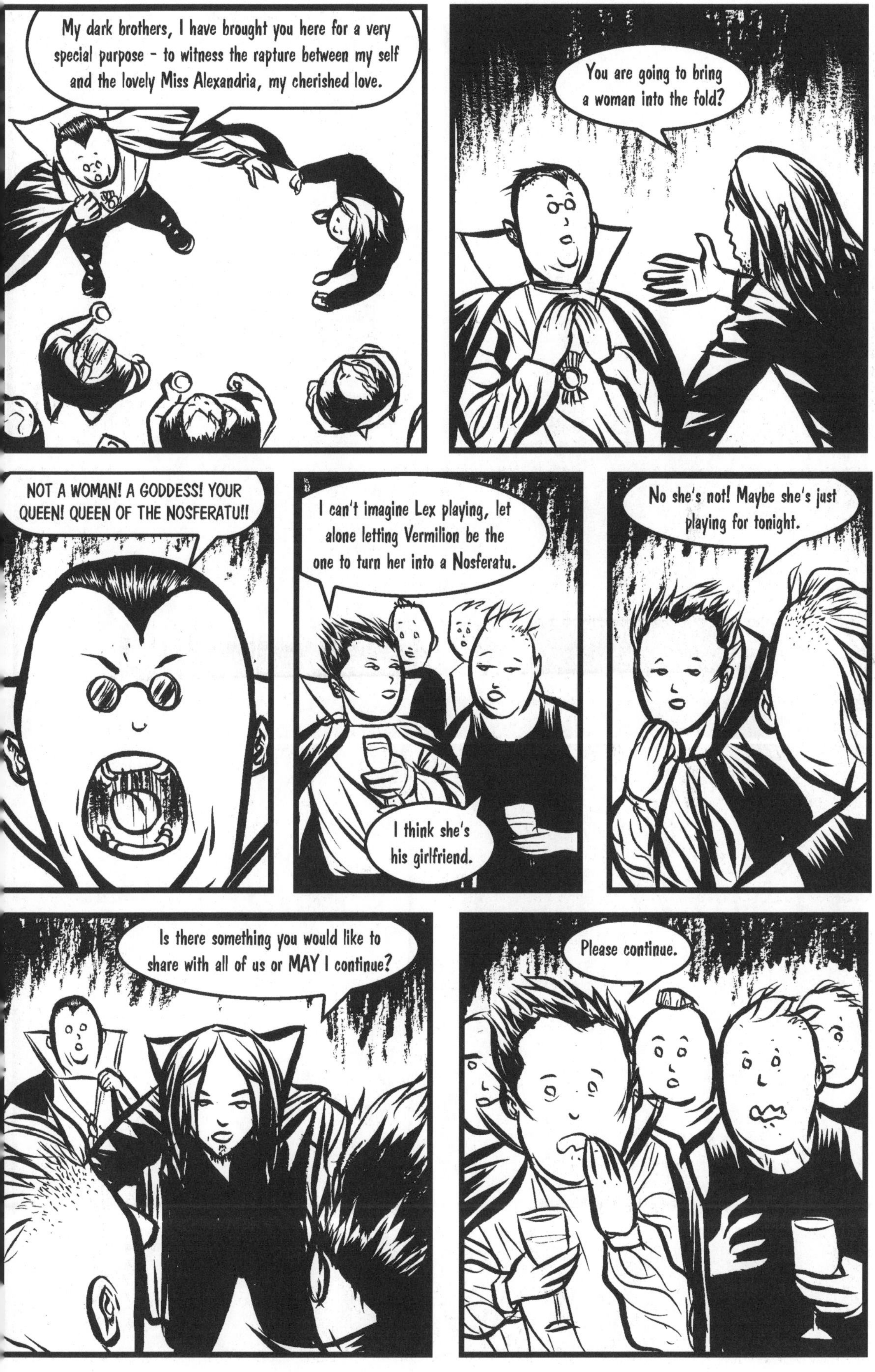
My dark brothers, I have brought you here for a very special purpose - to witness the rapture between my self and the lovely Miss Alexandria, my cherished love.
You are going to bring a woman into the fold?
NOT A WOMAN! A GODDESS! YOUR QUEEN! QUEEN OF THE NOSFERATU!!
I can't imagine Lex playing, let alone letting Vermilion be the one to turn her into a Nosferatu.
I think she's his girlfriend.
No she's not! Maybe she's just playing for tonight.
Is there something you would like to share with all of us or MAY I continue?
Please continue.

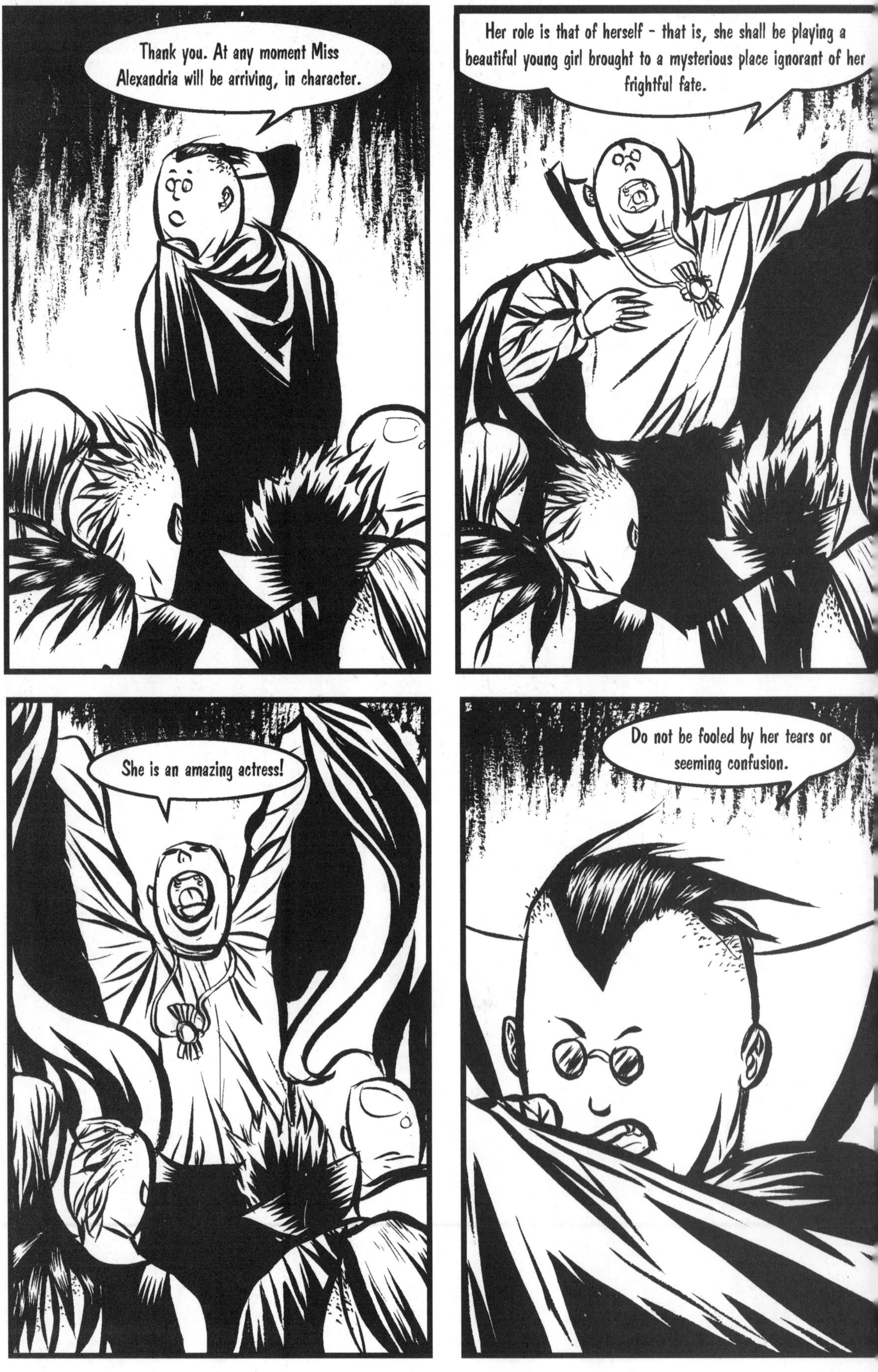
Thank you. At any moment Miss Alexandria will be arriving, in character.
Her role is that of herself - that is, she shall be playing a beautiful young girl brought to a mysterious place ignorant of her frightful fate.
She is an amazing actress!
Do not be fooled by her tears or seeming confusion.

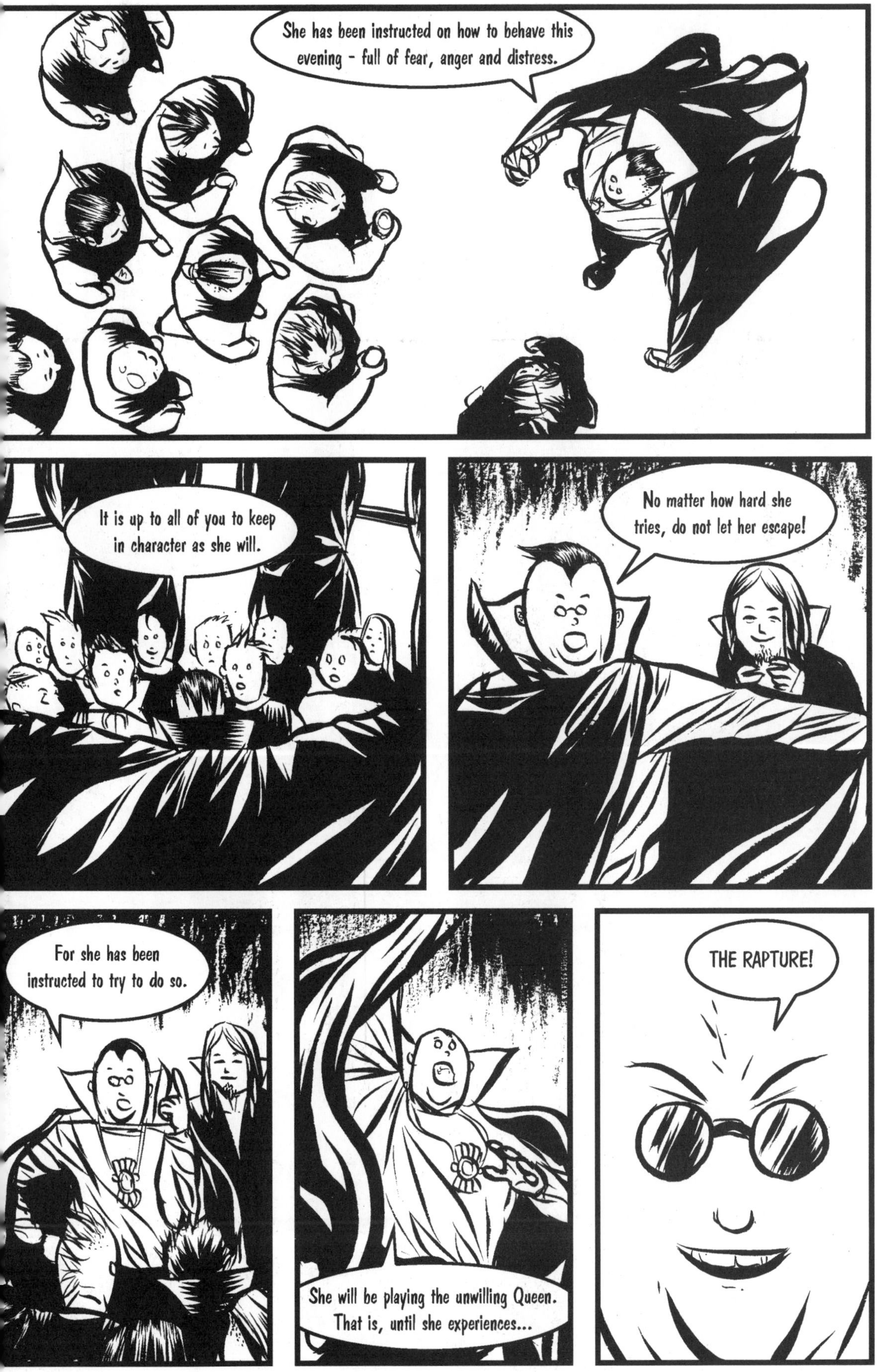
She has been instructed on how to behave this evening - full of fear, anger and distress.
It is up to all of you to keep in character as she will.
No matter how hard she tries, do not let her escape!
For she has been instructed to try to do so.
She will be playing the unwilling Queen. That is, until she experiences...
THE RAPTURE!

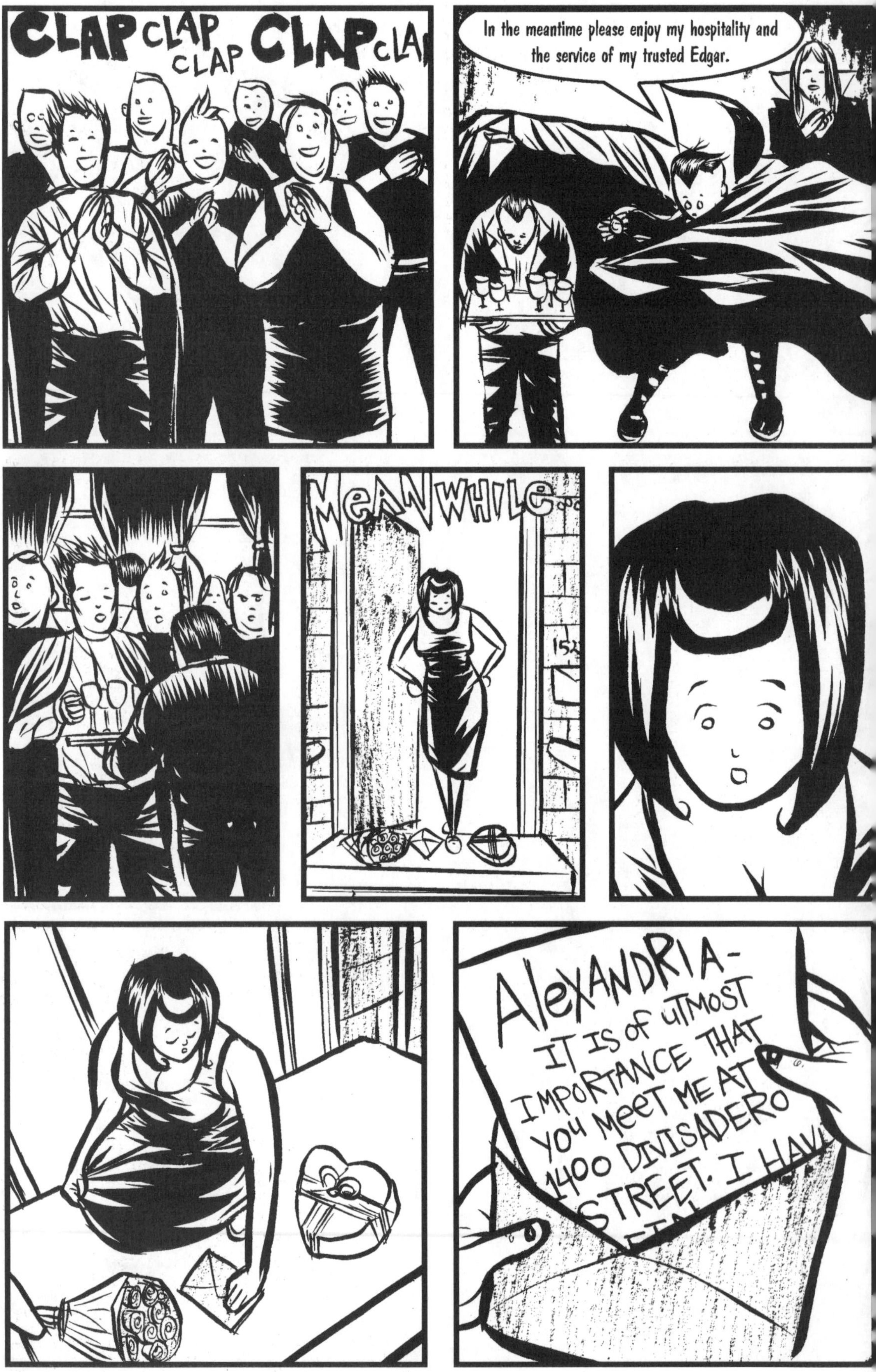

CLAP CLAP CLAP CLAP CLAP
In the meantime please enjoy my hospitality and the service of my trusted Edgar.
MEANWHILE...
152
ALEXANDRIA-
IT IS OF UTMOST IMPORTANCE THAT YOU MEET ME AT 1400 DIVISADERO STREET. I HAV

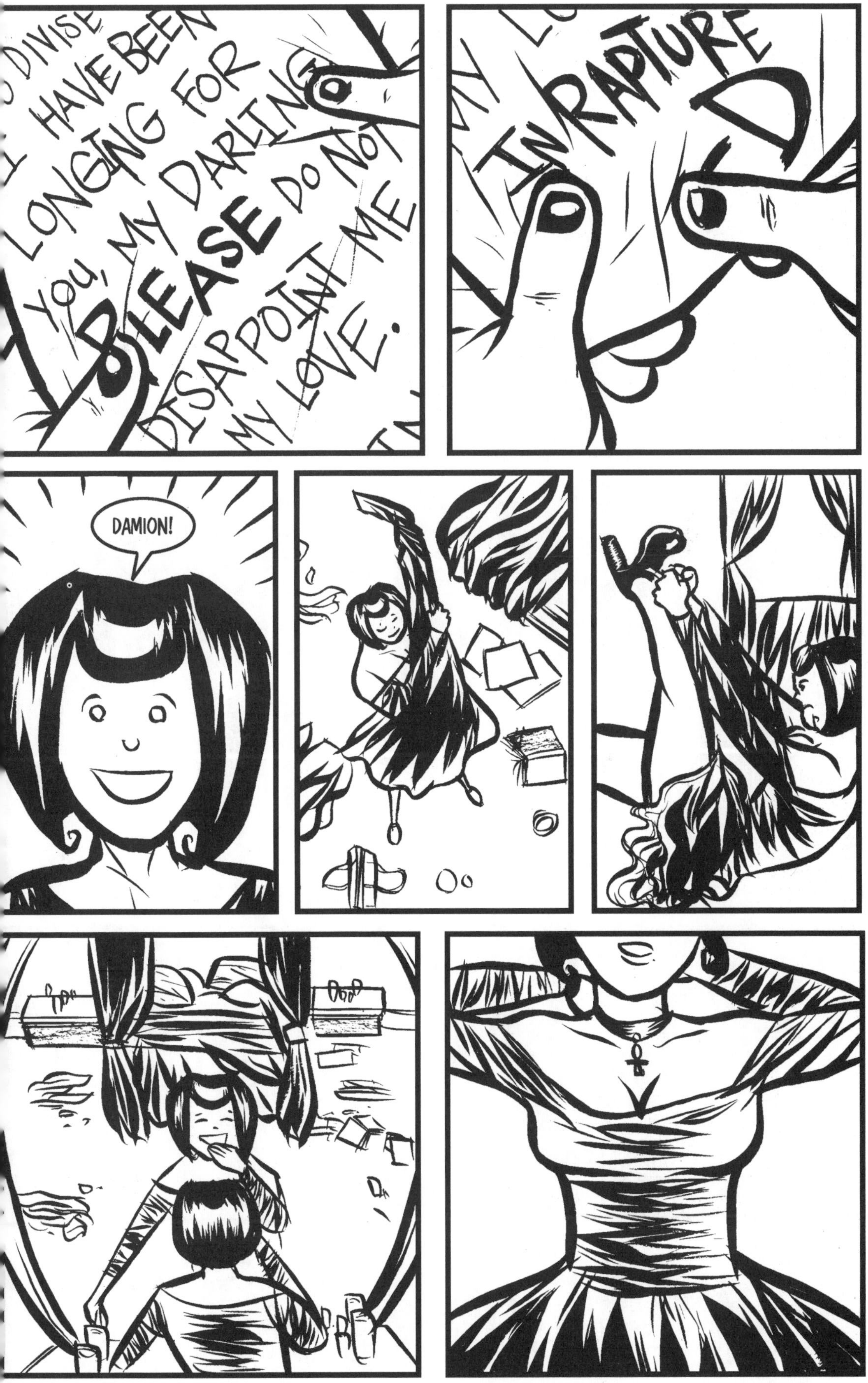
I HAVE BEEN LONGING FOR YOU, MY DARLING
PLEASE DO NOT DISAPPOINT ME MY LOVE.
IN RAPTURE
DAMION!

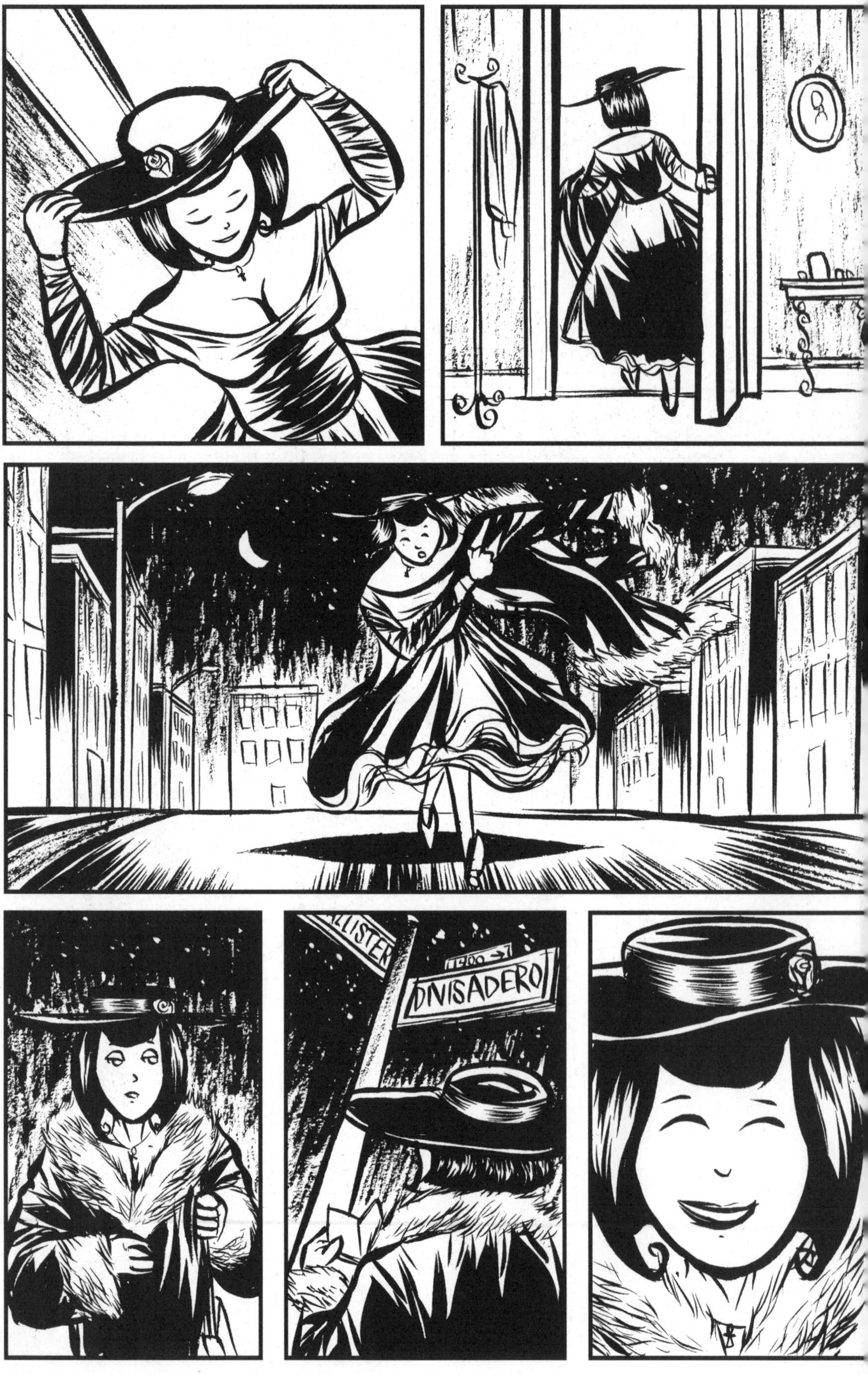
LLISTER
DNISADERO

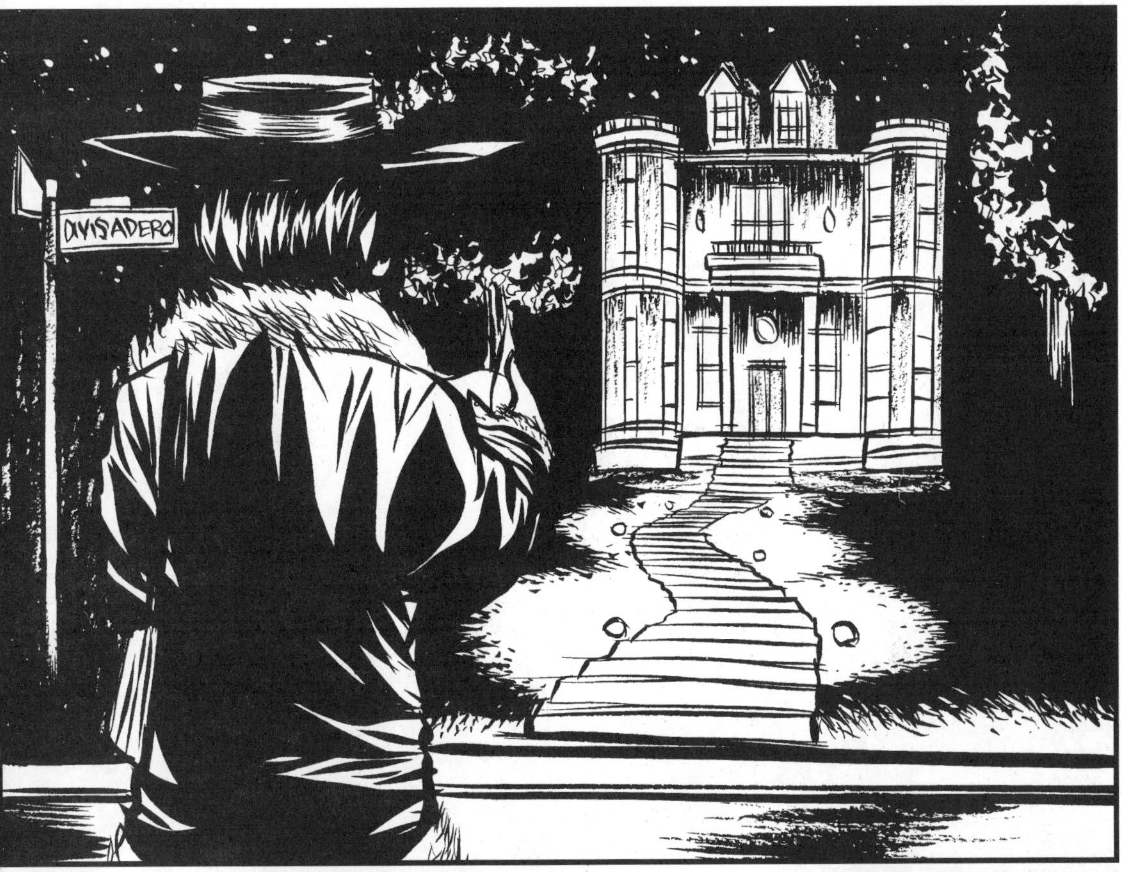
DIVISADERO

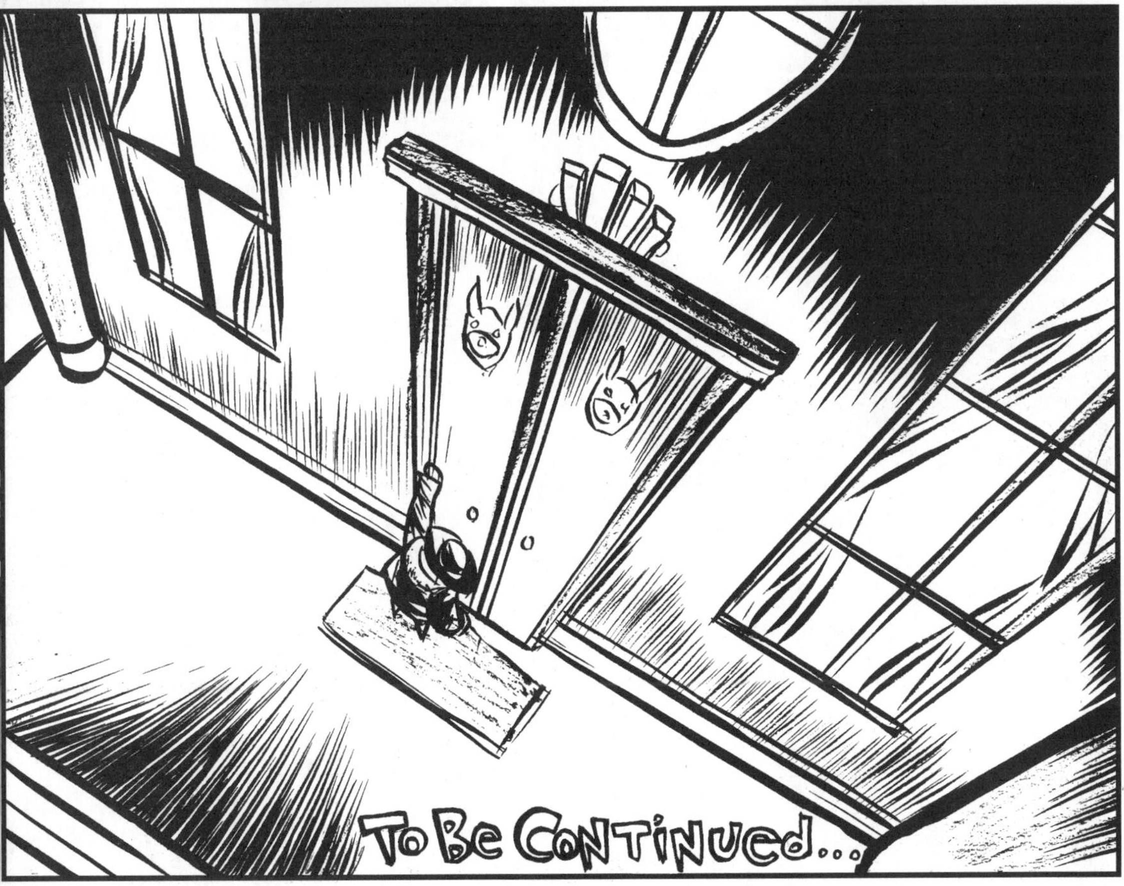
To Be Continued...

Chapter 12

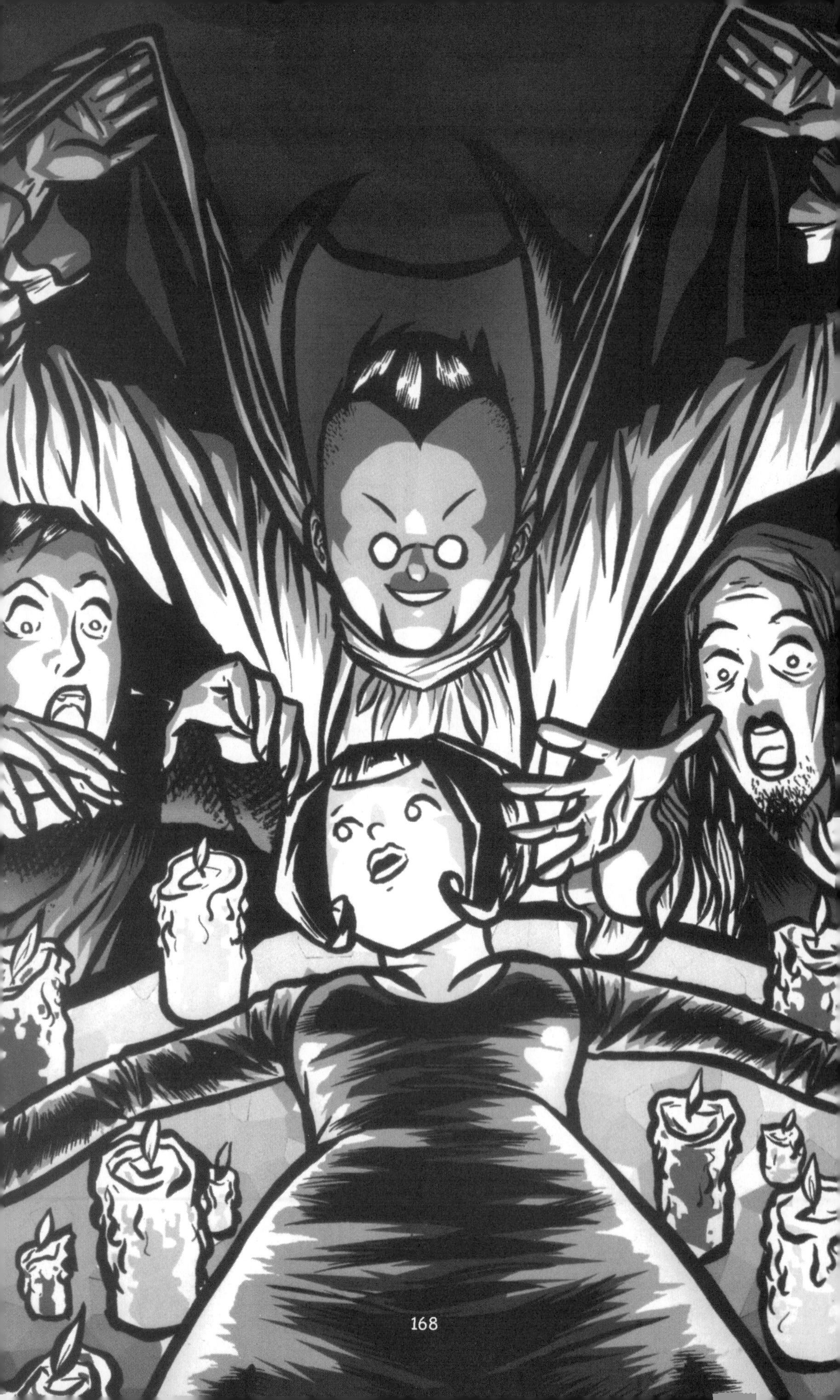

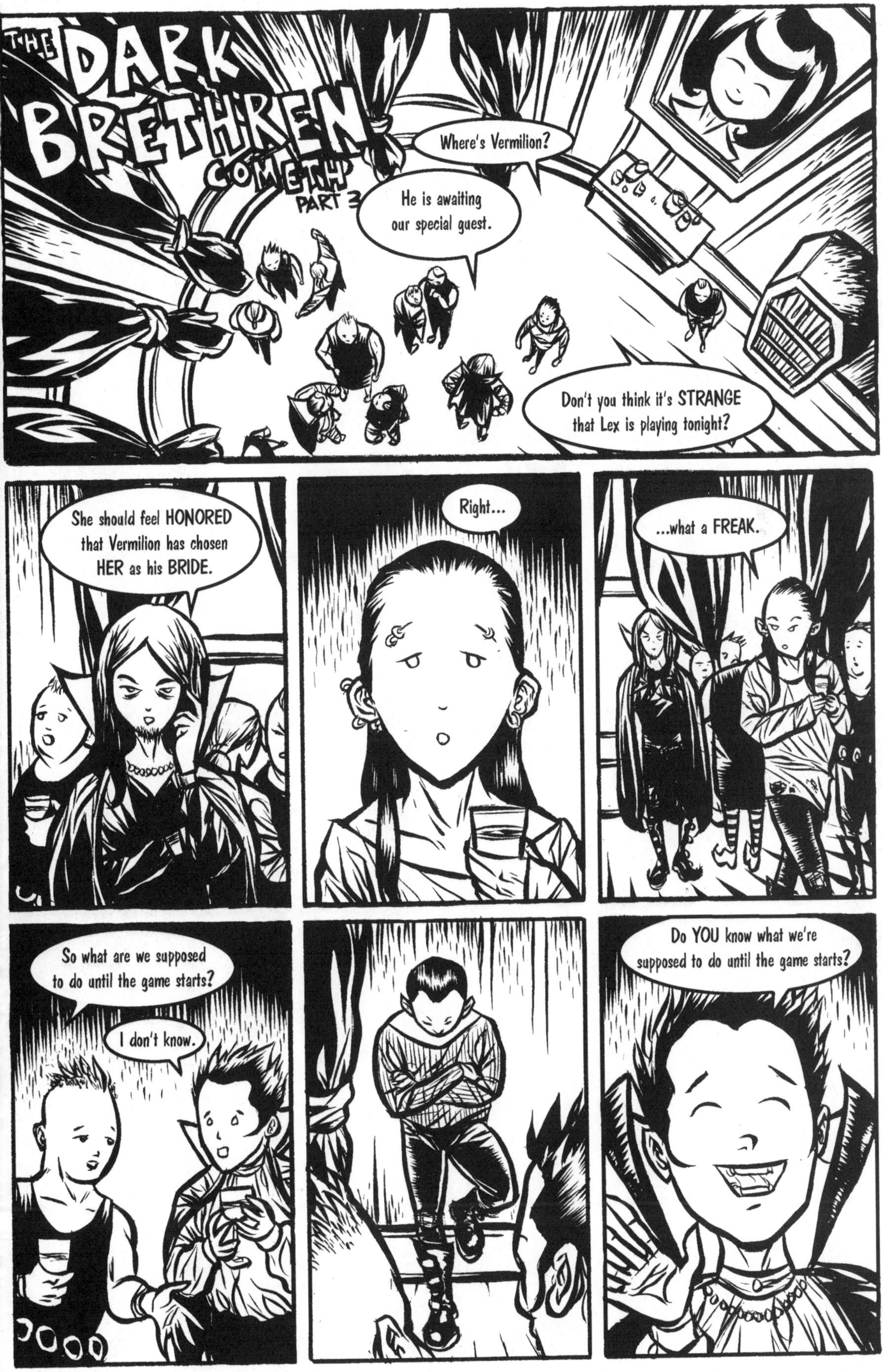
THE DARK BRETHREN COMETH
PART 3
Where's Vermilion?
He is awaiting our special guest.
Don't you think it's STRANGE that Lex is playing tonight?
She should feel HONORED that Vermilion has chosen HER as his BRIDE.
Right...
...what a FREAK.
So what are we supposed to do until the game starts?
I don't know.
Do YOU know what we're supposed to do until the game starts?

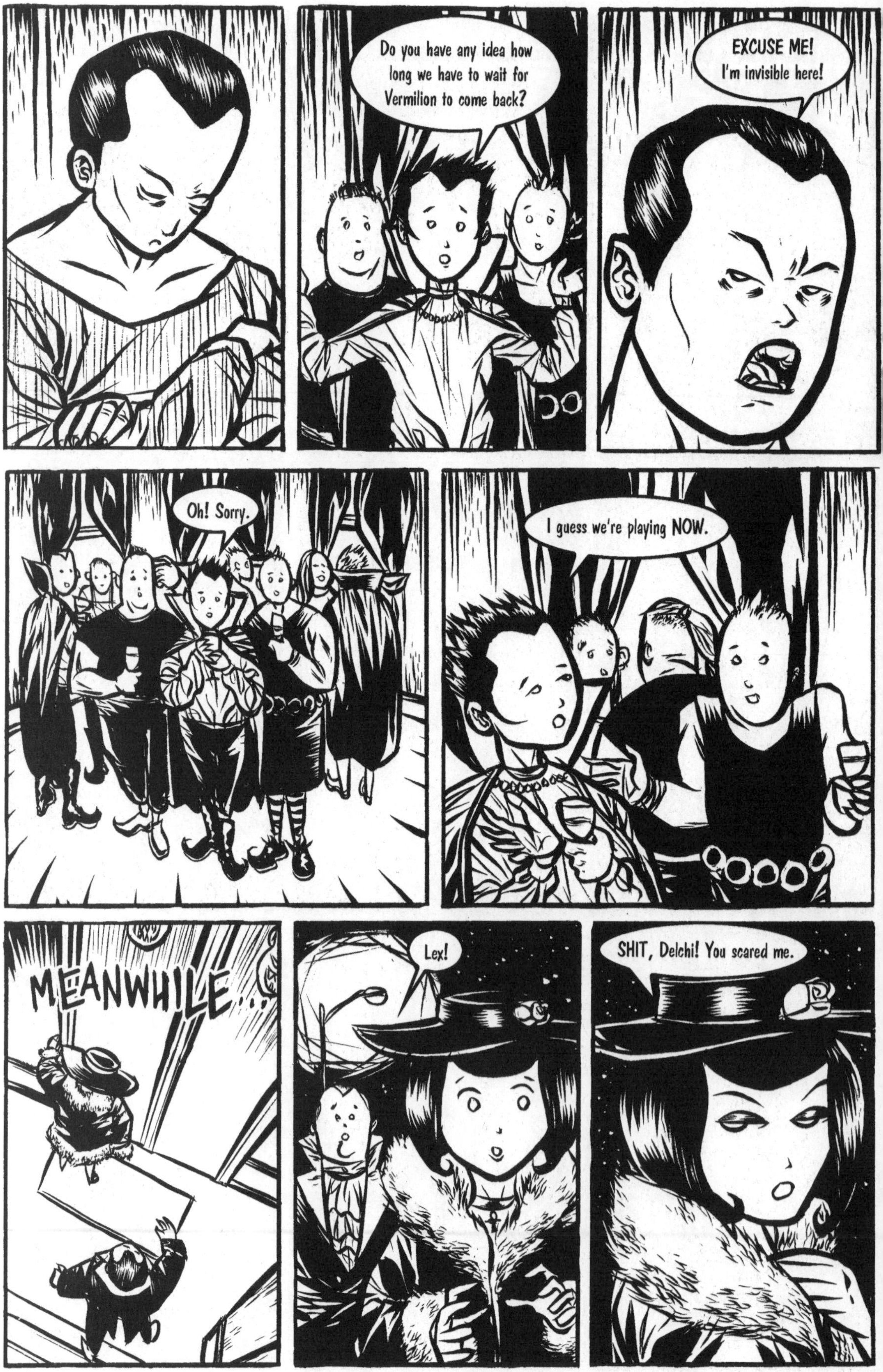
Do you have any idea how long we have to wait for Vermilion to come back?
EXCUSE ME!
I'm invisible here!
Oh! Sorry.
I guess we're playing NOW.
MEANWHILE...
Lex!
SHIT, Delchi! You scared me.

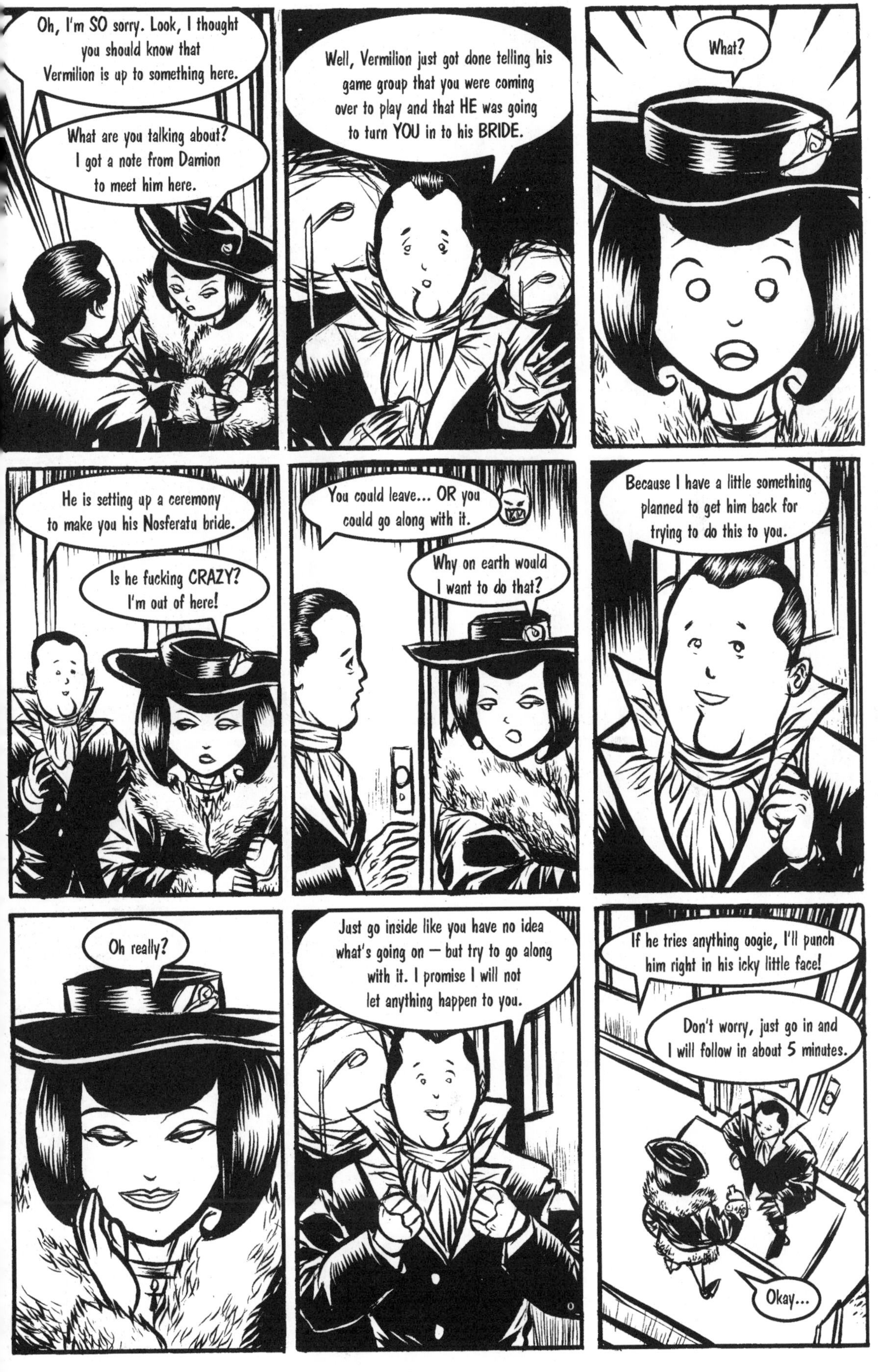
Oh, I'm SO sorry. Look, I thought you should know that Vermilion is up to something here.
What are you talking about? I got a note from Damion to meet him here.
Well, Vermilion just got done telling his game group that you were coming over to play and that HE was going to turn YOU in to his BRIDE.
What?
He is setting up a ceremony to make you his Nosferatu bride.
Is he fucking CRAZY? I'm out of here!
You could leave... OR you could go along with it.
Why on earth would I want to do that?
Because I have a little something planned to get him back for trying to do this to you.
Oh really?
Just go inside like you have no idea what's going on — but try to go along with it. I promise I will not let anything happen to you.
If he tries anything oogie, I'll punch him right in his icky little face!
Don't worry, just go in and I will follow in about 5 minutes.
Okay...

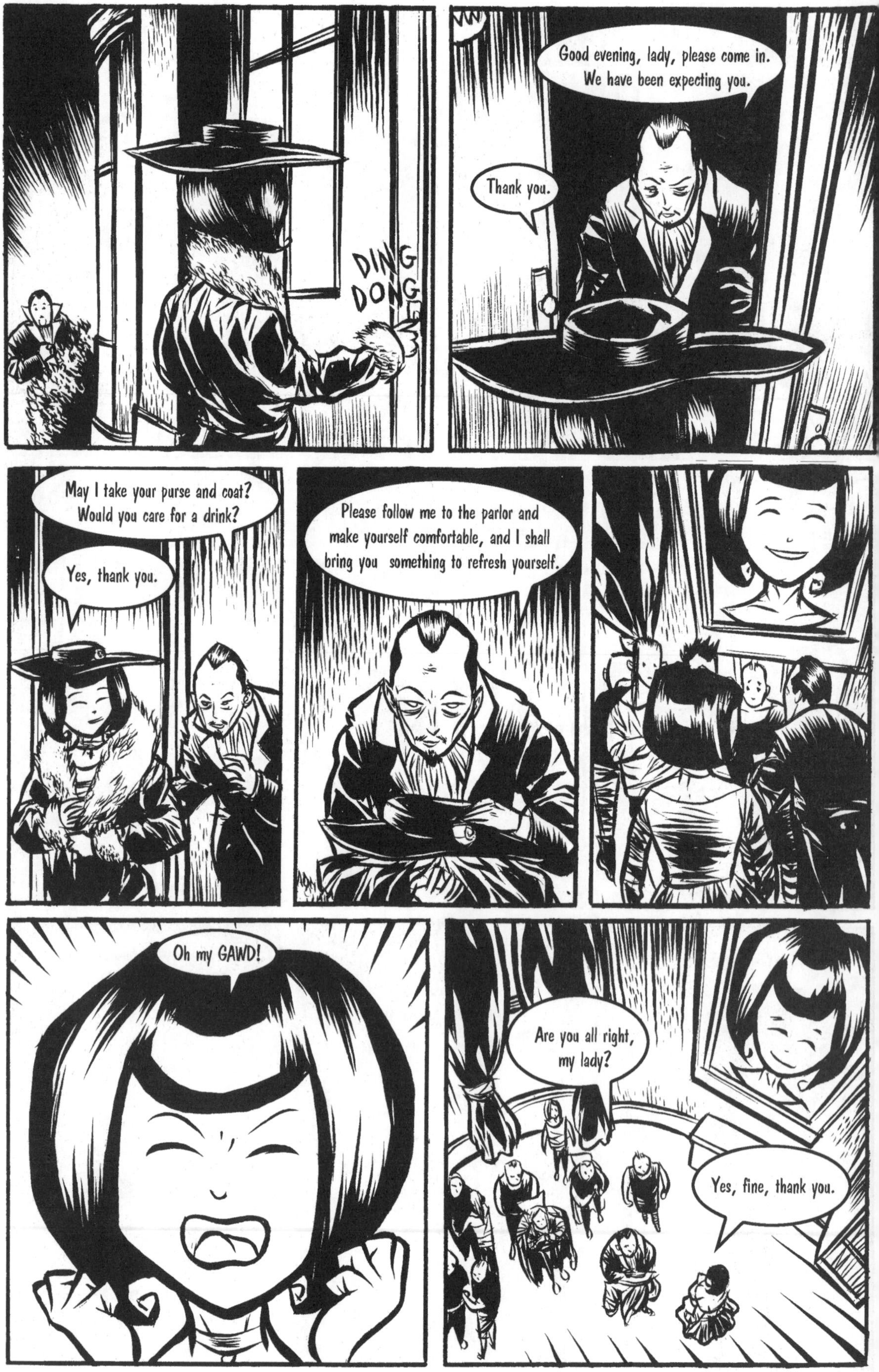
DING DONG
Good evening, lady, please come in. We have been expecting you.
Thank you.
May I take your purse and coat? Would you care for a drink?
Yes, thank you.
Please follow me to the parlor and make yourself comfortable, and I shall bring you something to refresh yourself.
Oh my GAWD!
Are you all right, my lady?
Yes, fine, thank you.

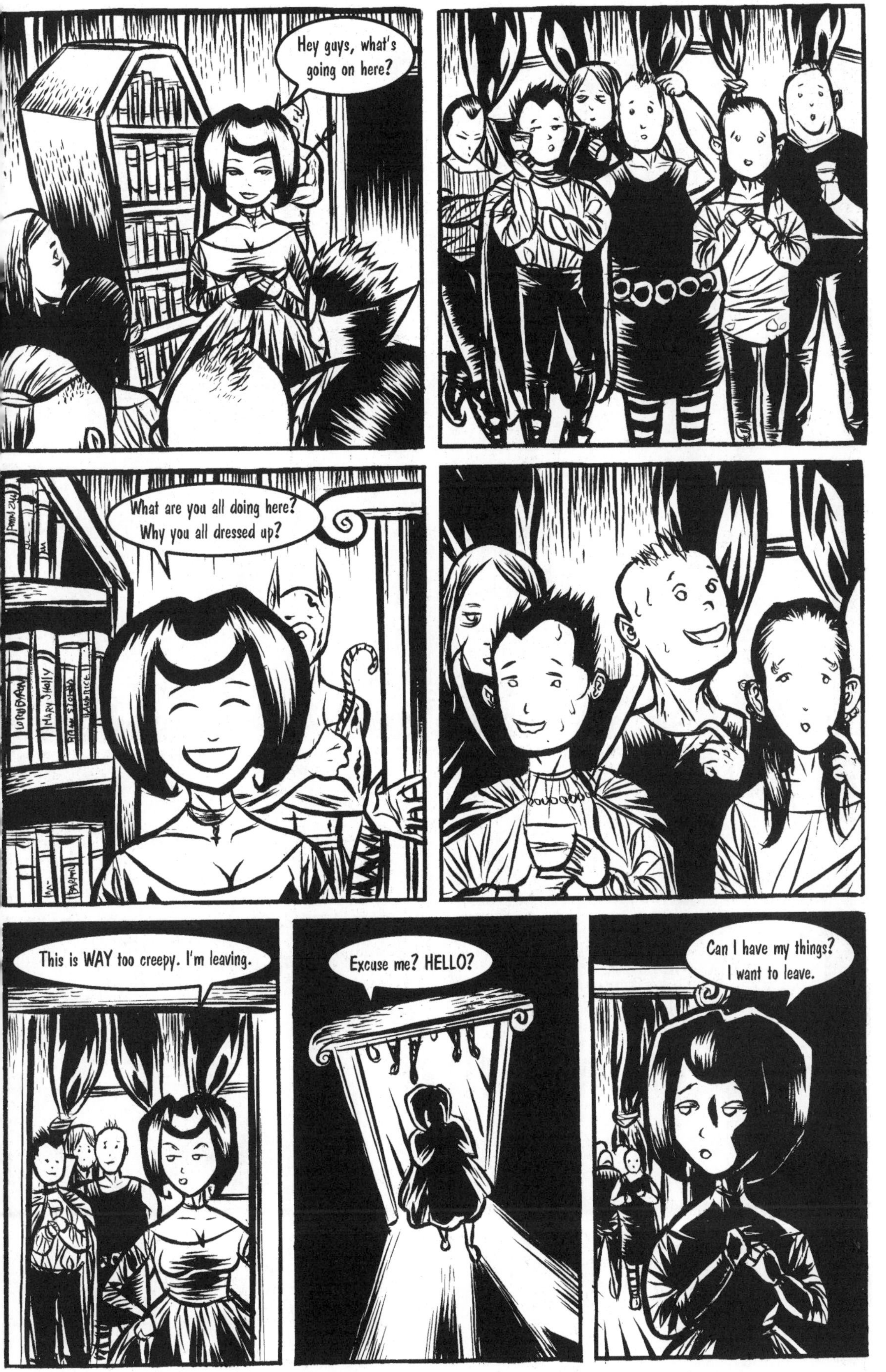
Hey guys, what's going on here?
What are you all doing here? Why you all dressed up?
This is WAY too creepy. I'm leaving.
Excuse me? HELLO?
Can I have my things? I want to leave.

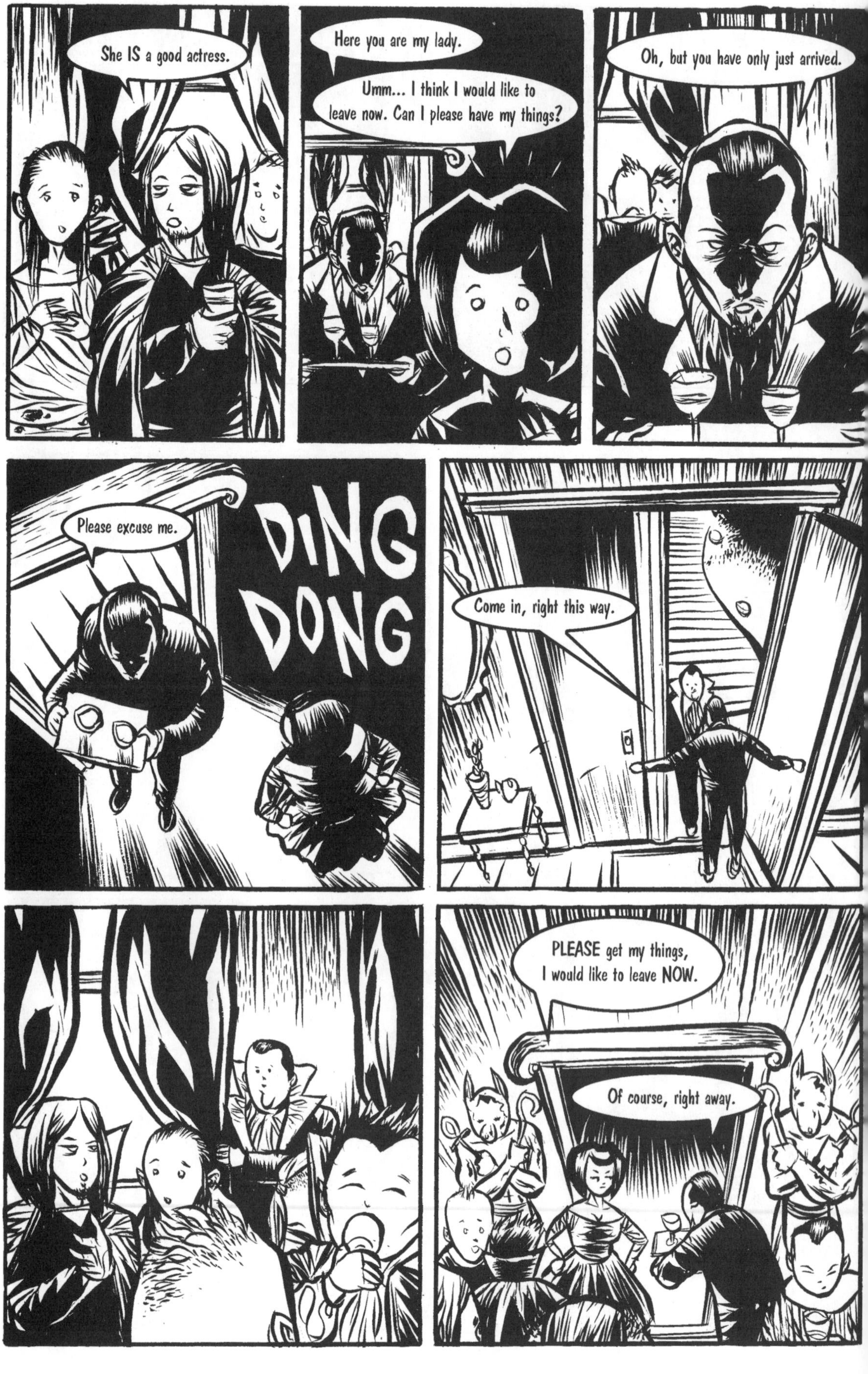
She IS a good actress.
Here you are my lady.
Umm... I think I would like to leave now. Can I please have my things?
Oh, but you have only just arrived.
Please excuse me.
DING DONG
Come in, right this way.
PLEASE get my things, I would like to leave NOW.
Of course, right away.

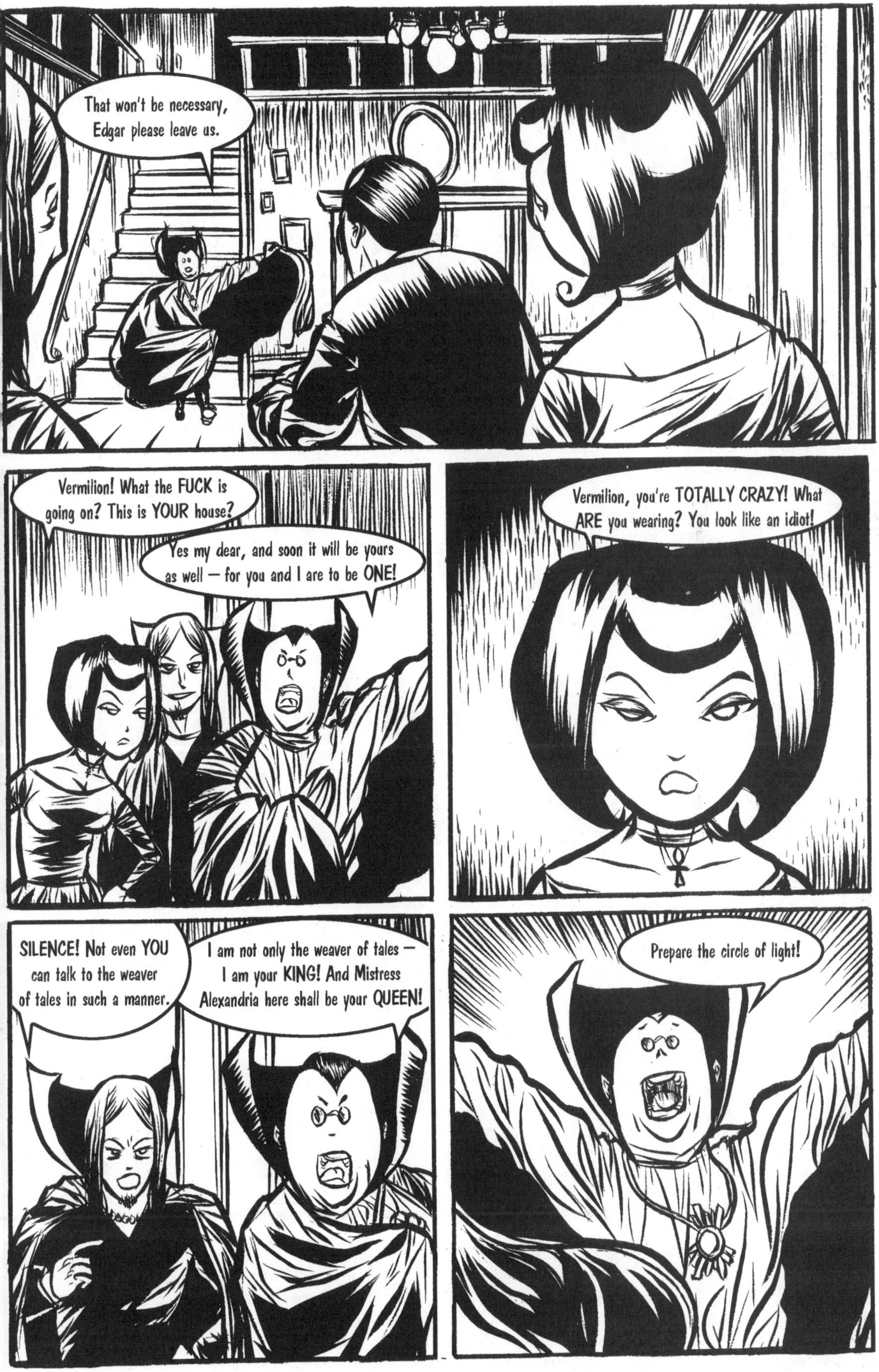
That won't be necessary, Edgar please leave us.
Vermilion! What the FUCK is going on? This is YOUR house?
Yes my dear, and soon it will be yours as well — for you and I are to be ONE!
Vermilion, you're TOTALLY CRAZY! What ARE you wearing? You look like an idiot!
SILENCE! Not even YOU can talk to the weaver of tales in such a manner.
I am not only the weaver of tales — I am your KING! And Mistress Alexandria here shall be your QUEEN!
Prepare the circle of light!

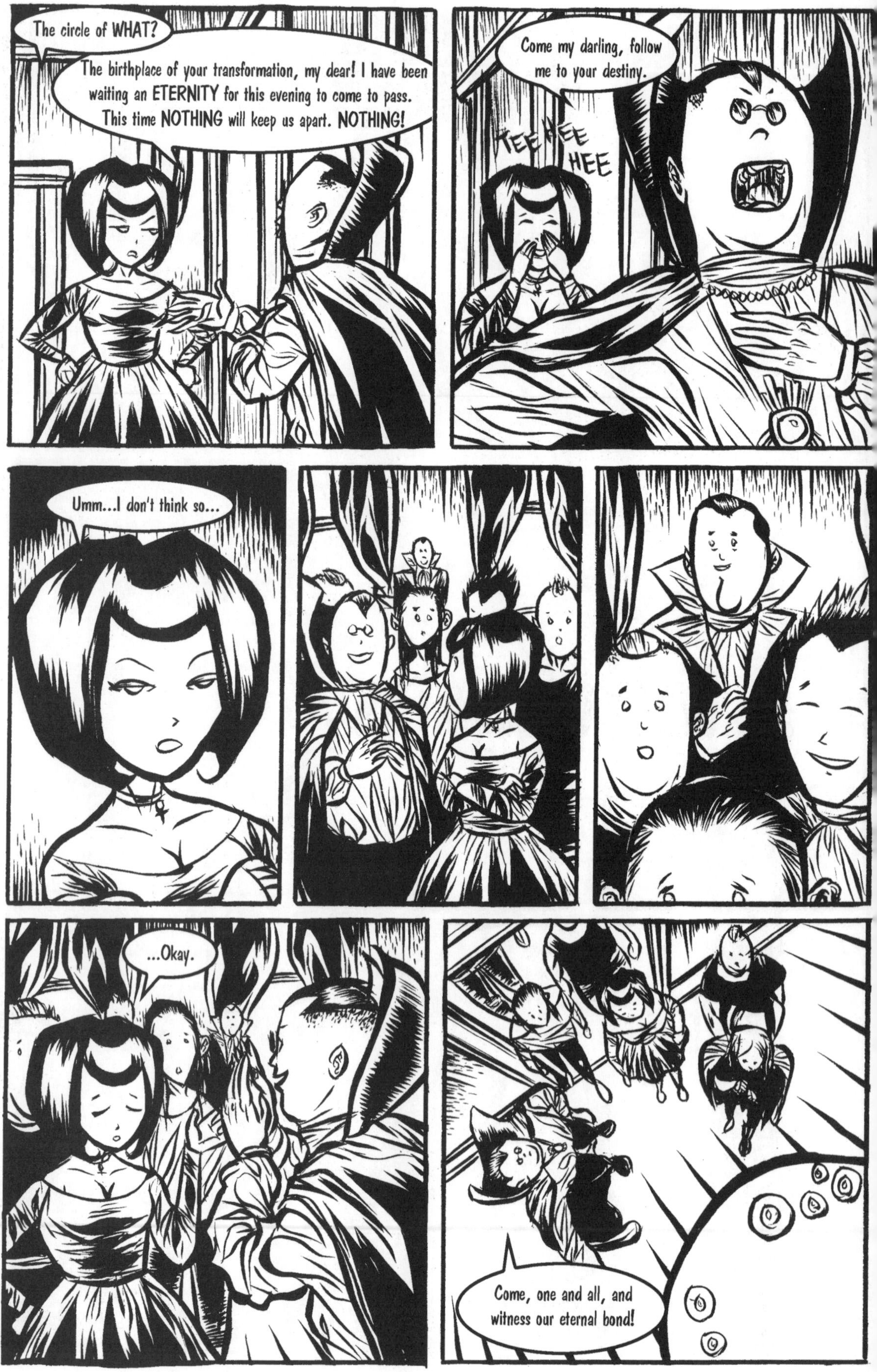

The circle of WHAT?
The birthplace of your transformation, my dear! I have been waiting an ETERNITY for this evening to come to pass. This time NOTHING will keep us apart. NOTHING!
Come my darling, follow me to your destiny.
TEE HEE HEE
Umm...I don't think so...
...Okay.
Come, one and all, and witness our eternal bond!

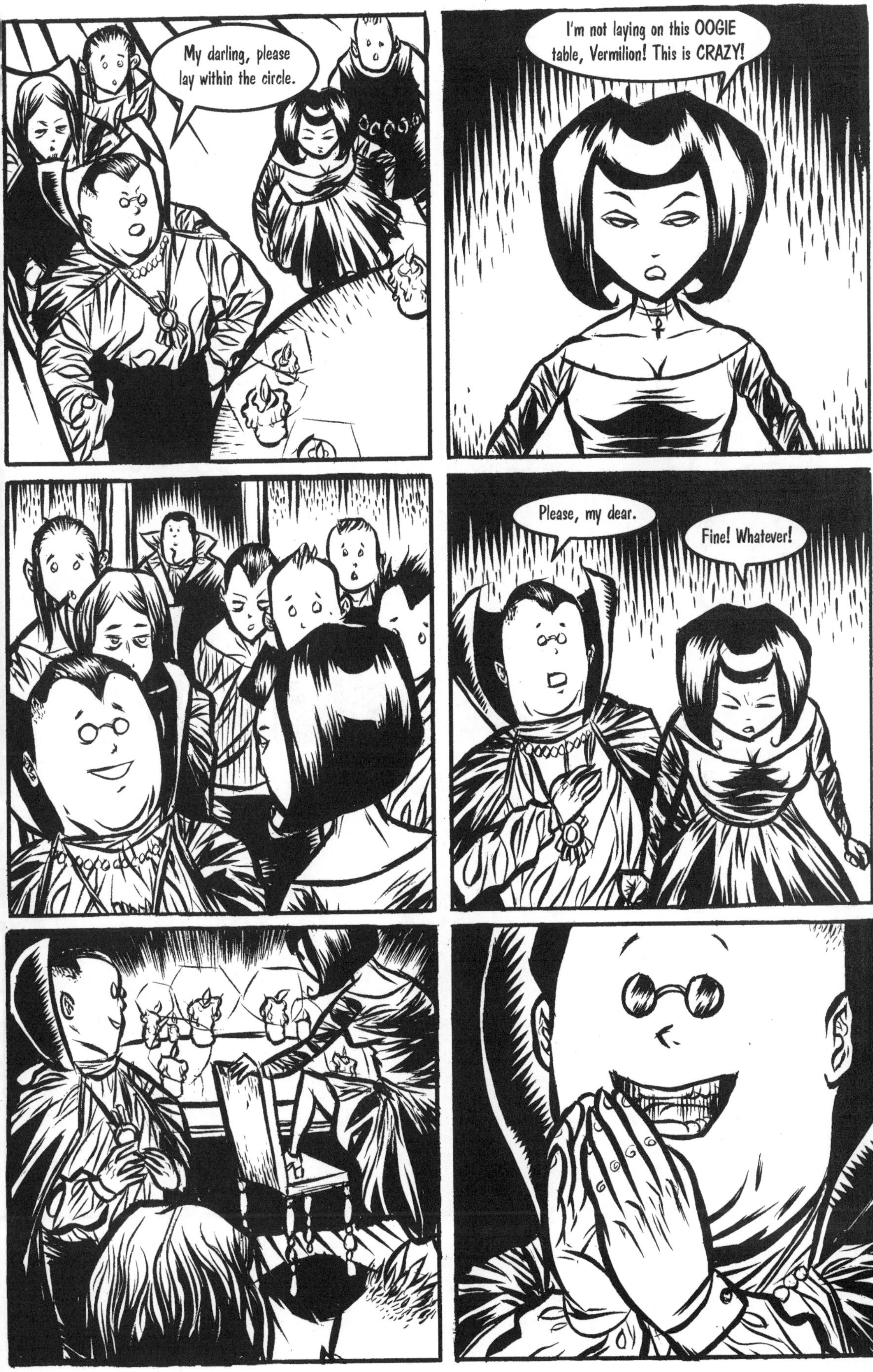
My darling, please lay within the circle.
I'm not laying on this OOGIE table, Vermilion! This is CRAZY!
Please, my dear.
Fine! Whatever!

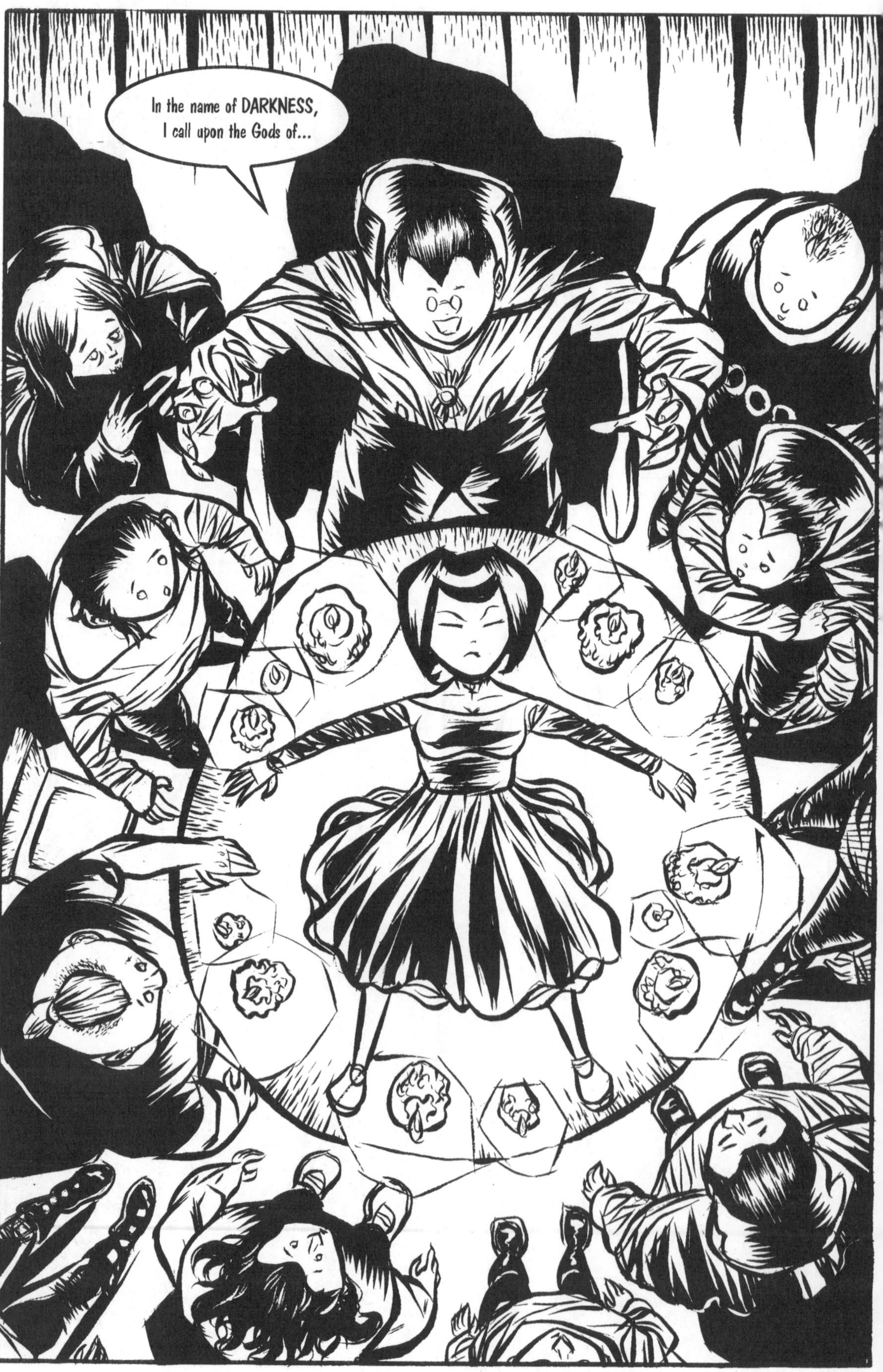
In the name of DARKNESS, I call upon the Gods of...

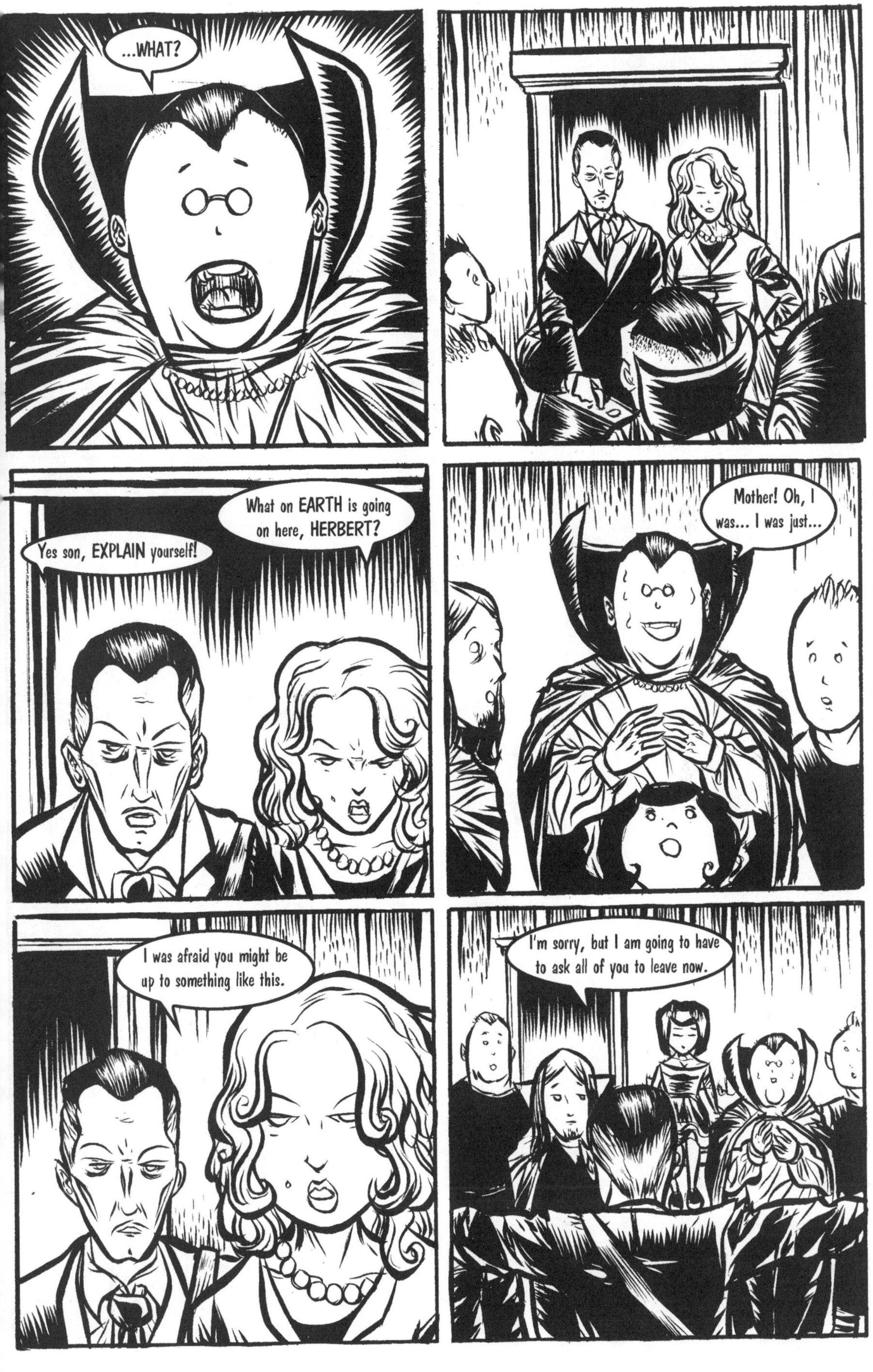
...WHAT?
What on EARTH is going on here, HERBERT?
Yes son, EXPLAIN yourself!
Mother! Oh, I was... I was just...
I was afraid you might be up to something like this.
I'm sorry, but I am going to have to ask all of you to leave now.

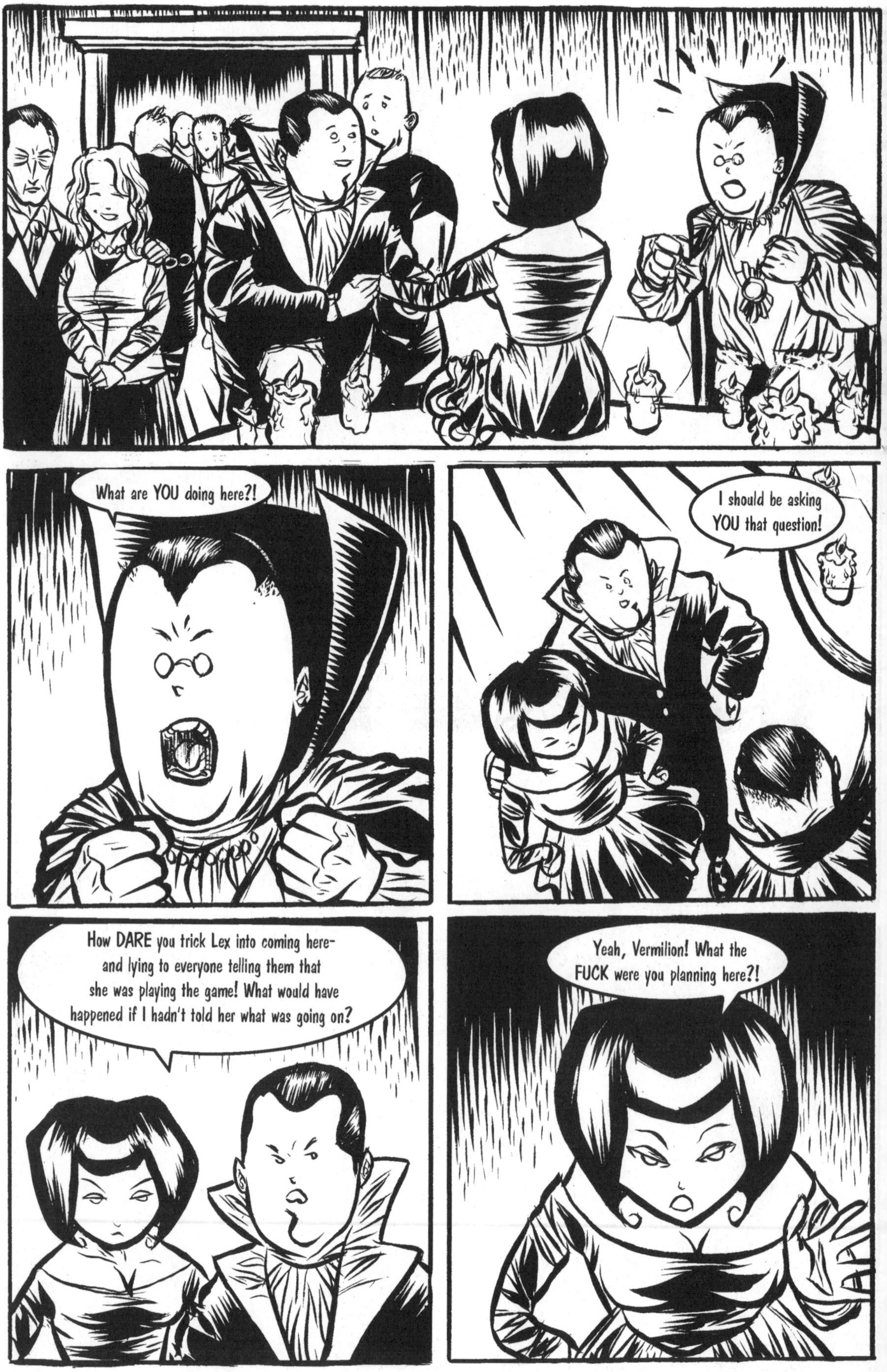
What are YOU doing here?!
I should be asking YOU that question!
How DARE you trick Lex into coming here- and lying to everyone telling them that she was playing the game! What would have happened if I hadn't told her what was going on?
Yeah, Vermilion! What the FUCK were you planning here?!

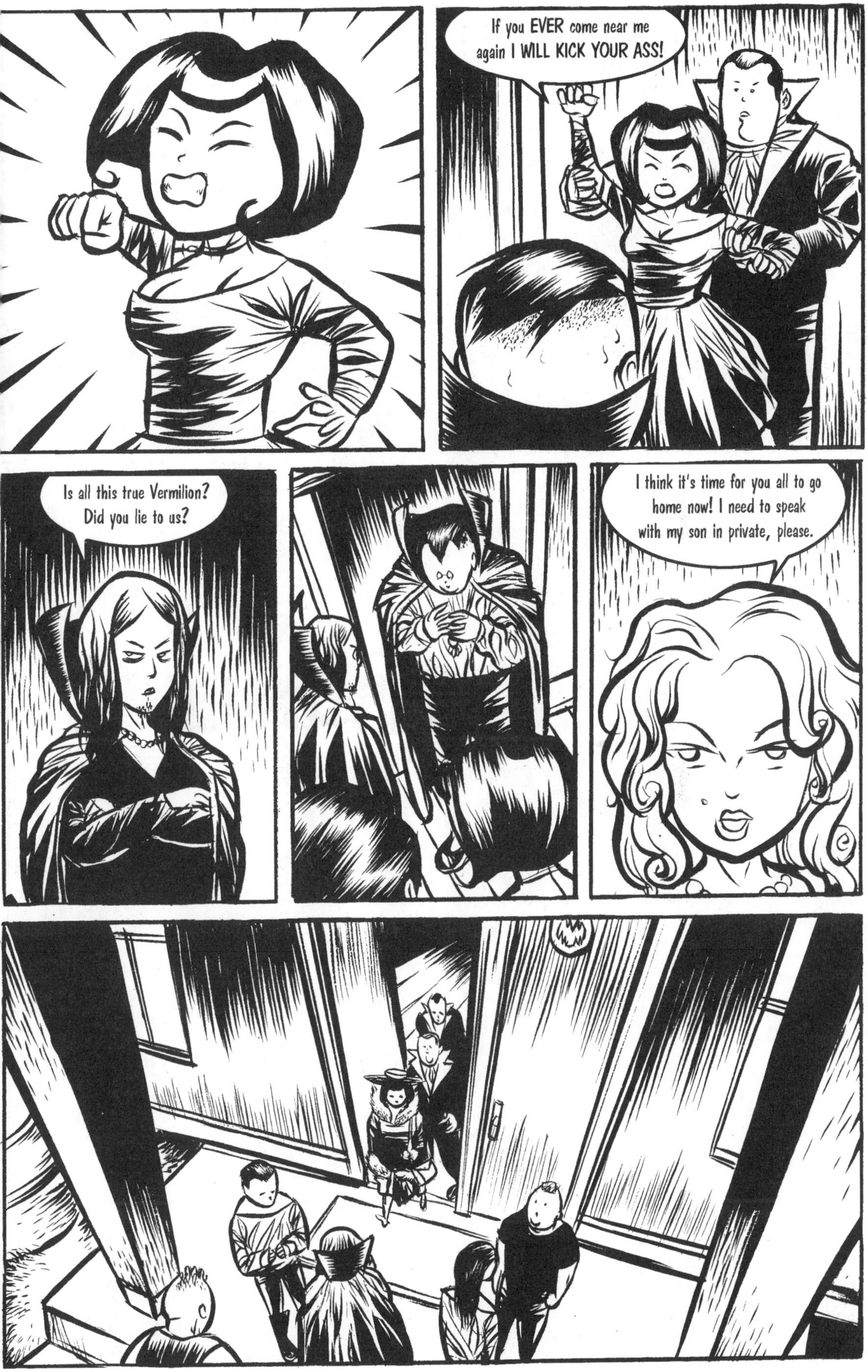

If you EVER come near me again I WILL KICK YOUR ASS!
Is all this true Vermilion? Did you lie to us?
I think it's time for you all to go home now! I need to speak with my son in private, please.

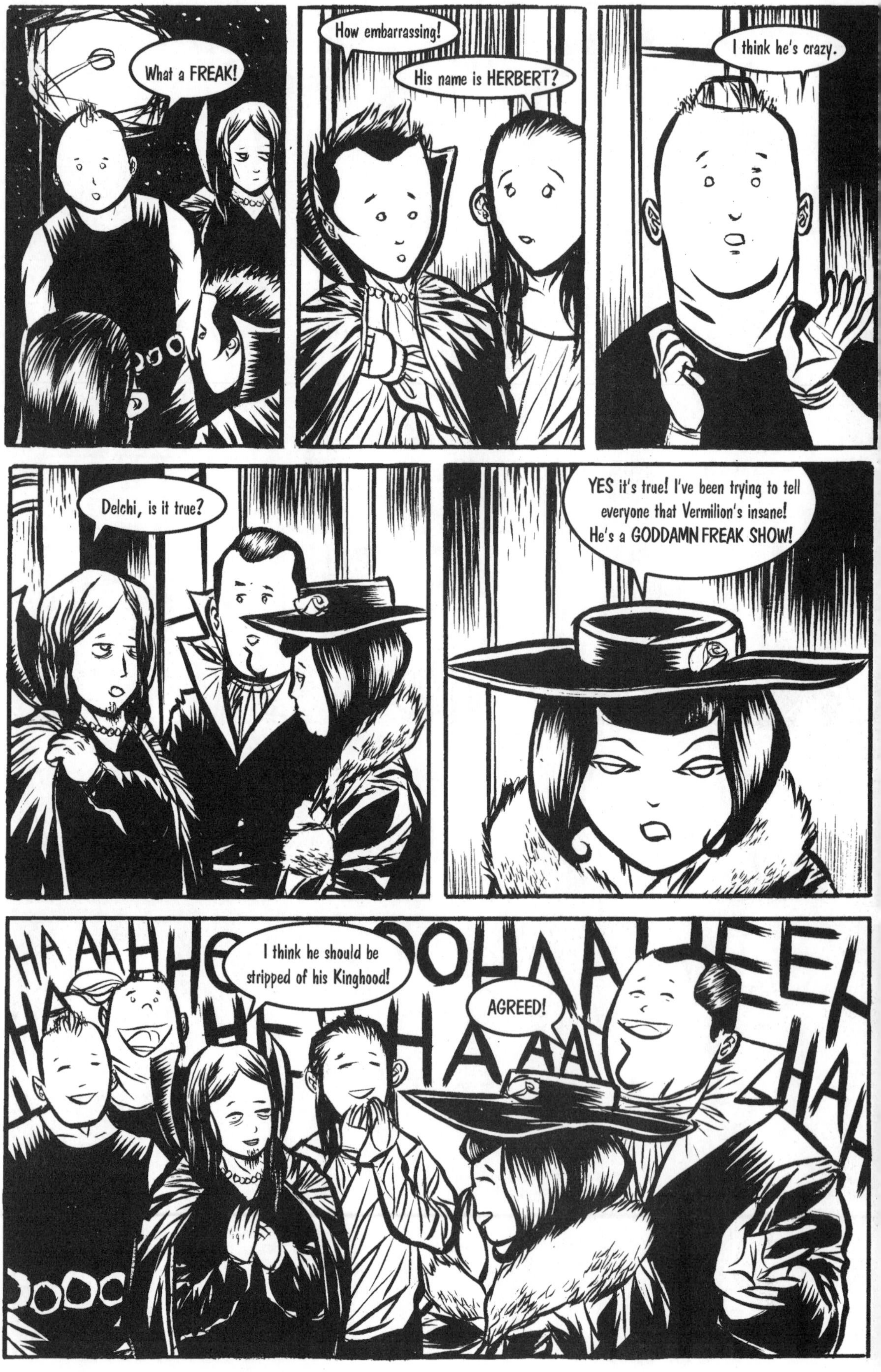
What a FREAK!
How embarrassing!
His name is HERBERT?
I think he's crazy.
Delchi, is it true?
YES it's true! I've been trying to tell everyone that Vermilion's insane! He's a GODDAMN FREAK SHOW!
I think he should be stripped of his Kinghood!
AGREED!

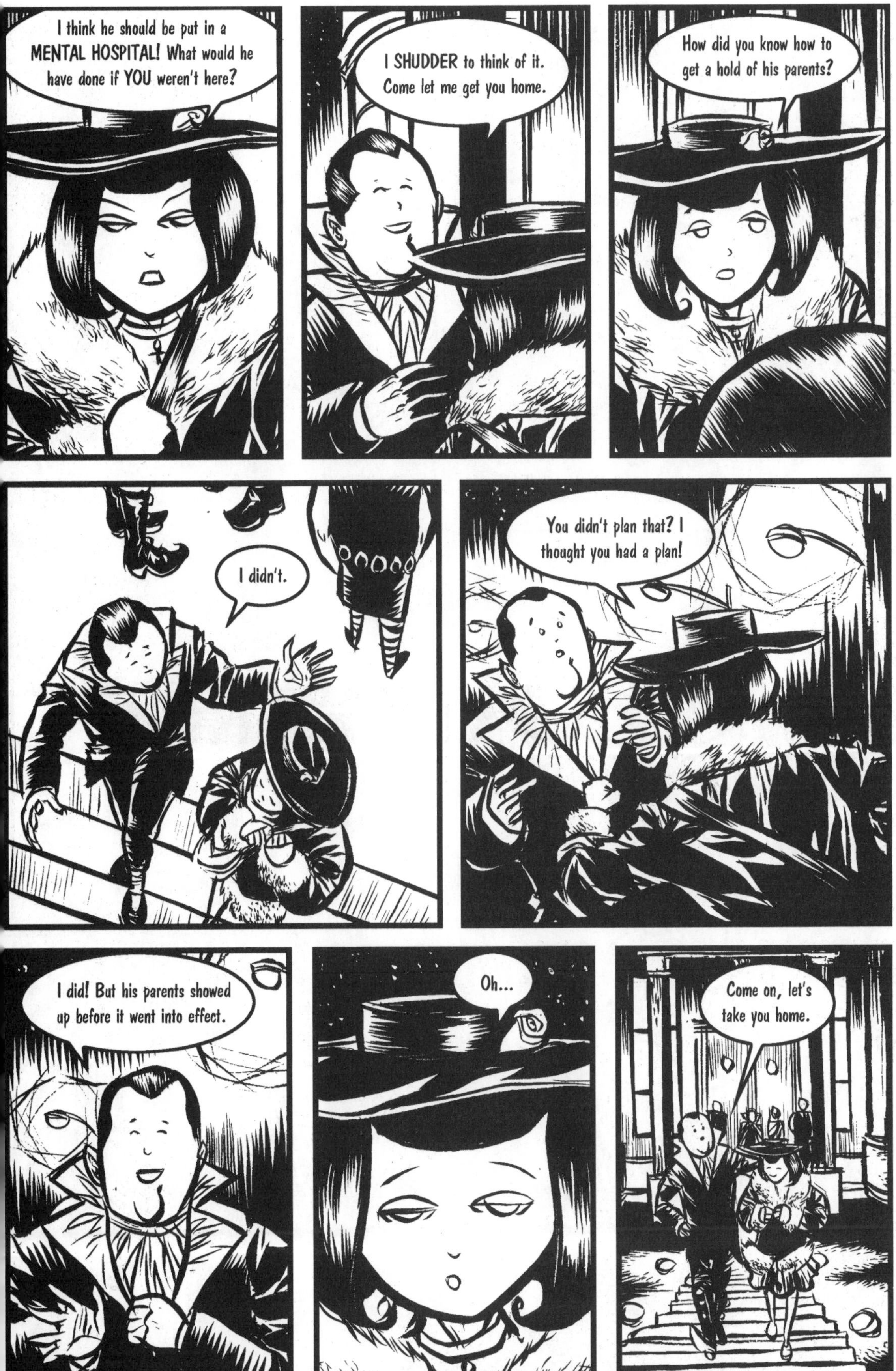

I think he should be put in a MENTAL HOSPITAL! What would he have done if YOU weren't here?
I SHUDDER to think of it. Come let me get you home.
How did you know how to get a hold of his parents?
I didn't.
You didn't plan that? I thought you had a plan!
I did! But his parents showed up before it went into effect.
Oh...
Come on, let's take you home.

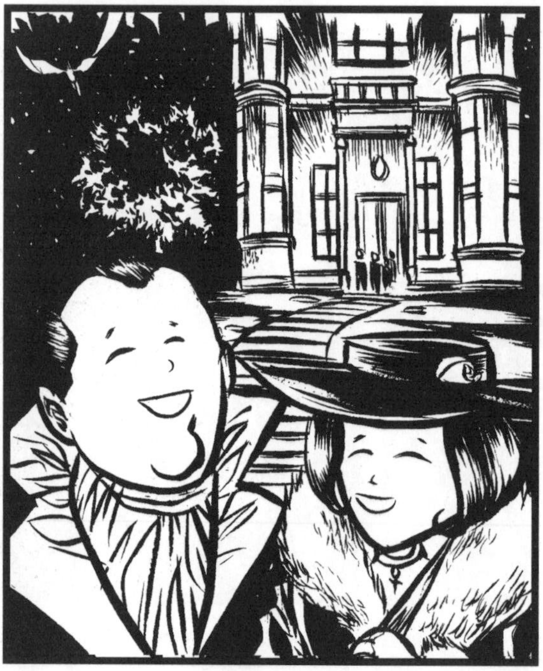

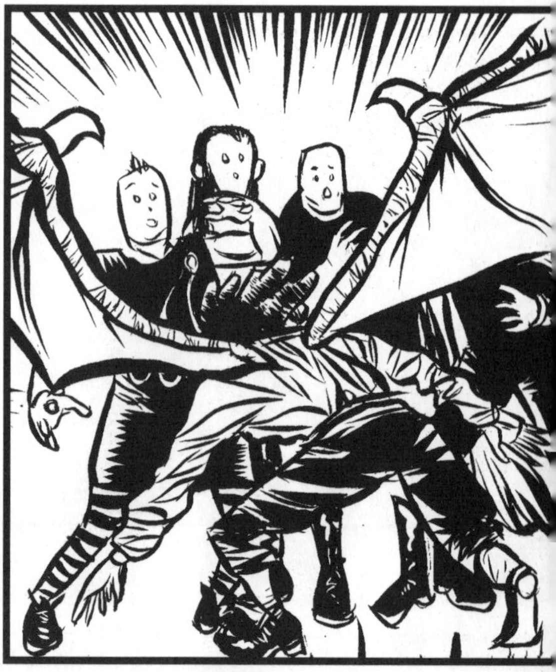

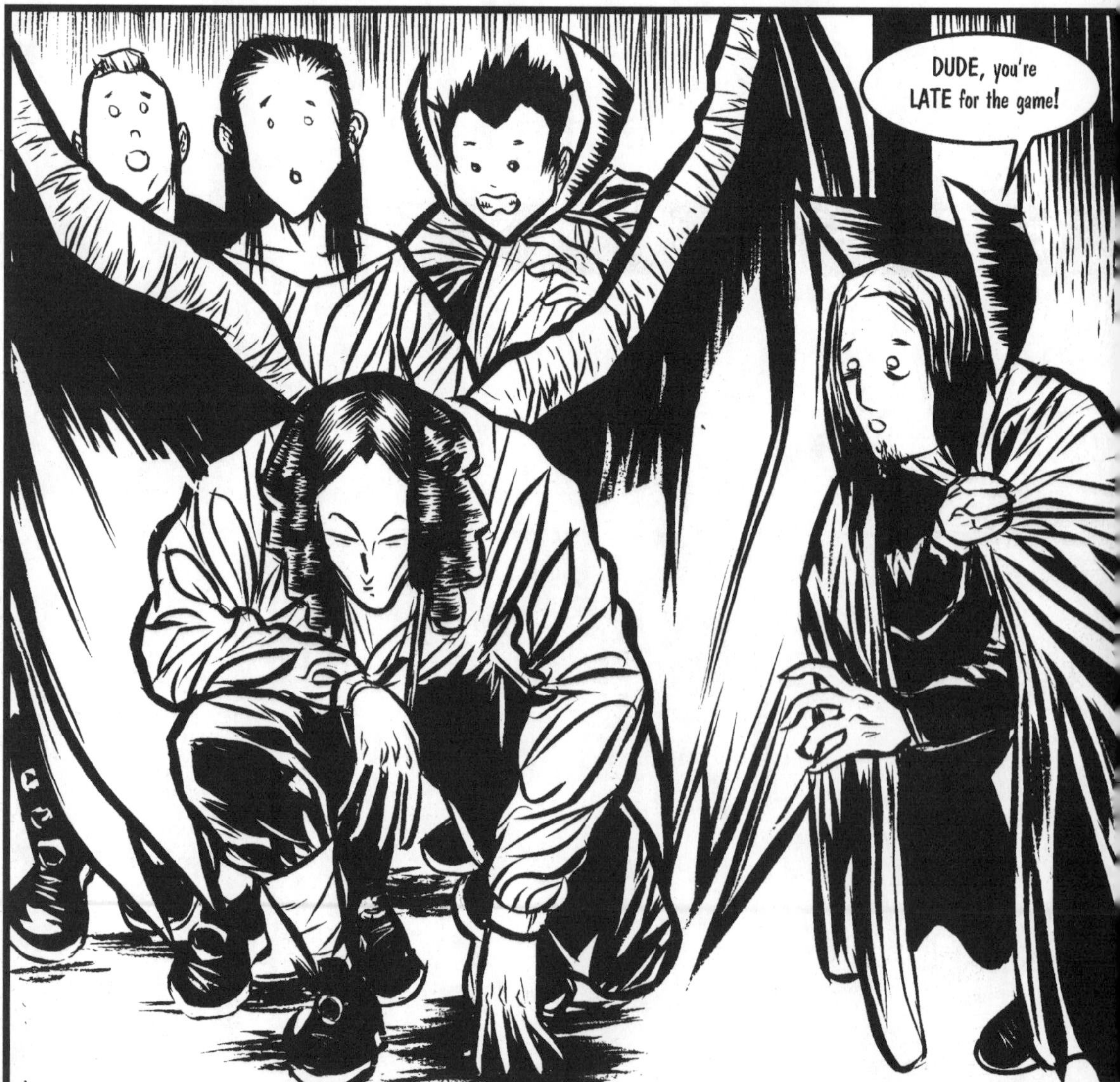
DUDE, you're LATE for the game!

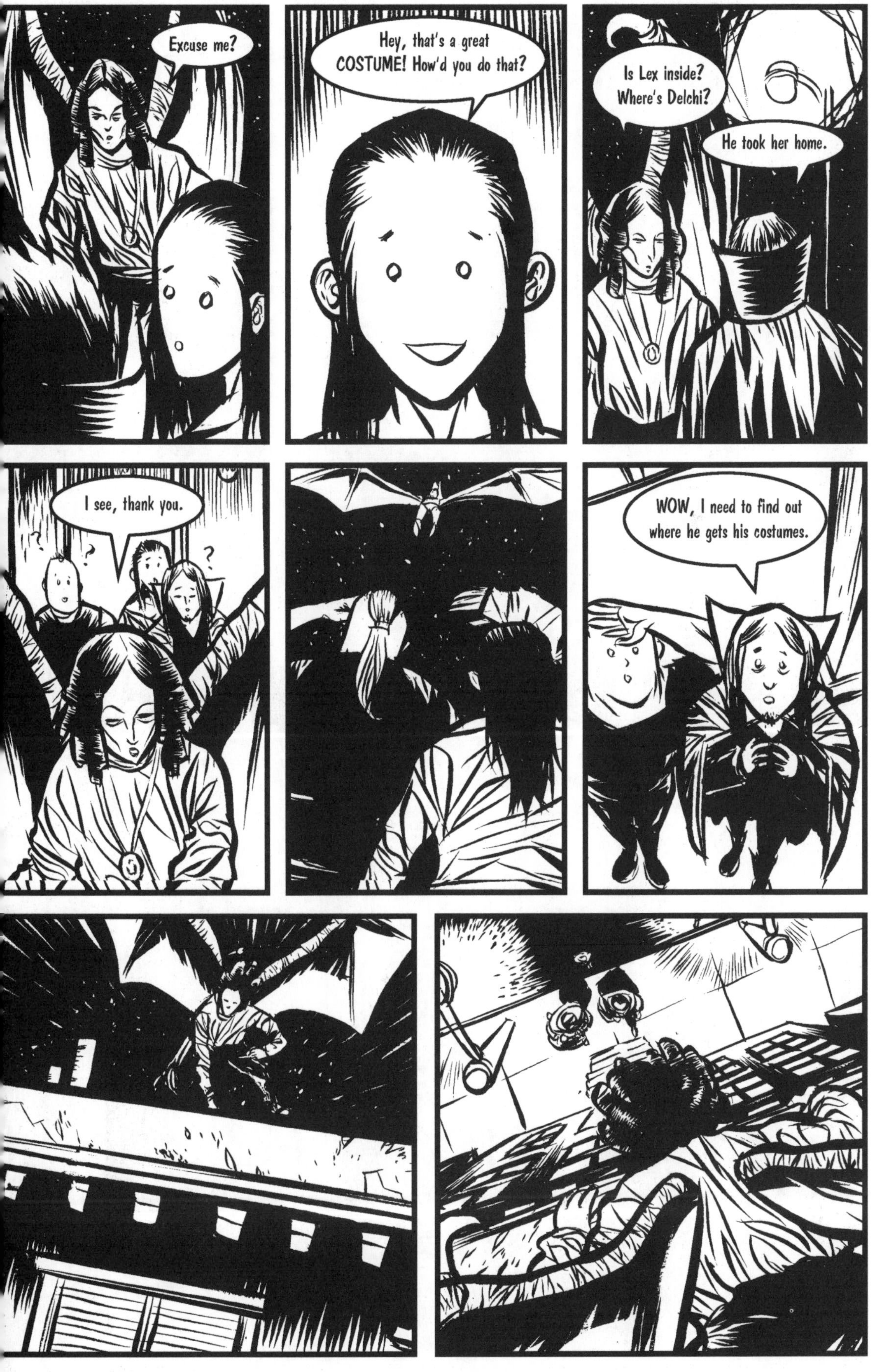
Excuse me?
Hey, that's a great COSTUME! How'd you do that?
Is Lex inside? Where's Delchi?
He took her home.
I see, thank you.
WOW, I need to find out where he gets his costumes.

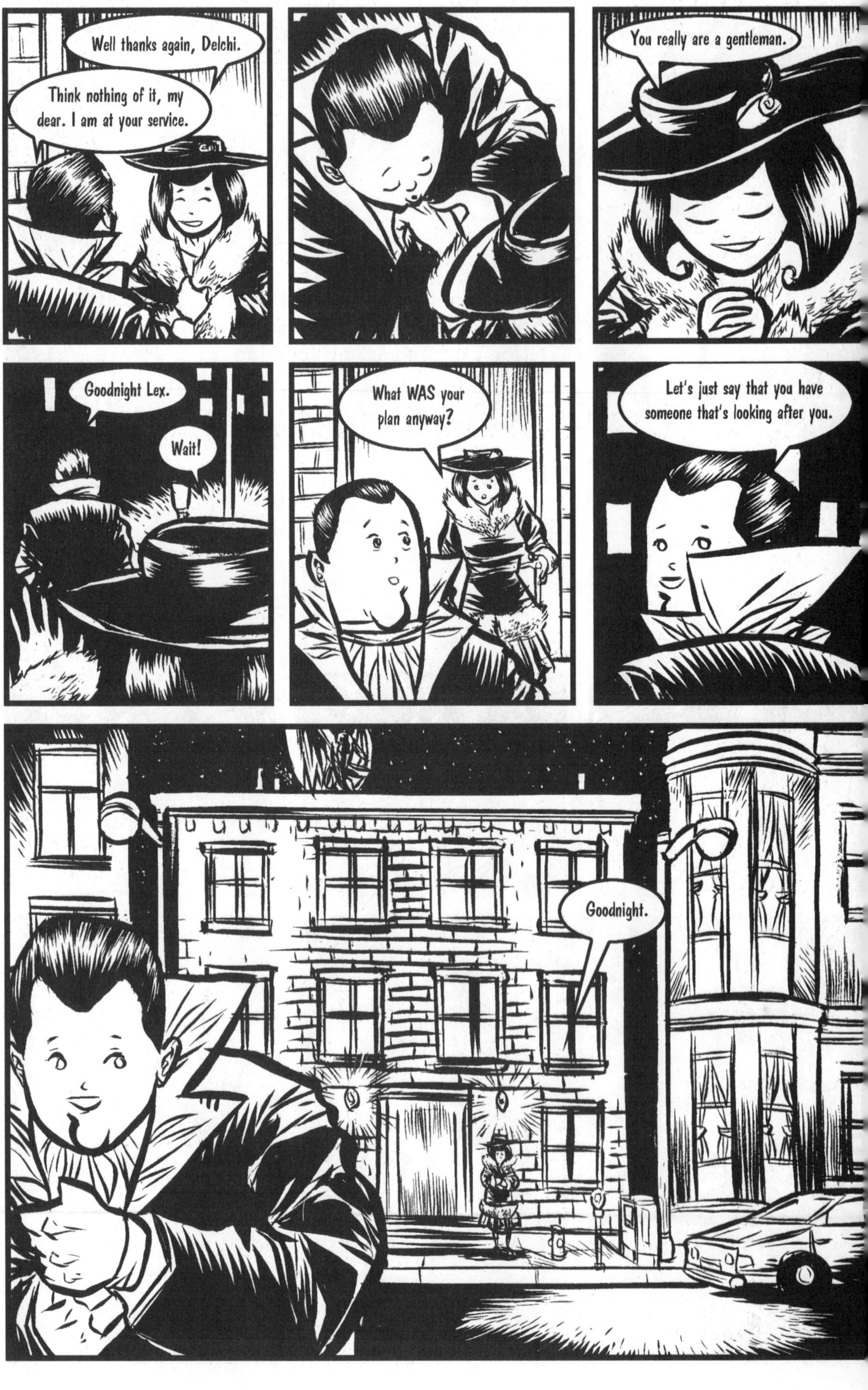
Well thanks again, Delchi.
Think nothing of it, my dear. I am at your service.
You really are a gentleman.
Goodnight Lex.
Wait!
What WAS your plan anyway?
Let's just say that you have someone that's looking after you.
Goodnight.

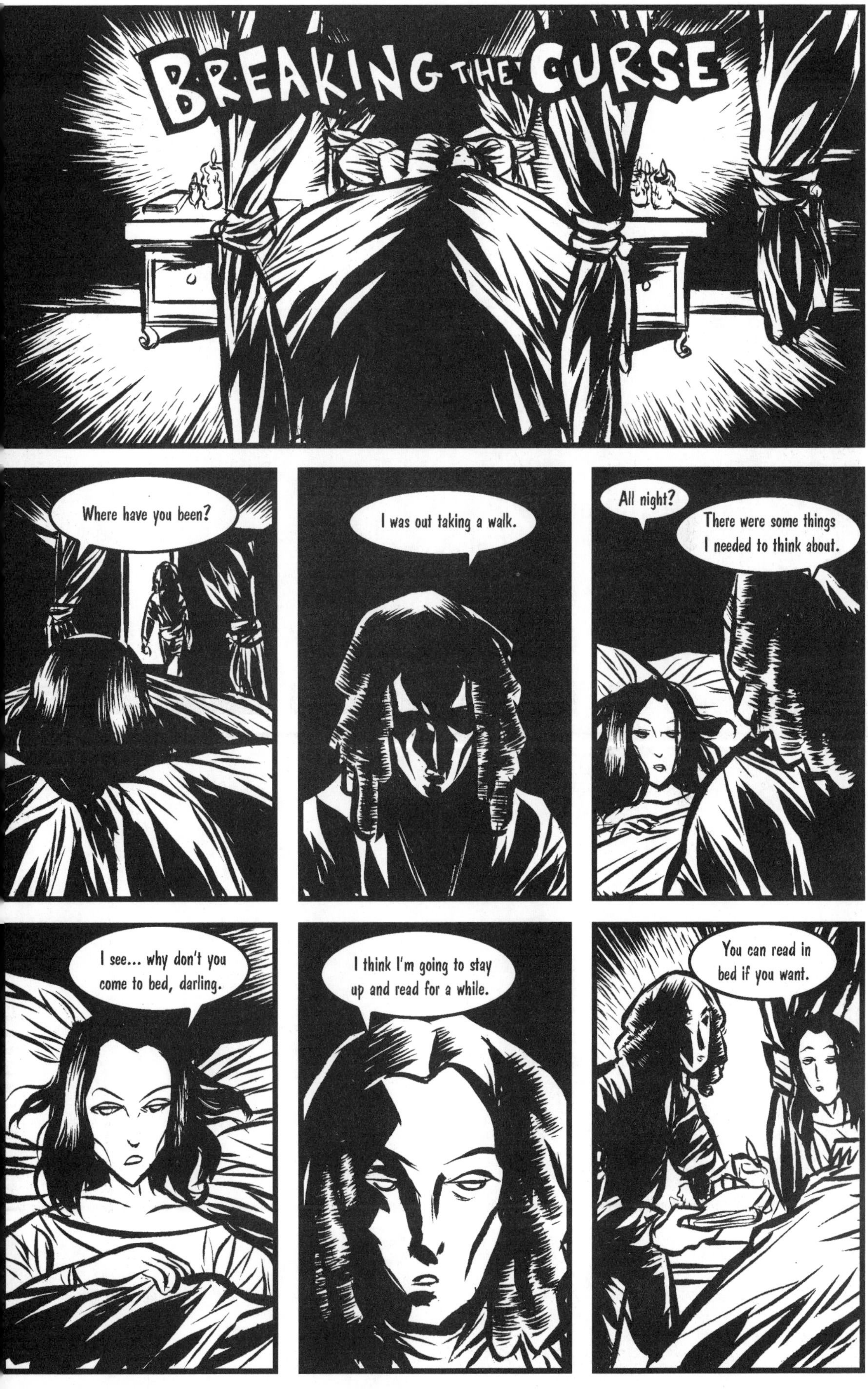

BREAKING THE CURSE
Where have you been?
I was out taking a walk.
All night?
There were some things I needed to think about.
I see... why don't you come to bed, darling.
I think I'm going to stay up and read for a while.
You can read in bed if you want.

No, I don't want to disturb you. Go back to sleep.

FRENCH
ROAST

GGGGRRRRRIIINND

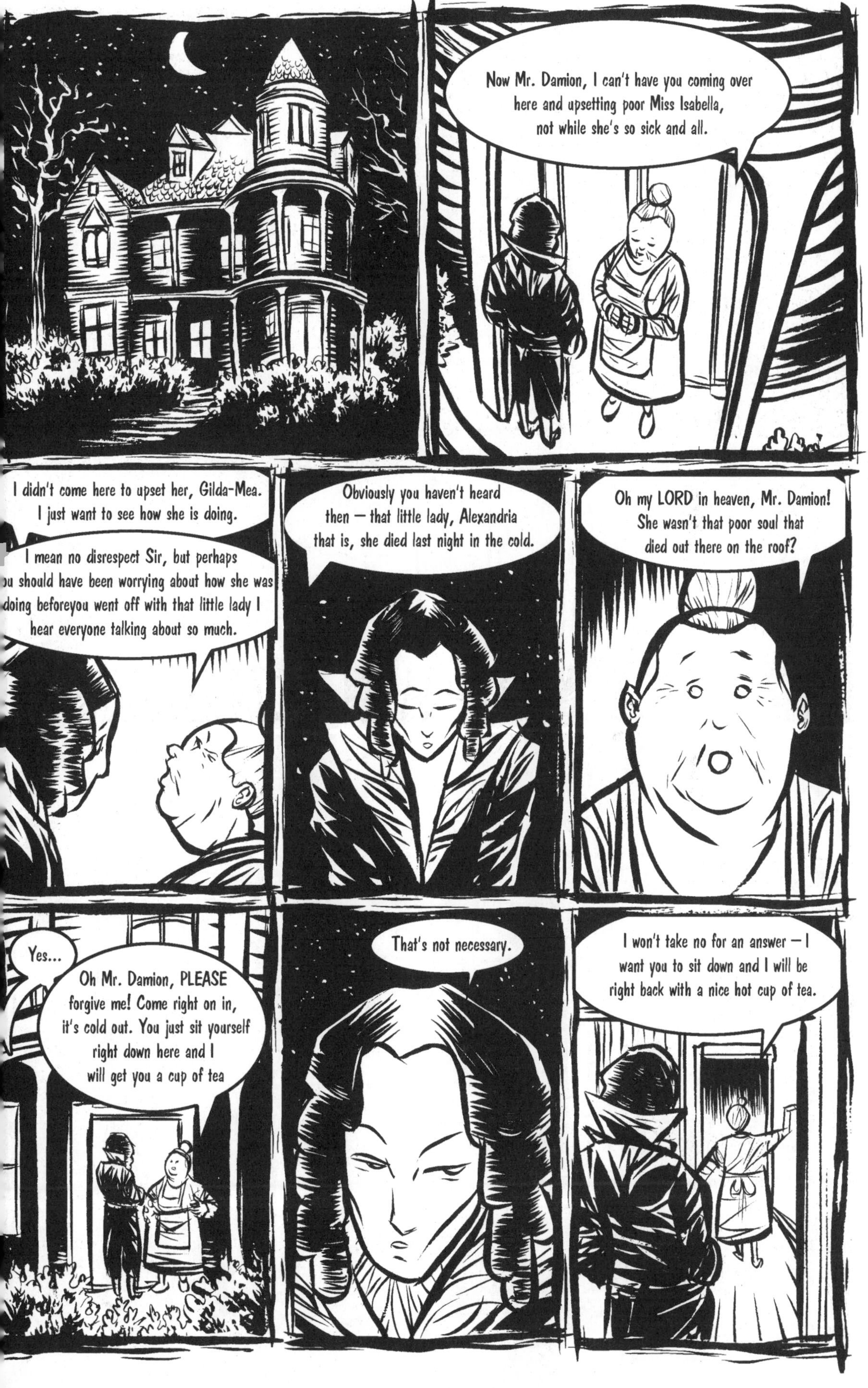
Now Mr. Damion, I can't have you coming over here and upsetting poor Miss Isabella, not while she's so sick and all.
I didn't come here to upset her, Gilda-Mea. I just want to see how she is doing.
I mean no disrespect Sir, but perhaps ou should have been worrying about how she was doing beforeyou went off with that little lady I hear everyone talking about so much.
Obviously you haven't heard then — that little lady, Alexandria that is, she died last night in the cold.
Oh my LORD in heaven, Mr. Damion! She wasn't that poor soul that died out there on the roof?
Yes...
Oh Mr. Damion, PLEASE forgive me! Come right on in, it's cold out. You just sit yourself right down here and I will get you a cup of tea
That's not necessary.
I won't take no for an answer — I want you to sit down and I will be right back with a nice hot cup of tea.

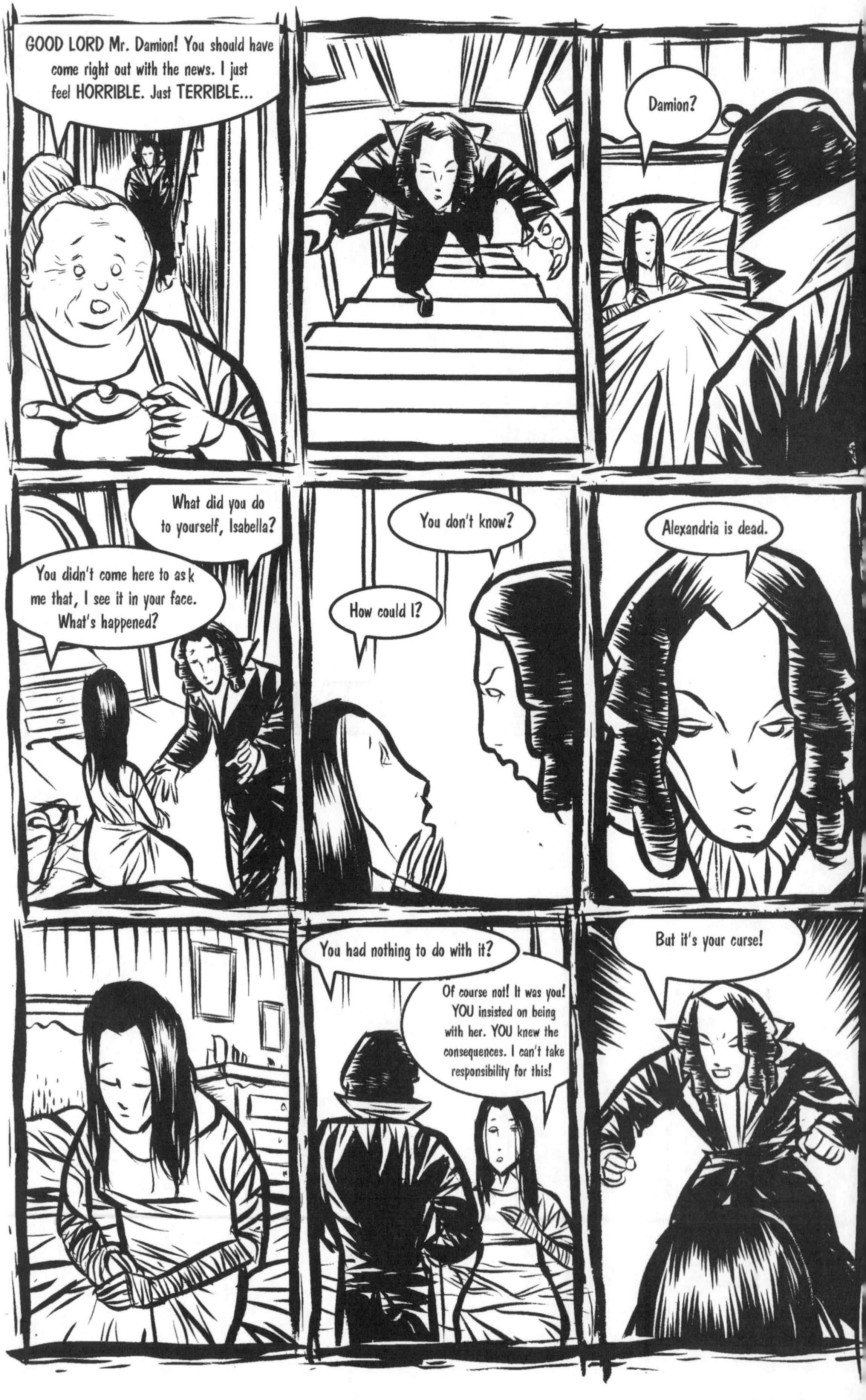
GOOD LORD Mr. Damion! You should have come right out with the news. I just feel HORRIBLE. Just TERRIBLE...
Damion?
What did you do to yourself, Isabella?
You didn't come here to as k me that, I see it in your face. What's happened?
You don't know?
How could I?
Alexandria is dead.
You had nothing to do with it?
Of course not! It was you! YOU insisted on being with her. YOU knew the consequences. I can't take responsibility for this!
But it's your curse!

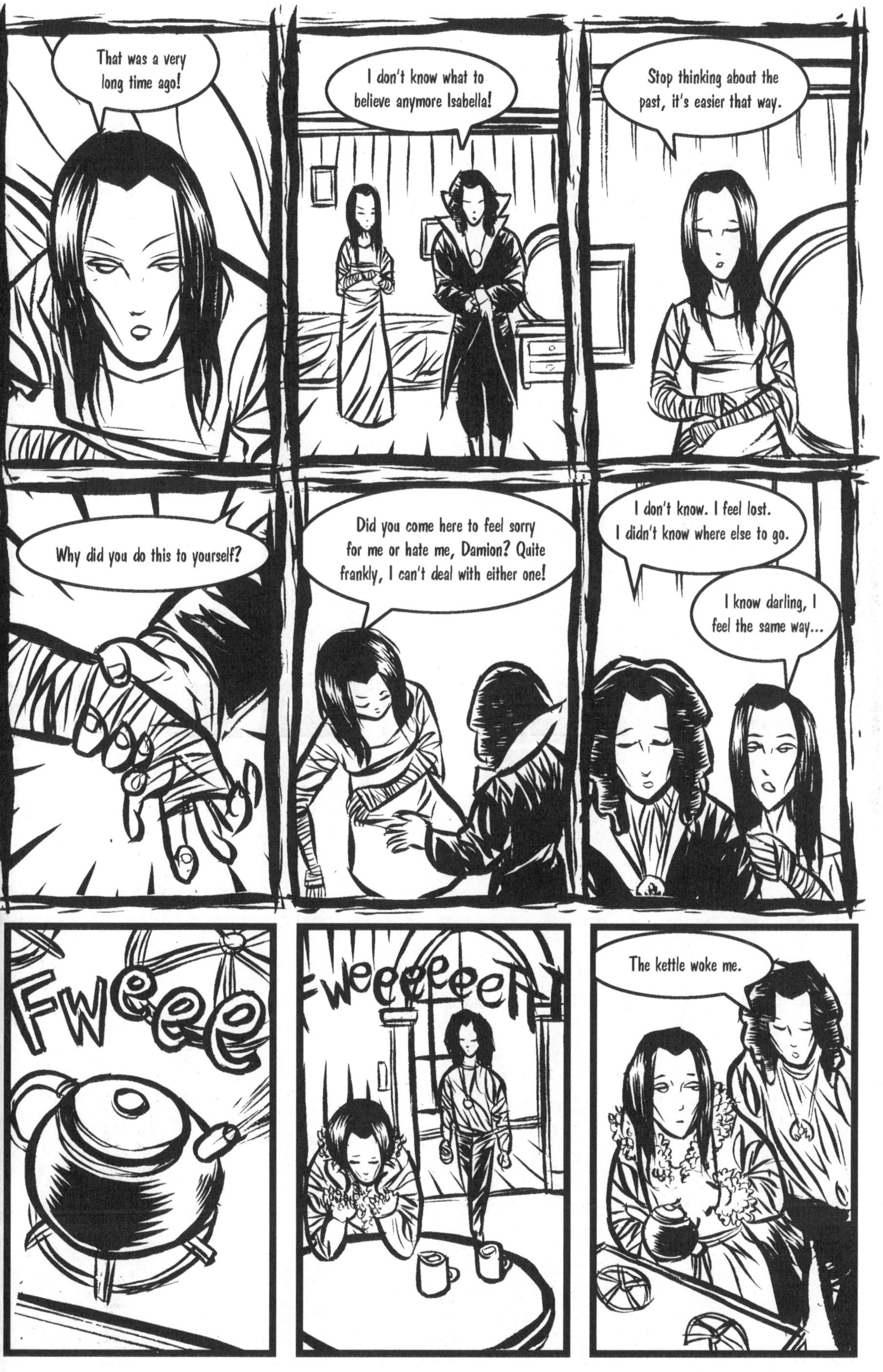
That was a very long time ago!
I don't know what to believe anymore Isabella!
Stop thinking about the past, it's easier that way.
Why did you do this to yourself?
Did you come here to feel sorry for me or hate me, Damion? Quite frankly, I can't deal with either one!
I don't know. I feel lost. I didn't know where else to go.
I know darling, I feel the same way...
Fweee
Fweeeeeet
The kettle woke me.

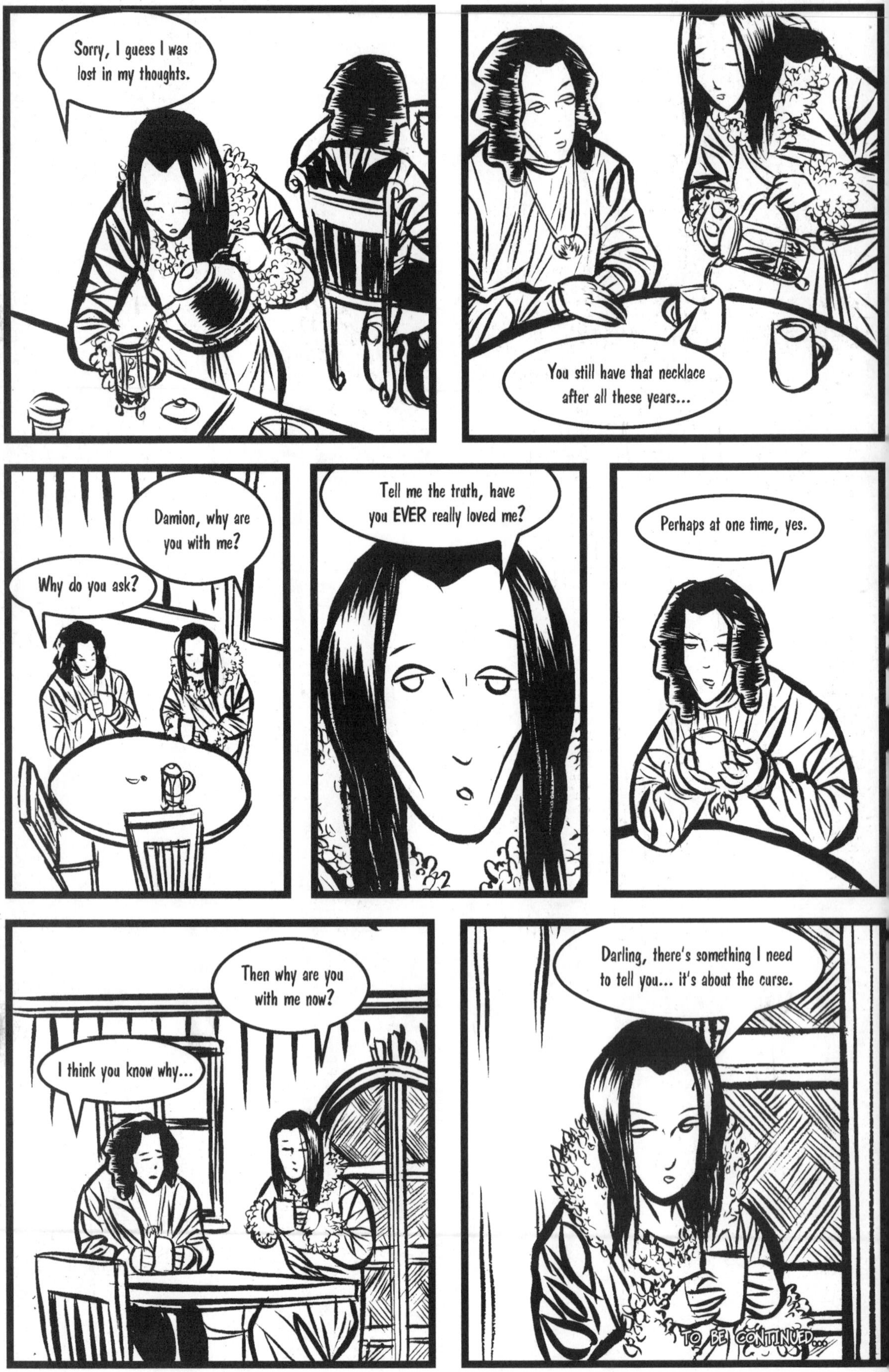

Sorry, I guess I was lost in my thoughts.
You still have that necklace after all these years...
Damion, why are you with me?
Why do you ask?
Tell me the truth, have you EVER really loved me?
Perhaps at one time, yes.
Then why are you with me now?
I think you know why...
Darling, there's something I need to tell you... it's about the curse.
TO BE CONTINUED...

John's Art

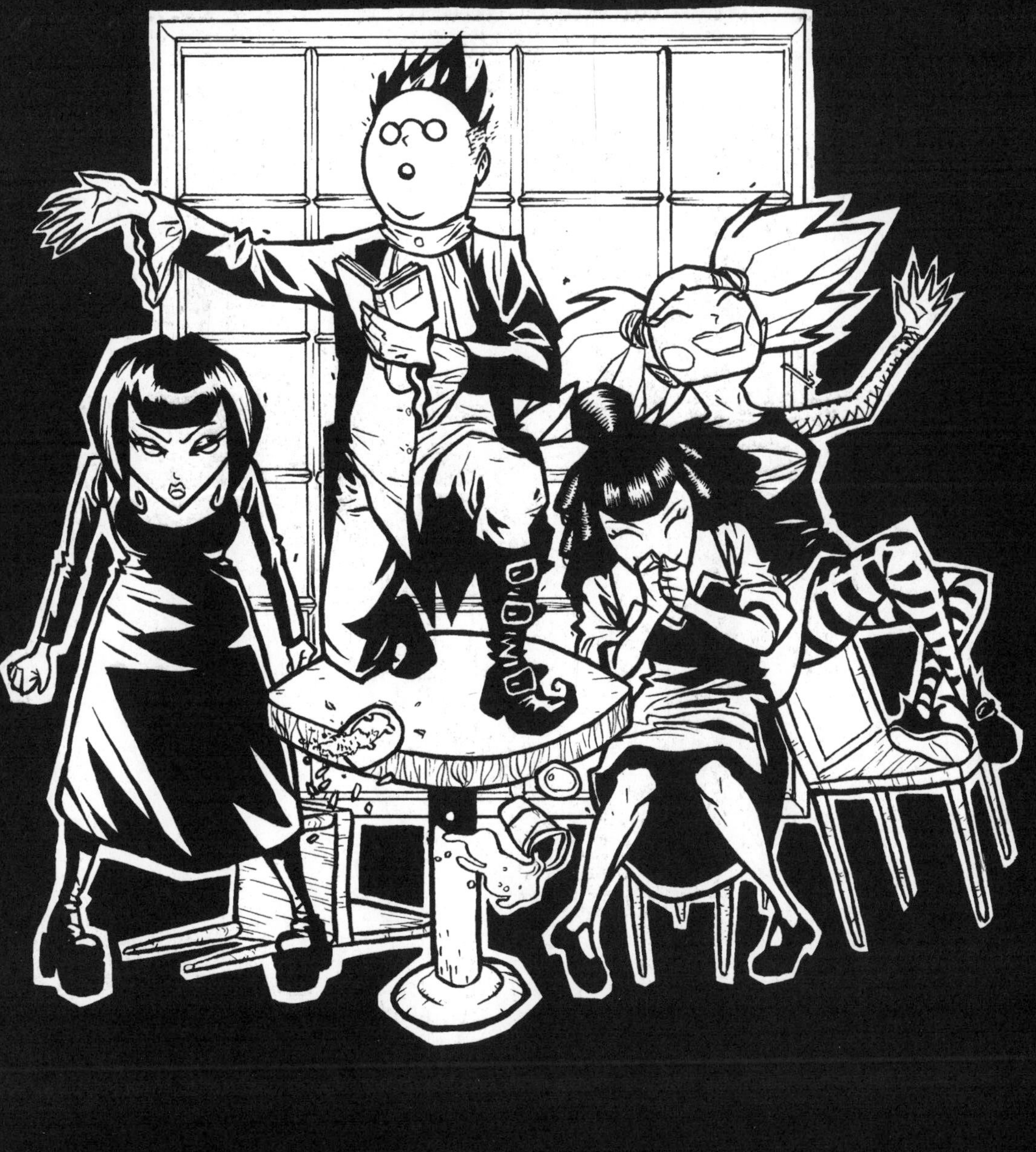

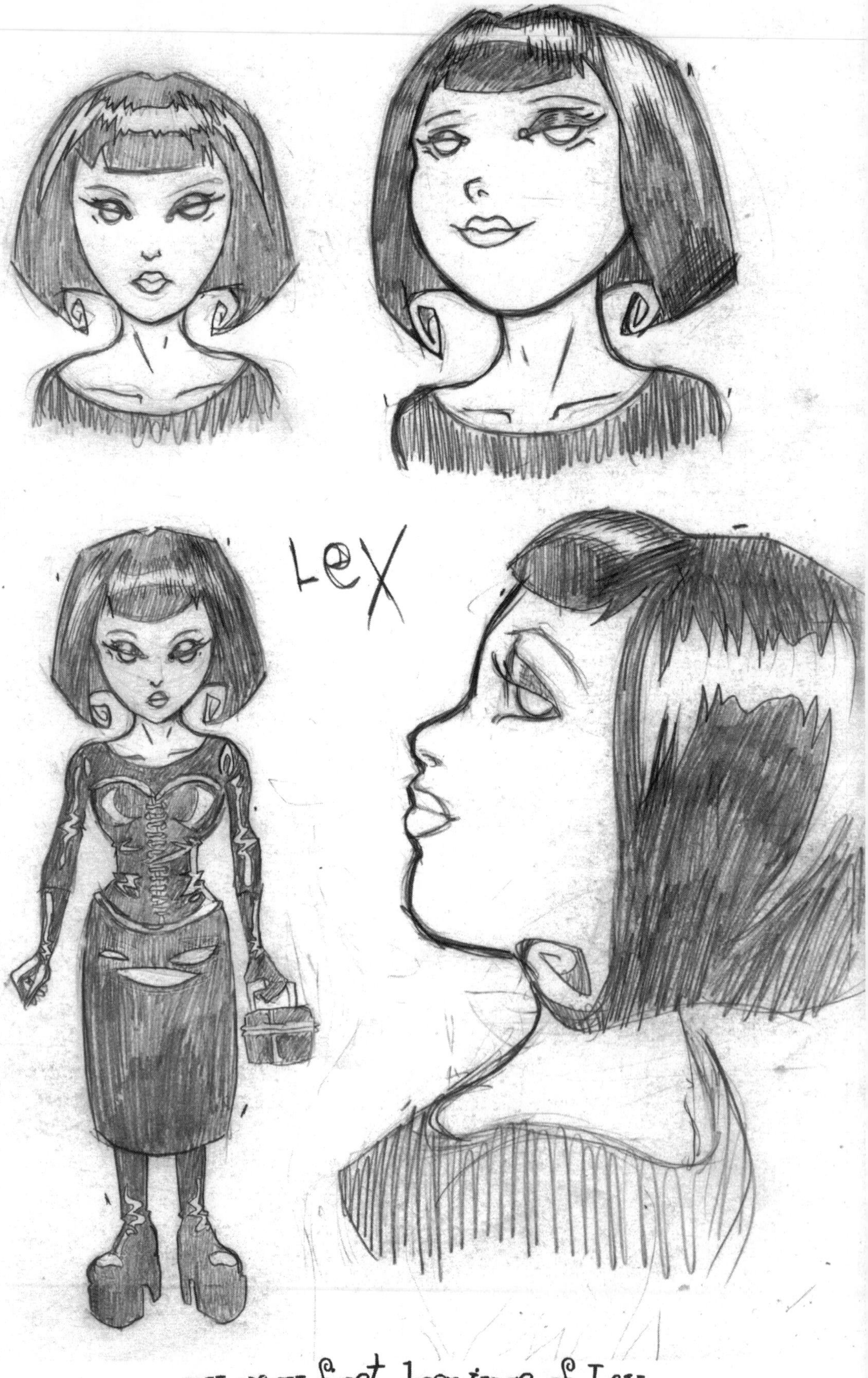
Lex

my very first drawings of Lex

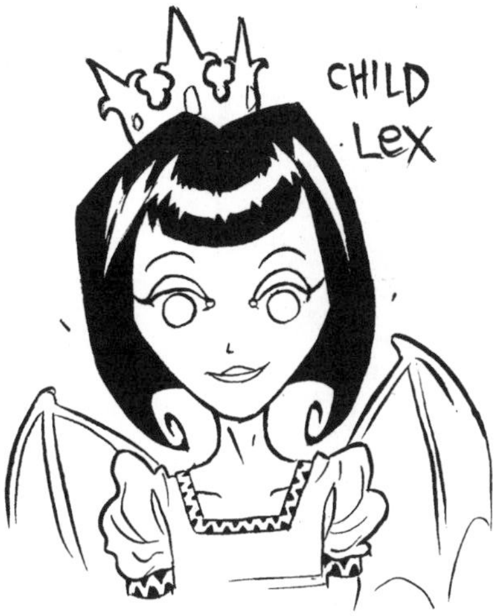
CHILD
LEX

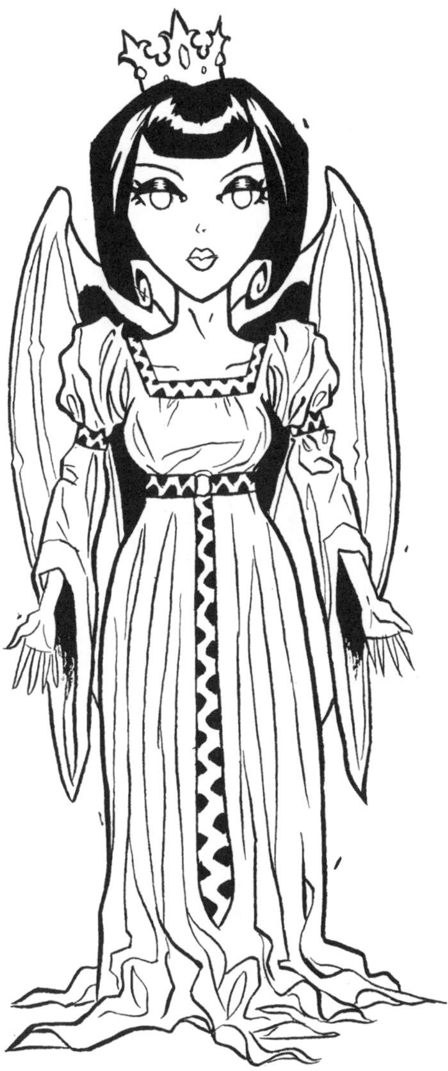

character designs of Lex for issue 7

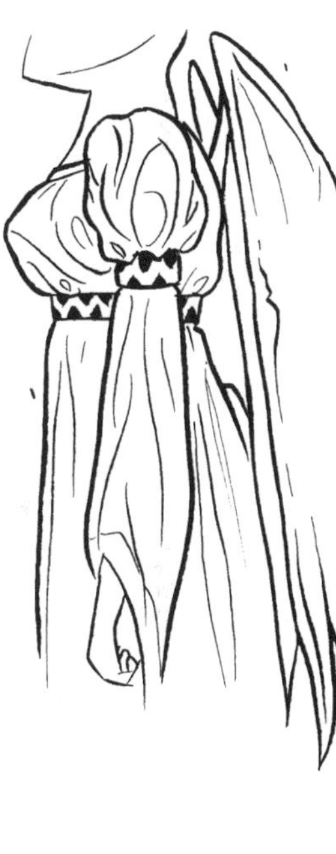

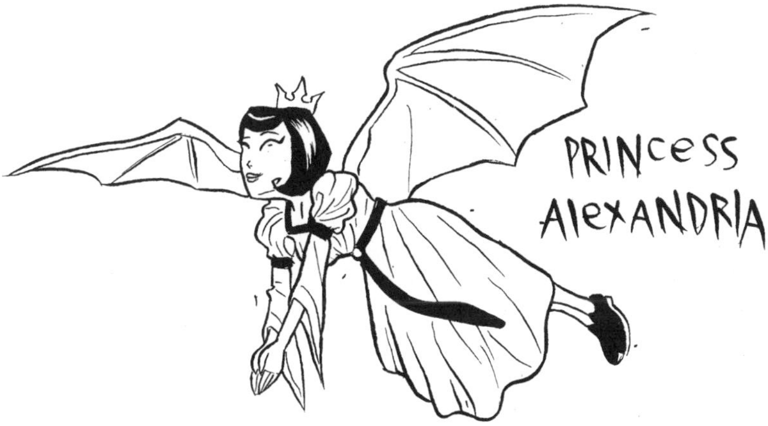
PRINCESS
ALEXANDRIA

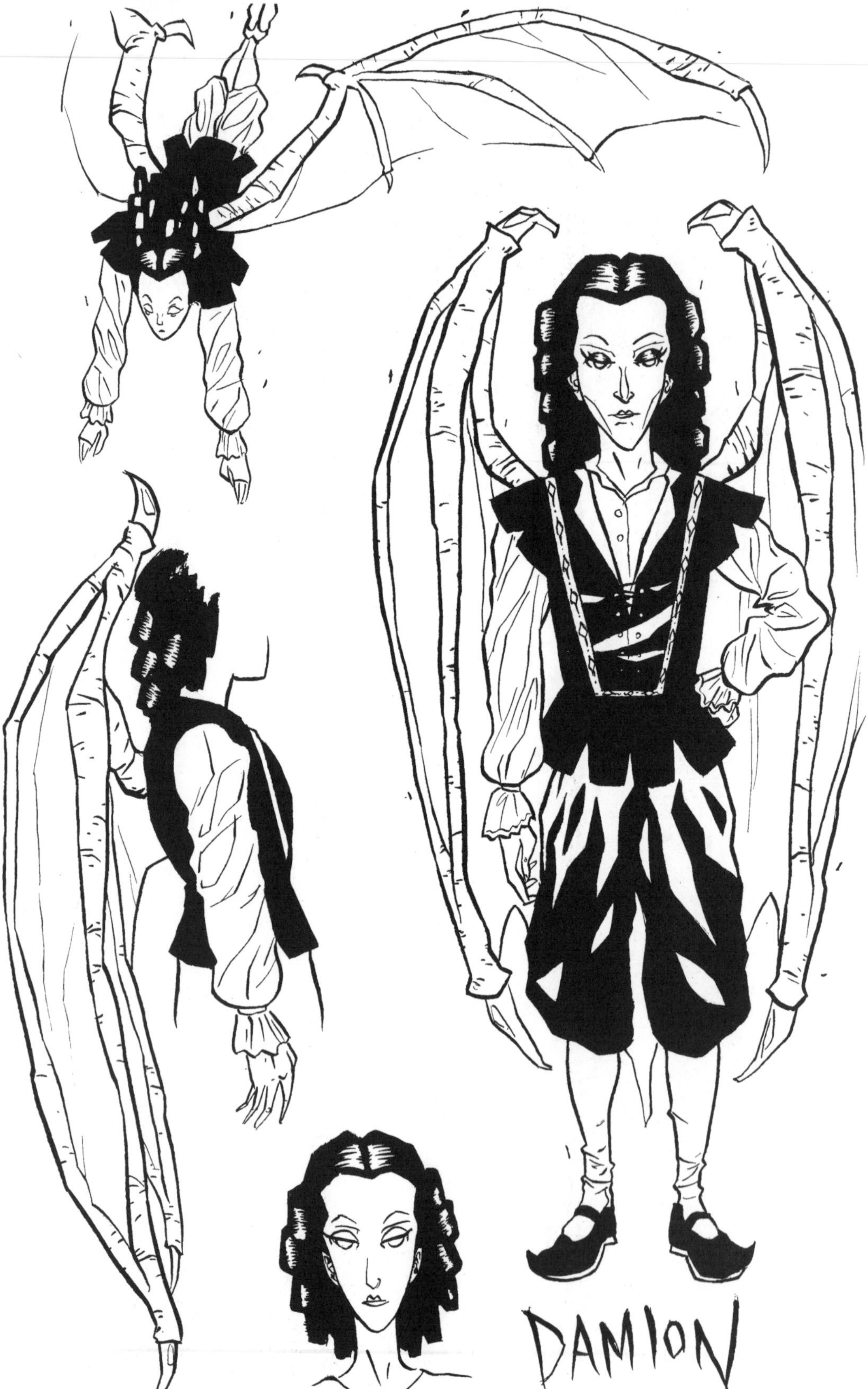
DAMION

Designs of Damion for issue 7

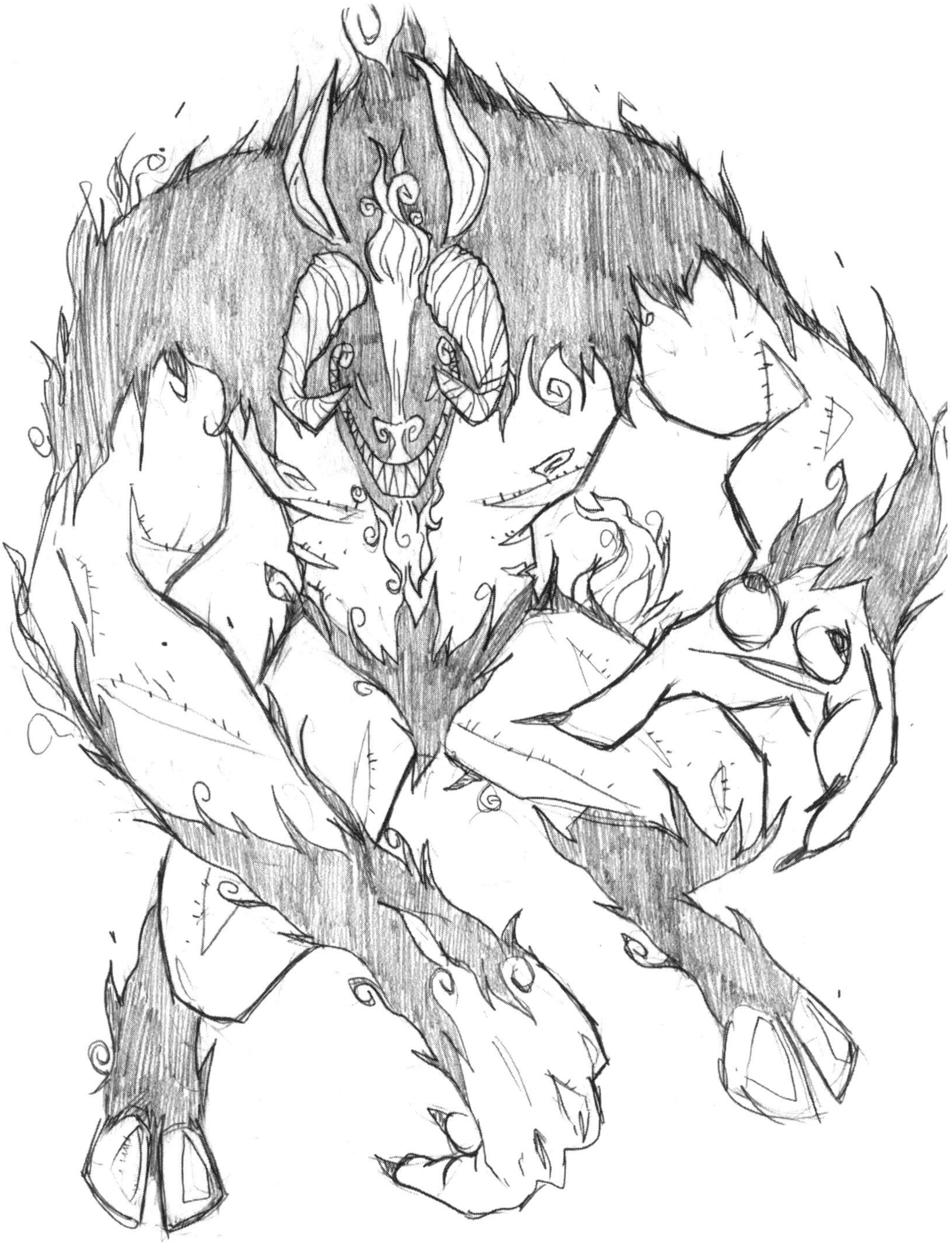

the Monster

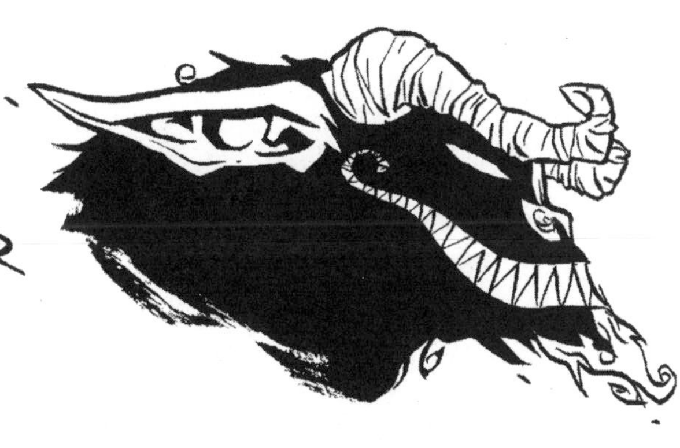

CHRYS

Some designs I
did before I
started
GloomCookie

SeBaSTiaN

more drawings that
I did before I
got the job

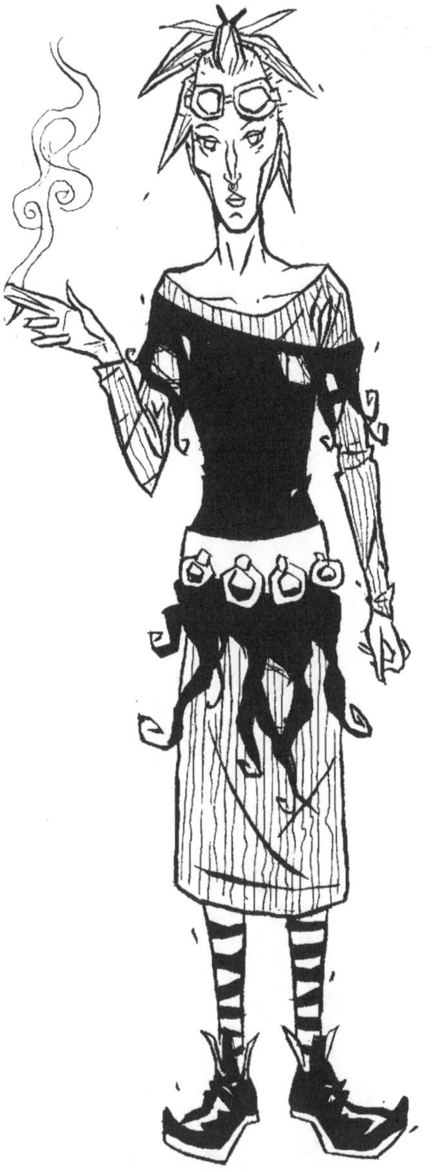

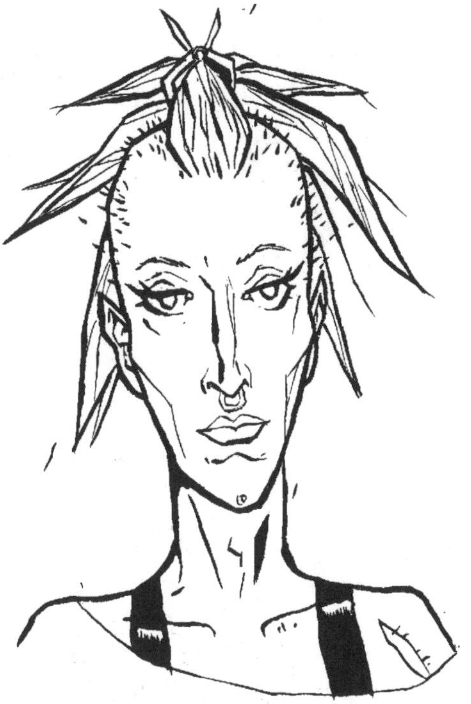

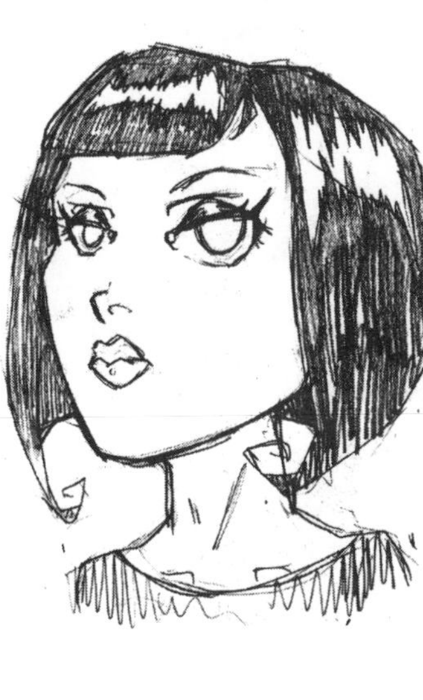

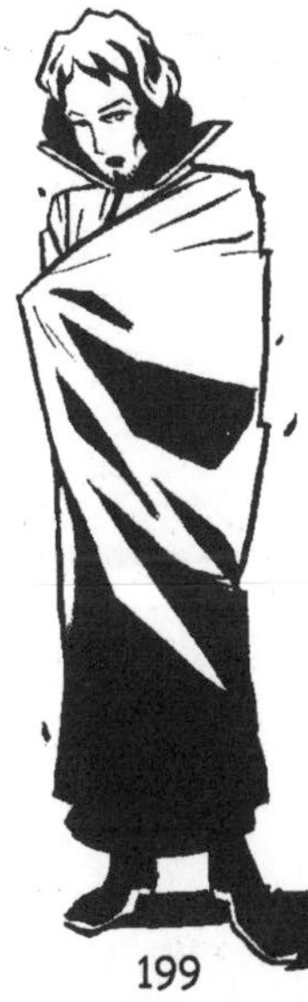

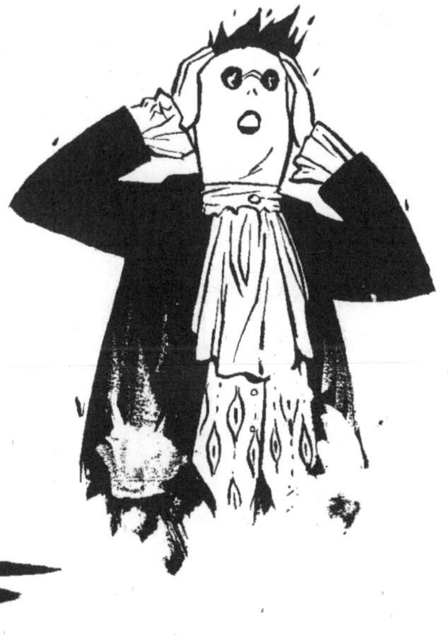

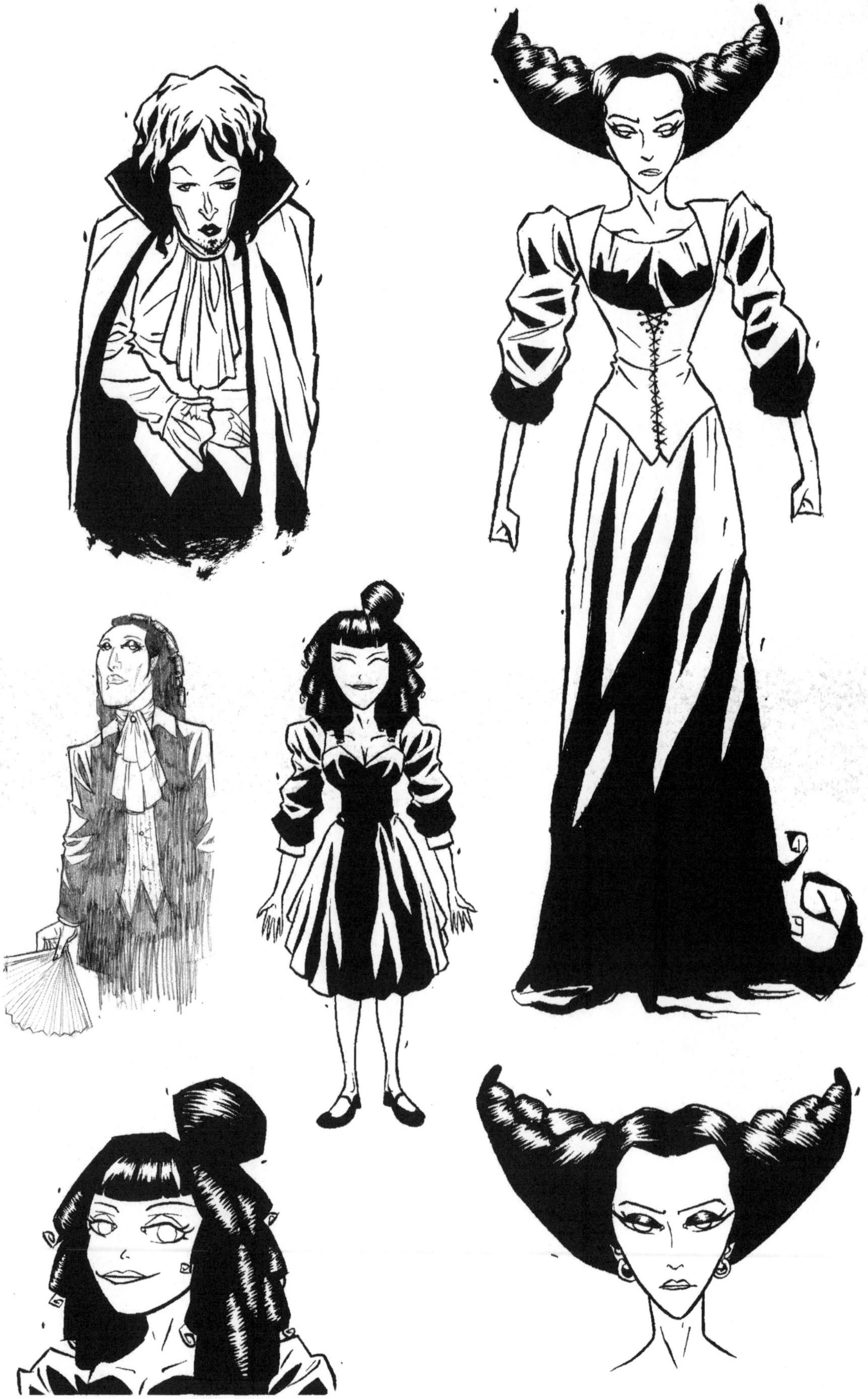

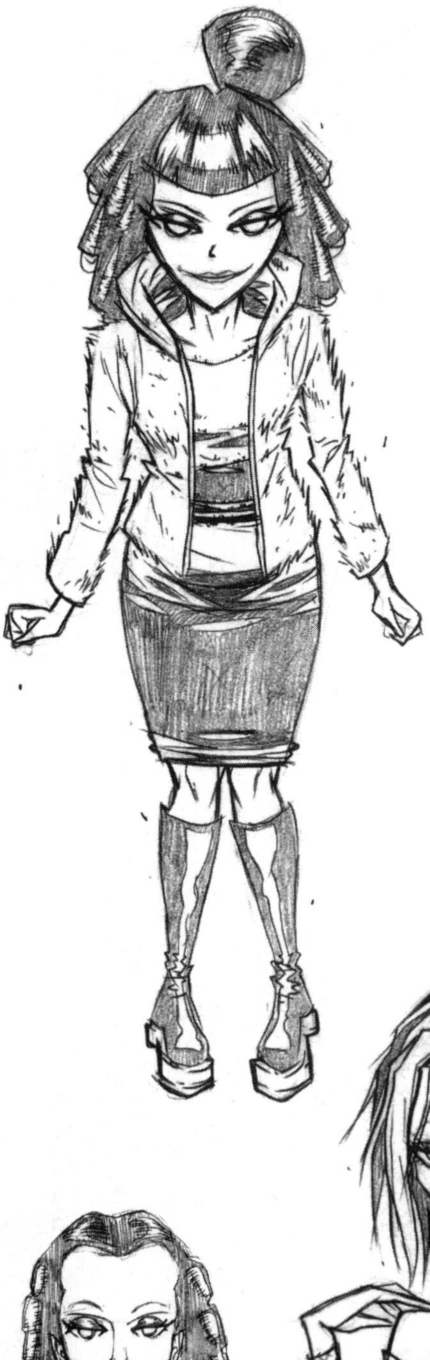
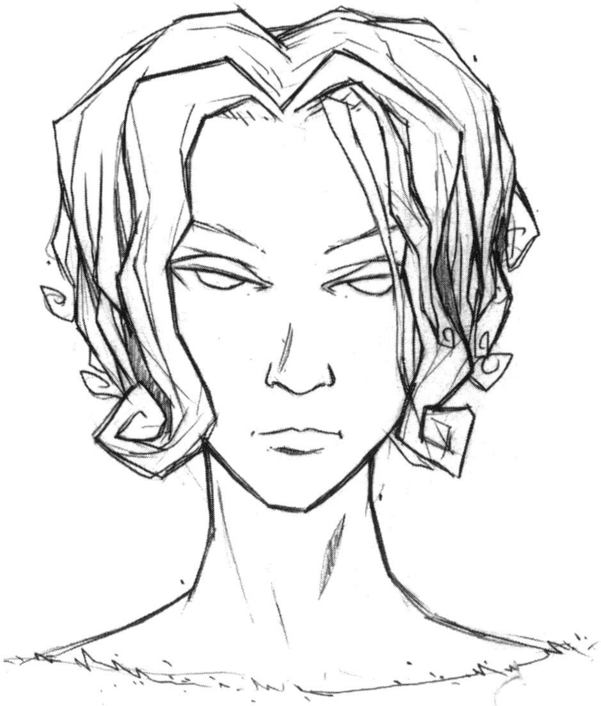
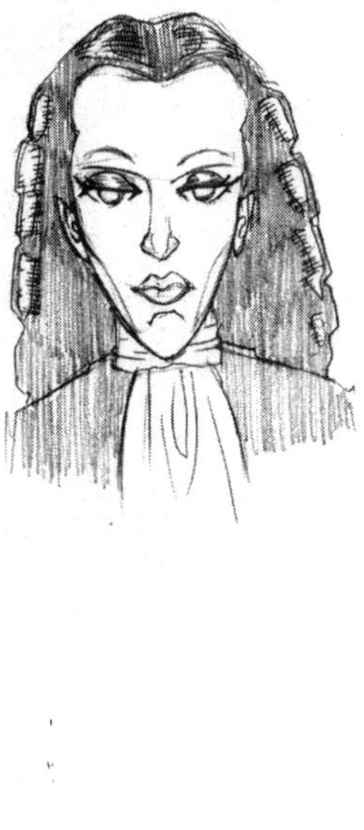
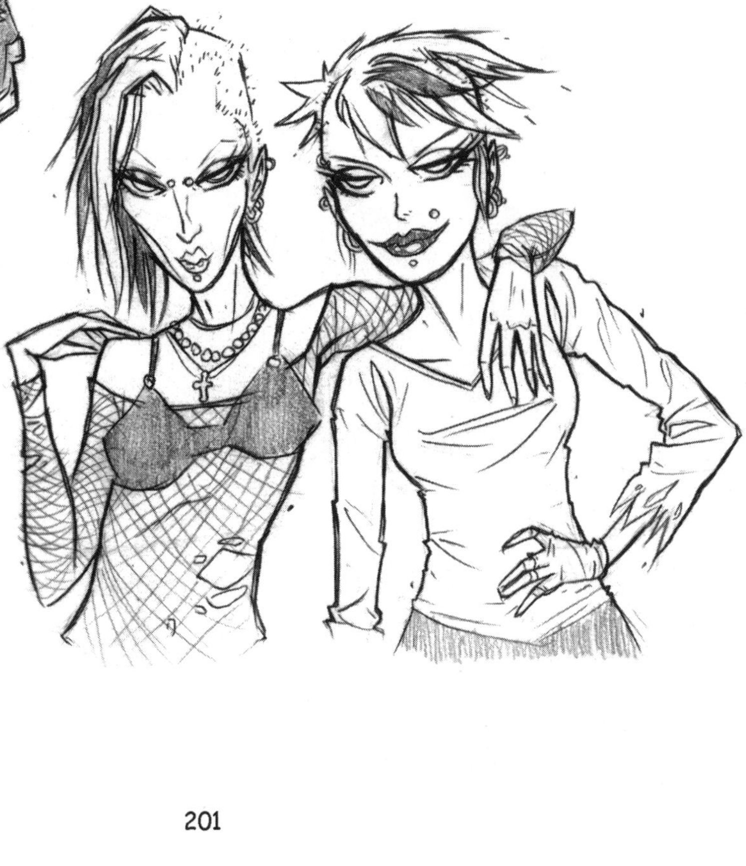

The TWINS

VINCENT

more inked
drawings

ISABELLA

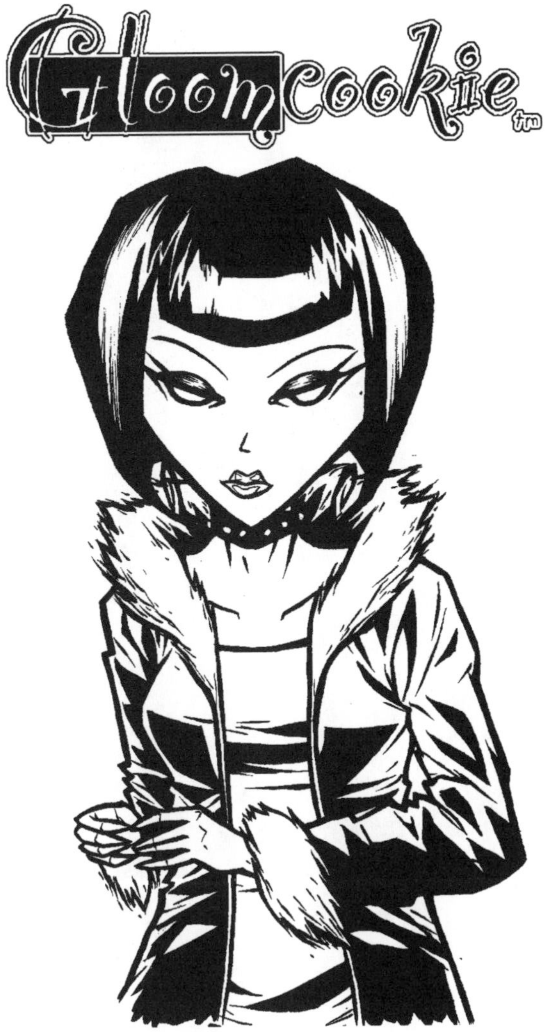
Gloomcookie

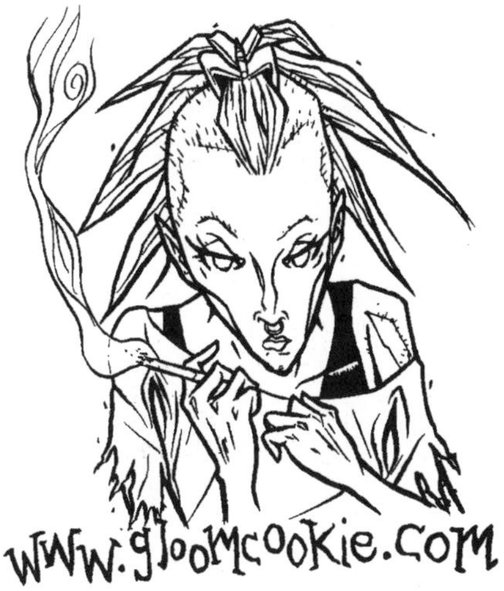
www.gloomcookie.com

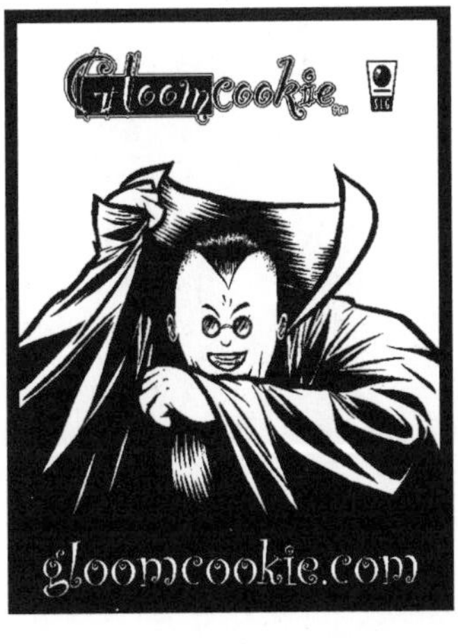
Gloomcookie
gloomcookie.com

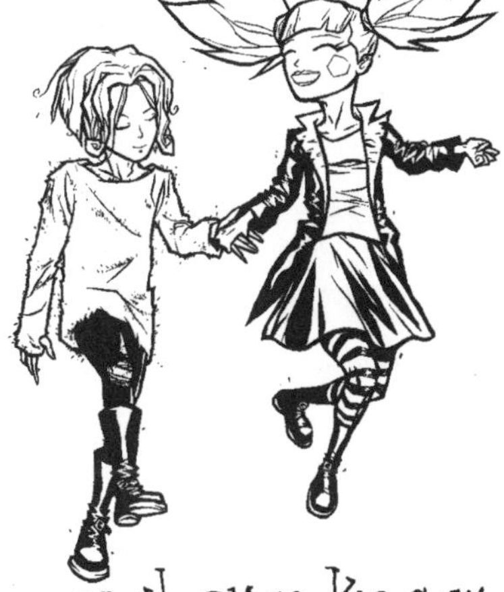
www.gloomcookie.com

stickers
I did for
various
conventions

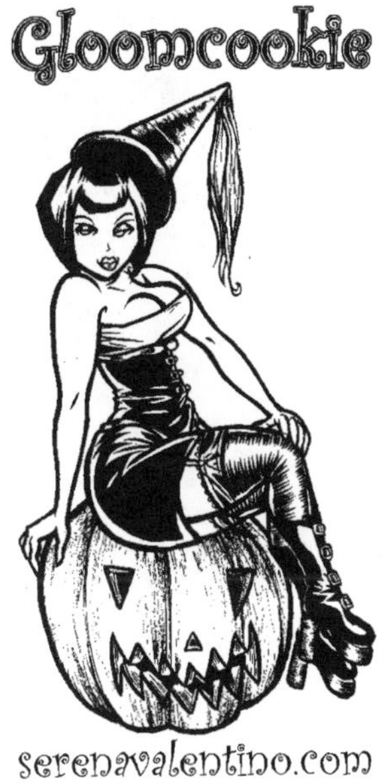
Gloomcookie
serenavalentino.com

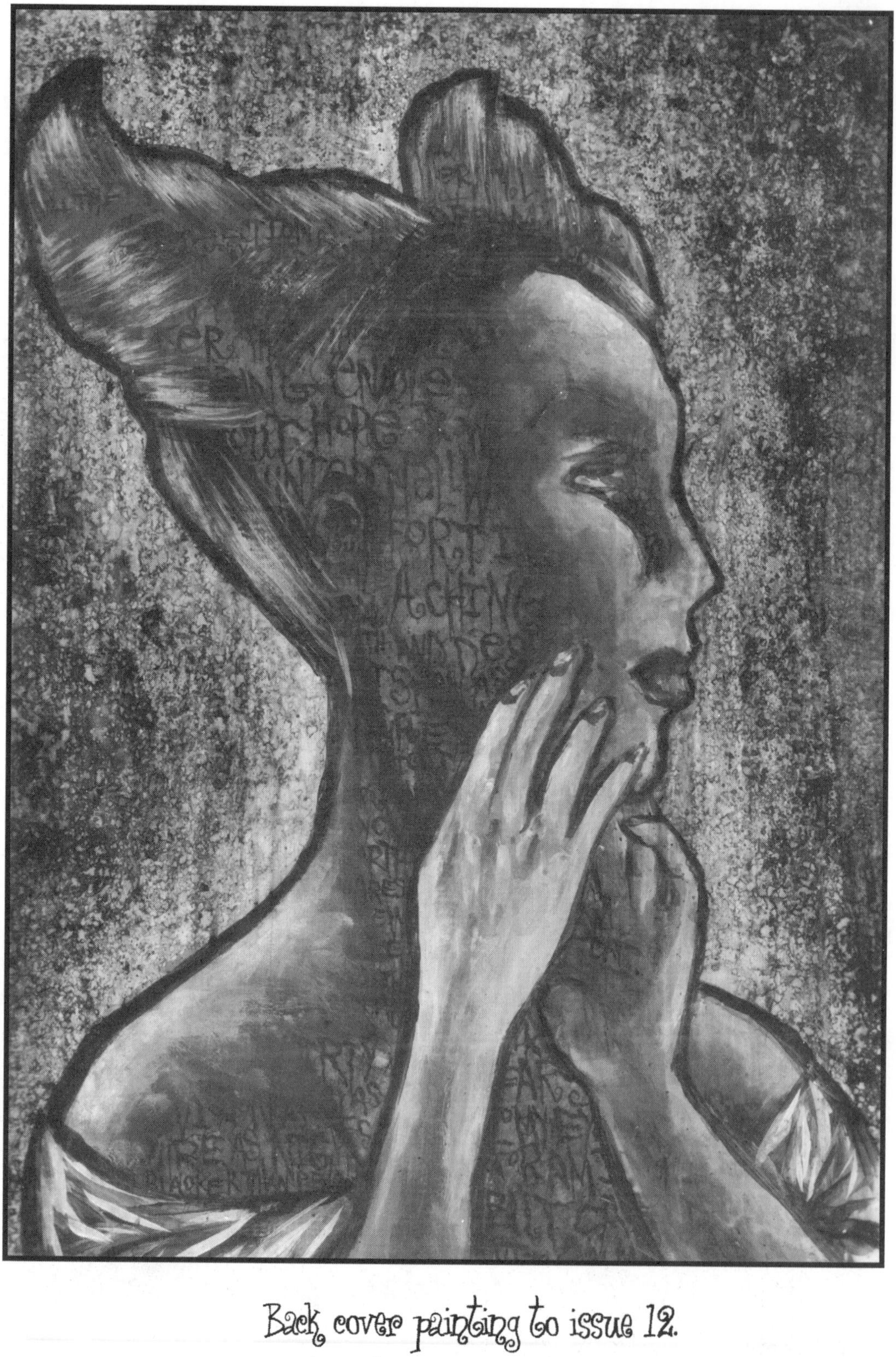

Back cover painting to issue 12.
Unfortunately, we can't print color
inside this graphic novel.

Pin Up Section

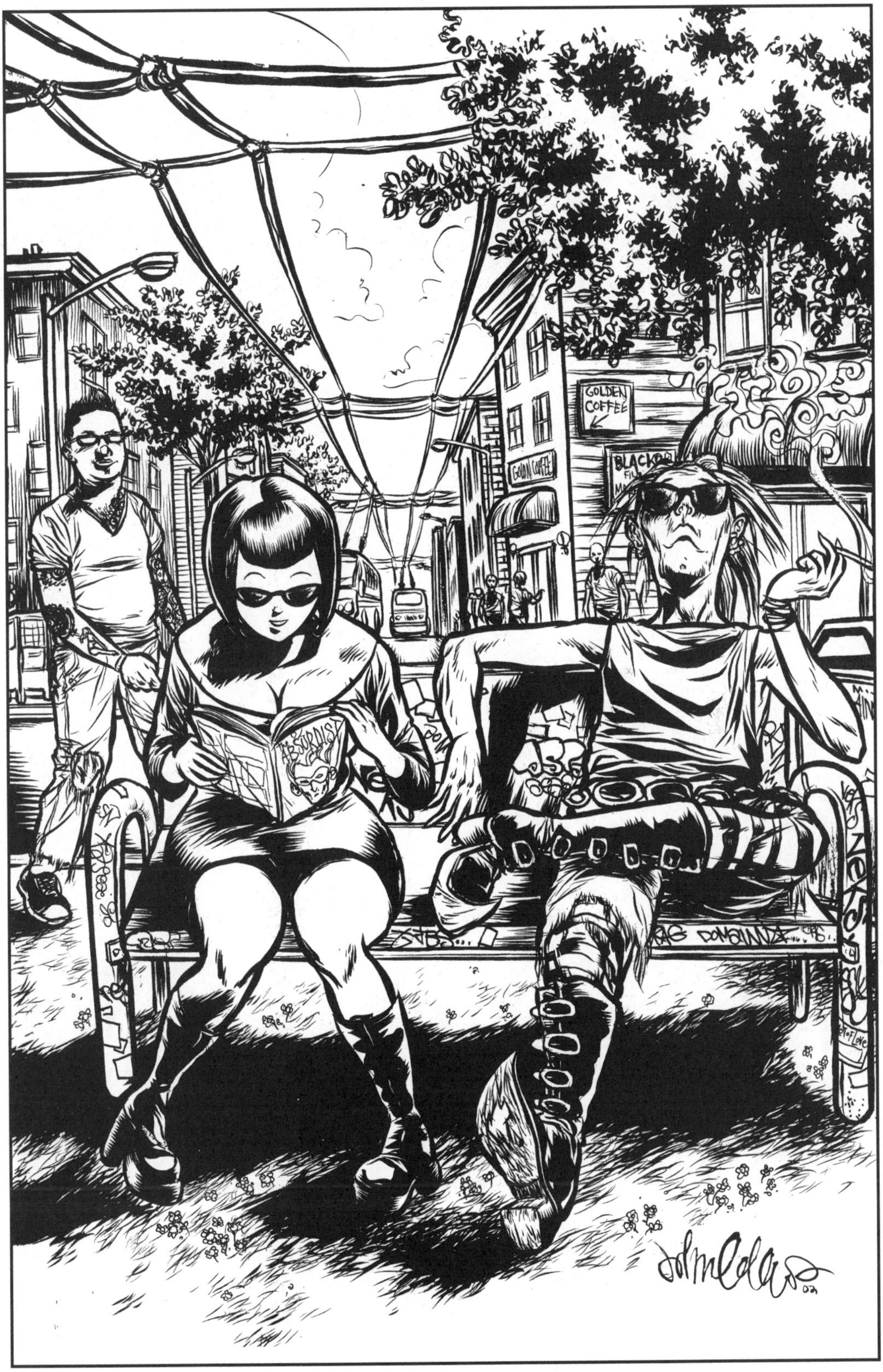
GOLDEN
COFFEE
GOLDEN COFFEE

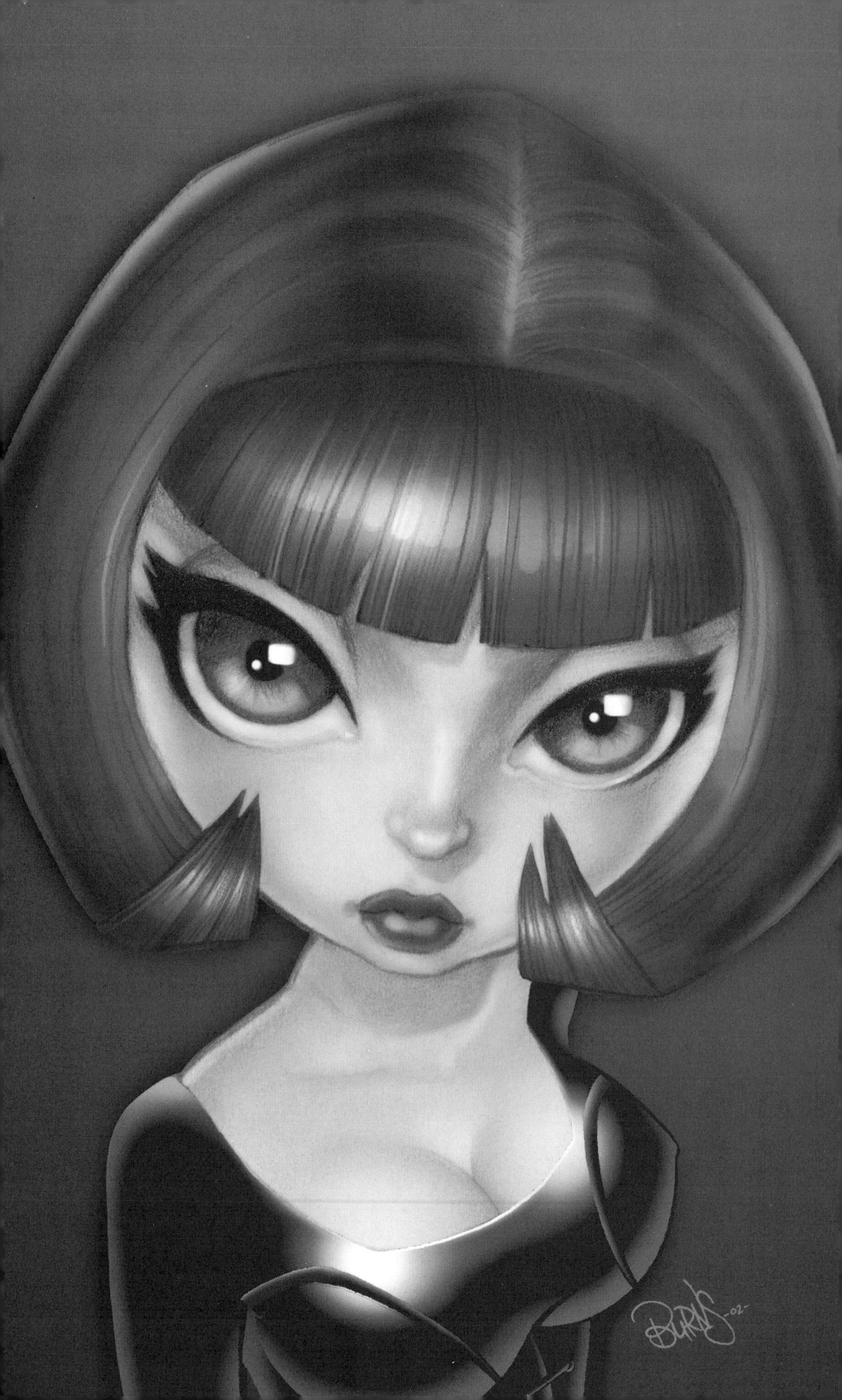

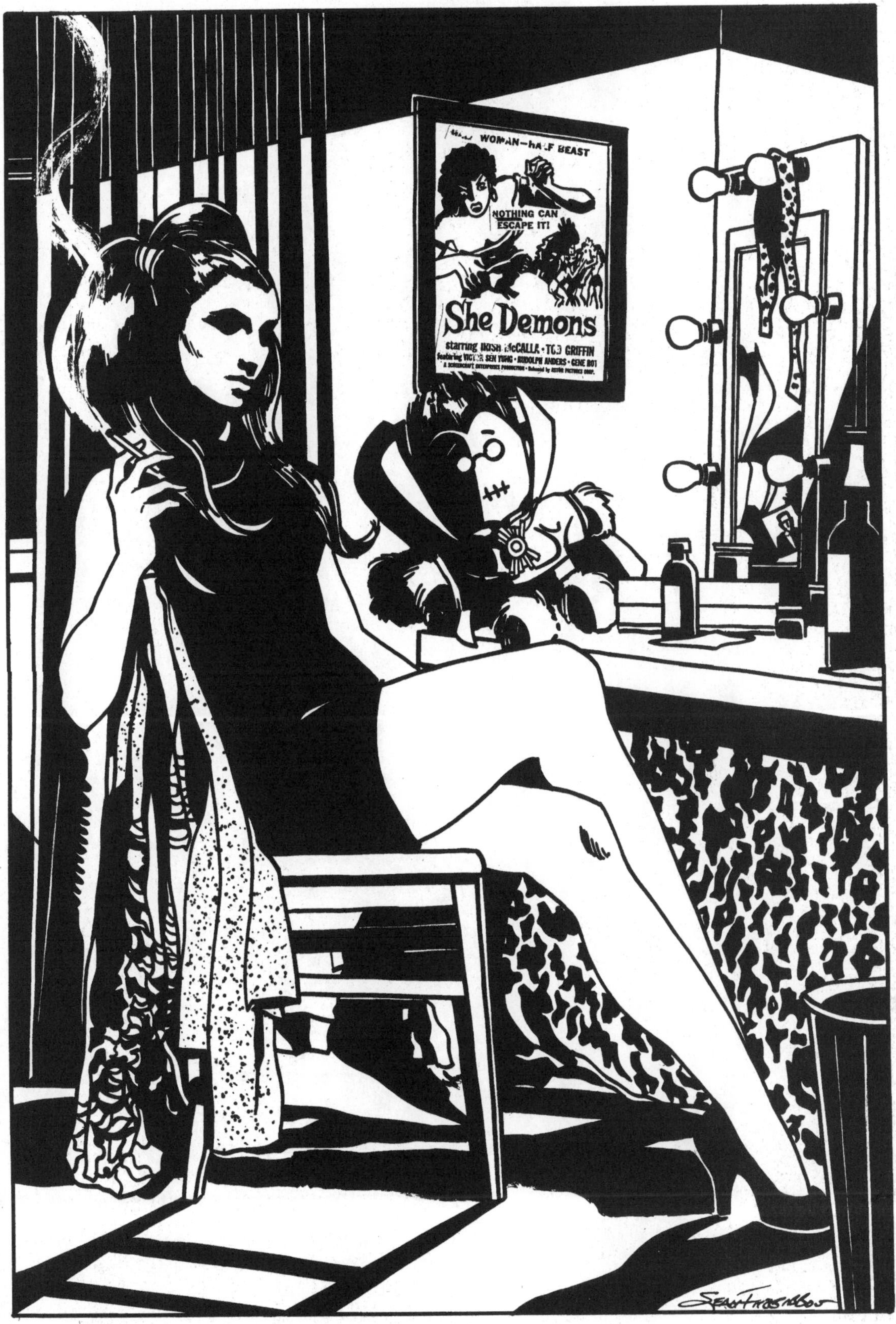
NOTHING CAN
ESCAPE IT!
She Demons
RUDOLPH ANDERS

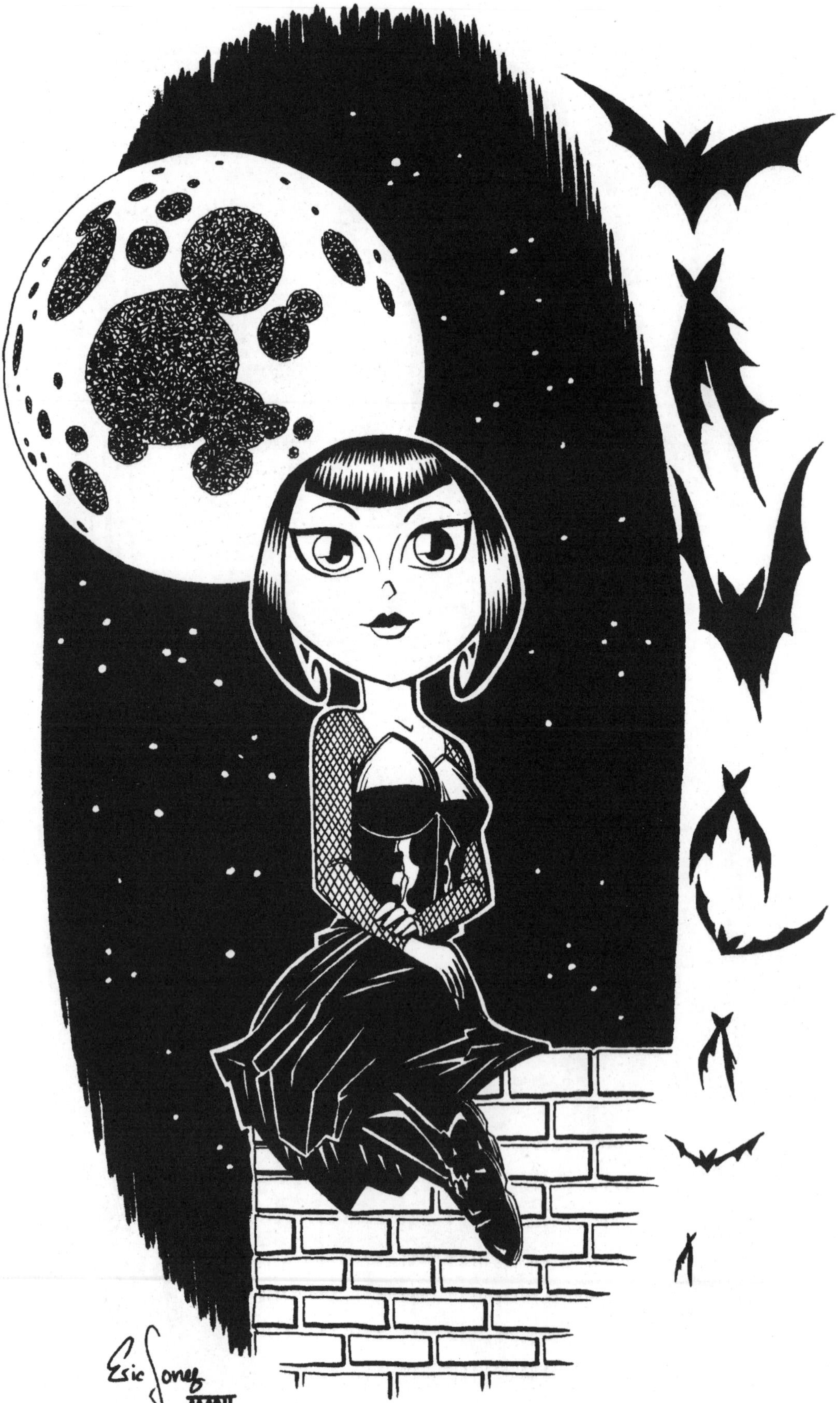
Eric Jones
MMII

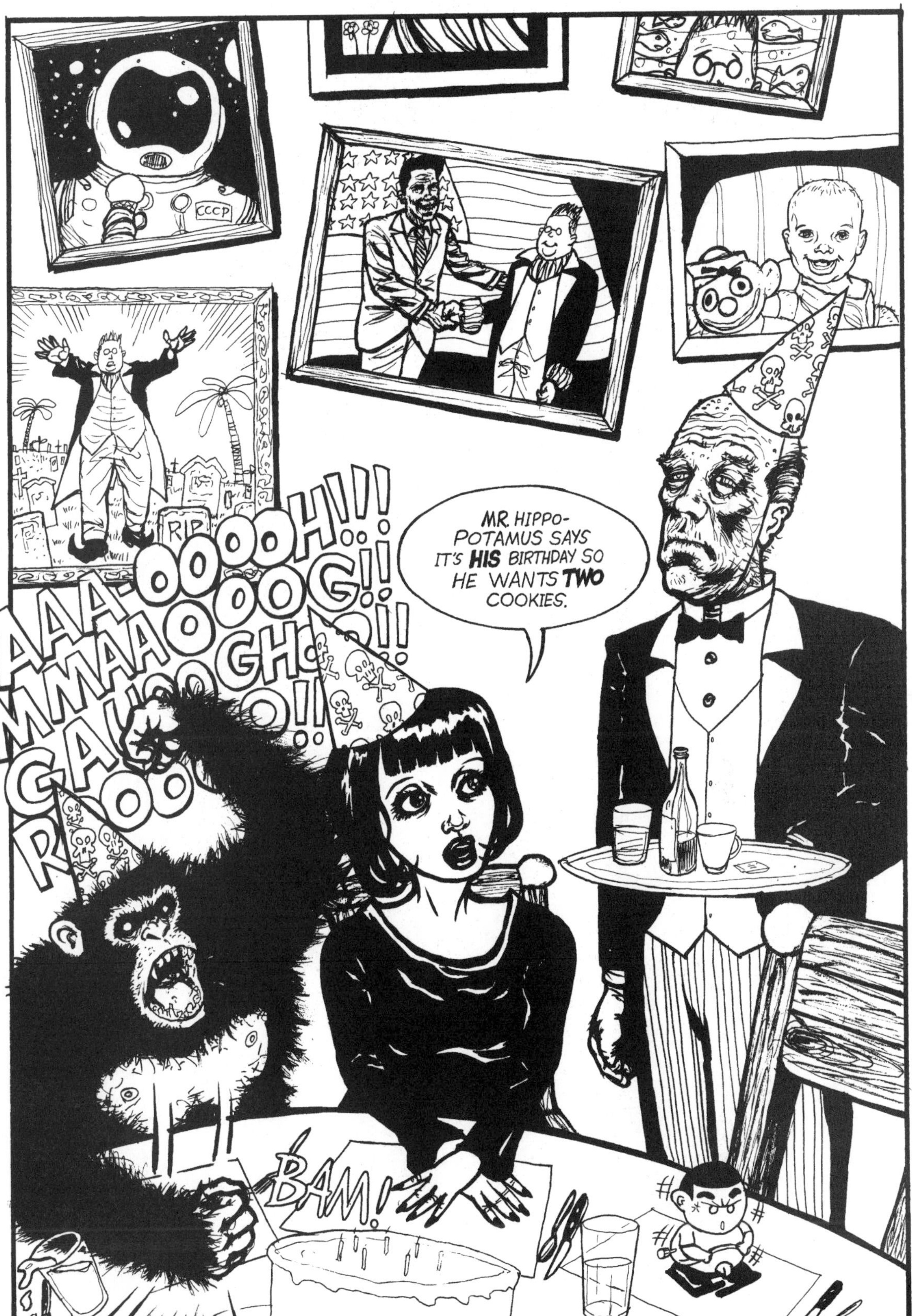
CCCP
AAA-OOOOH!!!
MMAAOOOOG!!!
GAUOOOGHOO!!
ROOOOOOO!!
MR. HIPPO-POTAMUS SAYS IT'S **HIS** BIRTHDAY SO HE WANTS **TWO** COOKIES.
BAM!

ALEX PETRETICH 2002

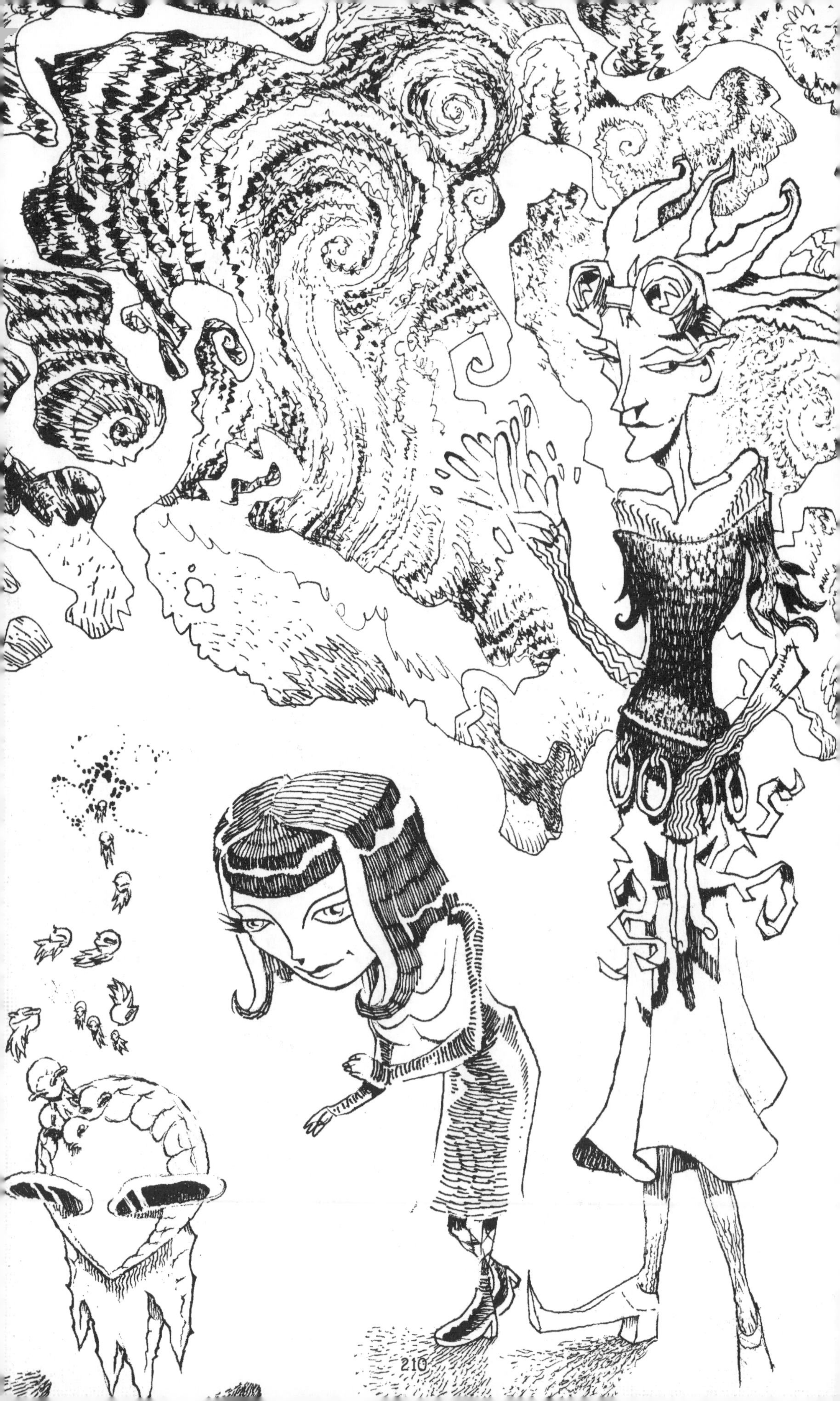

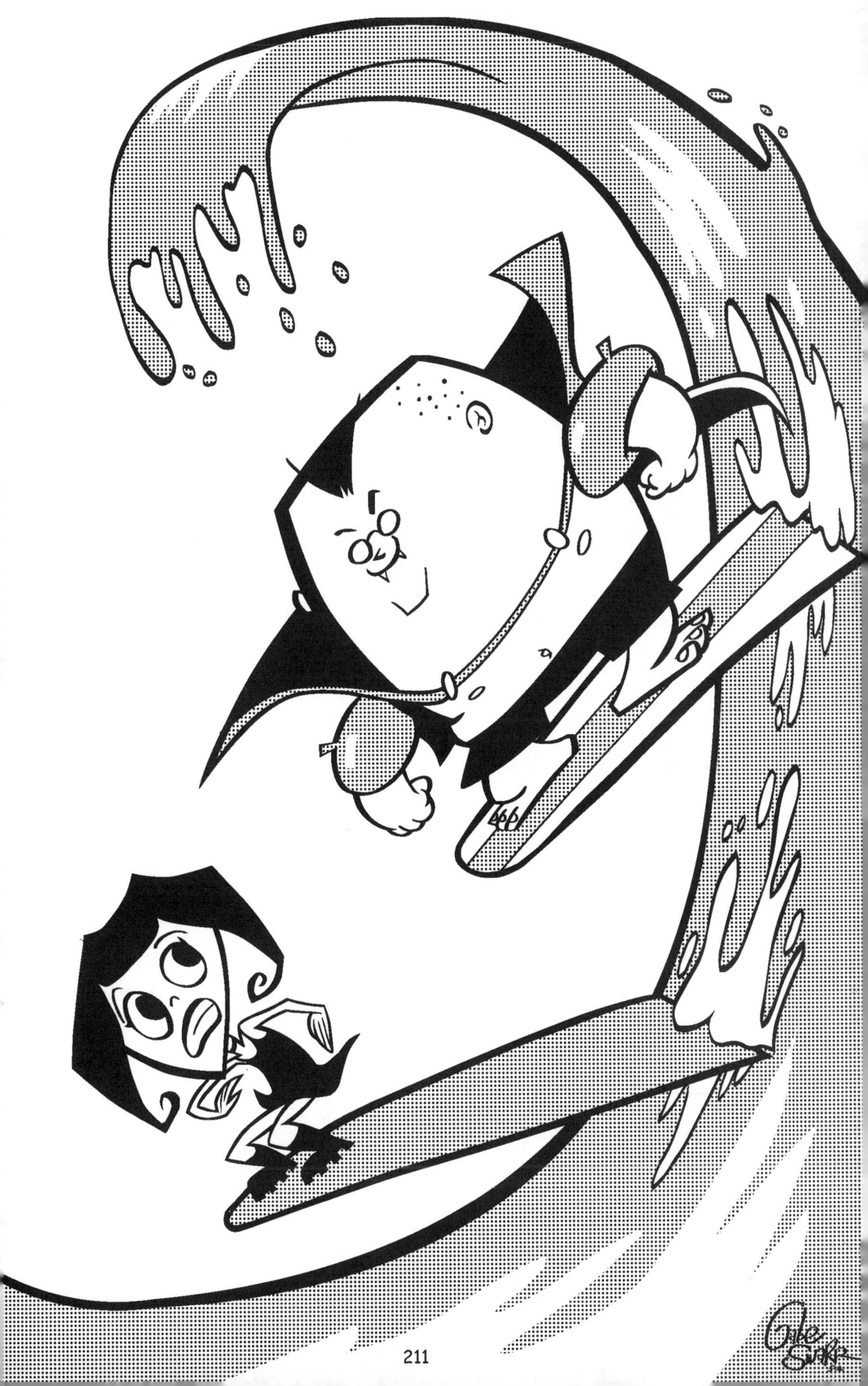

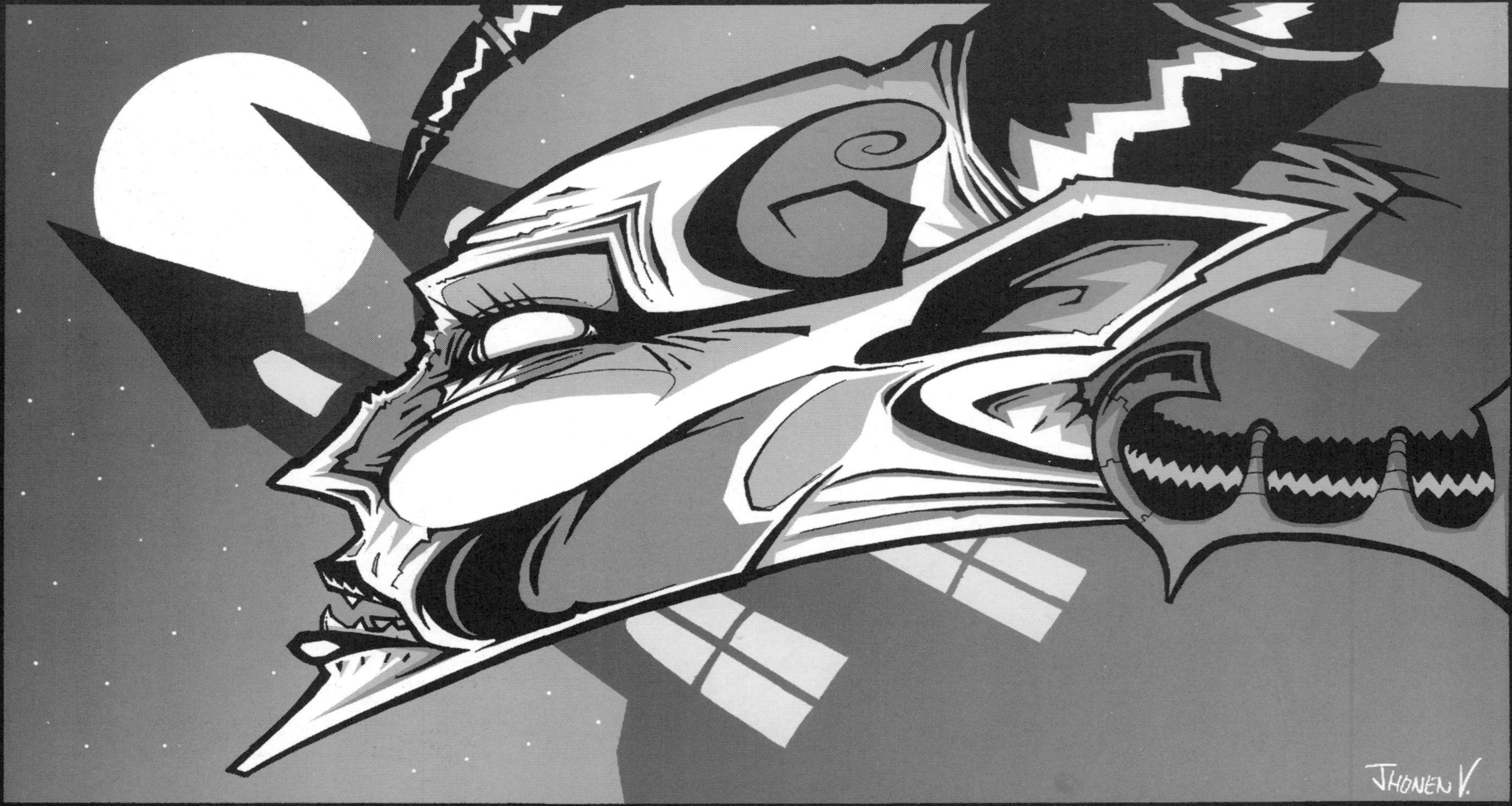
JHONEN V.

ISABELLA

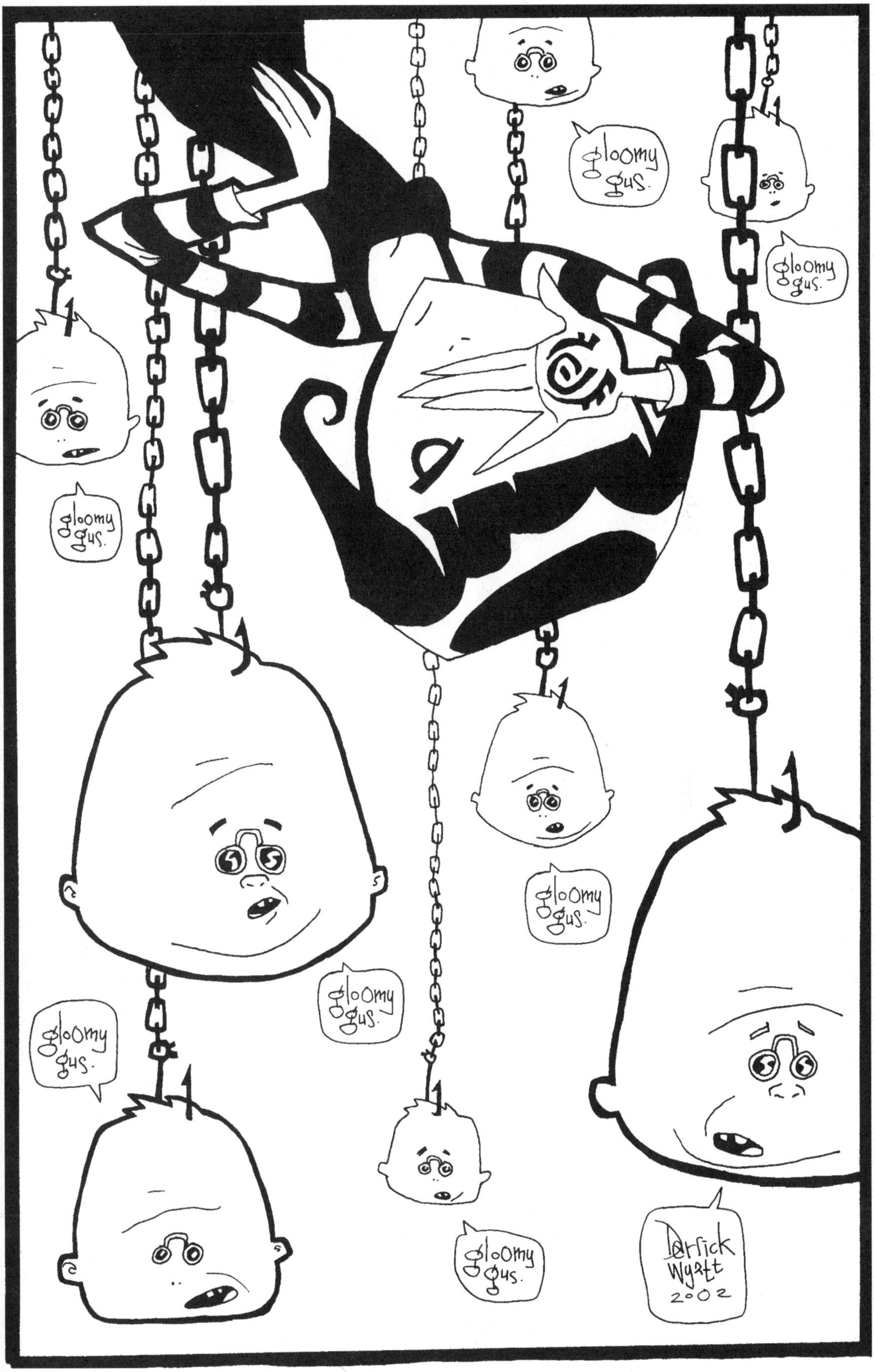
gloomy gus.
gloomy gus.
gloomy gus.
gloomy gus.
gloomy gus.
gloomy gus.
gloomy gus.
Derrick Wyatt 2002

Fan Art

Sydney
Huestis
(Serena's little sister)

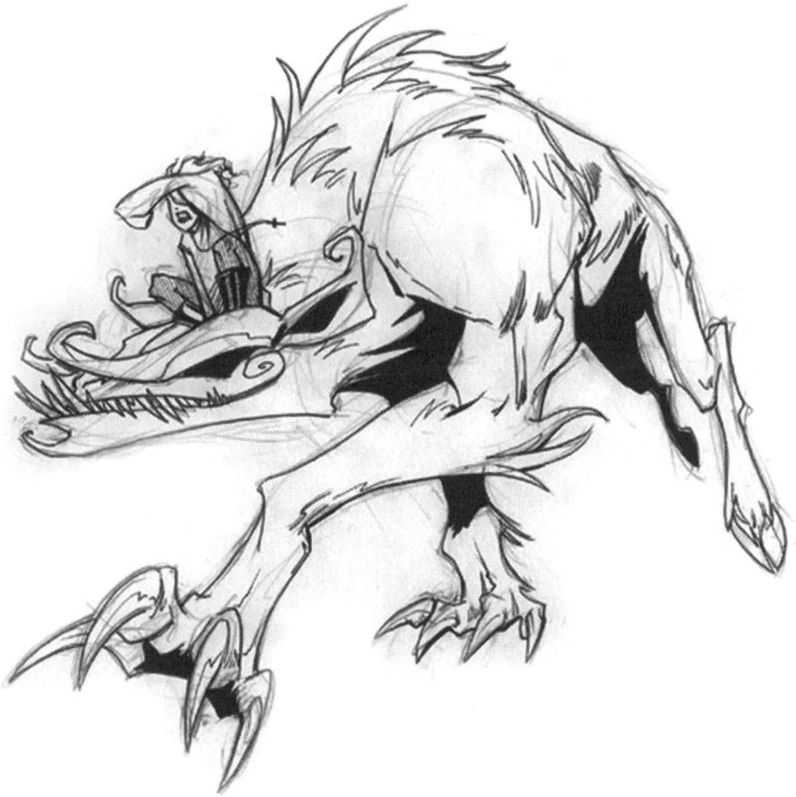

Harley Sparx

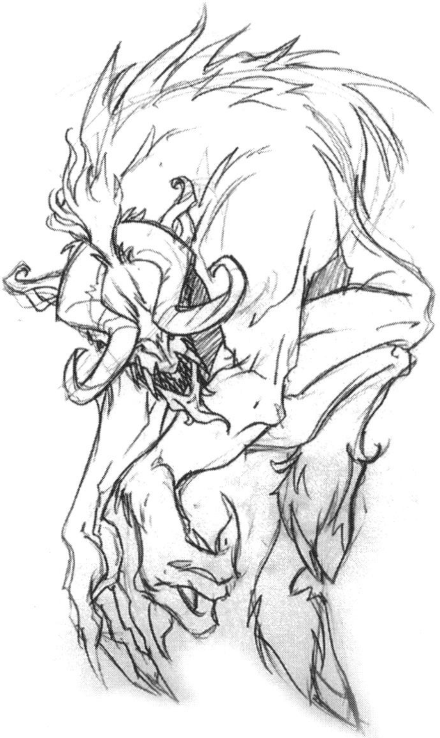

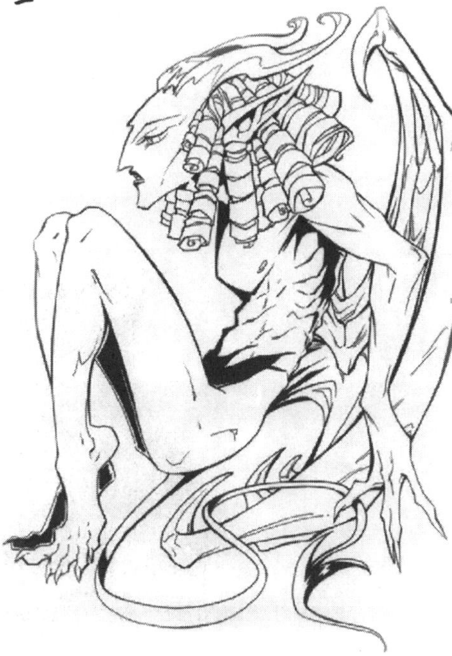

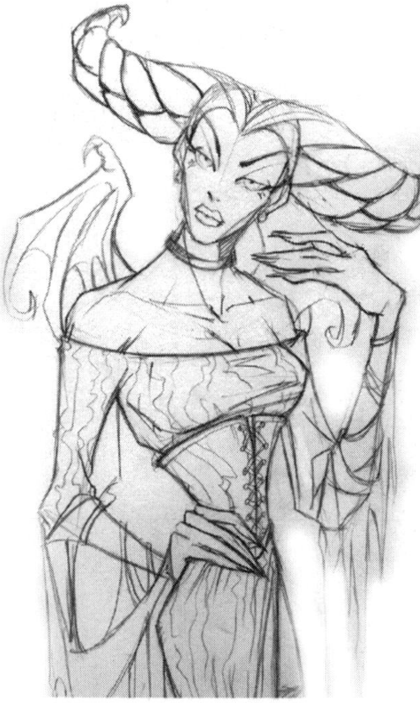

Harley Sparx

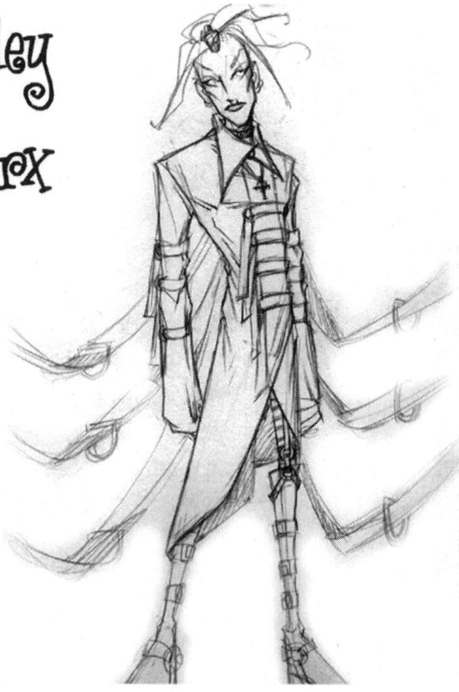

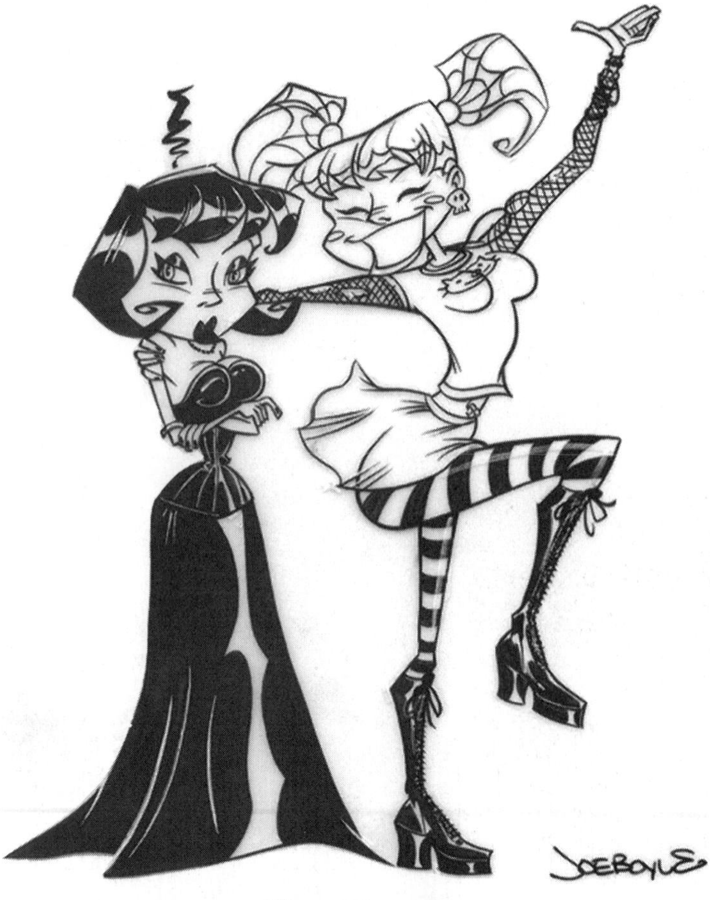
JOEBOYLE

Joe Boyle

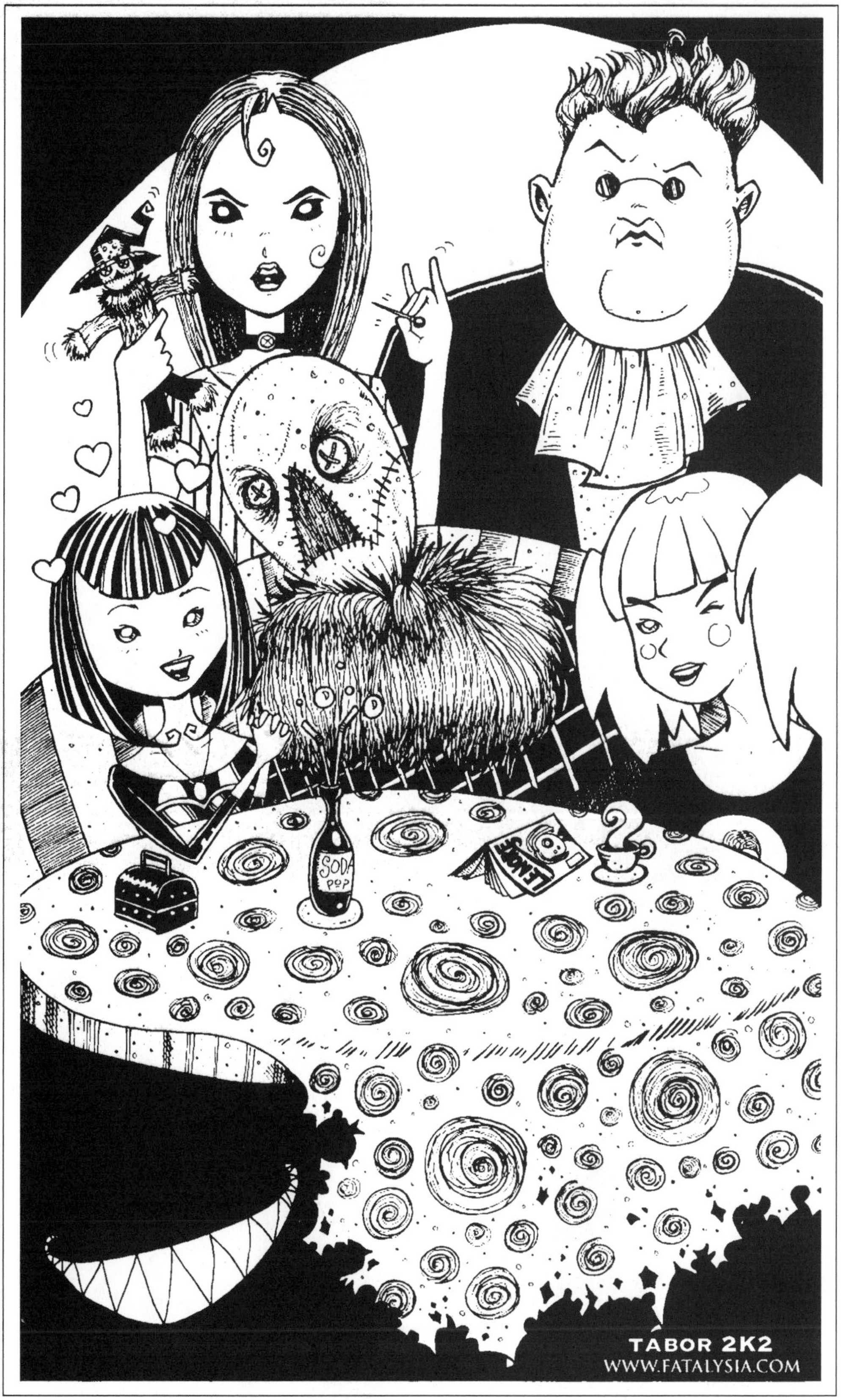
SODA POP
LENORE
TABOR 2K2
WWW.FATALYSIA.COM

Chris Tabor

Genevieve Bruneau

"Lex" G. Bruneau '02

Kim Redding

daddy's little girl

218

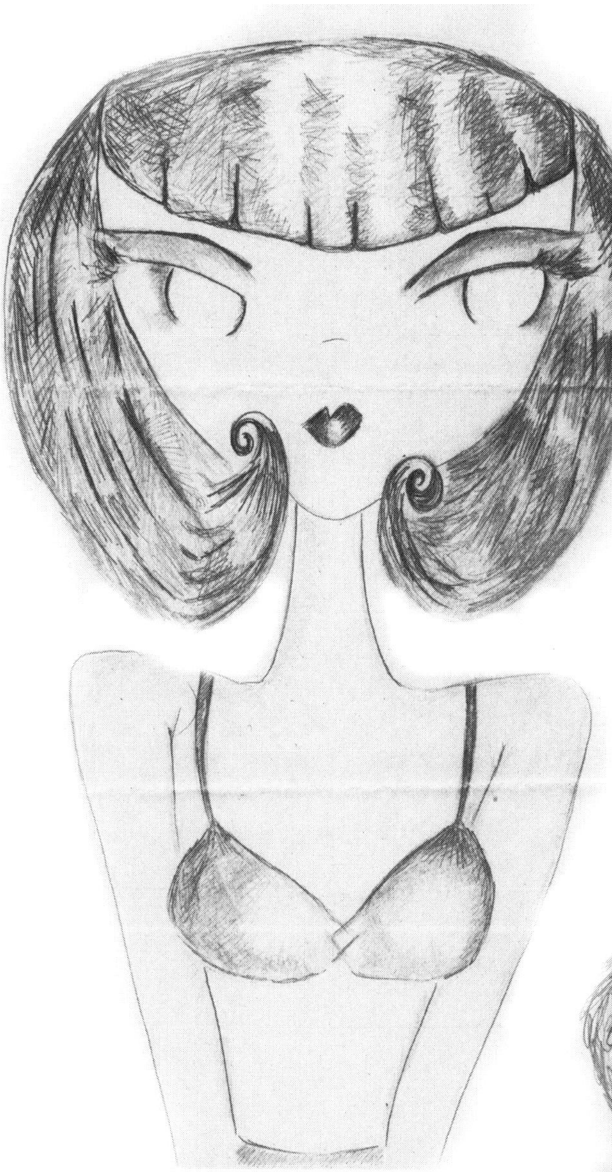

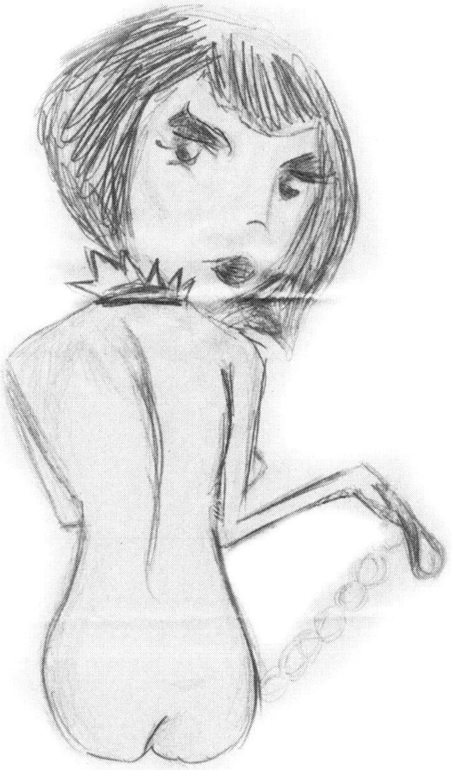

Kim
Redding

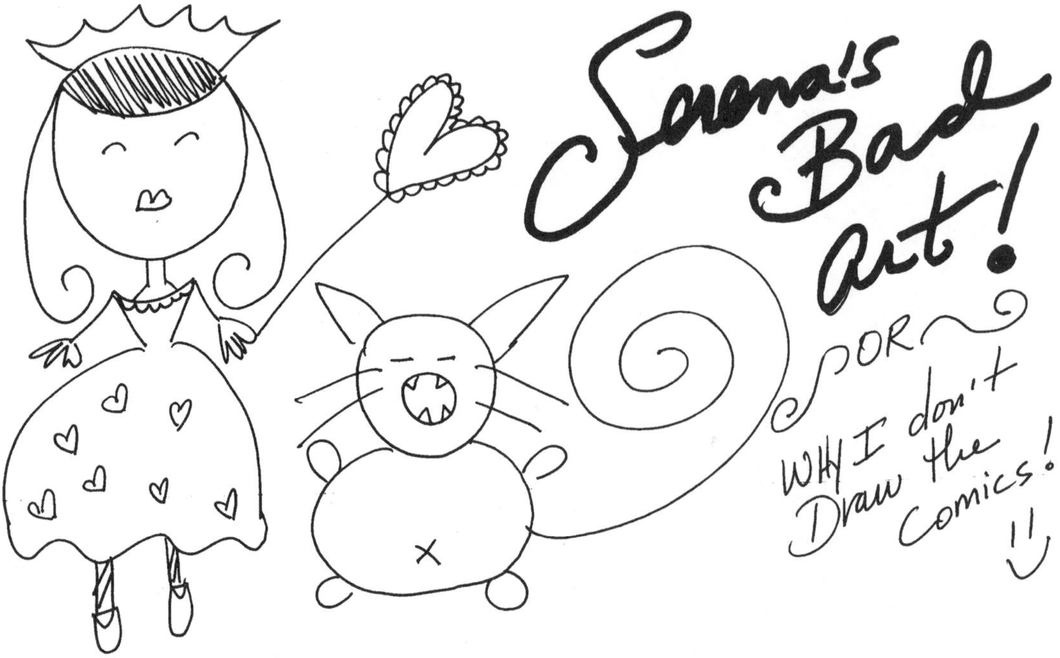
Serena's Bad Art!
OR
WHY I don't Draw the Comics!
!!

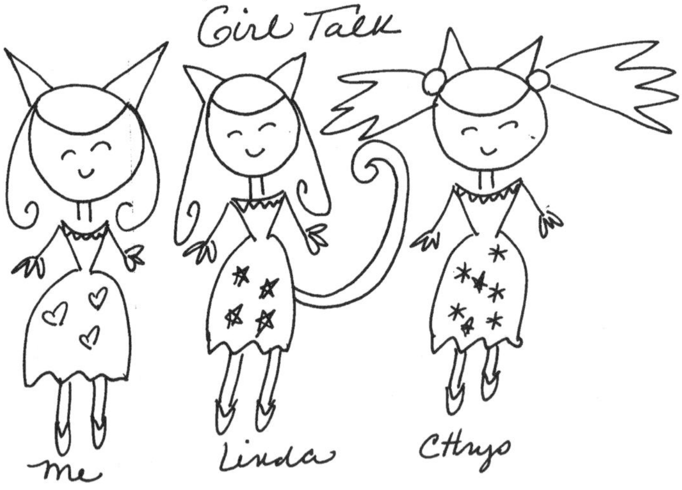
Girl Talk
me
Linda
Chiyo

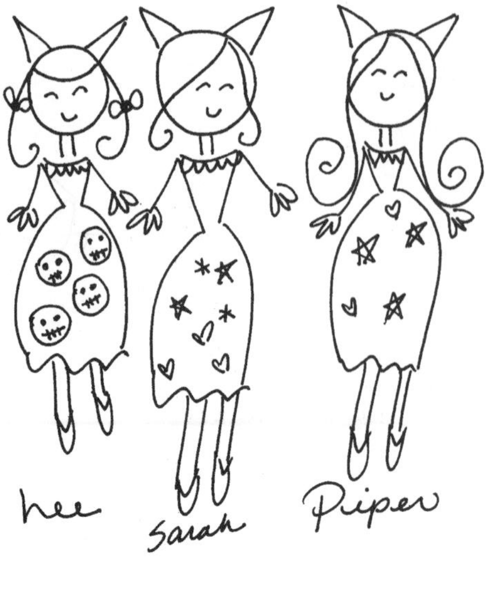
Sarah
Piper

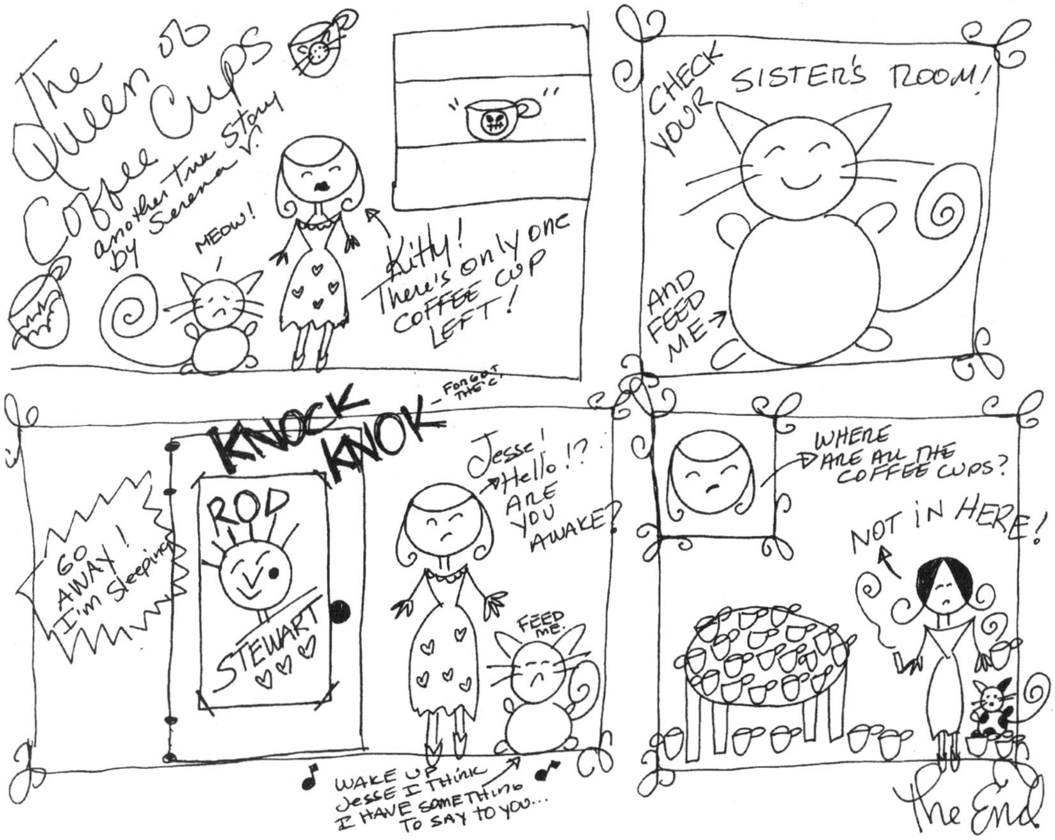
The Queen of Coffee Cups
another true story By Serena V.
MEOW!
Kitty! There's only one coffee cup left!
CHECK YOUR SISTER'S ROOM!
AND FEED ME
KNOCK KNOK
Forgot the C
ROD STEWART
GO AWAY! I'm Sleeping
Jesse! Hello!? ARE YOU AWAKE?
FEED ME.
WAKE UP JESSE I THINK I HAVE SOMETHING TO SAY TO YOU...
WHERE ARE ALL THE COFFEE CUPS?
NOT IN HERE!
The End

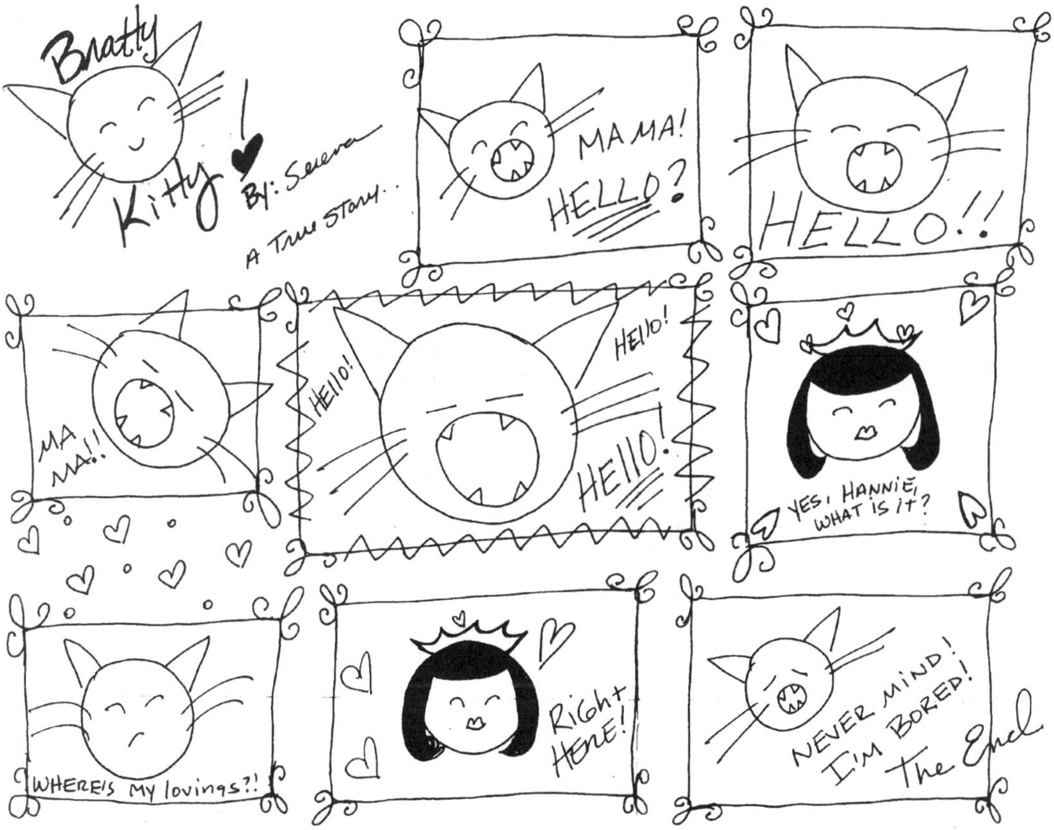
Bratty Kitty
By: Serena
A True Story...
MA MA! HELLO?
HELLO!!
MA MA!!
HELLO!
HELLO!
HELLO!
YES, HANNIE, WHAT IS IT?
WHERE'S My lovings?!
Right HERE!
NEVER MIND! I'M BORED!
The End

LEX PAPER DOLL

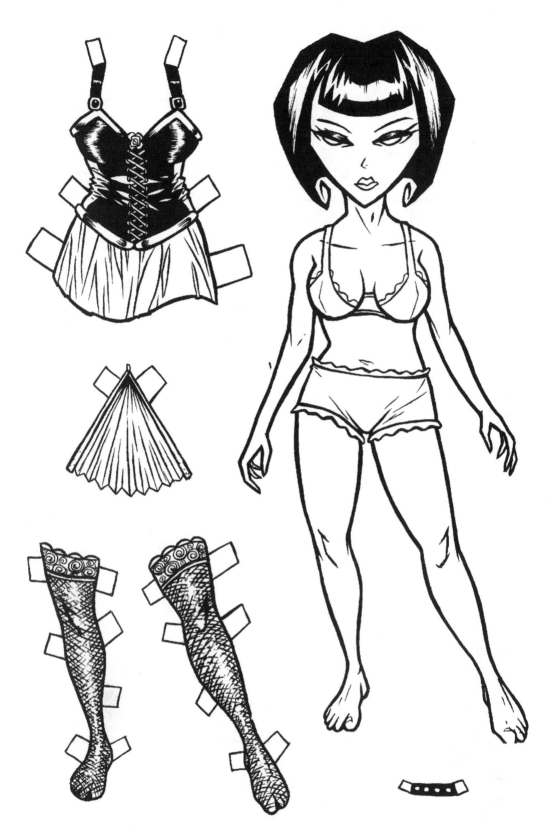

Special Thanks

WOW! I can't believe we have done twelve issues of GloomCookie... It seems only a short time ago that Ted and I were up all night at Kinko's photocopying the Lex & Max story to take to the Comic-Con the very next morning.

I remember standing in the San Diego airport that day, wondering to myself, "What am I doing here? Who is going to like this story?" Honestly, I wanted to just turn right around and fly home. I felt like puking. The prospect of walking around this gigantic convention center, handing out a little piece of myself for people to reject, frightened the hell out of me. But Ted was very enthusiastic about GloomCookie (regardless of my fears), and I thank him for that — and for being such a fantastic artist for the first six issues.

I still find it rather amazing that our little comic not only made it into the hands of Dan Vado at SLG (thanks to Roman Dirge), but that he actually wanted to publish it. I am sure Dan had some reservations, considering that I'd never written a damn thing before the Lex & Max story and the comic itself seemed more like a soap opera than anything else. . . .

I am very grateful that he took that risk. I thank you, Dan . . . for everything.

So it's twelve issues later, and John Gebbia took on the task of illustrating the past six issues you have in your little hands. I didn't envy his position and, quite frankly, I think he was rather brave to take it on. It was inevitable that people wouldn't like his style (at least at first) . . . no matter how amazing of an artist he is. Some people just don't like changes. But I have to say, John was a wonderful person to work with, and I thank him for what he brought to GloomCookie. For the record, I think he did an excellent job, and I thank him for that.

My love and thanks also go out to my husband Eric, the most supportive, loving, creative, sexy, and understanding best friend and husband a girl could ask for — I love you, darling! I would also like to thank Julia Dvorin for being the squishiest Editrix (and friend) ever! Happy 10th Anniversary, Julia! I love you and am so happy you are here to share this with me.

Love and thanks also go out to Joshua Archer for all of his love, help, and support. You're the yummiest, Joshie, I love you! More squishy thanks and love to my wonderful best girlies, Chrys, Sarah, Piper, Linda, Jesse, and Lee! I love you, sweeties! Thank you for all your support and love over the years. Umm . . . how many more times to you think I can fit the word "love" on this page?

More love and thanks to my mom, Brian, and all my friends and family who have been more supportive than they will ever know. Squishy thanks also to Delchi, for being such a sweetie, and not minding that I put him in the comic. Squishy thanks to Tommy, Landry, and Eric for being so sweet to me at conventions, listening to my fears and offering wonderful advice, insights, and making me laugh when I needed it.

Much love and thanks to Darick Robertson for your wonderful (and revealing) introduction, as well as for being such a dear friend. I love you, sweetheart! Squishy thanks to Bob, Jennifer, and everyone at SLG — as well as all the wonderful sweeties who contributed guest pages to this collection: Jhonen, Landry, Eric, Darick, Andy, and all of John's friends. And, of course, I would like to thank everyone who sent us fan art!

Squishy thanks to Jared for being such a yummy web ninja for the past two years! And thank you, Matthew, for taking over for him and doing such a spookarific-ninja job! You're both the yummiest! And the super-yummiest squish to one of my favorite girlies, Kris Strange, for all her help at GothCon! I love you, sweetie! Thanks for everything.

And lastly . . . I would especially like to thank all of you for reading our little comic and for your continuing support.
There would be no GloomCookie without all of you.

~Serena

First and foremost, I have to thank Dan and Serena for taking a chance with me. Also, I need to thank Bob for putting up with my incompetence with computers, and everyone else at SLG. Also, Marion for extracting any positiveness out of me and for being a pain in my ass, Gavin for keeping me drunk, Steve for letting me use his computer and burning me out, Mike and Mark for feeding me; Alex, Betsy, and Sofie Patretich, and Motabhon for making me fear for my life every time I leave my apartment.

I can't forget about my friends and family in Jersey — Pennis, Rudy, Cobb, Vud, Franz, Dave, Diesel, Tom, Janine, Chelz, rib crib, Nasiem, Ozwaldo Gonzalez, Roth, Shop-Rite liquors, West Essex, Peter Falco, dozing, showers, Bernardo in Chile (I hope you haven't gotten yourself killed), TMH, meat face, Mom and Dad for making me, stoag chats, the basement, Jesus H. Christ (my personal savior), HM for knocking some sense into me, Montclair, the bricks for making Essex County such a safe place to live in, Pado Grez, the joid (don't look out that window), Veronica Shy-Town for your fashion sense, and whoever else I never think of.

~John

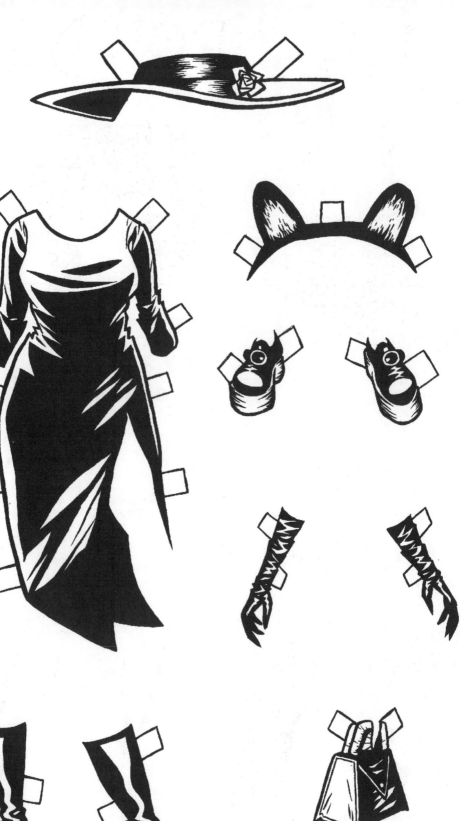